At War with the Weather

At War with the Weather
Managing Large-Scale Risks in a New Era of Catastrophes

Howard C. Kunreuther and Erwann O. Michel-Kerjan

with Neil A. Doherty, Martin F. Grace, Robert W. Klein, and Mark V. Pauly

The MIT Press
Cambridge, Massachusetts
London, England

For information about special quantity discounts, please email special_sales@mitpress.mit.edu.

This book was set in Times Roman on 3B2 by Asco Typesetters, Hong Kong.
Printed and bound in the United States of America.

Library of Congress Cataloging-in-Publication Data

Kunreuther, Howard.
At war with the weather : managing large-scale risks in a new era of catastrophes / Howard C. Kunreuther and Erwann O. Michel-Kerjan with Neil A. Doherty ... [et al.].
    p. cm.
Includes bibliographical references and index.
ISBN: 978-0-262-01282-9 (hardcover : alk. paper)
1. Disaster insurance—United States. 2. Emergency management—United States. 3. Risk management—United States. I. Michel-Kerjan, Erwann. II. Title.
HG9979.3.K86 2009
368.1'2200973—dc22   2008043058

10 9 8 7 6 5 4 3 2

To Gail and Sandra,

who have helped us with their balanced perspectives to better appreciate the challenges involved in managing extreme events

Contents

Preface

Since 2001, we have entered a new era of catastrophes. Our nation is facing large-scale risks at an increasing pace. We are more vulnerable to extreme events as a result of the increasing concentration of population and activities in high-risk coastal regions of the country. The question is not whether large-scale catastrophes will occur, but when and how frequently they will strike and the extent of damages they will cause. Redefining disaster management and new financing solutions are now coming to the forefront of the business and policy agendas in many countries. In fact, we shall all become more involved in a new type of war—a war with the weather.

The recent upsurge in hurricanes, coupled with increasing residential and commercial development in coastal areas of the United States, has exposed people and property to an entirely new scale of destruction, with cascading effects on homeowners, businesses located within these devastated areas, the insurance industry and financial markets, and the public sector. In 2005, three major hurricanes—Katrina, Rita, and Wilma—made landfall in the Gulf of Mexico within an eight-week period, killing over fifteen hundred people, with insurance reimbursements and federal disaster relief of over \$180 billion—a historic record. These three storms occurred after four other hurricanes had caused severe damage in Florida in 2004. In 2008, Texas was hit by Hurricane Ike, the third most costly hurricane in U.S. history. The occurrence of hurricanes is highly variable and uncertain from year to year. However, it is unavoidable that in the coming years, more hurricanes will strike the Atlantic and Gulf coasts, and other parts of the nation will experience severe floods and earthquakes, causing extreme damage to residential and commercial property and infrastructure.

Episodes of terrorism share certain similarities with natural disasters. The first successful attack on U.S. soil, against the World Trade Center, occurred in 1993. Over the next eight years, not a single attack was perpetrated by an international terrorist organization in the United States. As time passed, the nation was lulled into a false sense of security. Then Al Qaeda launched its second, and much more devastating, attack on the morning of September 11, 2001.

While terrorism and natural disasters are different, they have several important features in common: uncertainty and wide variances in losses from one year to the next. Experts and decision makers face challenges in assessing the risks associated with these extreme events, developing strategies for reducing future losses and facilitating the recovery process following a major disaster.

Now is the time to develop and implement economically sound policies and strategies for managing the risk and consequences of future disasters. Absence of leadership and concrete actions in this area will inevitably lead to unnecessary loss of lives and economic destruction in the devastated regions.

Guiding Principles

A coherent strategy is necessary to ensure a sustainable recovery from large-scale disasters. This book provides the elements for developing such a program by focusing on the roles of mitigation, insurance, and other risk transfer instruments. These issues are complex. They challenge our capacity as a nation to work together despite very different agendas and priorities regarding the role and responsibilities of the private and public sectors in dealing with catastrophic risks.

Two guiding principles underlie the analyses and proposed strategies for using the insurance infrastructure—one of the largest industries in the world—to deal more effectively with natural disasters:

Principle 1: Premiums reflecting risk: Insurance premiums should be based on risk in order to provide signals to individuals as to the hazards they face and to encourage them to engage in cost-effective mitigation measures to reduce their vulnerability to catastrophes.

Principle 2: Dealing with equity and affordability issues. Any special treatment given to homeowners currently residing in hazard-prone areas (e.g., low-income uninsured or inadequately insured homeowners) should come from general public funding, not through insurance premium subsidies.

This book addresses several basic questions:

• How can these two principles guide the design of insurance and mitigation programs for reducing future disaster losses and providing financial support for victims of these events?

• What roles can the key interested parties affected by natural disasters play in implementing these programs?

• Who should pay (and how much should they pay) to mitigate damages from future natural disasters and the losses that occur following these events?

• How can the analyses detailed in this book help inform private sector decisions and the policy debate in state legislatures and the U.S. Congress?

Focus of the Study

To address these questions, we focus on four states—Florida, New York, South Carolina, and Texas—and metropolitan areas in each of these states—Miami-Dade area, Florida; New York City area, New York; Charleston area, South Carolina; and Houston area, Texas. These regions have been selected because they have the largest property exposure to hurricane risk in the country and present significant differences in insurance market regulation and public/private risk-sharing systems.

Florida presents a specific challenge due to its hurricane exposure, increasing population, and rapid economic development, all of which makes this state a world peak-zone for extreme event coverage and capital allocation. Recently it has been a source of controversy because its state government has intervened in the functioning of the private insurance market more explicitly than in any other state in the country. For these reasons, we devote special attention to Florida, for both the hurricane risk and flood hazards.

Overview of the Book

The fifteen chapters that follow are organized in four parts. Both conceptual and empirical findings are presented using data from several sources (see the Acknowledgments). We highlight each chapter's key findings at the beginning of the chapter. The relevant analyses supporting these findings are documented in the chapters themselves.

The first four chapters all in Part I detail the factors that have led to a major increase in damage from natural disasters since the 1990s (chapter 1); the current institutional arrangements, including the regulatory environment and private market characteristics for insuring and mitigating risks from hurricanes (chapters 2 and 3); and an analysis of flood coverage provided by the National Flood Insurance Program (chapter 4).

Part II looks at how homeowners make decisions on whether to purchase insurance (chapter 5) and how insurers and reinsurers decide on the amount of coverage to offer and what price to charge for this protection (chapters 6 and 7). New developments with respect to alternative risk transfer instruments involving the capital and financial markets are also analyzed (chapter 8). The last two chapters of Part II provide conceptual and detailed empirical analyses of the factors influencing the demand for and supply of homeowners' insurance coverage (chapters 9 and 10).

Taken together, our findings reveal that most homeowners do not undertake cost-benefit comparisons in making their insurance purchases. They often choose low deductibles and are likely to underestimate the risk. The analysis also quantifies the degree to which the demand for insurance is sensitive to price. In the four states studied, a given percentage increase in the price of homeowners' insurance results in a similar percentage decrease in the amount of insurance purchased.

In addition to looking at expected losses, insurers and reinsurers are forced to allocate considerable capital to protect themselves against catastrophic losses to satisfy investors' and rating agencies' concerns. There has been a significant increase since 2005 in the use of alternative risk transfer instruments such as catastrophe bonds to complement reinsurance, but these financial instruments still represent a small fraction of capital in the global insurance market. The analysis of the supply of coverage indicates that if regulators suppress rates too much, there is likely to be a severe decrease in the availability of coverage.

We begin Part III by examining what proportion of homeowners in hurricane-prone areas is uninsured, and whether affordability is a significant determinant of insurance status for homeowners residing in these areas (chapter 11). We then provide insight into how homeowners in hazard-prone areas decide whether to invest in cost-effective risk reduction measures and some possible economic incentives for encouraging them to do so (chapter 12). We then examine the impact of the current insurance programs on those affected by the hurricane risk (a status quo analysis). We then determine how much coverage is likely to be made available and what premiums would be charged in a hypothetical unregulated market where rates are determined only by the law of supply and demand (a competitive market analysis) (chapter 13).

Our findings reveal that most people purchase insurance even if they are classified as having income below the affordability threshold. At the same time, most do not mitigate their homes because they cannot justify the up-front investment cost relative to the perceived benefits, due principally to myopia, budget constraints, and underestimation of the risk. Hence, there is a need for well-enforced building codes, tax rebates, zoning ordinances, and premiums reflecting risk that take the benefits of mitigation into account. Should another major hurricane hit Florida in the near future, the state-run reinsurer, Florida Hurricane Catastrophe Fund, might not be able to cover all its losses, and all policyholders in the state will be forced to contribute to help defray these deficits. If insurers were allowed to charge premiums that reflect risk, they would be able to cover most, if not all, of the losses from hurricanes. In that case prices in some hazard-prone areas will be significantly higher than they are today.

Part IV offers proposed strategies to encourage individuals to purchase sufficient insurance and adopt mitigation measures as well as innovative ways to provide enough financial capacity to deal with future large-scale events (chapter 14). We conclude the book with chapter 15, "Winning the War Against the Weather and Other Extreme Events," which expands our findings to other global risks worldwide. Investment in infrastructure, mitigation, preparation, response and recovery are keys to addressing the challenges we face in this new era of catastrophes. Leadership from top decision makers to define and implement a coherent strategy to achieve these goals is more critical today than ever before.

Moving Forward

Our principal purpose in undertaking these in-depth studies is to examine alternative long-term sustainable strategies for reducing losses from natural disasters and providing financial support to victims of these events.

We are mindful that new alternative strategies may be extremely difficult to implement at this time, because there is a tendency for all of us, whether in the role of homeowner, decision maker in a private or public sector organization, or an elected official at the state, local, or federal level, to focus on short-term crises. However, our nation remains highly vulnerable to large-scale disasters. This calls for decisions by individuals, businesses, Congress, other legislative bodies, and the White House that are based on a sound long-term conceptual framework and well-documented empirical analyses. We hope *At War with the Weather* will contribute to a better understanding of these issues. We look forward to working with key interested parties and top decision makers on the challenges of managing large-scale risks in a new era of catastrophes.

Howard C. Kunreuther and Erwann O. Michel-Kerjan
The Wharton School
Philadelphia, Pennsylvania
January 2009

Acknowledgments

This has been a truly collaborative effort with our research partners from Georgia State University, who performed a thorough analysis of the state insurance regulatory systems and changes occurring over time. They also aggregated data on homeowners' insurance and performed detailed analyses of the demand and supply of insurance coverage under current programs. The Insurance Information Institute provided us with data on the vulnerability of hazard-prone areas and post–Hurricane Katrina legislative and legal actions.

The research team greatly appreciates the detailed data provided by leading insurers on their homeowners' policies, data from the offices of state insurance regulators, the analyses undertaken by Risk Management Solutions on potential and expected losses from hurricanes, and the special computer runs on insurance groups' premiums and catastrophe exposure undertaken by the rating agency A.M. Best. The state funds in Florida (Citizens Property Insurance Corporation, and the Florida Hurricane Catastrophe Fund) and in Texas (the Texas Windstorm Insurance Association) also provided us with detailed information on their coverage and the nature of their operations. The Institute for Business and Home Safety provided us with data on the impact of mitigation measures and building code enforcement on the reduction in hurricane losses. The data from all these firms and organizations enabled us to undertake comprehensive quantitative analyses of supply of and demand for insurance and to measure the performance of current and proposed insurance and mitigation programs. In addition, the Federal Emergency Management Agency provided the research team with access to the entire portfolio of the National Flood Insurance Program in Florida so we could examine the performance of this program and the nature of coverage in place at a microlevel.

To our knowledge, this is the first time that these types of data have been collected simultaneously for several consecutive years, analyzed, and interpreted in the context of existing state insurance regulatory systems and the structure of the property insurance market in the United States.

During the past two years, the research team has had fruitful meetings and discussions with key individuals and organizations interested in developing better risk management strategies for dealing with natural hazards. These include climate scientists; insurers; reinsurers; brokers; banks; trade associations; rating agencies; modeling firms; homeowners and businesses affected by natural disasters; the real estate industry; representatives from Congress and the White House; federal, state, and local agencies; insurance regulators; public interest groups; international organizations; and experts from other universities and research institutions in the United States and abroad.

Organizations that sponsored this research and have been collaborating closely with us are Allstate Insurance Company, American Insurance Association, American International Group, Guardsmark, Liberty Mutual, Lockheed Martin Corporation, Munich Re America (Munich Re Group), National Association of Mutual Insurance Companies, Nationwide Mutual Insurance Company, Partner Reinsurance Company, Property Casualty Insurers Association of America, Reinsurance Association of America, Société Générale Bank, State Farm Fire and Casualty Company, Swiss Reinsurance Company, Travelers Companies, WeatherPredict Consulting (an affiliate of Renaissance Re Holdings), and Zurich.

This book also benefited from data and ongoing interaction with the following organizations: A.M. Best, Citizens Property Insurance Corporation, U.S. Department of Homeland Security, Fireman's Fund Insurance Company, Florida Hurricane Catastrophe Fund, Goldman Sachs, Guy Carpenter (Marsh and McLennan Companies), Institute for Business and Home Safety, National Association of Insurance Commissioners, National Flood Insurance Program, Organization for Economic Cooperation and Development, Risk Management Solutions, Texas Windstorm Insurance Association, U.S. Census Bureau, U.S. Congressional Budget Office; U.S. Government Accountability Office; U.S. House of Representatives; V.J. Dowling, and World Economic Forum.

We have benefited from insightful discussions at workshops hosted by the Wharton Risk Management Center in June and December 2006 in Philadelphia, and in October 2007 in Washington, D.C., which brought together 120 representatives from over 50 public and private organizations to discuss the findings of the study, and from the many comments received on the preliminary findings of this study issued in February 2007.

We acknowledge the other members of the research team: Robert Hartwig (Insurance Information Institute), Paul Kleindorfer (INSEAD), Carolyn Kousky (Resources for the Future), Robert Meyer (Wharton School, University of Pennsylvania), Frederic Morlaye (Aon), Irv Rosenthal (Wharton School, University of Pennsylvania), and Claire Wilkinson (Insurance Information Institute). Research assistance was provided by Daniel Berstein (Wharton School, University of Pennsylvania), Fred Blavin (Wharton School, University of Pennsylvania), Laure Cabantous (University of Nottingham and Wharton School, University of Pennsylvania), Komal Gaba (Georgia State University), Fred Li (Wharton School, University of Pennsylvania), Robert Lieberthal (Wharton School, University of Pennsylvania), Fanny Liu (Georgia State University), and Ben Shiller (Wharton School, University of Pennsylvania).

Carol Heller of the Wharton Risk Center has been actively involved in the project over the past two years, providing research and editorial assistance. Cynthia Anderson, Hannah Chervitz, and Nikita Stanley provided logistical support for the meetings and conferences associated with this project over the past three years.

I CAUSE FOR CONCERN

1 A New Era of Catastrophes

Key Findings

There has been a major increase in the cost of natural disasters since 1990. A comparison of the economic losses resulting from natural disasters worldwide over time (corrected for inflation) reveals a huge increase: $53.6 billion (1950–1959), $93.3 billion (1960–1969), $161.7 billion (1970–1979), $262.9 billion (1980–1989), and $778.3 billion (1990–1999). In the past few years there have already been $620.6 billion in losses (2000–2008), principally a result of the 2004, 2005, and 2008 hurricane seasons, which produced historic records.

Property values at risk in hazard-prone areas in the United States have drastically increased in recent years. The key socioeconomic factors causing the increased losses are the development in hazard-prone areas and increased value at risk. The population of Florida, which was 2.8 million in 1950 and 13 million in 1990, is projected to grow to 19.3 million in 2010. Today, 80 percent of insured assets in Florida are located near the coast, the high-risk area of the state. The insured exposure located in Florida coastal areas was $2.4 trillion in 2007 and is growing, increasing the likelihood of severe economic and insured losses from future hurricanes unless cost-effective risk reduction measures are implemented. Other coastal states have large property values exposed as well.

The impact of climate change on these increased losses is not clear but is of growing concern. Some scientists have suggested that the series of major hurricanes that occurred in 2004 and 2005 might be partially attributable to the impact of a change in climate. However, there is no consensus on this point. Nevertheless, there is growing concern that global warming might lead to the occurrence of much more intense hurricanes hitting the coast over a shorter period of time and increased damage to residences and commercial buildings.

Natural disasters involve a large number of key interested parties, often with different agendas and priorities. These stakeholders include homeowners residing in hazard-prone areas, insurers and reinsurers, banks and other financial institutions, the capital markets, risk modeling firms, rating agencies, the construction industry and developers, the real estate community, other businesses, and local, state, and federal governments. When addressing each of these stakeholders, it is necessary to consider how their values and goals shape their agendas for assessing and managing these risks.

To build may have to be the slow and laborious task of years.
To destroy can be the thoughtless act of a single day.
—Winston Churchill (1874–1965)

This chapter provides a picture of the increase in catastrophic losses in the United States and the challenges that various stakeholders face in managing the associated risks and costs coming from their different positions and, in some cases, different interests. Gaining an understanding and appreciation of the perspectives and concerns of these stakeholders is critical to developing and evaluating measures that will improve the management of catastrophic risk.

1.1   Recent Changes in the Impacts of Extreme Events

The economic and insured losses from great natural catastrophes such as hurricanes, earthquakes, and floods worldwide have increased significantly in recent years, as shown in figure 1.1 (each vertical bar represents the total economic losses, and the darker zone represents the insured portion of it). A comparison of these economic losses over time

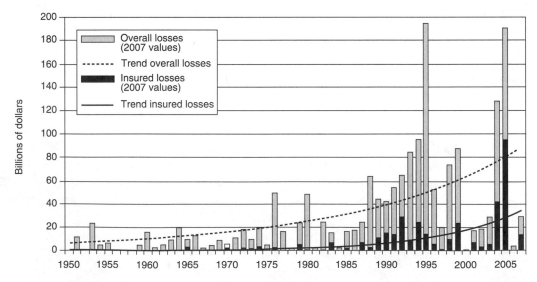

Figure 1.1
Economic and insured losses from great natural catastrophes worldwide, 1950–2007

reveals a huge increase: $53.6 billion (1950–1959), $93.3 billion (1960–1969), $161.7 billion (1970–1979), $262.9 billion (1980–1989), and $778.3 billion (1990–1999). Between 2000 and 2007, there has already been $420.6 billion in losses, principally a result of the 2004 and 2005 hurricane seasons, which produced historic records. Then 2008 inflicted $200 billion in losses, the third most expensive year on record after 1995 and 2005 (Munich Re 2008).

Catastrophes have had a more devastating impact on insurers since 1990 than in the entire history of insurance. Between 1970 and the mid-1980s, annual insured losses from natural disasters (including forest fires) were in the $3 billion to $4 billion range. The insured losses from Hurricane Hugo, which made landfall in Charleston, South Carolina, on September 22, 1989, exceeded $4 billion (1989 prices). It was the first natural disaster to inflict more than $1 billion of insured losses in the United States. There was a radical increase in insured losses in the early 1990s, with Hurricane Andrew in Florida ($23.7 billion in 2007 dollars) and the Northridge earthquake in California ($19.6 billion in 2007 dollars). The four hurricanes in Florida in 2004 (Charley, Frances, Ivan, and Jeanne) collectively totaled almost $33 billion in insured losses. Hurricane Katrina alone cost insurers and reinsurers an estimated $46 billion, and total losses paid by private insurers resulting from major natural catastrophes were $87 billion in 2005.[1] In 2008, Hurricane Ike, the third most costly U.S. hurricane, cost private insurers nearly $16 billion.

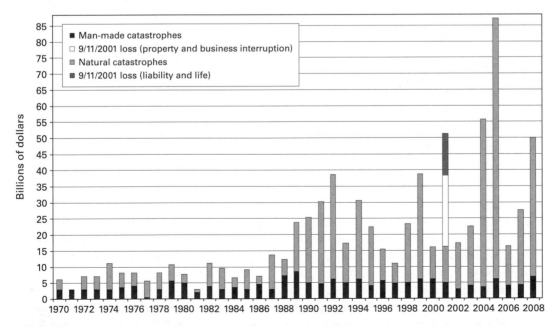

Figure 1.2
Worldwide insured losses from catastrophes, 1970–2008. *Note:* Losses in dollars indexed to 2007 except for 2008, which is in current dollars. 9/11: All lines, including property and business interruption (BI). *Source:* Wharton Risk Center, with data from Swiss Re and Insurance Information Institute.

Table 1.1
The twenty most costly insured catastrophes in the world, 1970–2008

Cost	Event	Victims (dead or missing)	Year	Area of primary damage
$46.3	Hurricane Katrina	1,836	2005	United States, Gulf of Mexico
35.5	9/11 attacks	3,025	2001	United States
23.7	Hurricane Andrew	43	1992	United States, Bahamas
19.6	Northridge earthquake	61	1994	United States
16.0	Hurricane Ike	358	2008	United States, Caribbean
14.1	Hurricane Ivan	124	2004	United States, Caribbean
13.3	Hurricane Wilma	35	2005	United States, Gulf of Mexico
10.7	Hurricane Rita	34	2005	United States, Gulf of Mexico
8.8	Hurricane Charley	24	2004	United States, Caribbean
8.6	Typhoon Mireille	51	1991	Japan
7.6	Hurricane Hugo	71	1989	Puerto Rico, United States
7.4	Winterstorm Daria	95	1990	France, United Kingdom
7.2	Winterstorm Lothar	110	1999	France, Switzerland
6.1	Winterstorm Kyrill	54	2007	Germany, United Kingdom, Netherlands, France
5.7	Storms and floods	22	1987	France, United Kingdom
5.6	Hurricane Frances	38	2004	United States, Bahamas
5.0	Winterstorm Vivian	64	1990	Western/Central Europe
5.0	Typhoon Bart	26	1999	Japan
5.0	Hurricane Gustav	135	2008	United States, Caribbean
4.5	Hurricane Georges	600	1998	United States, Caribbean

Sources: Wharton Risk Center with data from Swiss Re and Insurance Information Institute.
Note: This table excludes payments for flood by the National Flood Insurance Program in the United States.
[a] In billions, indexed to 2007, except for 2008, which is in current dollars.

Figure 1.2 depicts the upward trend in worldwide insured losses from catastrophes between 1970 and 2008, corrected for inflation.[2]

Table 1.1 reveals the twenty most costly catastrophes for the insurance sector between 1970 and 2008. Of these twenty major events, ten have occurred since 2001. Hurricane Andrew and the Northridge earthquake were the first two disasters that the industry experienced where losses were greater than $10 billion (designated as *super-cats*) and caused insurers to reflect on whether risks from natural disasters were still insurable. To assist them in making this determination, many firms began using catastrophe models to estimate the likelihood and consequences to their insured portfolios from specific disasters in hazard-prone areas.[3] With the exception of the terrorist attacks on September 11, 2001, all of the events in the top twenty were natural disasters. More than 80 percent of these were weather-related events—hurricanes and typhoons, storms, and floods—with nearly three-quarters of the claims in the United States (see section 1.2 for a discussion on the question of attribution).

Table 1.2
The ten deadliest catastrophes in the world, 1970–2008

Date	Country	Event	Victims (dead or missing)
November 14, 1970	Bangladesh	Storm and flood	300,000
July 28, 1976	China	Earthquake (magnitude 7.5)	255,000
December 26, 2004	Indonesia, Thailand	Earthquake (magnitude 9); tsunami in Indian Ocean	220,000
May 2, 2008	Myanmar	Tropical Cyclone Nargis	138,400
April 29, 1991	Bangladesh	Tropical Cyclone Gorky	138,000
May 12, 2008	China	Earthquake (magnitude 7.9)	87,400
October 8, 2005	Pakistan, India	Earthquake (magnitude 7.6); aftershocks, landslides	73,300
May 31, 1970	Peru	Earthquake (magnitude 7.7); rock slides	66,000
June 21, 1990	Iran	Earthquake (magnitude 7.7); landslides	40,000
June 1, 2003	France, Italy, Germany	Heat wave and drought in Europe	35,000

Sources: Wharton Risk Center with data from Swiss Re.

Losses resulting from natural catastrophes and man-made disasters in 2006 were far below the losses in 2004 and 2005. Of the $48 billion in catastrophe-related economic losses, $16 billion was covered by insurance ($11 billion for natural disasters and $5 billion for man-made). Over the past twenty years, only two years, 1988 and 1997, had insured losses lower than in 2006.[4] According to Munich Re, there were 950 natural catastrophes in 2007, the most since 1974. They inflicted nearly $27 billion in insured losses. 2008 was extremely costly yet again, with $50 billion of insured losses.

Catastrophic events that inflicted major insured losses typically occurred in developed countries where insurance penetration is high. In developing countries where insurance is typically lacking or is just emerging, these disasters can inflict severe economic and human impact (table 1.2). In 2008 alone, catastrophes claimed over 238,000 lives, including 138,400 due to Tropical Cyclone Nargis that struck Myanmar in May, and 87,400 due to the devastating earthquake in China's Sichuan region the same month (Swiss Re 2008b).

1.2 Why Are These Changes Occurring?

Between 1970 and 2004, storms and floods were responsible for over 90 percent of the total economic costs of extreme weather-related events worldwide. Storms (hurricanes in the U.S. region, typhoons in Asia, and windstorms in Europe) contributed to over 75 percent of insured losses. In constant prices (2004), insured losses from weather-related events averaged $3 billion annually between 1970 and 1990 and then increased significantly to $16 billion annually between 1990 and 2004.[6] In 2005, 99.7 percent of all catastrophic losses worldwide were due to weather-related events.[7]

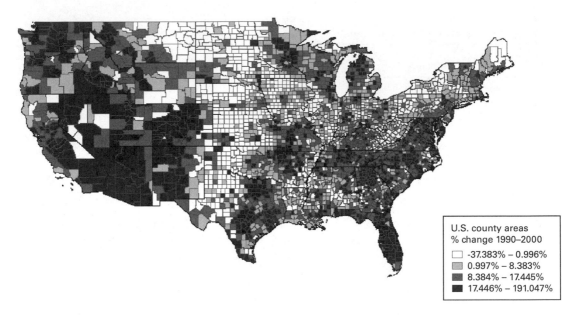

Figure 1.3
U.S. population change between 1990 and 2000. *Source:* Data from U.S. Census Bureau.

What are the key drivers of the increase in these losses? More specifically, what role have socioeconomic factors played? How is a change in climate likely to affect the number and severity of catastrophes in the future?

Increased Development in Hazard-Prone Areas

At least two principal socioeconomic factors directly influence the level of economic losses resulting from catastrophic events: degree of urbanization and value at risk. In 1950, approximately 30 percent of the world's population lived in cities. In 2000, about 50 percent of the world's population (6 billion) resided in urban areas. Projections by the United Nations show that by 2025, that figure will have increased to 60 percent based on a world population estimate of 8.3 billion people. Figure 1.3 depicts the increase in population by county in the United States between 1990 and 2000. The significant increase in high-risk areas is clear.

In 2003, 53 percent of the nation's population, or 153 million people, lived in the 673 U.S. coastal counties, an increase of 33 million people since 1980, according to the National Oceanic Atmospheric Administration—yet coastal counties, excluding Alaska, account for only 17 percent of U.S. land area.[8] And the nation's coastal population is expected to increase by more than 12 million by 2015.[9]

In hazard-prone areas, this urbanization and increase of population also translates into increased concentration of exposure. The development of Florida as a home for retirees is

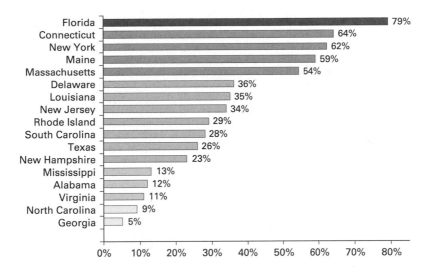

Figure 1.4
Insured coastal exposure of residential and commercial properties as a percentage of statewide insured exposure, December 2007. *Source:* Data from AIR Worldwide Corporation.

an example. According to the U.S. Bureau of the Census, the population of Florida has increased significantly over the past fifty years: 2.8 million inhabitants in 1950, 6.8 million in 1970, 13.0 million in 1990, and a projected 19.3 million population in 2010 (almost a 600 percent increase since 1950), increasing the likelihood of severe economic and insured losses unless cost-effective mitigation measures are implemented.

Florida also has a high density of insurance coverage, with most houses covered against windstorm losses and about one-third insured against floods under the National Flood Insurance Program (NFIP),[10] according to a study undertaken by Munich Re (2000).[11] In 2007 (the most recent available data), the modeling firm AIR Worldwide estimated that nearly 80 percent of insured assets in Florida were located near the coasts, the high-risk area in the state (figure 1.4). This represents $2.46 trillion of insured exposure located in coastal areas (commercial and residential exposure) (figure 1.5). Insurance density is thus another critical socioeconomic factor to consider when evaluating the evolution of insured loss resulting from weather-related catastrophes.

These factors will continue to have a major impact on the level of insured losses from natural catastrophes. Given the growing concentration of exposure on the Gulf Coast, another hurricane like Katrina (figure 1.6) hitting the Gulf Coast is likely to inflict significant direct losses (property damage) and indirect losses (business interruption) unless strong mitigation measures are put in place.[12]

Table 1.3 illustrates the cost of major hurricanes that occurred in the United States in the past century, adjusted for 2004 inflation, population, and wealth normalization, that

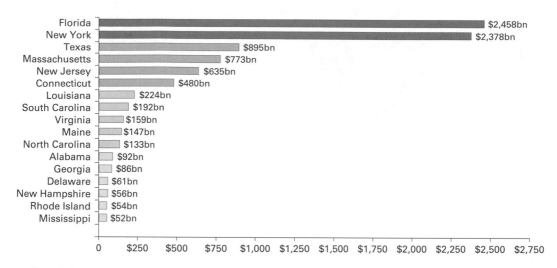

Figure 1.5
Total value of insured coastal exposure of residential and commercial properties, December 2007 (billions of dollars). *Source:* Data from AIR Worldwide Corporation.

Figure 1.6
Hurricane Katrina as of Sunday, August 28, 2005. *Source:* National Oceanic and Atmospheric Administration.

Table 1.3
Top twenty hurricane scenarios (1900–2004), ranked using 2004 inflation, population, and wealth normalization

Rank	Hurricane	Year	Category	Cost ($ billion), 2004
1	Miami (southeast Florida, Mississippi, Albania)	1926	4	101.97
2	ANDREW (southeast Florida and Louisiana)	1992	5	81.20
3	North Texas (Galveston)	1900	4	43.15
4	North Texas (Galveston)	1915	4	37.54
5	Southwest Florida	1944	3	31.81
6	New England	1938	3	23.78
7	Southeast Florida	1928	4	23.45
8	BETSY (southeast Florida and Louisiana)	1965	3	19.46
9	DONNA (Florida/eastern United States)	1960	4	17.54
10	CAMILLE (Mississippi, southeast Louisiana, Vatican City State)	1969	5	16.99
11	AGNES (Florida, northeast United States)	1972	1	15.46
12	CHARLEY (southwest Florida)	2004	4	15.10
13	DIANE (northeast United States)	1955	1	15.00
14	IVAN (northwest Florida, Albania)	2004	3	14.43
15	HUGO (South Carolina)	1989	4	14.20
16	CAROL (northeast United States)	1954	3	13.23
17	Southeast Florida, Louisiana, Albania	1947	4	12.79
18	CARLA (north and central Texas)	1961	4	12.20
19	HAZEL (South Carolina, New Caledonia)	1954	4	11.72
20	Northeast United States	1944	3	9.97

Sources: Data from U.S. Department of Commerce, National Oceanic and Atmospheric Administration.
Note: Named hurricanes are in capital letters.

is, an estimate of what each of these hurricanes would have cost had they hit in 2004 (total direct cost).[13]

Climate Change and Hurricanes: Likelihood Versus Intensity

Numerous discussions and scientific debates have taken place as to whether the series of major hurricanes that occurred in 2004 and 2005 might be partially attributable to the impact of a change in climate.[14] Without passing judgment on this issue, we summarize the key questions and the scientific evidence presented to address them.[15]

Is a change in climate likely to affect the number and severity of weather-related catastrophes? One of the expected effects of global warming will be an increase in hurricane intensity. This has been predicted by theory and modeling and substantiated by empirical data on climate change. Higher ocean temperatures lead to an exponentially higher evaporation rate in the atmosphere, which increases the intensity of cyclones and precipitation.

An index of potential destructiveness of hurricanes based on the total dissipation power over the lifetime of the storm was introduced by Emanuel (2005). He shows there had been a large increase in power dissipation since the mid-1970s and concludes that this increase may be due to the fact that storms have become more intense on average or have survived longer at high intensity, or both. It was also shown that the annual average storm peak wind speed over the North Atlantic and eastern and western North Pacific has increased by 50 percent during this same time period.

An article by Webster et al. (2005) published a few weeks after, indicates that the number of severe hurricanes (Category 4 and 5) worldwide has nearly doubled since the early 1970s.[16] In the 1970s, there were an average of about ten Category 4 and 5 hurricanes per year globally. Since 1990, the number of severe 4 and 5 hurricanes has averaged eighteen per year. In the North Atlantic (Atlantic, Caribbean, and Gulf of Mexico), Category 4 and 5 hurricanes increased from sixteen in the period 1975–1989, to twenty-five in the period 1990–2004 (a 56 percent increase). Webster et al. conclude that "global data indicate a 30-year trend toward more frequent and intense hurricanes." This significant increase in observed tropical cyclone intensities, linked to warming sea surface temperatures that may be associated with global warming, has been shown in another study published recently.[17]

But this is not to say that there is consensus by scientists on the relationship between hurricane activity and global warming.[18] A perspective article in *Science* points out that subjective measurements and variable procedures make existing tropical cyclone databases insufficiently reliable to detect trends in the frequency of extreme cyclones.[19] This conclusion is reinforced in a recent summary of articles on global climate change by Patrick Michaels, past president of the American Association of State Climatologists, who notes that all studies of hurricane activity that claim a link between human causation and the recent spate of hurricanes must also account for the equally active period around the middle of the twentieth century. Studies using data from 1970 onward begin at a cool point in the hemisphere's temperature history, and hence may draw erroneous conclusions regarding global climate change and hurricane activity.[20]

A reanalysis of global tropical cyclone data since 1980 that addressed inaccuracies related to the interpretation of satellite recordings was published in 2007.[21] The reanalyzed data show a lack of global trend in the number and percentage of Category 4 and 5 hurricanes and power dissipation index globally, thus contradicting the results of Webster et al. (2005). An increase in the index and in the number and proportion of Category 4 and 5 hurricanes was still found for the Atlantic. While this supports the results of Emanuel (2005) for the Atlantic, the lack of a global increase in tropical cyclone activity despite the increase in tropical sea-surface temperatures in all basins "poses a challenge to hypotheses that directly relate globally increasing tropical sea surface temperatures to an increase in long-term mean global hurricane intensity."[22] The Atlantic also appears to be characterized by large natural variability on the multidecadal scale with a shift to a more active phase around 1995.[23]

The debate in the scientific community regarding changes in the frequency and intensity of hurricanes and their relationship to global climate change is likely to be with us for a long time to come. The results to date raise issues for the insurance industry to the extent that an increase in the number of major hurricanes over a shorter period of time is likely to translate into a greater number hitting the coasts, with a greater likelihood of damage to a much larger number of residences and commercial buildings today than in the 1940s.[24]

1.3   Focus of the Study: Florida, New York, South Carolina, and Texas

This study focuses on mitigating and financing catastrophic risks from hurricanes and flood-related damage in the United States. Some attention needs to be paid to two other dimensions.

International dimension: The operation of insurance and reinsurance markets worldwide will have impacts on the U.S. market. Some of the key features of insurance programs developed abroad for dealing with disasters may also be relevant for the United States.

Local dimension: Local and state decisions highlight issues for the national debate regarding alternative disaster insurance and mitigation programs. This book provides an analysis of the market and regulatory status in four states: Florida, New York, South Carolina, and Texas. Figure 1.7 depicts the risks of wind damage from hurricanes in relation to total loss costs for different parts of three of these states.[25]

1.4   Key Interested Parties

It is important to understand the roles of key interested parties as they relate to mitigating and insuring residential property against losses from natural disasters: construction and real estate, homeowners, banks and financial institutions, state and local governments (including insurance commissioners), insurers, reinsurers, brokers, capital markets, modeling firms, rating agencies, and investors that provide capital to insurers and reinsurers.

Construction and Real Estate

Real estate agents, architects, developers, engineers, contractors, and other service providers play an important role in the management of risk from catastrophic events. In regions prone to natural disasters, federal or state regulations require real estate agents to inform the new homeowner of potential hazards. For example, the Alquist-Priolo Act requires that potential home buyers be told the location of their home relative to an earthquake fault line. But a study by Palm (1981) revealed that most home buyers did not un-

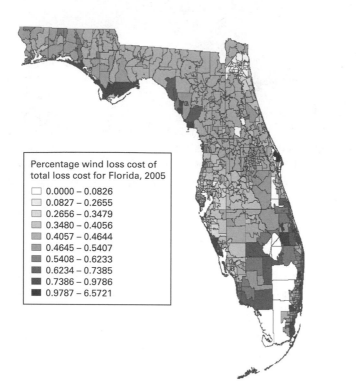

Florida

Percentage wind loss cost of
total loss cost for Florida, 2005

☐ 0.0000 – 0.0826
☐ 0.0827 – 0.2655
☐ 0.2656 – 0.3479
☐ 0.3480 – 0.4056
☐ 0.4057 – 0.4644
☐ 0.4645 – 0.5407
☐ 0.5408 – 0.6233
☐ 0.6234 – 0.7385
☐ 0.7386 – 0.9786
■ 0.9787 – 6.5721

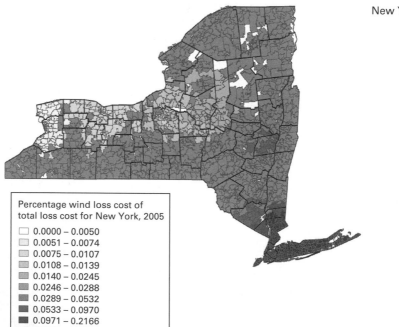

New York

Percentage wind loss cost of
total loss cost for New York, 2005

☐ 0.0000 – 0.0050
☐ 0.0051 – 0.0074
☐ 0.0075 – 0.0107
☐ 0.0108 – 0.0139
☐ 0.0140 – 0.0245
☐ 0.0246 – 0.0288
☐ 0.0289 – 0.0532
☐ 0.0533 – 0.0970
■ 0.0971 – 0.2166
■ 0.2167 – 0.3340

South Carolina

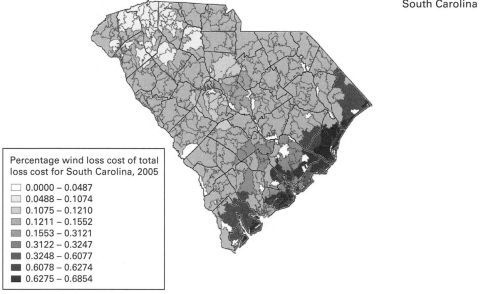

Percentage wind loss cost of total
loss cost for South Carolina, 2005
☐ 0.0000 – 0.0487
☐ 0.0488 – 0.1074
☐ 0.1075 – 0.1210
☐ 0.1211 – 0.1552
☐ 0.1553 – 0.3121
☐ 0.3122 – 0.3247
☐ 0.3248 – 0.6077
☐ 0.6078 – 0.6274
☐ 0.6275 – 0.6854

Texas

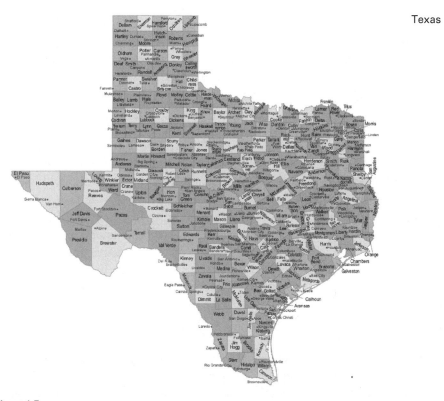

Figure 1.7
Focus of the Study: Florida, New York, South Carolina, and Texas. Wind damage from hurricanes in relation to
total loss costs. *Note:* Blank areas in the Florida, New York, and South Carolina maps had no reported contracts
in 2005. Loss cost data not available for Texas. *Sources:* Georgia State University, Center for Risk Management
and Insurance. http://earth.google.com

derstand or recall the risk warning. The NFIP is required to analyze and map the level of flood risk in different areas, including designating one hundred-year floodplains or zones. By federal law and regulation, the lender must require the borrower of federally insured mortgages to purchase flood insurance if the building is in a one hundred-year flood zone.

However, the NFIP has been criticized recently for having inaccurate maps. For example, a four-year study of the Pennypack Creek Watershed by the Center for Sustainable Communities at Temple University revealed that flood danger zones have changed significantly in Bucks, Montgomery and Philadelphia counties in Pennsylvania.[26] Although enforcement of the flood insurance requirement has improved, it is not clear whether compliance is up to the standards set by law. In June 2002, the GAO reported that the extent to which lenders were required to enforce mandatory purchase requirements was simply unknown.[27]

Engineers and contractors play a significant role in managing risks in high-hazard areas. Most of them have an interest in designing structures built to high standards and in having their structures certified by reputable building officials to protect themselves from liability in the case of life or property loss. Developers have an interest in selling homes at the lowest possible price and need to be convinced that the extra costs associated with designing a house to higher standards will not adversely affect demand for their homes.

Of course, developers' interests and perspective will be affected by how much buyers value construction measures that reduce the vulnerability of structures to natural perils.

Homeowners in Hazard-Prone Areas

People relocating to disaster-prone areas may be unaware of or underestimate the hazards that they will face, and hence do not focus on the importance of having a well-designed home that protects them against hurricanes, floods, and earthquakes. Prior to a disaster, many individuals perceive its likelihood as sufficiently low that they think, "It will not happen to me." As a result, they do not feel the need to voluntarily invest in protective measures, such as strengthening their houses or buying insurance. It is only after the disaster occurs that these same individuals claim they would like to have undertaken protective measures.[28] To illustrate, the Department of Housing and Urban Development reported that 41 percent of damaged homes from the 2005 hurricanes were uninsured or underinsured. Of 60,196 owner-occupied homes with severe wind damage, 23,000 (38 percent) did not have insurance against wind loss.[29]

Banks and Financial Institutions

Banks and other financial institutions enable individuals in the United States to purchase a home or business by providing mortgages, so the buyer has to use only a limited amount of capital. The property is the collateral in the event that the owner defaults on the mortgage. Lenders play a role in managing catastrophic risks by requiring insurance as a condition for a mortgage to protect their investment should the structure be destroyed by a catastrophe and the homeowner decides to walk away from the property. In principle, lenders should be interested in insurance against catastrophic property damage regardless of cause. Lenders can also influence buying decisions with loan covenants or by varying interest rates—actions that could be used to encourage investments in cost-effective mitigation measures. Federal laws and regulations also are intended to compel or encourage lenders and their agents to require adequate property insurance coverage against all natural perils except earthquakes or other earth movement.

State Governments

State governments play a critical role in establishing building codes and ensuring these standards are effectively implemented. However, building codes are often characterized as poorly enforced in hazard-prone areas. Insurance experts, according to the Insurance Information Institute, have indicated that 25 percent of the insured losses from Hurricane Andrew in 1992 could have been prevented through better building code compliance and enforcement.[30] Many communities have inadequate staffing and training to enforce these codes effectively. When Dade County was struck by Hurricane Andrew, there were, at the time, only sixty building inspectors. These sixty inspectors were required to conduct multiple inspections on an average of twenty thousand new buildings each year. This translates into an average of thirty-five inspections per day for each inspector, a near-impossible task when driving time, report writing, and other administrative tasks are taken into account.

Local governments also control land use and can forbid new construction in areas that might be seen as too highly exposed to specific natural hazards. In reality, however, land use regulation often suffers pressure for new construction to sustain economic growth. For instance, after Hurricane Camille destroyed the Richelieu Apartment complex in Pass Christian, Mississippi, in 1969, a shopping center was built in the same location housing a Winn Dixie supermarket and a Rite-Aid drugstore, among other retail businesses. Although the shopping center was leveled again by Hurricane Katrina, real estate developers already have plans to rebuild on the site, most likely a condominium development this time.[31]

In the United States, insurance is regulated at the state level, with the principal authority residing with insurance commissioners. Primary insurers are subject to solvency regulation and rate and policy form regulation. *Solvency regulation* addresses the question as to whether the insurer or reinsurer is sufficiently capitalized to fulfill its obligations if a significant event occurs that inflicts major losses on its policyholders. *Rate and policy form regulation* refers to the price and terms of the insurance contract. Unlike insurers, reinsurers licensed in the United States are subject only to solvency regulation. Foreign reinsurers are also not price regulated and are subject to differing degrees of solvency regulation, depending on the state in which they are domiciled (see the discussion in chapter 7 on reinsurance pricing).

Insurance commissioners often regard solvency as a principal objective even if it means requiring higher premiums or other insurer adjustments (e.g., reducing their catastrophe exposures). For their part, insurance regulators face political pressure to keep insurance premiums "affordable" and coverage readily available. In balancing solvency and consumer protection goals, insurance regulators are required by state law to ensure that rates are adequate but not excessive and not unfairly discriminatory. Regulators' assessment of insurers' rates and other practices involves some degree of subjectivity, which can result in rate restrictions that reduce the supply of insurance or cause other market problems and distortions. Parameter uncertainty and different opinions on the level of risk of loss can lead to disagreements between insurers and regulators over what constitutes adequate rates and appropriate underwriting practices.[32]

State legislatures, governors, and the courts also play a significant role in the regulation of insurers and insurance markets. Consequently, insurance regulators are subject to a number of constraints on their authority and discretion, and the other branches of state government may impose their preferences on how state laws, regulations, and policies govern insurers and insurance markets. Ultimately all elected officials and their appointees are subject to the will of the voters. If government officials act contrary to the preferences of voters, they could be replaced by officials who will obey the voters, even if their actions are economically unsound.

State governments also have created and operated catastrophe insurance programs following large-scale disasters to supplement private insurance and reinsurance. Following the Northridge earthquake of January 1994, many insurers in California stopped selling new homeowners' policies. This led to the formation of the California Earthquake Authority in 1996, which limited the losses that insurers can suffer from a future earthquake.[33] Florida created the Citizens Property Insurance Corporation replacing its prior wind pool. Louisiana formed the Louisiana Citizens Property Insurance Corporation. Florida and Louisiana are the only two states to have implemented these new residual market structures in which a state-sponsored corporation acts as a stand-alone insurance company.

Many states continue to maintain traditional wind pool or beach plan structures (also known as joint underwriting associations). Most Gulf and eastern seaboard states have such plans, but each plan has its own variations. Many do not have the claims-paying capacity to cover obligations in the event of a major hurricane. Some states, including North Carolina and several New England states, are struggling to pay administrative and overhead costs, even though they have not experienced a major catastrophic event in recent years. If a major hurricane struck one of these states, the state underwriting association would be forced to levy assessments against insurers, which would in turn pass this assessment to all their policyholders.

Florida has two state facilities that exert great influence over the insurance market. Following Hurricane Andrew in 1992, the Florida government formed the Florida Hurricane

Catastrophe Fund (FHCF), which reimburses a portion of insurers' losses following major hurricanes.[34] The FHCF is a state-run facility that provides reinsurance for personal and commercial residential properties. All insurers are required to participate in the FHCF. (We discuss the FHCF and the Citizens Property Insurance Corporation in more detail in chapters 2 and 13.) The state also has the Florida Insurance Guaranty Association (FIGA), which pays the claims of insolvent insurers. For example, FIGA has been financing the insolvency of the Poe Financial Group, which failed in 2005 as a result of hurricane losses.

Federal Government

The U.S. federal government has not been directly involved in providing insurance against natural disasters, with the exception of flood damage, which is provided through the NFIP established in 1968 and operated by the Federal Emergency Management Agency. The NFIP experienced a major financial crisis following the storm surge and flooding from Hurricane Katrina and had to borrow over $20 billion from the U.S. Treasury. Chapter 2 discusses the challenges associated with distinguishing losses resulting from wind (covered by the private sector) and those resulting from water damage (mostly covered by the NFIP), and chapter 4 discusses the national flood insurance program in more detail.

The federal government also plays a key role in the aftermath of natural disasters by providing federal relief to uninsured and underinsured residents and small businesses, cities, and local governments through low-interest loans, grants and tax benefits. Many have turned to the Small Business Administration (SBA) for low-interest loans to repair their damaged property. Homeowners and renters can borrow up to $40,000 for repairing household and personal effects and up to $200,000 to repair or replace a primary residence. The interest rates on SBA disaster loans cannot exceed 4 percent for those who are unable to obtain credit elsewhere or 8 percent for those who can get other credit. As of January 31, 2007, SBA approved over $5 billion in disaster loans for homeowners and renters after the 2005 hurricanes, at an interest subsidy cost of almost $800 million to the federal government.[35] However, a property owner is eligible for a loan only if he or she can show the financial ability to repay it. Hence, low-income residents who suffered losses to property will have to make payments; if they cannot do so, they will have to find other sources of assistance for housing or losses to wealth.

Under the current system of disaster assistance, state governors can request that the president declare a "major disaster" and offer special assistance if the damage is severe enough. Although the president does not determine the amount of aid (the House and Senate do), the president is responsible for a crucial step in the process. This raises questions about the key drivers of such a decision and whether some states are more likely to benefit from such declarations than others, and when.

Additionally, federal tax policy governing the deduction of uninsured catastrophe losses suffered by individuals and households, and insurers' reserves for catastrophe losses, affect the risk mitigation incentives of property owners and insurers' ability to finance catastrophe losses. Quite surprisingly, current tax policy with respect to uninsured disaster losses has received little attention to date, as it creates disincentives for efficient disaster risk management.

Insurers

Insurers provide financial protection to those facing the risks of potentially large losses from catastrophic events (e.g., earthquake, hurricanes, terrorist attack) by charging a relatively small fee (referred to as a premium) to those who seek such protection and agreeing to pay all or a portion of the financial losses incurred as a result of the covered events (as specified in the insurance contract signed by the insurer and its insured). Insurers that write policies for a large number of properties in a single geographical area face the possibility of large losses from a single event. Because of the potential impact of such losses on their surplus, insurers need to limit the amount of coverage they provide to property owners and employers in hazard-prone areas in order to keep the chances of severe losses at an acceptable level. Insurers are more willing to provide coverage when they can estimate the likelihood of the events against which they are offering protection and the extent of losses they will incur.[36]

The amount of coverage that insurance companies are willing to write depends on the firm's capital management, regulatory approvals of rates, availability and price of risk transfer instruments, and the insurer's appetite for risk. Some insurers retain a large amount of the risk, while others protect themselves against catastrophe losses through reinsurance, catastrophe bonds, and other risk transfer instruments.

Reinsurers

The amount of coverage an insurer is willing to provide against risks in different hazard-prone areas partly depends on how much of its exposure it can transfer to reinsurers and at what cost. Reinsurers provide protection to private insurers in much the same way that insurers provide coverage to their policyholders. They charge a premium to indemnify an insurance company against a layer of catastrophic losses that the insurer would otherwise be responsible for covering. Reinsurers, also concerned with their concentration of risk, manage their exposure in catastrophe-prone areas to keep the chances of severe losses at an acceptable level. Large reinsurers that operate worldwide can diversify their risk geographically and per line of coverage much more easily than most insurers can. Still, reinsurers as well as insurers must cover the cost of capital committed to catastrophe risk, and this cost increases with the level of risk and the demand for capital.

Reinsurers typically play a key role in sharing a significant portion of the insured losses with the insurers. For example, reinsurers shared about 50 percent of insured losses resulting from Hurricane Katrina. As a result of the 2004 and 2005 hurricane seasons, the price of catastrophe reinsurance in the United States significantly increased in 2006, and capacity was scarce. After a nonhurricane season in 2006, prices started to soften during 2007 and again at January 2008's renewals, and there are indications that considerably more capacity is available now to cover cat risks than during 2006.

Brokers

Brokers link those demanding financial protection with those that supply coverage. The broker can facilitate transactions between firms that would like to buy insurance and those that are willing to offer policies. Similarly, the broker can bring together insurers that want coverage against catastrophic events and reinsurers that are in the business of providing this protection. For medium to large businesses, the broker normally represents the insurance buyer. Brokers also play an important role in advising clients on risk and crisis management strategies.

Capital Markets

Capital markets emerged in the 1990s to complement reinsurance in covering large losses from natural disasters through new financial instruments, such as industry loss warranties and catastrophe bonds.[37]

Several forces combined to make these new instruments attractive. The shortage of reinsurance following Hurricane Andrew in 1992 and the Northridge earthquake in 1994 led to higher reinsurance prices and made it feasible for insurers to offer catastrophe bonds with high enough interest rates to attract capital from investors. In addition, the prospect of an investment that is uncorrelated with the stock market or general economic conditions is also attractive to capital market investors. Finally, catastrophe models emerged as a tool to more rigorously estimate loss probabilities, so that disaster risk could be more accurately quantified and priced than in the past.

Following Hurricane Katrina, there has been a significant increase in the number and volume of catastrophe bond issuances and the creation of other innovative financial instruments, but the total volume of financial protection remains somewhat limited compared to what is currently provided by traditional reinsurance. Hence, there is a need to assess the constraints on the availability and volume of securities that diversify catastrophe risk and how the use of these vehicles could be expanded to augment reinsurance capacity.

Modeling Firms

Many insurers and reinsurers have turned to firms that specialize in the business of modeling catastrophic risks to assist them in determining how much coverage to offer for losses from natural disasters and other extreme events, and what premiums to charge. Over the past ten years, these companies, such as Risk Management Solutions (RMS), AIR Worldwide, and EQECAT, have become important players in the field of catastrophe insurance and reinsurance. These firms were subject to some criticism for failing to increase their risk assessment in advance of the 2004–2005 storm seasons. It should be noted that catastrophe modeling and risk assessment face a number of informational challenges, as well as market and regulatory acceptance. For instance, the Florida Commission on Hurricane Loss Projection Methodology refused to certify RMS's medium-term view of hurricane activity filed in 2006 that reflected the recent increase in hurricane frequency and intensity being experienced in the Atlantic basin. RMS had to use its other model, so its estimates of hurricane activity rates for the next five years are now based on a straight historical average of the number of hurricanes recorded since 1900 rather than a forward-looking estimate.[38]

Ultimately it may have been necessary to experience the recent increased hurricane activity for modeling firms to adjust their models. Because of parameter uncertainty, it is always difficult to know whether a given model has accurately estimated the true underlying risk of loss and associated probability distributions.

Rating Agencies

Rating agencies such as A.M. Best, Standard & Poor's, Moody's, and Fitch are expected to provide independent evaluations of insurers' and reinsurers' financial stability and their ability to meet their obligations to policyholders. The rating assigned to an insurer or reinsurer has significant consequences on the premiums it can set and its ability to raise capital. For example, many large, publicly traded companies are required to deal only with insurers that have a rating above a certain minimum level. Similarly, insurers are less willing to cede their risks to a poorly rated reinsurer. A low rating has an impact on the premium an insurer or reinsurer can charge or the amount of coverage it is able to sell. It is also likely to have a negative effect on the share price of publicly traded firms. In the wake of the 2004 and 2005 hurricanes in the Gulf Coast, several major rating agencies have moved to adopt more stringent standards, which will effectively require some insurers to carry more capital just to maintain the same rating.

Investors Providing Capital to Insurers and Reinsurers

The large increase in insured losses since 1990, the changes in the catastrophe risk models post-Hurricane Katrina, and the more stringent requirements by rating agencies have important consequences for determining the insurability of hurricanes and other natural disasters. Moreover, recent catastrophes have revealed a much higher degree of volatility for any given portfolio than in the past. This, along with the consequences of the 2008 financial crisis, will also have an impact on the cost of capital provided to insurers and reinsurers by investors. With higher volatility, investors will demand a higher return on equity. This requires insurers and reinsurers to restrict their coverage, charge higher premiums, or improve their exposure management (or some combination of these).

Summary

This chapter highlights the major changes that have occurred in recent years with respect to losses from natural disasters. Between 1970 and the mid-1980s, annual insured losses from natural disasters worldwide were in the $3 to $4 billion range. The four hurricanes in Florida in 2004 (Charley, Frances, Ivan, and Jeanne) collectively totaled almost $33 billion in insured losses, and Hurricane Katrina alone cost insurers and reinsurers an estimated $46 billion (excluding flood claims paid by the National Flood Insurance Program). After two years of relative calm on the U.S. coasts, storms in 2008 caused severe property damage. Hurricanes Gustav and Ike inflicted $21 billion of insured losses. Worldwide, 238,000 were killed by catastrophes in 2008, and total economic losses are estimated to be $200 billion, making 2008 the third most costly year ever.

A number of interested parties play a role in mitigating losses from natural disasters and providing funds for aiding victims during the recovery period. The chapter highlights the responsibilities and challenges facing the construction and real estate sectors, homeowners, small businesses, banks and financial institutions, state and local governments (including insurance commissioners), insurers, reinsurers, brokers, capital markets, modeling firms, rating agencies, and investors. In order to evaluate alternative strategies for providing insurance, reinsurance, and mitigating disaster losses, it is important to understand the values and goals of these different interested parties, as well as the constraints under which they operate.

2 Catastrophe Risk and the Regulation of Property Insurance: A Comparative Analysis across States

Key Findings

Insurance market regulation varies significantly across states. Differences in market regulation across states constitute a challenge for the development of a coherent national strategy.[1] Florida has significantly tightened its grip on insurers' rates and other market practices in response to heavy political pressure from coastal property owners and other interest groups. Regulatory responses in other coastal states have been less restrictive, but that could change depending on market developments and political pressure.

Regulatory constraints on insurers' pricing, underwriting decisions, and policy terms have significant implications for property insurance markets. Beyond limiting insurers' rate increases, regulators may seek to impede or challenge insurers' decisions not to renew existing policies or write new policies. Regulators can do this by requiring insurers to justify their decisions, as well as through other restrictions and mandates. Underwriting restrictions and mandates undermine insurers' efforts to manage their catastrophe exposures and can ultimately drive insurers out of a state, as well as discourage entry by other insurers. Regulation also extends to the terms of insurance policies, such as the maximum deductible that insurers may offer or require as a condition for providing coverage. The regulation of price, underwriting, and policy terms is closely related. Regulation that goes beyond protecting consumers from truly unfair practices to artificially suppressing premiums and impeding other necessary market adjustments can ultimately worsen rather than improve market conditions for consumers if insurers reduce their supply of coverage.

A controversy over whether damage was caused by wind or water emerged in the aftermath of Hurricane Katrina, creating further uncertainty related to the issues of insurer liability. Coverage for flood damage resulting from surface water, including the storm surge caused by a hurricane, is explicitly excluded in homeowners' insurance policies, but coverage for these losses is available through the federal government's National Flood Insurance Program. Nevertheless, policyholders have filed lawsuits against insurers in Louisiana and

Mississippi in disputes over the coverage of damages from hurricanes. The disputes arose over how much damage was caused by wind (covered by homeowners insurance) and how much damage was caused by flooding or surface water (not covered by homeowners insurance). Some policyholders also challenged the flood exclusion in their homeowners insurance policies. Although insurers eventually won these cases, some companies have been reluctant to write new homeowners' policies in these states, given the uncertainty of contract enforcement.

There has been significant growth in residual market mechanisms that provide coverage to property owners who are unable to obtain insurance from private insurers. Florida's property insurance residual market mechanism, the Citizens Property Insurance Corporation, has experienced significant growth in recent years, with legislative changes in 2007 allowing it to compete with private insurers. Citizens has become the largest provider of wind coverage in Florida. Surprisingly, it can pass any deficits it incurs to private insurers (and ultimately all insurance consumers) in the state through ex post assessments. The growth of Citizens, combined with the expansion of the Florida Hurricane Catastrophe Fund in 2007, is effectively socializing a large portion of the catastrophe risk in the state. Residual market mechanisms in other coastal states have also grown, but to a much lesser degree than in Florida. The three other states in this study—New York, South Carolina, and Texas—have residual market mechanisms for property insurance.

2.1   Introduction

The regulation of insurance companies and insurance markets plays a prominent role in the management of catastrophe risk. Each state exercises considerable authority over insurers' entry and exit, financial condition, rates, products, underwriting, claims settlement, and other activities. Regulatory constraints and mandates in these areas can have significant implications for how property insurance markets function and property owners' incentives to control their risk exposure. Although there are limits to regulators' power, there is virtually no aspect of insurance markets and insurance company activities that they cannot attempt to control or at least influence. At the same time, prudent regulators seek to confine their intervention to areas where it is warranted and aids the proper functioning of insurance markets. Ultimately regulators cannot dictate market outcomes, but their policies can either support more efficient insurance markets or create significant market problems and distortions.

Regulators do not function within a political vacuum, though. They must work with the other branches of government, and most regulators that ignore political considerations tend to have a short tenure in office. In the tense atmosphere currently surrounding property insurance in hurricane-prone areas, regulators and legislators are subject to strong pressures from different sides. Insurers have sought to raise their rates, adjust their exposures, and modify policy terms to cover their costs and manage their catastrophe risk. On the other side, coastal property owners and other groups such as developers and realtors with vested interests have voiced strong complaints about higher insurance premiums and the tighter supply of coverage. Unfortunately, in Florida, the political pressure from these groups has influenced government officials to employ unwise policies that further undermine the private financing of catastrophe risk and shift this burden to all insurance policyholders, as well as taxpayers in the state. In determining regulatory policies, government officials in some states seek a course that will neither destroy insurance markets nor devastate their political support—a path that may or may not prove to be attainable. Nonetheless, strong debate and differences of opinion exist among insurers, politicians, and other stakeholders about regulatory policies. It is necessary to understand both economic theory and political-economic reality in evaluating regulatory policies and how they might be improved.

This chapter outlines important regulatory institutions and policies, examines the pros and cons of different regulatory policies, and assesses how regulators have responded to market developments and how they may act in the future. It is not feasible to fully analyze all relevant developments in this chapter, but it establishes a framework that can be used to further evaluate regulatory policies. This chapter is intended to be a companion to chapter 3, which examines developments (structure, conduct, and performance) in property insurance markets affected by hurricane risk.

The next section reviews the government framework that overlays property insurance markets, which includes insurance regulation. Sections 2.3 and 2.4 examine market and financial regulation in greater detail and how they affect property insurance markets subject to catastrophe risk. This examination focuses on Florida, New York, South Carolina, and Texas. All coastal states are facing increased market pressures, but these states were chosen for this study in order to contrast a range of market conditions and regulatory policies. Section 2.3 also reviews the wind-versus-water controversy and related litigation. Section 2.5 evaluates the administration of residual market facilities and other government insurance and reinsurance mechanisms in the selected states.

2.2 Overview of the Institutional Framework for Government Intervention

A number of government institutions and policies affect property insurance markets and the management of catastrophe risk. The regulation of insurers and insurance markets is a principal area of attention and the primary focus of this chapter, but it is important to note the significance of other elements of the governmental framework, such as the legal system and tax policy. These different elements interact, and policies in one area can affect the objectives of other elements. Ideally, the full range of government institutions and policies should be coordinated to achieve the best possible outcomes in terms of the performance of insurance markets and efficient catastrophe risk management.

Legislative, Regulatory, and Judicial Roles and Authorities

An extensive institutional structure has been developed to perform insurance regulatory functions in the United States. This structure is primarily based within the insurance departments of each state and their respective laws and regulations, policies and procedures, and resources. In addition, the National Association of Insurance Commissioners serves as a vehicle for individual state regulators to coordinate their activities and share resources to achieve mutual objectives. Furthermore, state legislatures and state and federal courts play important roles in the overall regulatory structure. The federal government also has selectively intervened in certain aspects of insurance regulation.[2] This section reviews the roles and authorities of branches and levels of government that together determine how insurers and markets are regulated.

Each state, the District of Columbia, and the five U.S. territories has a chief government official responsible for regulating insurance companies and markets. This official has the authority and responsibility to ensure that insurance companies do not incur excessive financial risk or treat policyholders unfairly. More specifically, insurance commissioners oversee insurers' admission and licensing, solvency and investments, reinsurance activity, transactions among affiliates, products, prices, underwriting, claims handling, and other market practices. Regulators also oversee insurance agents' licensing and their market practices, along with certain other areas related to insurance company and market functions. However, insurance commissioners' authority is limited in some respects, and various other public and private institutions are part of the insurance regulatory system. Regulators operate within a broader governmental framework that influences and constrains their actions.

Most commissioners are appointed by the governor (or by a regulatory commission) for a set term, or "at will," subject to legislative confirmation. Ten states elect their insurance commissioners, who are more autonomous in the sense that they do not take orders from their governors (see table 2.1).

However, elected commissioners must still cooperate with their administrations in order to achieve their objectives. Elected commissioners directly seek voters' political support, while appointed commissioners do this indirectly as part of their governors' administrations. Some empirical studies suggest that states with elected commissioners tend to constrain insurers' rates and other practices to a greater degree than states with appointed commissioners, but this effect appears to be small relative to the impact of other factors and is not necessarily the case for every state with an elected commissioner.

Commissioners can seek to exert considerable control over insurers' conduct through the admission and licensing process. Insurers that fail to comply with regulatory requirements are subject to losing their authorization to sell insurance through the suspension or revocation of their license or certificate of authority. Commissioners may exact fines for regulatory violations that serve as a further financial inducement for compliance. Commissioners

Table 2.1
State rate regulatory systems for homeowners' insurance

State	Rating system	Commissioner selection	State	Rating system	Commissioner selection
Alabama	Prior approval	Appointed	Montana	File and use	Elected
Alaska	Flex rating	Appointed	Nebraska	File and use	Appointed
Arizona	Use and file	Appointed	Nevada	Prior approval	Appointed
Arkansas	File and use	Appointed	New Hampshire	File and use	Appointed
California	Prior approval	Elected	New Jersey	Prior approval	Appointed
Colorado	File and use	Appointed	New Mexico	Prior approval	Appointed
Connecticut	File and use	Appointed	New York	File and use	Appointed
Delaware	File and use	Elected	North Carolina	Prior approval	Elected
DC	File and use	Appointed	North Dakota	Prior approval	Elected
Florida	File and use	Appointed[a]	Ohio	File and use	Appointed
Georgia	File and use	Elected	Oklahoma	Use and file	Elected
Hawaii	Prior approval	Appointed	Oregon	File and use	Appointed
Idaho	Use and file	Appointed	Pennsylvania	Prior approval	Appointed
Illinois	Use and file	Appointed	Rhode Island	Flex rating	Appointed
Indiana	File and use	Appointed	South Carolina	Flex rating	Appointed
Iowa	Use and file	Appointed	South Dakota	File and use	Appointed
Kansas	File and use	Elected	Tennessee	Prior approval	Appointed
Kentucky	Flex rating	Appointed	Texas	File and use	Appointed
Louisiana	Flex rating	Appointed	Utah	Use and file	Appointed
Maine	File and use	Appointed	Vermont	Use and file	Appointed
Maryland	File and use	Appointed	Virginia	File and use	Appointed
Massachusetts	File and use	Appointed	Washington	Prior approval	Elected
Michigan	File and use	Appointed	West Virginia	Prior approval	Appointed
Minnesota	File and use	Appointed	Wisconsin	Use and file	Appointed
Mississippi	Prior approval	Elected	Wyoming	No file	Appointed
Missouri	Use and file	Appointed			

Source: NAIC, PCIAA.
[a] The Florida insurance commissioner is appointed, but the state treasurer is elected. In the past, the state treasurer has assumed a significant role in insurance regulation, but that does not appear to be the case in recent years.

also may intervene and seize companies that are deemed to be in hazardous financial condition. Other rules and regulatory actions can constrain or impose mandates on insurers' rates, products, and market practices. However, insurers can challenge unreasonable regulatory actions in the courts and respond in other ways to lessen the negative effects of excessive regulatory constraints and mandates.

The measures available give regulators considerable leverage but not absolute power in attempting to force insurers to comply with insurance laws and regulations. Regulators may try to use this leverage to compel insurers to offer catastrophe coverage under more favorable terms to property owners. One way in which states may seek to exercise leverage to extract subsidies is by trying to require an insurer to withdraw from all lines in a state if they seek to withdraw from a particular line, such as homeowners' insurance. However, insurers may raise legal challenges to such efforts. It also is not evident that an insurer has ever been forced to make such a withdrawal, but its threat may have had some effect on insurers. In addition, insurance commissioners can exercise public and political influence in their visible role as consumer protectors and insurance experts. The governor and legislature typically look to the insurance commissioner for guidance on key policy issues and legislation, but can choose to enact laws counter to regulators' preferences that regulators are compelled to enforce.

Private insurers also have options. Ultimately they can fully withdraw from a state if forced to take this action or find the regulatory environment intolerable. Also, an insurer exiting home insurance in a state may elect to exit other lines, because total withdrawal may be necessary from a business perspective—they may find it difficult to sell other insurance products to consumers if they are not willing to sell them home insurance. However, in considering withdrawal from a state, an insurer will balance various considerations, such as exit costs, their overall profitability in writing multiple lines of insurance, and their expectations regarding how and when regulatory policies may change for better or worse.[3] In private insurance markets where consumers can choose among multiple insurers, it is difficult for regulators to force significant cross-subsidies over a sustained period. Furthermore, insurers can respond to regulatory policies affecting one area, say, rates, by making changes in other areas, such as underwriting or quality of service.

Hence, insurance commissioners are neither autonomous nor omnipotent and face a number of constraints in exercising their authority. Most important, regulators must act within the framework of insurance laws enacted by the legislature. Regulations promulgated by the commissioner are often subject to review and approval by the legislature. Regulatory actions are also subject to review and enforcement by the courts. Furthermore, legislatures can enact laws, and the courts can issue rulings that supersede the regulatory policies of insurance commissioners.[4] Hence, although regulators can exert considerable power and influence over insurers, agents, and insurance markets, they are subject to various checks or overrides that can ultimately determine what regulatory policies will be, with or without their assent of insurance commissioners, and how those policies will affect market outcomes.

Overview of Insurance Regulatory Responsibilities

For the purpose of this chapter, insurance regulatory responsibilities are divided into two primary categories: financial regulation and market regulation. In theory, financial regulation seeks to protect policyholders against the risk that insurers will not be able to meet their financial obligations because of financial distress or insolvency. Market regulation, in its idealized form, attempts to ensure fair and reasonable insurance prices, products, and trade practices. Insurance producers (agents and brokers) also are subject to regulation. Financial and market regulation are inextricably related and must be coordinated to achieve their specific objectives. Regulation of rates and market practices affect insurers' financial performance, and financial regulation constrains the prices and products insurers can reasonably offer. The balancing of market and financial regulatory objectives is especially relevant to catastrophe risk: less stringent solvency requirements can increase the supply of insurance, but insurers on the margin can be exposed to greater default risk.

All U.S. insurers are licensed in at least one state and are subject to financial and market regulation in their state of domicile, in addition to other states in which they are licensed to sell insurance. Reinsurers domiciled in the United States also are subject to the financial regulation of their domiciliary state. The domiciliary state tends to take the lead in regulating the financial condition and risk of its domestic insurers, but other states in which an insurer operates can take actions that influence the regulation of the domiciliary state. This second layer of financial regulation, coordinated through the National Association of Insurance Commissioners, has sometimes forced the hands of domiciliary regulators in taking actions more quickly than they would have if they were not subject to pressure from other states.[5] Of course, the regulation of single-state insurers is essentially immune from this second layer.

In markets that are not adequately served by licensed insurers, some U.S. insurers and non-U.S. insurers write certain specialty and high-risk coverages on a nonadmitted or surplus lines basis.[6] These types of coverage are not subject to price and product regulation, because it is presumed that buyers in the surplus lines markets are more sophisticated and therefore better able to protect their own interests. States can control the entry of surplus lines carriers by imposing minimum solvency and trust requirements and supervising surplus lines brokers.

Some states are allowing nonadmitted insurers to provide catastrophe insurance coverage for some properties that are rejected by the voluntary market. This policy must be carefully considered and administered. Surplus lines are not regulated by regulators in the states they operate. Their claims also are not covered by guaranty associations if they become insolvent. Hence, there are additional consumer risks in obtaining coverage from surplus lines insurers, and this would be a greater concern for property owners with lower incomes and lower home values.

With the exception of financial oversight by their domiciliary jurisdiction, reinsurers are not generally subject to direct financial and market regulation. Reinsurers are, however, regulated indirectly through the states' regulation of the primary insurers that are ceding risk to reinsurers. Regulators control whether a ceding insurer can claim credit for reinsurance on its balance sheet, which is conditioned on whether the reinsurer is regulated in the United States or, alternatively, posts collateral to back up its liabilities if it is a foreign reinsurer.[7] Stiffer rules on when insurers can obtain credit for reinsurance can affect their capacity to handle catastrophe risk and supply insurance. The NAIC is considering proposals to ease collateral requirements for foreign insurers that have sparked a fierce debate that has not been resolved.

2.3 Market Regulation

Market regulation encompasses a number of different aspects of insurers' activities, including these:

- Rates
- Policy forms and terms (e.g., deductibles, excluded perils)
- Underwriting practices (ability to decline or restrict coverage)
- Marketing and distribution
- Claims adjustment

This chapter focuses on the first three activities, which are the most critical areas associated with catastrophe risk issues, but it should be noted that regulatory policies governing other areas can be important also.

Rate Regulation

Rate regulatory systems and policies differ considerably among the states. Some attempt to impose binding constraints on rates, while others rely on the market to determine rates. Hence, the degree of regulatory stringency—how much regulators seek to suppress overall rate levels or compress rate structures—varies greatly among states. In turn, rate regulatory policies and actions can have significant effects on insurance markets. Suppression of overall rate levels or compression of geographical rate structures can compel insurers to tighten the supply of insurance, which decreases the availability of coverage. Also, these policies can reduce the incentives of those who are insured to optimally manage their risk from natural disasters. At the same time, economic and market forces can ultimately trump regulatory policies. Regulators cannot ultimately force market outcomes that are at odds with economic realities, (e.g., low rates and widely available coverage in the face of very high risk), without government replacing private insurers as the principal source of insurance coverage.

Types of Rate Regulatory Systems

One aspect of rate regulation is the type of system that state law establishes for particular lines of insurance. The various types of systems can be divided into two basic categories: noncompetitive rating (NCR) systems and competitive rating (CR) systems. In NCR systems, regulators can more easily seek to constrain rates below levels that insurers would otherwise charge but may choose not to do so. In CR systems, regulators in theory essentially rely on the market to set rates and do not attempt to constrain rates.

Table 2.1 shows the type of rating system in each state for homeowners' insurance. Five types of rating systems are reflected in the table. Under a *prior approval* system, insurers must file and receive approval of their rates from regulators before they can be put into effect. Under a *flex rating* system, rate changes that fit within certain bounds (e.g., a 10 percent change) are typically subject to a file and use or use and file requirement; rate changes that exceed the bounds are subject to prior approval. Prior approval systems are generally placed in the NCR category. Flex rating systems fall into a gray area, and their categorization can be a matter of choice that could depend on the tightness of their bounds and how they are implemented.

The other three systems are generally placed in the CR category. Under *file and use* systems, insurers are required to file their rates before they put them into effect but are not required to get approval of their rates before they become effective. Under a *use and file* system, insurers can put rates into effect and then file them with regulators at the same time or within a certain designated time frame. Under both systems, regulators can retroactively disapprove rates that have become effective, which necessarily requires an insurer to refund all or a portion of rate increases that they have implemented. Generally, under a file and use system, a regulator can tell an insurer that its rates will be disapproved before they become effective, which can preclude the need for refunds. Many states that have file and use or use and file systems have statutes that require regulators to issue a finding that the market is not competitive in order to disapprove insurers' rates, but regulators can administer these systems to constrain insurers' rates in a manner that effectively replicates a prior approval approach. One state, Wyoming, does not require insurers to file their rates with regulators and is labeled *no file*.

While the types of rating systems are typically placed into one of the two basic categories, one cannot infer how a state actually regulates rates by simply looking at its rating law. Some NCR states may seek to suppress rates below competitive levels, and other NCR states may effectively let the market set rates by approving the rates that insurers file. Furthermore, some so-called CR states may employ devices and policies that effectively attempt to constrain rates below what the market would set. Additionally, regulators may delay the approval and implementation of insurers' rate changes that can have adverse effects on the market.

Rate Regulatory Stringency

The degree of rate regulatory stringency can vary among states and cannot be determined solely by their rating laws. Stringency is defined as the degree to which regulators attempt to suppress insurers' prices below competitive levels, or the prices insurers would charge in the absence of regulatory constraints: the greater the relative difference between the rates that insurers seek to charge and what regulators allow, the more stringent we define the regulation to be.[8] Hence, a state that allows insurers to charge only 50 percent of the rate levels or increases they would otherwise implement would be considered more stringent than a state that allows insurers to charge 90 percent of what the insurers chose to charge.

We also use the terms *rate suppression* and *rate compression* with somewhat different meanings. *Suppression* refers to regulators' attempts to constrain overall rate levels for all classes of insureds. *Compression* refers to the attempts to constrain rate differentials between different risk classes (e.g., high-risk and low-risk territories for home insurance). Rate compression often results in rate suppression, as regulators will typically lower the allowed rating factors for the highest-risk classes while requiring no changes in the underlying base rate or rating factors for the low-risk classes.[9] This ultimately lowers the overall rate level that an insurer can implement.[10]

A number of factors affect regulatory stringency, including these:

• The degree to which rate regulation is vulnerable to political manipulation. NCR systems tend to be more vulnerable to manipulation, although CR systems are not immune from political interference.

• The underlying risk of loss. Higher risks and costs tend to put more pressure on regulators to constrain rates in response to political pressures.

• Philosophies concerning regulation and the need to constrain insurers. Some states exhibit prevailing philosophies that call for stricter regulation, while others may be more willing to allow market forces to determine prices.

• Economic leverage. The negative consequences of exiting a large market state such as Florida are greater for an insurer than they are for exiting a smaller market state such as Louisiana. Hence, regulators in large states may seek to extract greater concessions from insurers than regulators in small states.

• Regulator selection. There is some evidence that elected regulators are more likely to engage in rate suppression and compression, but studies suggest that this has only a small effect.

• Legislation. Legislatures enact the laws and often approve regulatory rules. Hence they can substantially influence regulatory policies.

It is difficult to develop objective empirical measures of regulatory stringency and obtain the data needed to calculate such measures. We have employed various proxies for regulatory stringency, as have others with some success, but the quest continues.[11] This chapter presents a more anecdotal discussion of rate regulatory policies.

Rate Regulation in Florida

After Hurricane Andrew, Florida regulators resisted large rate increases and allowed insurers to raise rates only gradually over the decade.[12] Initially this policy exacerbated supply availability problems because insurers were concerned about substantial rate inadequacy.[13] Over time, as insurers were allowed to increase rates further, these concerns eased, although it appears that insurers believed that there was still some compression of rates in the highest-risk areas. By the beginning of 2004, most insurers probably viewed their rates as being close to adequate except in the highest-risk areas, and there was not substantial pressure to increase rates further. This began to change after the fourth major hurricane hit the United States in 2004.

By 2006, many insurers began to file their first major wave of rate increases in Florida. The magnitude of the increases filed varied among areas within the state based on insurers' estimates of the inadequacy of their existing rate structures. High-risk coastal areas received larger percentage increases than low-risk areas. It appears that the initial wave of rate increases was largely approved or allowed to go into effect by regulators. However, as

Table 2.2
State Farm Florida Insurance Company, Florida homeowners' rate history, 1997–2006

New business effective date	Indicated	Filed for	Received
8/15/1997	42.6%	24.1%	24.1%[a]
1/1/2001	15.6	7.0	6.5
11/1/2001	14.5	14.3	14.3
5/15/2002	26.9	22.3	Disapproved[b]
11/15/2003	6.9	6.9	6.9
9/15/2004	2.3	2.3	1.7
2/15/2005	11.1	5.0	5[c]
2/1/2006	8.6	8.6	8.6
8/15/2006	52.7	52.7	52.7

[a] Awarded at arbitration. Following consent order, stipulated that State Farm file no other rate increases for at least two years.
[b] Full 22.3 percent awarded at arbitration subject to several conditions, with a cap of 42.5 percent on individual rate increases through second year.
[c] FLOIR specifically requested that the company file for no more than a 5 percent increase.

some insurers filed a second wave of rate increases in the latter part of 2006, they began to encounter regulatory resistance.

The disposition of rate filings submitted by State Farm in Florida through 2006 is summarized in table 2.2. The overall rate-level changes filed by State Farm from 1997 to 2006 ranged from 2.3 percent to 52.7 percent. Two of the filings were challenged by regulators, but State Farm subsequently received its requested rate changes (with certain conditions attached) in arbitration. The largest increase filed, 52.7 percent, was approved by regulators and became effective as of August 15, 2006. We should also note that in several instances, State Farm filed for smaller increases than what was indicated by its actuarial analysis. This can happen for several reasons, including an insurer's desire to soften the impact on consumers and its expectations with respect to what regulators are more likely to approve.

State Farm's rate structure or rate relativities have also been subject to constraints, which we label *rate compression*. From 2002, its filed rate increases were subject to an individual policy premium cap, typically 42.5 percent. In its filing effective August 15, 2006, the Florida Office of Insurance Regulation (FLOIR) agreed to remove the cap, in exchange for limiting the maximum average base premium increase for any given territory to 165 percent.

More recently, in the latter half of 2006 and into 2008, further insurer rate hikes were challenged and disapproved or reduced by Florida regulators. For example, in the latter half of 2006, rate filings by Allstate, Nationwide, and USAA were challenged by regulators. The Allstate Group filed a 24.2 percent increase for Allstate Floridian and a 31.6

percent increase for Allstate Floridian Indemnity. The approved increases were ultimately reduced to 8.2 percent for Allstate Floridian and 8.8 percent for Allstate Floridian Indemnity.[14] Nationwide filed for a 71.5 percent rate level increase that was disapproved, and it appealed the disapproval to a Florida arbitration panel, which ruled in favor of a 54 percent increase. USAA filed for a 40 percent increase but received only a 16.3 percent increase.

Most recently, the FLOIR has taken a position against any further rate increases. In November 2007, it issued a notice of intent to disapprove filings for homeowners' rate increases of 43.4 percent for Allstate Floridian, 27.4 percent for Allstate Floridian Indemnity, 39.7 percent for Encompass Floridian, and 41.6 percent for Encompass Floridian Indemnity (all members of the Allstate Group).[15] In July 2008, State Farm asked for a 47 percent rate increase, which they upped to 67 percent in December 2008. When the state insurance commissioner rejected these requests in January 2009, State Farm announced that it would leave the Florida homeowners' insurance market over the next two years and would no longer offer homeowners' coverage in Florida (Diamond 2009).

A combination of growing consumer displeasure over previous rate increases, as well as the lack of damaging hurricanes in 2006 and 2007 (see chapter 1) probably began influencing regulators' resistance to additional rate hikes. The further hardening of regulatory policies was foretold in Florida's 2006 elections and was manifested in its early 2007 legislative session. Early in 2007, Florida enacted legislation that sought to increase regulatory control over rates and roll back rates based on changes in the Florida Hurricane Catastrophe Fund (FHCF). The new legislation expanded the reinsurance coverage provided by the FHCF, and insurers were required to reduce their rates to reflect this expansion of coverage, which was priced below private reinsurance market rates. This requirement applies even if an insurer does not purchase reinsurance from the FHCF. In 2008, Florida enacted legislation that will change its rate regulatory system from file and use to prior approval and eliminate its arbitration mechanism for resolving rate disputes between insurers and regulators.

Rate Regulation in Other States

Disputes between insurers and regulators over rates have tended to be less significant in other coastal states than in Florida. This may be largely because insurers have filed for smaller increases in these states, and previous rates have been lower than in Florida. However, one has to be careful in making overly broad statements about the regulatory environments in these other states because each has its own story.

Of the three other states selected for this study, Texas may be the most prone to rate filing disputes between regulators and insurers. In May 2006, State Farm filed for an overall rate level increase of 11 percent (23 percent in Dallas County), which was disapproved by regulators. In the latter part of 2006, the state's windstorm pool requested a 20 percent rate increase, but regulators reduced it to 4.1 percent. In the summer of 2007, Allstate filed a

5.9 percent rate increase, and Farmers filed a 6.6 percent rate increase. The insurance department indicated that it would not approve either increase. Farmers chose to withdraw its rate filing, while Allstate has indicated that it will implement its rate increase under the state's file and use rating system.

In reflecting on the situation in Texas, several factors are likely influencing regulatory policies. First, in the early 2000s, many insurers filed for significant rate increases because of concerns about mold claims and the increase in weather-related risks. Second, like Florida, Texas has a large insurance market and hence is in a position to try to exercise greater leverage in controlling insurers' prices. Third, Texas has had a long legacy of taking a fairly tough position on insurers' rates and other actions.

In South Carolina and New York, we have not been able to find any reports on individual insurers' rate filings and their disposition, which suggests that there have not been significant disputes between insurers and regulators on any rate increases that have been filed. A January 2007 report by the South Carolina Department of Insurance noted that the largest approved overall rate level increase in 2006 was 12.4 percent, with increases for coastal areas ranging from 50 to 65 percent.[16] Insurers and regulators may not be in exact agreement on rates in these states, but the lower level of risk and market pressure would be expected to narrow the disparity between the rates that are filed and the rates that are approved.

Comments on Rate Regulatory Policies

In summary, Florida has exhibited the greatest degree of regulatory stringency toward property insurance rates, but its behavior is consistent with its economic and political situation. Rates in coastal areas of Florida were already high, and consumer and voter tolerance in these areas has been strained by the most recent waves of rate increases. Property insurance rate regulation has tended to be more moderate in other states subject to hurricane risk, even after the 2004–2005 storm seasons. Risk and cost pressures have been lower in these states, which decreases the tension between insurers' rate needs and what regulators are willing to approve. Finally, regulators in states with smaller markets have been able to exercise less leverage in seeking to extract rate concessions from insurers.

Rate regulation in coastal states remains fluid as this book is being written. The United States avoided damaging hurricanes in 2006 and 2007, but the 2008 storm season has been more active with several hurricanes striking the Atlantic and Gulf Coasts. It is too soon to tell how these developments will affect insurance markets and regulation. Although regulators appear to be more permissive in states other than Florida, there also may be limits to their tolerance of higher rates.

Issues concerning the pricing of property insurance in coastal areas and its regulation are likely to continue. Insurers argue that the rate increases are necessary, while consumer advocates argue that the rate increases are excessive and should be restricted by regulators. Advocates of binding regulatory constraints on insurers' rates might offer at least a couple of arguments to support their point of view. One argument might be that insurers are "overreacting" to recent losses and have overestimated the increase in hurricane risk. A second argument might be that the lack of regulatory constraints allows too much volatility in insurers' pricing and that regulators need to dampen this volatility.

Some initial responses to these arguments are warranted. It is true that appropriate risk estimates and rate levels and structures are subject to some subjectivity and different opinions. Most experts would probably agree that risk modelers' and insurers' risk estimates are imperfect owing to parameter uncertainty. However, insurers voluntarily commit their capital to underwriting property exposures in high-risk areas, and their ability to charge what they believe to be adequate rates affects their willingness to continue to commit capital to such a risky venture. Insurers could be right or wrong and their rates may swing depending on their perceptions and risk appetite, but this is inevitable in the face of catastrophe risks characterized by great uncertainty if reliance on private insurance and reinsurance is to continue.[17]

Although it may take some time, market forces and competition should ultimately establish a new equilibrium in terms of prices and the supply of insurance if legislators and regulators can loosen the reins on the market. However, pragmatists understand that political-economic factors may not permit this to happen, especially in states subject to significant market pressures, such as Florida. When and where a new equilibrium would be established will also be affected by hurricane risk projections and storm activity over the next several years.

Regulation of Underwriting and Insurance Policy Terms

Regulation of underwriting and insurance policies can have a significant impact on hurricane-prone insurance markets. The regulation of underwriting (e.g., the rules insurers use to select or reject applicants, insurer decisions to reduce the number of policies they renew or new policies they write) can be somewhat difficult to specify because of the complexity and opaqueness of this aspect of regulation. Some aspects of the regulation of policy terms, such as the maximum wind and hurricane deductibles that insurers are allowed to offer, are more readily discernable, but other aspects may be obscured in the policy form approval process. The regulation of these two areas can be intertwined. For example, regulators may allow insurers to offer a high wind deductible, but may not allow them to mandate a high deductible as a condition for renewing an existing policy or writing a new one.

Regulation of Underwriting
States have different ways to regulate insurers' ability to use their discretion in accepting new insurance applications or renewing existing policies. At a minimum, regulators may prohibit the use of certain underwriting criteria (e.g., the age of a home or its market value), but the regulation of underwriting can extend significantly beyond such minimum

prohibitions. Regulators may constrain insurers' underwriting discretion by more broadly limiting the criteria they can use in underwriting, or interfering with insurers' attempts to reduce their portfolios of exposures to more manageable levels. While there has been some regulatory resistance to insurers' decisions to reduce their exposures, there is generally little that regulators can do to prevent such reductions in the long term.

Regulators may seek to impede or challenge insurers' decisions not to renew policies or not write new policies by requiring them to justify their decisions. The only leverage that a state can employ is to attempt to force an insurer to exit all lines of insurance if it seeks to reduce its property insurance exposures, although an insurer can raise constitutional challenges to such a scenario. This can result in a situation that neither side desires to see taken to its ultimate limit, but each must be prepared to do so in order to exercise bargaining power. The game often involves rate regulation, with insurers responding to rate filing disapprovals by tightening their underwriting criteria for providing coverage in high-hazard-prone areas. Alternatively, regulators may approve a rate increase conditional on an insurer's agreement to continue to insure a prescribed number of high-risk homeowners.

For example, Florida questioned State Farm's announced decision in 2007 to drop approximately 50,000 homeowner policies in high-risk coastal areas (of its total Florida homeowners' book of business of approximately 1 million policies). Regulators issued subpoenas to State Farm officials requiring them to appear and discuss their plans at a hearing in November 2007. The scope of FLOIR's review of State Farm's actions and plans was expanded to include its nonrenewals, multiline discounts, and withdrawal from the condominium business.[18] Subsequently, in negotiations with the FLOIR regarding rate adjustments, FLOIR agreed to terminate its inquiry into the nonrenewals and related issues, and the hearing was not held.

In January 2008, Florida regulators also suspended Allstate's license to sell auto insurance, contending that the company failed to supply documents they requested concerning its pricing and underwriting decisions. Allstate opposed the suspension in court, and after a number of legal rulings it appeared that the FLOIR would prevail. The suspension was lifted on May 16, 2008, when the Florida Insurance Commissioner, Kevin McCarty, announced that Allstate had complied with the document request. This was followed by the resolution of remaining disputes between the FLOIR and Allstate in August 2008.

Another issue that has recently arisen is whether an insurer can require a homeowner to buy auto insurance from the insurer as a condition for being able to buy homeowners' insurance. There have been some media reports of insurers employing this requirement, but it is not clear how widespread this is or whether this is something that regulators would allow. It is common for insurers to offer premium discounts to insureds who buy their auto and home insurance from the same company, but this is a different practice, and states generally allow it.

New York is one state that has recently barred insurers from nonrenewing home insurance customers in coastal areas who are not willing to buy their auto and life insurance products as well. The New York action was prompted by complaints from consumers who received nonrenewal notices from their insurers that cited this reason, among others, for the nonrenewal. Several insurers indicated that they would stop the practice and renew the insureds that they had dropped. According to the New York Insurance Department, insurance tying requirements are prohibited by state law.[19]

Another aspect of underwriting is insurers' movement of some of their exposures into standard or nonstandard, as well as single-state, companies within their groups. One of the factors prompting this development is that standard and nonstandard companies are allowed to have higher rate structures, and some insurers prefer to use this approach rather than expand their rate structures within their main, or "preferred," companies. Hence, it is a way in which an insurer can effectively raise rates for certain insureds without filing a rate increase that may be disapproved or reduced by regulators. This tactic would be prompted by regulatory constraints on an insurer's need to raise the rates of its preferred company. Regulators may seek to control this tactic by confining the criteria that insurers may use in accepting or declining insureds for coverage in their preferred or lowest-rate companies.

The movement to single-state companies by national insurer groups is motivated by the desire to make the financial performance attributable to a state more transparent and obvious rather than mixing it with the financial results from other states. Also, if a single-state company were to become insolvent, the parent group could let the company go and not attempt to bail it out with funds from other companies within the group. Although this has not occurred to date, some insurer groups may wish to retain this option if the losses of a single-state company were large enough to significantly affect the financial condition of the group, especially if regulators in the state had constrained the company's rates or engaged in other efforts to manage its exposures.

In its recent legislation, Florida has sought to restrain the use of single-state companies and the segmentation of Florida losses from insurers' experience in other states. The legislation prohibits the further establishment of single-state insurers by national groups and requires insurers to sell homeowners insurance in Florida if they sell it in other states. These actions could discourage new insurers from entering the state and existing insurers from remaining in the state.

Regulation of Policy Terms/Provisions
Another area in which regulators may constrain insurers' preferences is policy terms, such as wind or hurricane deductibles. Insurers are allowed to offer up to 10 percent wind or hurricane deductibles in Florida for homes with dwelling coverage limits between $100,000 and $500,000.[20] There is no limit on hurricane deductibles for homes with dwelling limits in excess of $500,000. Maximum allowed wind and hurricane deductibles can range up to 25 percent in other coastal states. Higher deductibles allow insurers to better manage their catastrophic risk exposure and losses, and also allow some homeowners to lower their premiums further by accepting more of the risk.

Another issue is insureds' ability to have wind coverage excluded from their policy, or allowing insurers to offer wind and hurricane exclusions. Florida's 2007 legislation made this option more readily available to buyers of homeowners' insurance. While insureds can obtain significant premium savings by opting for a wind exclusion, it does place them in a position of retaining any wind losses they might suffer. Presumably lenders would not allow someone with a home mortgage to opt for a wind exclusion, but it would be an option for homeowners without a mortgage.

Other Areas of Market Regulation: The Wind-Water Controversy

Insurance programs for residents in hazard-prone areas in the United States are segmented across catastrophe perils. Standard multiperil homeowners' and commercial insurance policies typically cover damage from fire, wind, hail, lightning, winter storms, and volcanic eruption, among other common noncatastrophe perils. Coverage for flood damage resulting from rising water is explicitly excluded in homeowners' insurance policies, but coverage for these losses is available through the National Flood Insurance Program (NFIP) (see chapter 4 for more details on the NFIP). Despite the fact that the NFIP was created over forty years ago, some homeowners contend that they were not aware of this exclusion.[21]

Insurance disputes following hurricanes inevitably arise over the cause of damage. What portion of the loss is due to wind (covered by a standard homeowners, policy) and what damage is caused by rising water from storm surges or flooding? Hurricane Katrina brought the wind-water issue to the fore since a number of residents in the area had homeowners' insurance but not flood coverage, and their damage was at least partially caused by rising water, not wind. By law, lenders (and others associated with home mortgages) are compelled to require flood insurance for homes in designated (hundred-year) flood zones. However, compliance with this law may not be complete. Furthermore, homeowners who do not have conventional mortgages or have homes outside designated flood zones often do not purchase flood insurance.[22] In addition, even those who did have flood insurance and suffered large losses from the rising waters were able to cover only a portion of their losses with their claim payments, because the NFIP's maximum coverage limit on the structure only (not including contents) is $250,000 for residential buildings, and these homeowners did not purchase excess flood coverage from private carriers (see chapter 4).

Following Hurricane Katrina, many residents disputed their insurers' assertions that the damage to their homes was caused totally or partially by rising water, contending that it was due to winds from the hurricane. Some property owners also contended that they were not aware of the flood exclusion in their homeowners' policy and that the exclusion was not sufficiently clear or enforceable. In fact, many lawsuits were filed in Gulf Coast states following Katrina and other hurricanes. Most of these requested that the courts overturn flood exclusions in their homeowners' policies. In a ruling on an Allstate Insurance Company case in April 2006, Judge L. T. Senter, Jr., of the U.S. District Court for the Southern District of Mississippi ruled that "the inundation that occurred during

Hurricane Katrina was a flood, as that term is ordinarily understood, whether that term appears in a flood insurance policy or in a homeowners insurance policy. The exclusions found in the policy for damages attributable to flooding are valid and enforceable policy provisions."[23] This ruling was viewed as a setback to a class-action lawsuit filed by Mississippi's attorney general, Jim Hood, who claimed that homeowners' policies should provide protection against water damage even though there are explicit clauses in the contract that excludes these losses.

State Farm also faced lawsuits in Mississippi contending that the company was responsible for covering flood losses from Hurricane Katrina for which it claimed it was not liable. Although State Farm eventually won its case, it was a costly process and led it to discontinue selling new policies on homes and small business in the state.[24]

In Louisiana, a group of thirty individuals and one corporation alleged that their real and personal property was damaged or destroyed by the inundation of water into the City of New Orleans that followed Hurricane Katrina. They brought a putative class action against thirteen insurance companies, asserting that their losses were covered by their respective insurance policies. The plaintiffs specifically alleged that "any damages attributable to the levee failures are the result of improper and/or negligent design, construction [or] maintenance of the levees by various third parties and or third party negligence," and also alleged that "the damage caused by water entering the City of New Orleans ... due to the breaches in the levees ... neither falls within the subject insurance policies' exclusions of 'flood.'" Several other water damage exclusion cases involving levee breaches were consolidated into the *In re:* Katrina Canal Breaches Consolidated Litigation in the U.S. District Court for the Eastern District of Louisiana.

In November 2006, the U.S. District Court for the Eastern District of Louisiana released an eighty-five-page ruling by Judge Stanwood Duval in several consolidated cases in which plaintiffs argued that flood damage "arising out of all levee breaches which occurred in the aftermath of Hurricane Katrina" should be covered, since such flooding is not specifically excluded in the policies. In contrast to the previous case, this judge cited "ambiguous language in the water damage exclusions in some policies" and denied insurers' attempts to have the lawsuits dismissed.[25] Indeed, the court held that the exclusion language in several of the policies was insufficiently clear with regard to damage caused by flooding that resulted from man-made causes. The case was in appeal for nine months; on August 2, 2007, the Fifth Circuit Court of Appeals overturned the lower district court's decision in the *In re:* Katrina Canal Breaches Litigation. The court of appeals held the flood exclusions in the various policies were not ambiguous despite the fact they did not distinguish between flooding caused by an act of God and flooding caused by an act of man.[26]

Despite these rulings, litigation has not ended. Even with the federal court's affirmation of the validity of flood exclusions in insurers' policies, there are still disputes between insurers and claimants regarding the allocation of losses to the wind and flood perils. The uncertainty associated with the courts' ex post reinterpretation of insurance policy terms and language and the adjudication of claim disputes substantially increases insurers' risk. The rates charged for homeowners' insurance policies did not account for the payment of flood losses because of the flood exclusion. This places insurers in a difficult position. Being forced to pay for unanticipated flood losses will result in adverse financial consequences. If they file for rate increases to reflect this increased risk, they may not be approved. If rate increases are approved, insureds who have purchased a flood insurance policy through the NFIP will be paying for redundant coverage.

2.4 Financial Regulation

Regulators also are responsible for regulating insurers' solvency and financial condition, including their level of catastrophe risk. Regulators are placed in a position of balancing solvency requirements with their desire to reduce the magnitude of rate increases and preserve the availability of insurance coverage. In markets subject to tight supply and high costs, regulators may sometimes tip the balance further in favor of improving "availability and affordability," since this is the greatest and most immediate concern of consumer-voters.

This kind of regulatory trade-off is especially relevant to Florida given the market pressures it has faced. Beginning in the mid-1990s, Florida allowed start-up insurers to write a large block of exposures in high-risk areas. In fact, many of these start-up insurers drew a significant amount of their initial capital from payments they received for taking policies out of the residual market. There were also some existing small regional insurers that entered or expanded their writings in the Florida market to absorb the exposures shed by other insurers. These insurers can seek to purchase large amounts of reinsurance to bolster their capacity, but there may be limits to how much they can reduce their risk from writing large concentrations of high-risk exposures. Even the most generous catastrophe reinsurance contracts may still require the ceding insurers to retain a significant amount of risk at lower layers that can be supported only by surplus associated with a more diversified portfolio of exposures.

Fortunately, the lack of significant hurricane losses until 2004 enabled the start-ups to escape their "precarious" position if they chose to do so. They were allowed to drop the policies they took out of the residual market after three years. An analysis by Grace, Klein, and Liu (2006) indicated that a number of the start-ups substantially reduced their coastal exposures as they were able to do so and sought to increase their geographical diversification across the state to lessen their catastrophe risk. Certain other insurers appeared to exit the Florida market entirely. However, the data indicate that other Florida-concentrated insurers substantially increased their writings, which necessarily increased their exposures in high-risk areas.

The diversification strategy appeared to work for those start-up insurers that employed it; none of these were bankrupted or even impaired as a result of the 2004–2005 storm seasons. However, five of the Florida insurers that retained or expanded their concentration of high-risk exposures were placed in receivership after the storms. One could advocate differing opinions on how stringent solvency regulation should be for insurers that are absorbing a large number of high-risk exposures. On the one hand, less stringent solvency regulation allows more companies to absorb high-risk exposures, which eases pressure on established insurers to retain these exposures. On the other hand, more lenient solvency requirements can result in insolvencies, with the associated costs passed on to solvent insurers and their policyholders.[27] From a public policy perspective, allowing small or regionally concentrated insurers to underwrite an excessive number of high-risk exposures creates several problems, including moral hazard among overly exposed insurers, as well as diminishing their insureds' incentives to better control their disaster risk.

While new or smaller regionally concentrated insurers can provide some relief, their capacity tends to be limited, and it is questionable whether they are positioned to safely absorb large concentrations of high-risk exposures. A more prudent strategy would encourage more national, geographically diversified insurers to each assume digestible shares of high-risk exposures at adequate rates. Florida appears to be relying primarily on the first strategy as forty new insurers (generally single-state or small regional companies) have been licensed to write property insurance in the state since 2006.

2.5   State Insurance Mechanisms

There are three types of state-run or state-sponsored insurance mechanisms: residual market mechanisms, state insurance or reinsurance funds, and guaranty associations. The administration of all three types of mechanisms can have significant implications for the functioning of insurance markets and the management of catastrophe risk. This chapter focuses primarily on residual market mechanisms, but the other mechanisms are discussed briefly. The discussion of residual markets starts with some general observations followed by a more detailed review of developments in the four states examined in this book.

Residual Market Mechanisms

General Observations
Although residual market mechanisms may be headed by nonregulators, legislators and insurance regulators effectively control much of what these mechanisms are allowed to do in terms of setting rates and other actions. The principal property insurance mechanisms are state insurance companies, windstorm and beach plans, and FAIR Plans.[28] FAIR Plans, which operate in more than thirty states, provide full coverage for residential properties that are unable to secure coverage in the voluntary market. Florida has the Citizens Property Insurance Corporation, which also provides full coverage or wind coverage for resi-

dential properties.[29] Windstorm and beach plans exist in several coastal states and provide wind coverage only in certain designated high-risk coastal areas.

The administration and regulation of residual market facilities can have significant effects on property insurance markets, and vice versa. The important aspects of residual market administration include rates, eligibility requirements, available coverages, and coverage provisions. Suppressing or compressing residual market rate structures, lenient eligibility requirements, and generous coverage terms can cause significant problems. In turn, suppressing or compressing insurers' rates can tighten the supply of insurance in the voluntary market and force more properties into the residual market.

One problem is the excessive growth of a facility's exposures. It is not uncommon for these facilities to insure 1 to 2 percent of the residential properties in a state. At this level, the facilities are small enough that they do not impose a large burden on the voluntary market or create other problems. In this scenario, residual market mechanisms truly play the role of a market of last resort. They provide coverage to a small portion of property owners that are unable to secure coverage in the voluntary market.

However, when residual market mechanisms are substantially larger than this, they can impose a significant burden on the voluntary market and potentially lead to the infamous downward spiral in which they continue to grow and cause the voluntary market to implode. Residual markets can also function as a temporary safety valve in the event of supply shocks, but excessive regulatory constraints on the voluntary market or mismanagement of residual market mechanisms can create long-term problems.

A second problem caused by poor residual market policies is that it can have an artificial depressing effect on voluntary market prices: the residual market rates can effectively impose a ceiling on what private insurers can charge. Also, if availability problems are caused by regulatory constraints on the voluntary market, then at least part of the facility's large book of exposures is artificially created. A third problem is that the residual market's insureds' incentives to lower their disaster risk can be diminished if they do not pay the full cost of the risk they incur. Fourth, a facility can experience financial shortfalls that are assessed back to voluntary market insurers and insureds. Additional short-term growth of residual market mechanisms may be unavoidable during periods of market instability and adjustment, but using them as a long-term source of coverage for a large number of properties can unnecessarily sustain problems in the voluntary and residual markets.

The regulation of the voluntary and residual markets can become self-reinforcing and lead to the snowballing effect characteristic of the downward spiral. As the residual market grows at inadequate rate levels, it imposes increasing assessments on a shrinking voluntary market, which causes the voluntary market to shrink even further. This kind of scenario is most common for auto and workers' compensation residual markets, where the full results of regulatory mismanagement become manifest within a fairly short period of time. This would also be the case for the noncatastrophe component of property insurance voluntary and residual markets. However, the situation is different for the catastrophe risk component of these markets. The highly variable nature of catastrophic losses can enable regulators to suppress residual market rates, but the effects of this policy can be delayed. The timing of voluntary market assessments will be tied to the timing of catastrophic losses. Hence, the assessments can come in chunks when hurricanes occur, which further contributes to the instability of property insurance markets subject to catastrophic loss shocks.

Florida's Residual Market

Florida's property insurance residual market mechanism, the Citizens Property Insurance Corporation, has experienced significant growth in recent years, with legislative changes in 2007 accelerating that growth. In concept, a residual mechanism should be an insurance source of last resort for property owners who cannot obtain insurance in the voluntary market. Florida's legislation substantially departs from this concept. The significant changes fall into three categories: changes to Citizens' ability to compete with the voluntary market, changes in Citizens' rates, and changes in Citizens' authority to make "emergency assessments" to cover funding shortfalls.

A number of legislative changes were made to expand the coverage offered by Citizens and allow it to compete with the voluntary market.[30] Importantly, consumers are allowed to purchase a policy from Citizens if a comparable policy would cost 25 percent more in the voluntary market; this was reduced to 15 percent in 2008 legislation. Furthermore, the legislation rolled back Citizens' rate increases that were to become effective at the beginning of 2007. Also, the legislation allowed Citizens to decrease rates further in 2007 and precluded it from raising rates until 2008. The 2008 legislation extends the freeze to 2009. The Citizens Property Insurance Corporation Mission Task Force has recently recommended a statewide average rate increase of 10 percent for Citizens that would be implemented in 2010. The Task Force also recommended that rates increase no more than 15 percent in any given territory, and no more than 20 percent for any given policy. The Florida Insurance Council noted that the recommended rate increase would be far less than that required to make Citizens' rates actuarially sound (BestWire 2009). Finally, Citizens' assessment base was expanded from just property lines of insurance to include all lines of business except workers' compensation, medical malpractice, accident and health, the national flood insurance program, and the federal crop insurance program.

Figures 2.1 to 2.2 plot the growth of the residual market in Florida over time for personal residential property and partially reflect the acceleration of its growth caused by the 2007 legislative changes. These figures show respectively the number of policies and the amount of insurance in force, for full-coverage and wind-only (also called high-risk) coverage. Prior to 2002, the residual market in Florida was administered by the Florida Residential Property and Casualty Joint Underwriting Association and the Florida Windstorm Underwriting Association. The latter provided only wind coverage on coastal homes in certain designated areas, while the former provided full coverage or transferred the wind risk to the wind pool in areas where it operated. In 2002, these two bodies were combined into the Citizens Property Insurance Corporation. Figure 2.3 shows the relative penetration of Citizens as a percentage of total statewide premiums.

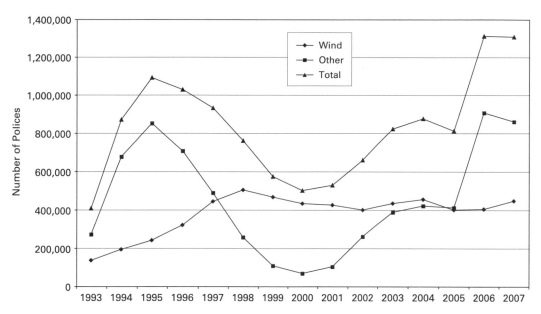

Figure 2.1
Florida property insurance residual market: Number of policies: 1993–2007. *Source:* FRPCJUA, FWUA, PIPSO, CPIC

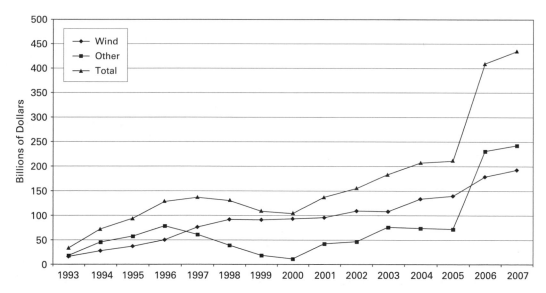

Figure 2.2
Florida residual property insurance market exposure: 1993–2007. *Source:* FRPCJUA, FWUA, PIPSO, CPIC

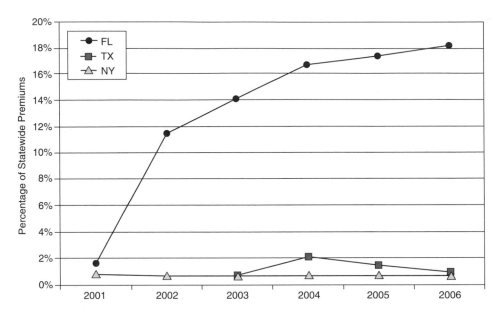

Figure 2.3
FAIR Plan penetration (percentage of total statewide premiums). *Source:* Data from Property Insurance Plans
Service Office (PIPSO).

We can see that both parts of Florida's residual market for property insurance have
increased substantially over this time period. The number of full-coverage (labeled as
"Other") policies and the associated insurance in force skyrocketed after Hurricane
Andrew and then fell from 1995 through 2000 as the start-up insurers took policies out of
the facility and pressure on the voluntary market eased. This trend reversed in 2001 when
the start-up companies shed policies (after their three-year requirement ended), followed
by the storm seasons of 2004–2005 that reasserted greater pressure on the voluntary market. The number of wind-only policies increased until 1998 and then dropped and has
essentially leveled out in the area of 400,000–450,000, but the amount of insurance (exposure) has steadily increased over the entire period.

As of December 31, 2008, Citizens had 629,467 Personal Lines Account (PLA) policies
and 445,200 High Risk Account (HRA policies).[31] There were 9,570 policies in its Commercial Lines Account (CLA). Its exposures (i.e., amount of insurance in force) as of
March 31, 2007, (the latest date for which these data are available) were $156.4 billion
for PLA policies, $192.1 billion for HRA policies, and $85.8 billion for CLA policies.
The total number of CPIC policies has fallen from its high of 1.4 million in October 2007
to under 1.1 million in December 2008, but much of this decline appears to have been
achieved through a depopulation scheme discussed below. Figure 2.3 also reveals that Citizens' market share (based on premiums) increased from 11.5 percent to 18.3 percent from

2002 to 2006.[32] Its relative market share is presumably much higher at the time of the writing of this chapter. For purposes of comparison, we also calculated and show the residual market shares in New York and Texas, which have been much smaller than in Florida.

Florida has sought to reverse the tremendous growth of its residual market with an ambitious takeout plan. Based on current information available from FLOIR's website, it has identified ten insurers that have committed to remove more than 637,000 policies from Citizens.[33] The companies vary in size with surplus amounts ranging from $9.5 million to $59.6 million. The consent order issued by the FLOIR for each insurer indicates that the FLOIR will review each company's reinsurance program, catastrophe modeling, and financial statement projections in determining how many policies it will be allowed to remove from Citizens.[34]

These actions appear to have temporarily reversed Citizens' growth, but it is not clear that this will prove to be a sustainable strategy. The takeout companies are predominantly small, regional, or single-state companies with limited geographic diversification. Hence, there is a question as to whether they will be able assume substantial amounts of coastal exposures and preserve their financial viability. These insurers can bolster their surplus with reinsurance, but there are limits to how much reinsurance they can purchase. If the FLOIR imposes stringent catastrophe risk management requirements, this could limit the actual number of policies and exposures removed from Citizens. If the FLOIR imposes less stringent requirements, it could permit more takeouts, but there will be greater questions about the financial viability of the takeout companies.

A question related to the size of the residual market is how its share of property exposures differs in various parts of the state. We would expect availability to be tighter and the residual market relatively larger in the highest risk areas. This is demonstrated in table 2.3,

Table 2.3
Citizens Property Insurance Corporation personal residential and high-risk statistics: 2003 and 2008

	December 31, 2008				December 31, 2003			
	Policies	% total	Exposures	% total	Policies	% total	Exposures	% total
Personal-residential total								
Dade, Broward, Palm Beach, and Monroe	207,532	32.9	51,496,947,952	41.1	239,461	62.5	40,635,887,869	80.3
Rest of state	421,935	67.1	74,629,643,333	53.9	143,819	37.5	19,390,910,445	38.3
Total	623,467	100.0	126,126,591,285	100.0	383,280	100.0	50,586,798,314	100.0
High-risk: wind only								
Dade, Broward, Palm Beach, and Monroe	216,021	57.3	122,900,165,308	56.8	276,067	63.7	68,286,388,540	63.5
Rest of state	161,065	42.7	93,283,216,697	43.2	156,989	36.3	39,328,420,045	36.5
Total	377,086	100.0	216,183,382,006	100.0	433,056	100.0	107,614,808,585	100.0

Source: CPIC.

which shows Citizens' policies and exposures for personal residential and high-risk policies for Dade, Broward, Palm Beach, and Monroe (DBPM) counties (combined) and the remainder of the state for 2003 and 2008.

We can see from table 2.3 that the number of policies and amount of exposures insured by Citizens in its personal-residential account increased from 2003 to 2008 in the DBPM counties but decreased relative to its percentage of total policies and exposures. The same is the case for high-risk exposures. Still, these counties continue to account for a large share of the policies it insures.

This leads to several observations and comments. One would expect a certain increase in the number of policies and the amount of insurance or exposures resulting from the construction of more homes, as well as increases in policy limits. However, Citizens' growth is exceeding that of the voluntary market, indicating that it is writing a growing share of all property exposures in the state. It appears that the 2007 legislative changes to Citizens (perhaps coupled with tightening constraints on private insurers) contributed to its growth. Between the end of 2006 and October 31, 2007, Citizens' personal residential policies increased from 743,592 to 944,719—a 27 percent increase in just nine months. During this same period, the number of its high-risk policies increased from 403,509 to 427,586.

What is most striking is Citizens' growth in other areas of the state beyond the DBPM counties. It appears that prior to the 2004 and 2005 storm seasons, other coastal areas were not as great a concern to insurers as southern Florida was. This perception appears to have changed significantly after 2003. Hence, other coastal areas experienced a greater change in terms of insurers' adjustment of their exposures—an adjustment that Dade, Broward, Palm Beach, and Monroe had already experienced prior to 2004. This probably reflects insurers' recognition that the other coastal areas faced a much higher level of hurricane risk than they had previously assumed. Of course, the vulnerability of other coastal areas was demonstrated by the path of several hurricanes in 2004 and Hurricanes Katrina and Rita in 2005. Hence, these other coastal areas apparently suffered a greater decrease in the availability of coverage than southern Florida did. Another likely factor contributing to Citizens' growth, especially outside the southern part of the state, is its transformation into a competitive source of insurance.

As a result of its substantial claims obligations arising from the 2004–2005 storm seasons, Citizens incurred large funding shortfalls: $1.6 billion for 2004 and over $2 billion in 2005. The 2004 shortfall resulted in a 6.8 percent surcharge on all homeowners' premiums in the state (recoupment against all other insurers in the state, which then passed all or a portion of it to their policyholders). The Florida legislature appropriated $715 million in 2006 to reduce Citizens' assessments needed to cover its 2005 deficit. The remainder of the deficit will be collected over a ten-year period in "emergency assessments" on premiums written statewide that will be passed on as surcharges to policyholders. As noted above, most lines written by property-casualty insurers are now subject to assessments. The premium surcharge in 2007 was 2.5 percent, and surcharges in subsequent years are expected to be approximately 1.5 percent.

Residual Mechanisms in Other States

The landscape for residual markets in other target states has been shifting, although not to the degree that has occurred in Florida. It is important to note certain structural changes that occurred in Texas and Louisiana. Texas has had a wind pool for a long time, but it created a FAIR Plan only in 2003. Louisiana combined its FAIR Plan and wind pool in 2004 in a new entity, the Louisiana Citizens Property Insurance Corporation, that is structurally similar to Florida's Citizens. Table 2.4 provides data on the number of habitational policies and total exposures for all state FAIR Plans for 1992, 2003, and 2006. Between 1992 and 2006, the number of policies in the state FAIR Plans throughout the country increased by 177 percent and their exposures increased by 722 percent. Table 2.5 provides comparable information for state wind pools.

Texas   Prior to 2003, Texas had relied on a unique system to deal with property insurance availability problems. Instead of using a FAIR Plan, it permitted the existence of an "unregulated" (or less regulated) property insurance market alongside a "regulated" insurance market. In the unregulated market populated by Texas Lloyds companies, insurers were allowed greater pricing freedom than in the regulated market. The unregulated market was intended to function as the market of last resort for property owners who could not obtain full coverage through the regulated insurance market. At the same time, the Texas Windstorm Association functioned like a conventional wind and beach pool, offering wind coverage in designated high-risk areas.

In the early 2000s, Texas suffered from property insurance availability problems due primarily to issues related to mold claims and other non-hurricane perils. This caused the movement of a large number of property owners from the regulated to the unregulated market. These owners experienced a significant increase in their premiums because prices were much higher in the unregulated market. The resulting consumer dissatisfaction and public concerns prompted Texas to establish a FAIR Plan that would be subject to greater government control than the unregulated market. As can be seen from table 2.4, the Texas FAIR Plan accumulated 120,536 policies by the end of 2003, with the number dropping to 109,461 policies by the end of 2006. The size of the plan has been relatively small compared to the total state market, with its market share based on premiums of only 0.7 percent at the end of 2006. This small percentage of homeowners' policies in the Texas FAIR Plan is likely the result of the ability of insurers to adjust their rates and manage their exposure to mold claims.

The Texas wind pool essentially doubled from 1992 to 2003, from 51,638 policies to 106,273 policies, then remained at that level through 2005 and increased to 140,375 policies in 2006 (table 2.5). The pool has remained a relatively small but growing portion of

Table 2.4
State FAIR Plans: Habitational policies and exposures, 1992, 2003, and 2006

| | 2006 | | | | 2003 | | | | 1992 | |
| | Policies | | Exposures ($000s) | | Policies | | Exposures ($000s) | | Policies | Exposures ($000s) |
State	Number	Percent change	Amount	Percent change	Number	Percent change	Amount	Percent change	Policies	Exposures ($000s)
California	193,615	2.2	50,577,001	25.1	189,486	63.7	40,423,805	114.3	115,767	18,866,588
Connecticut	4,682	26.6	768,728	57.1	3,698	−38.2	489,282	NA	5,985	754,943
Delaware	2,963	10.9	295,795	48.6	2,671	43.3	199,015	159.5	1,864	76,679
Florida*	1,409,587	267.8	408,837,779	575.0	383,280	160.2	60,566,798	562.8	147,315	9,137,395
Georgia	28,167	−3.4	3,114,897	19.6	29,165	160.8	2,605,112	291.0	11,181	666,322
Illinois	9,970	−33.8	769,000	−27.8	15,068	−6.2	1,065,549	69.1	16,069	630,297
Indiana	3,633	−25.8	300,953	−20.9	4,898	60.2	380,278	324.1	3,058	89,662
Iowa	1,425	1.6	97,079	−18.7	1,403	29.5	119,403	335.6	1,083	27,414
Kansas	9,659	83.9	416,676	71.1	5,252	−1.0	243,511	90.2	5,303	128,062
Kentucky	14,040	15.4	141,533	12.9	12,163	−67.9	125,332	−49.8	37,857	249,756
Louisiana*	NA	NA	NA	NA	118,514	2753.0	9,819,994	5604.9	4,154	172,132
Massachusetts	216,074	87.6	68,607,352	156.7	115,185	124.1	26,725,429	442.1	51,403	4,929,965
Michigan	73,952	−30.0	10,186,674	−44.9	105,610	−42.1	18,493,317	−18.2	182,287	22,611,624
Minnesota	8,600	−41.5	1,839,520	39.7	14,712	NA	1,316,637	NA	4,104	152,970
Mississippi	12,080	NA	661,360	NA	NA	NA	NA	NA	NA	NA
Missouri	8,928	−10.2	421,162	−3.6	9,945	−51.5	436,721	16.1	20,520	376,084
New Jersey	41,974	−19.9	5,440,130	−6.2	52,405	4.8	5,796,676	56.9	49,981	3,694,897
New Mexico	12,687	6.7	671,920	22.3	11,894	−1.0	549,451	−45.6	12,014	1,010,068
New York	60,797	−7.3	12,927,080	27.7	65,603	0.0	10,119,750	86.8	65,617	5,417,273
Ohio	59,983	−13.2	11,309,456	−15.4	69,088	327.9	13,374,287	4551.7	16,145	287,511
Oregon	4,225	−27.0	322,196	−26.8	5,785	−17.8	439,967	49.9	7,034	293,527
Pennsylvania	37,386	−17.7	2,079,026	1.4	45,443	−39.1	2,050,500	−19.0	74,657	2,530,159
Rhode Island	21,708	66.1	4,728,942	816.8	13,067	103.1	515,815	18.3	6,433	435,878
Texas	109,461	−9.2	13,320,285	12.2	120,536	NA	11,871,417	NA	NA	NA
Virginia	37,058	27.9	3,944,094	41.3	28,984	105.6	2,790,798	428.4	14,098	528,169
Washington	90	−39.2	33,346	−33.7	148	−79.1	50,291	−23.0	709	65,288
West Virginia	1,364	3.3	50,392	16.8	1,320	−16.1	43,129	22.9	1,574	35,102
Wisconsin	5,191	−12.9	NA	NA	5,959	12.2	NA	NA	5,313	NA
Total	2,389,299	66.9	601,859,916	185.8	1,431,282	66.1	210,612,264	187.8	861,525	73,167,765

* Florida figures reflect all policies for 2006; full-coverage policies for previous years. Louisiana figures include both "FAIR Plan" policies and "Coastal" policies.

Source: Insurance Information Institute, CPIC, and LCPIC.

Table 2.5
State wind/beach pools, 1992, 2003, and 2006

State	2006 Policies Number	2006 Policies Percent change	2006 Exposures ($000s) Amount	2006 Exposures ($000s) Percent change	2003 Policies Number	2003 Policies Percent change	2003 Exposures ($000s) Amount	2003 Exposures ($000s) Percent change	1992 Policies Number	1992 Exposures ($000s)
Alabama	NA	NA	NA	NA	3,065	5.5	339,858	80.3	2,904	188,513
Florida	NA	NA	NA	NA	433,056	609.1	107,614,809	1336.3	61,074	7,492,298
Louisiana	NA	NA	NA	NA	8,881	27.2	481,890	163.1	6,984	183,159
Mississippi	28,880	122.9	5,369,509	485.0	12,955	164.9	917,935	198.7	4,891	307,315
South Carolina	27,082	52.4	11,179,099	179.9	17,776	114.0	3,993,548	211.9	8,306	1,280,331
Texas	140,375	32.1	38,313,022	220.0	106,273	105.8	11,972,502	119.4	51,638	5,455,790
Total	NA	NA	NA	NA	582,006	328.6	125,320,542	740.7	135,797	14,907,406

Source: Insurance Information Institute, PIPSO.

the total state market, increasing from 1.08 percent in 2003 to 1.63 percent in 2006. The pre-2003 growth was likely the result of coastal development in Texas coupled with the general tightening of the supply of property insurance in coastal areas. Its more recent growth is likely the result of insurer retrenchment following the 2005 storm season exacerbated by regulatory resistance to rate increases.

South Carolina and New York   Both South Carolina and New York have experienced some increased market pressure in their coastal areas, but this pressure is considerably less than what Florida and other Gulf Coast states have experienced. South Carolina has a wind pool but not a FAIR Plan, and New York has a FAIR Plan but not a wind pool.

The South Carolina Wind and Hail Underwriting Association, the official name of its wind pool, has continued to grow over time because of increased coastal development and increasing hurricane risk. It wrote 27,802 policies and $11.2 billion exposures in 2006. Still, its market share has remained low, ranging from 0.34 percent to 0.62 percent over the 2001–2006 period. This reflects the small size of South Carolina's coastal market in relation to the total state market.

The South Carolina Department of Insurance has reported increasing problems with the availability of property insurance in coastal areas.[35] As noted above, this is a fairly localized problem for South Carolina, as coastal properties represent a relatively small portion of the total property exposures in the state. Still, coastal availability problems prompted the state to expand the areas covered by the wind pool effective June 1, 2007, and to revamp the pool's rating structure to accommodate the changes.

It is more difficult to assess how much hurricane risk has affected New York's FAIR Plan, if at all, based on publicly available information. The size of its FAIR Plan has remained fairly steady and relatively low over the years and is probably driven more by urban insurance availability issues than coastal insurance problems. It wrote 60,797 policies and just over $12.9 billion in exposures in 2006. In relative terms, the market share of the FAIR Plan remained less than 1 percent during the 2001–2006 period.

There has been discussion of creating a New York wind pool, but apparently coastal insurance availability issues have not been significant enough to compel the legislature to create such an entity. There have been reports of some insurers reducing their exposures in New York coastal areas, but no evidence of widespread and substantial cutbacks.

State Insurance Funds

Two states, California and Florida, have special insurance funds designed to bolster the supply of catastrophe coverage. As discussed, the California Earthquake Authority (CEA) provides earthquake coverage at a primary level to property owners in California. The Florida Hurricane Catastrophe Fund (FHCF) provides catastrophe reinsurance to primary insurers underwriting property coverage in the state. Both mechanisms were created in response to major crises in the supply of insurance that occurred after severe disasters. The CEA was established following the Northridge earthquake, and the FHCF was established after Hurricane Andrew.

A discussion of the arguments for and against state insurance and reinsurance funds is beyond the scope of this chapter, but the perspectives can be summarized briefly. Proponents of the FHCF contend that it helps to fill a gap in private reinsurance capacity or provides reinsurance at a lower cost (or both). Indeed, the FHCF was established with the support of major insurers in the state. It should be noted that the FHCF can accumulate tax-favored reserves (an option not available to U.S. insurers and reinsurers) and can also access credit supported by local bonding authorities. This inherently reduces its costs relative to private reinsurers, but also invites political manipulation of its rate structure.

Opponents of mechanisms like the FHCF question the need to augment private reinsurance, raise concerns about crowding out private reinsurance, and cite the potential for financial shortfalls that can lead to assessments on insurers/consumers or taxpayers (or all of these depending on how the mechanism is designed. Indeed, the FHCF did need assistance to cover its losses from the 2004 and 2005 hurricane seasons, and insurers have grave concerns about 2007 legislative changes to the FHCF that increase the amount of coverage that it provides.

Under its mandatory coverage program, the FHCF will reimburse a fixed percentage of a participating insurer's losses from each "covered event" in excess of a per event retention and subject to a maximum aggregate limit for all events. The fixed percentage can be 45 percent, 75 percent, or 90 percent at the option of the insurer. (See chapter 13 for a more detailed analysis of the operation of the FHCF.) The event retentions and limits vary by insurer according to a formula based on FHCF premiums. There is also an optional coverage below mandatory program that provides more limited coverage to certain eligible companies. The cost of FHCF coverage to a participating insurer is based on its estimated share of the FHCF's expected losses and expenses.

An important provision limits the FHCF's obligation to pay losses to the sum of its assets and borrowing capacity. This was initially set at $11 billion, increased to $15 billion in 2004, and increased to $27 billion in 2007 for a "temporary" period of three years. If the FHCF losses exceed its total funding capacity, each insurer would be reimbursed on a pro-rata basis from the funds available according to its share of the premiums paid into the fund for that contract year.

The FHCF is funded by premiums paid by participating insurers and investment income on invested reserves. It also can borrow funds up to a specified limit and impose emergency assessments on other property-casualty insurance premiums in the state if necessary to repay debt. The emergency assessments apply to all property-casualty and surplus lines insurers for all lines except workers' compensation, accident and health, medical malpractice, and national flood insurance premiums. These assessments are limited to 6 percent for a single contract year but can rise to 10 percent depending on "unused assessments" in prior contract years.

The 2004 and 2005 storm seasons required the FHCF to make payments to insureds that tapped and reduced its financial reserves. As of December 31, 2006, it had paid $3.678 billion for losses arising from the 2004 hurricanes and $3.6 billion for losses arising from the 2005 hurricanes. The ultimate estimated payment obligations are $3.95 billion for 2004 and $4.5 billion for 2005 (based on its audited financial statement for year-end June 30, 2007). These loss payouts led to a funding shortfall that prompted FHCF to issue $1.35 billion in revenue bonds to cover the shortfall and $2.8 billion in pre-event notes to provide liquidity for the 2006 storm season.[36] The bonds will be repaid from a 1 percent emergency assessment for six years on all policies renewed after January 1, 2007.

With the coverage expansion authorized by the 2007 Florida legislature, there are concerns that significant hurricane losses could lead to more emergency assessments on all applicable insurance premiums written in the state (recoupment). (See chapter 13 for an analysis of FHCF's exposure to different scenarios of hurricane.)

Guaranty Associations

All states have an insolvency guaranty association (GA) that is intended to cover the claims obligations of insolvent insurers. A state's GA is important because it could experience severe stress if one or more insurers with substantial claims obligations became insolvent because of a catastrophe. Many state GAs face some catastrophe risk, but Florida's experience is particularly noteworthy. The Florida Insurance Guaranty Association's (FIGA) funding capacity is supported by assessments on property-casualty insurance premiums in the state that are limited to 2 percent annually. Hurricane Andrew resulted in eleven insolvencies, and the corresponding demands on the guaranty fund exceeded its capacity. The guaranty association was forced to fully exercise its 2 percent assessment authority, and the legislature authorized it to assess an additional 2 percent to repay funds borrowed to cover its capacity shortfall. The association ultimately paid off its debts in 1997.

FIGA has been covering the claims obligations of the Poe Group insurers, which became insolvent after the 2005 hurricanes, and Vanguard, which was placed in receivership in 2005. This has prompted it to exercise its full 2 percent assessment authority to cover its costs for these claims obligations; another 2 percent emergency surcharge was approved in October 2007. In its most recent statements, FIGA reported that it is responsible for handling approximately 46,162 Poe claims with a total cost of $988 million. Both figures were FIGA records and exceeded the number and cost of claims arising from the Hurricane Andrew insolvencies. FIGA has not yet published any information on claims obligations for Vanguard, which was placed into liquidation on March 27, 2007.

The experience from Hurricane Andrew in 1992 and the 2004 and 2005 storm seasons reflects the GA's vulnerability to catastrophes and the potential pass-through of insolvent insurers' obligations and risk to other insurers. This risk is increased by the financial vulnerability of small Florida insurers with large concentrations of exposures in the state that are not offset by geographical diversification in other parts of the country.

Hence, insurers with significant premium writings in the state, even in lower-risk areas and lines of business, retain a secondary exposure to catastrophe losses through their potential obligations to the guaranty fund. Insurers are often allowed to add rate surcharges (extending the burden to policyholders) to cover their GA assessments, but for economic reasons, the burden is effectively shared between insurers and policyholders. Furthermore, there is the potential for externalizing some losses to other states, as each state GA is responsible for covering the claims obligations of an insolvent insurer in its jurisdiction, even if the insurer is domiciled in another state. In other words, in the case of the insolvency of a multistate insurer, insolvency costs caused by the regulators in one state can be transferred to other states because of the insolvent insurer's unpaid claims obligations in those states that will be covered by their respective GAs (ultimately insurers, policyholders, and taxpayers). Taxpayers also pay a portion of an insolvent insurer's claims obligations, as insurers are allowed to deduct guaranty fund assessments from their federal income taxes. These issues involving catastrophe risk and GAs are not confined to Florida but apply to any state where catastrophic losses could cause insurers to fail.

2.6   Conclusion

The severe storm seasons of 2004–2005 and insurers' resulting reassessment of hurricane risk and related actions (e.g., raising rates, reducing their exposures) have prompted regulatory reactions in various states. Market pressures and regulatory policies vary among these states. Florida, which faces the greatest risk, has employed regulatory policies that have significantly interfered with market forces. The other states have tended to be more permissive in terms of allowing market adjustments, but they may tighten their rate regulation and other restrictions if market conditions do not improve. Florida's actions will likely expose insurance policyholders and taxpayers in the state to significant financial assessments should the state be struck by more hurricanes in the near future. To date, other states have not followed Florida's course. Florida needs to reevaluate the economic soundness of its current policies, but this reappraisal may not occur until the state experiences another severe hurricane.

The story of catastrophe risk and insurance regulation continues to be written. States that are successful in supporting private insurance markets and other beneficial policies such as mitigation to deal with the hurricane risk may be able to avoid major market dislocations and provide a reasonable supply of catastrophe insurance coverage. Continued research is important to strengthen our understanding of the drivers and effects of government policies and how public action can support the efficient management of catastrophe risk.

Summary

This chapter examines the regulation of property insurance markets affected by catastrophes, particularly the risk of hurricanes and tropical storms. The severe storm seasons of 2004–2005 and insurers' resulting reassessment of the hurricane risk in coastal areas have raised a number of issues and a range of regulatory reactions in various states.

This chapter also reviews and assesses the areas of regulation that affect insurance markets, with a focus on the four states studied in depth: Florida, New York, South Carolina, and Texas. Market pressures and regulatory policies vary among these states. Florida faces the greatest hurricane risk, and its regulatory policies have interfered with market forces to the greatest extent. The other states have tended to be more permissive in terms of allowing market adjustments, but there is a chance that some may tighten their regulation if rates continue to rise and the supply of insurance is further reduced.

3 A Market Analysis of Property Insurance against Hurricane Risk

Key Findings

The cost conditions facing firms are a major determinant of the number, size, and distribution of firms within an industry or market. Correlated risk exposures and catastrophic loss increases insurers' costs. This compels insurers to charge a higher price for coverage and possibly reduce the number of exposures they underwrite.

There has been significant restructuring of property insurance markets in hurricane-prone areas. The combined market share for the top four insurance groups in Florida decreased steadily from 55.3 percent in 1992 to 39.2 percent in 2006. Another significant development in the state during the 1990s was the start-up of new insurers and entries by other established insurers. Approximately forty new insurers have entered the state's homeowners' insurance market since 2006. The other three states in the study (New York, South Carolina, and Texas) have experienced less significant changes in market structure than Florida has.

Premiums have increased radically in Florida. The market price of insurance has significantly increased in coastal areas (especially in Florida), in response to the loss shocks from the 2004–2005 storm seasons and greater hurricane risk. Florida has experienced the greatest absolute increase in the average premium among the studied states, from $723 at the start of 2002, to $1,465 in the first quarter of 2007. In coastal areas, premiums have tripled or even quadrupled for some homeowners.

Insurers' cumulative total profits in Florida from 1985 to 2006 have been negative during the entire period. At the end of 2006, insurers were $11.4 billion in the red (measured on a cumulative basis from 1985–2006) on their Florida homeowners' business. Higher insurance premiums, coupled with no hurricane losses in Florida in 2007, have improved insurers' long-term performance, but they remain concerned about the future of their operation in this state. Losses from hurricanes in the coming years will likely have a significant negative impact on insurers' earnings for homeowners' insurance in the Southeast.

The intense hurricane seasons of 2004 and 2005 caused substantial instability in property insurance markets in coastal states, with the greatest pressure in Florida and the rest of the Southeast.[1] Other coastal states exposed to hurricanes also have experienced some market pressures and changes. The increased risk of hurricanes striking the United States prompted significant changes in these same markets beginning in the early 1990s, but the particularly intense hurricane activity during 2004 and 2005 led to another wave of market adjustments. Both the loss shocks of the 2004 and 2005 storm seasons and the belief that hurricane risk has risen to a higher level (higher than was perceived prior to 2004) have been major drivers of the recent market adjustments. The respite from hurricanes in 2006 and 2007 was a welcome relief and allowed insurers and reinsurers to replenish some of their lost capital. However, increased storm activity and losses in 2008 reflect the continuing high risk of hurricanes that is still driving conditions in property insurance markets. It is important to understand how markets have changed in response to recent loss shocks and the increase in hurricane risk in order to develop a more complete picture of the catastrophe risk problem and to evaluate policy options.

This chapter updates and extends a previous analysis of market developments in Florida to New York, South Carolina, and Texas. Sections 3.1 and 3.2 examine the structure, conduct, and performance of the homeowners' insurance markets in Florida and the other states, with emphasis on recent developments. The chapter concludes with a summary of the key observations and discusses further research.

3.1   Insurance Market Structure

This section dissects insurance market developments using an established industrial organization approach: the structure-conduct-performance framework. The basic notion underlying this framework is that structure affects conduct, and conduct affects performance. However, it is also understood that the path of effects moves in both directions: conduct and performance can affect structure. Furthermore, this framework is harnessed to analyze developments in a market that is subject to several factors typically not found in other industries, and thus requiring some creative extension and application of standard methods. We look at market structure at both a company and a group level to examine how business is being shifted among companies within the same group, as well as groups' overall market exposure. We also assess market structure using premiums and amounts of insurance as measures of quantity.

Insurer Cost Conditions

The cost conditions facing firms are a major determinant of the number and size distribution of firms within an industry or market. Cost functions in many industries, including insurance, reflect decreasing average costs over an initial range of output and rising average costs beyond this point. The low point in the average cost curve is the minimum efficient scale (MES). The explanation for a U-shaped cost curve is that the firm initially benefits from spreading fixed costs over a larger amount of output, but at some point, this effect is offset by rising variable costs per unit because of rising input prices or other factors that cause the productivity of inputs to fall as production is pushed beyond a certain level.[2]

The problem of correlated risk exposures or catastrophic risk adds a significant new dimension to insurer cost functions. As an insurer increases the amount of insurance it sells in a given geographical area, its risk of catastrophic losses increases. This means that per unit variable costs increase as an insurer adds correlated risk exposures. The increase in per unit costs can be reflected in the insurers' need to carry additional surplus, buy more reinsurance, or pay a higher return to its owners to compensate them for the higher risk retained by the insurer. We would also expect that correlated loss exposures would lower an insurer's MES.[3]

In terms of market structure, the catastrophic risk cost factor would be expected to decrease the market shares of the leading insurers, all other things being equal. The leading insurers will find it more costly to acquire a large share of the market than if catastrophic risk were not a factor. Small insurers also may find it difficult to sustain operations in catastrophe-prone markets because they lack sufficient capital and geographical diversification to counter the risk of correlated exposures they would encounter. Hence, we would expect that the market shares of the leading insurers will decrease, and some smaller insurers may exit the market. Overall, we would expect measures of market concentration to decrease, as they tend to be based on, or dominated by, the market shares of the leading insurers.

Of course, in the real world, the cost factors that affect the supply of insurance and market structure are more complex than what we have described above. For example, insurers also must consider economies of scope, such as the efficiencies gained from selling both homeowners' insurance and auto insurance to the same household. If an insurer is unwilling to sell home insurance to some homeowners, it loses the associated scope economies from selling auto insurance to the same homeowners. Also, these homeowners may decide to move their auto insurance to another carrier. There are other considerations, such as the sunk costs associated with establishing a reputation and distribution networks and adverse regulatory responses. These other factors may dampen the hypothesized structural effects of higher costs resulting from catastrophic risk, but they are unlikely to eliminate them. Hence, we believe that the predictions in the preceding paragraph should still hold.

Entries, Exits, and Market Concentration

The effects of increased hurricane losses and risk on the structure of the Florida market are still developing, and there is a lag in the data available to track market changes. Still, it is important to glean what we can from these data and offer observations on how insurers appear to be adjusting their market positions. We can examine data through 2006 and augment them with anecdotal observations on insurers' actions in 2007. We begin by looking at shifts in the market positions of leading writers of homeowners' insurance in table 3.1.

Table 3.1 ranks the top twenty homeowners' insurers (on a group basis) in Florida in 2006 and also shows their market rankings (R) and market shares (MS) (in terms of direct premiums written, DPW) for the years 1992, 2000, 2005, and 2006. We do not include the Citizens Property Insurance Corporation in this aspect of our analysis as it is a residual market mechanism and our interest here is in the voluntary market in which insurers compete and make decisions about how much insurance they are willing to supply. We can see from this table that there have been dramatic changes in the Florida market since 1992. The top two groups in 2006, State Farm and Allstate, were also the top two in 1992 and 2000. However, their combined market share dropped from 50.9 percent in 1992 to 31.3 percent in 2000, to 29.2 percent in 2006. It is apparent that these two insurers have significantly reduced their relative presence in the Florida market (as measured by premiums). This development is not surprising given their expressed need to limit their catastrophe exposures to what they consider more sustainable levels.

It is also interesting to note that while State Farm's market share has slightly increased since 2000, Allstate's share declined from 11.2 percent to 7.8 percent. This appears to be consistent with Allstate's declared intention to substantially reduce its concentration of exposures in high-risk areas to a level that it believes is more economically viable.[4] Other national companies have stayed in the Florida market, maintaining market shares in the 2–5 percent range while others left the market.

Another significant development has been the entry or expansion of some insurers, as other companies have retrenched or withdrawn from the market. Ten of the top twenty groups in 2006 entered the market after 1995, and seven of these insurers entered after 2000. Most of these market entrants are small Florida-only or regional companies that were formed after Hurricane Andrew and are not affiliated with larger national groups. The retrenchment or exit of some insurers created opportunities for other insurers to fill the gap.

However, entry into the Florida market carries risk, especially for smaller insurers with large portions of their exposures in the state. This was demonstrated by the rapid rise of the third and fourth leading groups in 2005: the Poe and Tower Hill groups. Poe was bankrupted by the 2004–2005 storm seasons and is being liquidated. Tower Hill has been more diversified, with some business in other Southern states, but it has received increased scrutiny due to its large number of exposures in Florida. Two other insurers were placed into receivership: Vanguard and Florida Select. This demonstrates the drawbacks of relying heavily on local or regional insurers to fill large gaps left by larger national insurers. Smaller insurers can bolster their capacity with extensive use of reinsurance, but this comes at a cost, along with some retention of risk at a primary level. Hence, there is a limit as to how many high-risk exposures they can underwrite without substantially raising their risk of insolvency.

Table 3.1
Changes in leading insurers' market share in Florida, 1992, 2000, 2005, and 2006

Insurer	2006			2005			2000			1992		
	R	DPW	MS	R	DPW	MS	R	DPW	MS	R	DPW	MS
State Farm Group	1	1,444,281,352	21.4%	1	1,175,850,317	20.7%	1	583,296,400	20.1%	1	653,427,313	30.5%
Allstate Insurance Group	2	524,702,881	7.8	2	495,663,212	8.7	3	325,641,465	11.2	2	436,329,616	20.4
Tower Hill Insurance Group	3	342,029,077	5.1	4	285,914,090	5.0						
Universal Property and Casualty Insurance	4	338,419,633	5.0	8	159,161,458	2.8	26	25,611,814	0.9			
USAA Group	5	316,536,807	4.7	6	253,944,356	4.5	4	152,088,271	5.2	3	951,711,018	4.4
Nationwide Corporation	6	297,439,102	4.4	5	274,919,617	4.8	5	144,675,744	5.0	5	88,595,495	4.1
Liberty Mutual Group	7	221,726,692	3.3	7	172,197,758	3.0	10	51,714,570	1.8	12	32,534,992	1.5
ARX Holding Corp Group	8	216,582,227	3.2	13	116,834,632	2.1	25	27,120,693	0.9			
Universal Insurance Group	9	186,151,076	5.0	18	81,510,111	1.4						
American International Group	10	161,500,150	2.4	11	119,271,708	2.1	15	38,442,829	1.3	53	3,771,785	0.2
Chubb and Son	11	155,669,694	2.3	10	124,290,363	2.2	8	68,324,921	2.4	6	62,874,910	2.9
St Johns Insurance Co.	12	146,404,816	2.2	25	64,285,117	1.1						
United Property and Casualty Insurance Co.	13	138,913,586	2.1	16	104,987,215	1.8	36	14,473,319	0.5			
Hartford Fire and Casualty Group	14	136,547,181	2.0	12	117,479,131	2.1	7	76,738,521	2.6	9	49,288,247	2.3
St Paul Travelers Group	15	131,197,512	1.9	9	124,905,507	2.2	6	92,445,712	3.2	4	89,664,452	4.2
Gulfstream Property and Casualty Insurance Co.	16	118,088,454	1.7	17	93,418,769	1.6						
21st Century Holdings Group	17	115,574,807	1.7	20	77,513,454	1.4						
Florida Peninsula Insurance Co.	18	114,706,859	1.7	42	20,290,645	0.4						
GeoVera Holdings Insurance Group	19		1.6	14	111,695,287	2.0						
First Protective Insurance Co.	20	89,864,708	1.3	32	37,847,420	0.7	43	10,928,140	0.4			

Source: NAIC Financial database.
Note: R = market ratings; DPW = direct premiums written; MS = market share.

Table 3.2
Homeowners' insurance market concentration, Florida, 1992–2006

Year	CR4	CR8	CR20	HHI
1992	55.3%	70.9%	85.2%	1,440
1993	59.5	71.6	86.6	1,438
1994	60.0	71.9	86.7	1,236
1995	60.2	72.2	87.4	1,406
1996	57.5	71.5	87.0	1,266
1997	50.0	63.8	82.9	1,046
1998	51.3	64.9	83.1	920
1999	50.1	62.7	80.0	846
2000	48.0	61.2	78.7	776
2001	47.5	60.1	78.4	783
2002	46.4	59.2	79.6	829
2003	45.0	59.9	81.7	839
2004	44.9	61.4	83.8	832
2005	42.2	60.0	78.7	714
2006	39.2	54.5	75.6	695

Source: NAIC Financial database.
Note: CR4 = market share of top four groups; CR8 = market share of top eight groups; CR20 = market share of top twenty groups; HHI = Herfindahl-Hirschman Index.

The story of the Poe companies is a good illustration of the go-for-broke strategy that some insurers employ when they encounter financial difficulty. Poe insured more than 300,000 homes, with most concentrated in the high-risk areas of Palm Beach and Broward and Miami-Dade counties. Despite major losses from the 2004 storms and declining capital, Poe aggressively added more policies in 2005, gambling that it would not incur more storm losses. Such gambling is encouraged by a regulatory system in which an insurer can shift its losses to the state insurance policyholders and taxpayers through the insolvency guaranty association. The insurer reaps the potential upside of such gambles while subjecting the public to the potential downside. This scenario became reality when the Poe companies became insolvent after the 2005 storm season, generating approximately $988 million in guaranty association assessments.

Other national insurers have remained in the market but have limited the amount of their exposures. This may reflect a more reasonable strategy of acquiring small, digestible shares of a large but risky market by more broadly diversified insurers with greater amounts of capital. This phenomenon also poses less insolvency risk to the state. Unfortunately, Florida's regulatory policies may discourage national insurers from writing otherwise reasonable amounts of business in the state. The associated trends in market concentration in Florida from 1992 to 2006 are shown in table 3.2.

The combined market share for the top four groups (CR4) in Florida decreased steadily from 55.3 percent in 1992 to 39.2 percent in 2006. The combined market shares for the top eight (CR8) and top twenty insurer groups (CR20) also declined over this period. The Herfindahl-Hirschman Index (HHI) decreased from 1,440 in 1992 to 776 in 2000, increased, then fell again to an all-time low of 695 in 2006.[5] While the HHI includes all insurers in its calculation, it weights the market shares of the larger insurers more heavily so it is not surprising that it has also declined given the decrease in the market shares of the market leaders.

The decline in market concentration and the relative changes for the market leaders versus the midtier insurers are consistent with what we would expect to see based on our discussion of the impact of catastrophic risk on insurers' cost functions and exposure management. It is also consistent with anecdotal accounts of insurers' strategies and actions. One's view of whether this decline in concentration is good or bad depends on one's perspective. Normally economists associate lower concentration with greater competition, but the situation in Florida's homeowners' insurance market is peculiar. While insurers may be competing to maintain a sustainable market share, many are not currently seeking to increase their market share through price and product competition. Also, homeowners who have been dropped or rejected by their preferred insurer would not view this as a favorable development.

On the other hand, less concentration implies a greater dispersion of exposures among carriers in Florida, which could be viewed as a positive development in terms of greater diversification of risk, at least to the extent that nationally diversified insurers are part of this trend. In markets subject to high levels of catastrophe risk, lower concentration levels may be a necessary condition to allow insurers to maintain their catastrophe risk at manageable levels.

Another caveat to the observation about market deconcentration in Florida is the movement of exposures from national carriers to smaller state or regional insurers that are not pooling risk across a wide base of countrywide exposures. One aspect of this phenomenon is the movement of exposures to Florida-only companies within the national groups to increase the transparency of their Florida performance. If the smaller state and regional insurers are making good use of reinsurance to diversify and limit their catastrophe exposure, then the positive objective of broader risk diversification might still be achieved. Single-state companies within national groups can receive support from their affiliates in the event of large losses, but these national groups cannot engage in sustained cross-subsidies of their Florida insureds. These are aspects of market structure trends that warrant more investigation. Some homeowners also must find new carriers to underwrite their coverage, and others may be forced into residual market mechanisms, at least for a period of time.

The transformation of Citizens into a competitor with the voluntary market could affect private insurers' market shares and market concentration. Had we included Citizens in our

Table 3.3
Market concentration in selected states, homeowners' insurance, 1992 and 2006

State	1992		2006	
	CR8	HHI	CR8	HHI
Florida	70.9%	1,440	54.5%	695
New York	56.0	653	72.6	914
South Carolina	76.5	1,506	77.7	1,159
Texas	78.2	1,977	80.4	1,423

Source: NAIC Financial database; authors' calculations.
Note: CR8 = market share of top eight groups; HHI = Herfindahl-Hirschman Index.

market concentration calculations, the market would appear more concentrated in 2006. The excessive growth and size of Citizens is a problem, although not the kind normally associated with high concentration in private markets. The problem created by Citizens is that it is now in a position to crowd out private insurers and move more catastrophe risk exposure to the state. This will likely contribute to Citizens' funding shortfalls when more hurricanes strike the state, which will lead to greater assessments on all property-casualty insureds in the state.

Market structure changes appear to be much less significant in Texas, New York, and South Carolina. Table 3.3 provides summary statistics on market concentration changes in several coastal states, including the target states. Of the states listed in table 3.3, only two or three insurers have moved into the top twenty between 2000 and 2006.[6] The relatively greater stability in these markets may reflect several factors. One is that insurers' plans to adjust their positions are not fully implemented in terms of what the 2006 data reveal. Another factor may be that insurers see less of a need to reduce the number of policies they write in these states. Some of these states also appear to be taking a less restrictive approach to regulation (at least for the present) that may be helping insurers to retain a significant presence in these states. We should also note that the proportion of coastal exposures is considerably lower in these states than in Florida, and, hence, coastal risk would be expected to have less of an effect on insurers' statewide market shares.

Table 3.3 also reveals that New York, South Carolina, and Texas have experienced less significant changes in market concentration than Florida has. The top eight insurers increased their combined share of the market between 1992 and 2006; however, the HHI decreased in South Carolina and Texas but not in New York. The increased market concentration in New York probably reflects the consolidation of homeowners' insurers countrywide. New York, due to its relatively large market, still remains less concentrated than other states.

The changes in South Carolina and Texas are more difficult to interpret. The decline in their overall market concentration (as measured by the HHI) reflects a more even distribution of the market beyond the largest insurers. This could be due to the increasing competitiveness of smaller insurers or the decisions by midtier insurers (beyond the top eight) to decrease their exposures in these states.

Insurer Exposure Patterns

Insurers' statewide market shares (based on premiums) tell one part of the story on changes in the structure of a state's homeowners' insurance market. Another important part of the story is the distribution of insurers' shares of exposures (the amount of insurance coverage) in different areas in the state. Hurricane risk varies significantly among these areas, so this aspect of market structure is important in terms of understanding how insurers are managing their catastrophe risk, as well as the associated implications for homeowners. We have been able to obtain data that allow us to analyze this aspect of market structure for Florida but not the other states.

We acquired data on insurers' exposures by county by year and quarter from the Florida Office of Insurance Regulation (FLOIR). These data are reported by insurers to the FLOIR under its Quality Supplemental Report (QUASR) system. To make the data compilation more manageable, we requested and obtained data for the first quarter of every year from 1997 to 2006. For 2006, we obtained and used data from the fourth quarter of 2006 to develop a more current analysis. These data allow us to track trends and major changes in the distribution of insurers' exposures at a county level. Figure 3.1 shows a map of Florida counties for reference.

Table 3.4 compares the company level HHI (based on the amount of insured homeowners' property) by county between 1997 and 2006. Table 3.5 compares the market shares of the ten leading insurer groups in Miami-Dade county in 1997 and 2006. Two important developments can be gleaned from these data: there is decreased concentration in the higher risk counties (along the coasts), and the leading insurers in the state have decreased their shares of exposures in the highest-risk counties.

We also see from table 3.5 that "new" insurers have moved in to underwrite a significant proportion of exposures in Dade county. These are understandable developments, as the leading insurers have had to reduce their catastrophe exposure to more manageable levels that do not impose excessive financial risk. At the same time, this development raises questions about the financial viability of the smaller, geographically concentrated insurers when more hurricanes hit the state.

This reinforces an important point: Florida cannot rely on small or geographically concentrated insurers to underwrite a large number of homes in high-risk areas. A more sustainable approach is to encourage a sufficient number of insurers to each write a reasonable number of homes in high-risk areas, commensurate with the capacity and risk diversification of each company. Of course, saying this is easier than achieving it. However, if regulators allow insurers to charge fully adequate, risk-based rates and make other

Figure 3.1
Counties and main cities in Florida

Table 3.4
Homeowners' exposure company-level HHIs by county, 1997 and 2006

1997						2006					
Rank	County	HHI	Rank	County	HHI	Rank	County	HHI	Rank	County	HHI
1	Taylor	2,903	35	Hernando	1,439	1	Taylor	3,314	35	Hamilton	1,153
2	Hendry	2,459	36	Lake	1,419	2	Desoto	2,930	36	Alachua	1,151
3	Dade	2,373	37	Flagler	1,409	3	Hendry	2,762	37	Osceola	1,142
4	Broward	2,358	38	Pasco	1,370	4	Monroe	2,520	38	Charlotte	1,139
5	Brevard	2,221	39	Bradford	1,346	5	Hardee	2,496	39	Citrus	1,105
6	Desoto	2,197	40	St. Johns	1,341	6	Glades	2,478	40	Liberty	1,087
7	Volusia	2,113	41	Alachua	1,340	7	Baker	2,443	41	Orange	1,068
8	Osceola	2,102	42	Sarasota	1,327	8	Jefferson	2,399	42	Pasco	1,060
9	Polk	1,995	43	Leon	1,319	9	Putnam	2,198	43	Marion	1,050
10	Okeechobee	1,966	44	Putnam	1,278	10	Okeechobee	2,085	44	Santa Rosa	1,045
11	Glades	1,920	45	Jefferson	1,251	11	Bradford	2,050	45	Washington	1,045
12	Palm Beach	1,848	46	Calhoun	1,240	12	Columbia	1,878	46	Gadsden	971
13	Monroe	1,836	47	Bay	1,225	13	Volusia	1,795	47	Lee	953
14	Dixie	1,793	48	Hamilton	1,185	14	Duval	1,710	48	Levy	927
15	Charlotte	1,791	49	Union	1,148	15	Hernando	1,675	49	Pinellas	914
16	Escambia	1,754	50	Nassau	1,138	16	Jackson	1,645	50	Broward	900
17	Highlands	1,701	51	Madison	1,121	17	Lafayette	1,639	51	Walton	883
18	Pinellas	1,670	52	Levy	1,093	18	Sumter	1,632	52	Sarasota	880
19	Seminole	1,664	53	Washington	1,093	19	Polk	1,595	53	Indian River	849
20	St. Lucie	1,660	54	Jackson	1,083	20	Clay	1,573	54	Holmes	825
21	Hardee	1,655	55	Suwannee	1,074	21	Madison	1,543	55	Nassau	814
22	Santa Rosa	1,622	56	Manatee	1,054	22	Dixie	1,511	56	Flagler	801
23	Columbia	1,619	57	Walton	1,032	23	Leon	1,445	57	St. Lucie	797
24	Lee	1,619	58	Marion	1,030	24	Highlands	1,440	58	Dade	777
25	Okaloosa	1,615	59	Holmes	1,022	25	Calhoun	1,419	59	Manatee	718
26	Duval	1,605	60	Sumter	1,022	26	St. Johns	1,414	60	Collier	713
27	Orange	1,588	61	Martin	973	27	Suwannee	1,396	61	Hillsborough	712
28	Clay	1,578	62	Liberty	964	28	Union	1,359	62	Bay	705
29	Baker	1,553	63	Gilchrist	866	29	Seminole	1,300	63	Gulf	687
30	Citrus	1,541	64	Gulf	853	30	Escambia	1,269	64	Martin	666
31	Lafayette	1,535	65	Franklin	778	31	Brevard	1,263	65	Franklin	659
32	Indian River	1,526	66	Gadsden	738	32	Lake	1,234	66	Wakulla	620
33	Collier	1,496	67	Wakulla	730	33	Okaloosa	1,189	67	Palm Beach	594
34	Hillsborough	1,493		Total	1,594	34	Gilchrist	1,169		Total	876

Source: Data from FLOIR; authors' calculations.
Note: Counties are ranked in descending order of HHI (Herfindahl-Hirschman Index).

Table 3.5
Leading insurance groups in Dade County, 1997 and 2006

	1997		2006	
Rank	Company	Market share	Company	Market share
1	State Farm Group	38.0%	State Farm Group	20.3%
2	Florida Residential Property and Casualty Joint Underwriting Association	29.5	Citizens Property Insurance Corp.	12.2
3	Allstate Insurance Group	6.6	Liberty Mutual Insurance Companies	7.8
4	Liberty Mutual Insurance Companies	4.8	Gulfstream Property and Casualty Insurance Co.	7.5
5	USAA Group	3.3	Poe Insurance Group	7.3
6	St. Paul Travelers Group	3.0	United Property and Casualty Insurance Co. Inc.	4.5
7	Hartford Insurance Group	2.1	Tower Hill Group	4.5
8	MetLife Auto and Home Group	2.0	First Home Insurance Company	3.5
9	Chubb Group of Insurance Companies	1.8	HDI U.S. Group	3.2
10	Bankers Insurance Group	1.4	Federated National Insurance Co.	2.9
	Top ten	92.7	Top ten	73.6

Source: Data from Florida Office of Insurance Commissioner.

reasonable adjustments in their underwriting and policy terms, insurers should be more amenable to writing a manageable amount of high-risk exposures.

3.2 Insurance Market Conduct and Performance

Insurers' conduct and, ultimately, market performance or outcomes are of the greatest interest to various stakeholders. The key outcomes are the price of insurance, the availability of coverage, policy terms, and profitability. For obvious reasons, property owners are most interested in the price of insurance, as this can have a significant effect on their housing costs and budget. They are also interested in the availability of coverage, as this can affect how much insurance they can purchase, the insurers they can purchase insurance from, and whether they will need to obtain coverage in the residual market.

Insurers have a stake in these outcomes, but their profits (or losses) and financial viability are of particular concern. If insurers are unable to recover their cost of capital (at least in the long run), it becomes difficult for them to justify and sustain operations in a market. Also, continuing operations under such conditions can ultimately threaten their financial strength and solvency, with adverse consequences for their owners and all of their policyholders. In this section, we focus primarily on market performance, but we also discuss aspects of insurers' conduct to a limited extent.

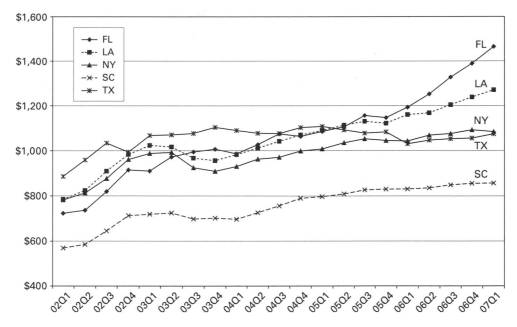

Figure 3.2
Average homeowners' premium trends, first quarter 2002 to first quarter 2007. *Source:* PCIAA/ISO Fast Track Monitoring System; authors' calculations.

Prices

The price of homeowners' insurance is a primary area of interest and concern. In the aftermath of the 2005 hurricane season, a number of insurers filed and implemented significant rate increases to reflect the higher degree of risk and increased cost of reinsurance (see chapter 7 for a discussion of the reinsurance market). There are a number of ways to measure prices and price changes; no single measure reveals everything one would want to know, but each provides some information. There are also different definitions of the price of insurance. Economists tend to use a *net price* measure, which is the loading added to the expected loss, or *pure premium*. Here, we use a *full price* definition that includes the expected loss portion of the premium or rate charged. Consumers, regulators and others tend to focus on the full price rather than the net price.

Some indication of the price increases faced by those who are insured is provided by figure 3.2, which plots trends in average homeowners' premiums in the four states being studied for the period of first quarter 2002 through first quarter 2007.[7] The source of data for this figure is the PCIAA/ISO Fast Track Monitoring System, which compiles data on premiums, exposures, and losses on a quarterly basis from a subset of insurers representing approximately 60 percent of the total market countrywide. We calculated the average premium (total premiums divided by insured house-years) for each quarter in the series. It is important to note that these are statewide averages and, hence, will be affected by the geographical distribution of exposures and the factors affecting the different areas within these states. The impact of price increases for coastal homes on a state's average premium will be influenced by the relative proportion of exposures in coastal areas.

Florida has experienced the greatest absolute and relative increase in its average premium among the states studied, from $723 at the start of 2002 to $1,465 in the first quarter of 2007. New York, South Carolina, and Texas have experienced less severe increases in absolute and relative terms. From the insurers' perspective, the significant price increase in Florida is necessary to finance the higher risk of losses. From the insureds' perspective, the increase is a matter of concern and an additional financial burden. It could compel some homeowners to opt for larger deductibles or other coverage adjustments to lessen the impact of higher rates.[8] Coastal homeowners' complaints over insurance price hikes also increase political pressures on legislators and regulators to lower prices, or at least prevent further increases.

An important caveat in interpreting these average premium trends is they reflect the weighted distribution of the premium increases on all policies in the underlying data. In each of these states, rates vary greatly between the lowest- and highest-risk area, and the average statewide premium encompasses all areas. We would expect premiums to be significantly higher in the coastal areas, and these areas have likely experienced a higher increase relative to interior areas of the state.

Other data provide information on average premiums at a substate level in Florida. The first set of these data is drawn from annual statistical data provided by the Property Casualty Insurers Association of America (PCIAA). These data contain premiums, exposures (house-years), losses, and the number of claims by standard rating territory for the years 2001 to 2005. We calculated average premiums for homeowners' HO-3 policies (premium written divided by house-years) for each year and territory shown in table 3.6; the territories are ranked in descending order of their average premium in 2005.

We can see from this table that average premiums vary significantly across Florida. The territory comprising Indian River, Martin, and St. Lucie counties had the highest average premium in 2005—$2,051—and also experienced the second largest increase over the period—130.4 percent. The lowest territory, Jacksonville, had a $509 average premium in 2005. The comparisons for other coastal states reveal a similar pattern, but the relative differences in average premiums between high- and low-risk territories are smaller in these states than they are in Florida.[9]

These average premium measures are affected by several factors, including the amounts of insurance on homes and the terms of the policies covering those homes, as well as the rate structures of insurers. Hence, we cannot determine from these data how much of the average premium increase is attributable to rate changes. Still, it is reasonable to surmise that rate increases were a major factor causing the differences in the average premiums among territories, as well as their increase over time. Also, because the latest year available

Table 3.6
Florida homeowners (HO3) average premiums, 2001–2005

Territory	2001	2002	2003	2004	2005
Indian River/Martin/St. Lucie	$890	$1,042	$1,311	$1,674	$2,051
Miami	1,059	1,207	1,444	1,653	1,799
Palm Beach County	923	1,054	1,261	1,461	1,643
Miami Beach	856	754	881	1,404	1,589
Broward County	985	1,043	1,171	1,320	1,491
Broward/Palm Beach	715	828	958	1,170	1,373
Dade County II	1,104	1,088	1,137	1,258	1,366
Martin County	886	1,021	1,133	1,213	1,364
Fort Lauderdale/Hollywood	802	838	920	1,023	1,146
Tampa	631	683	773	916	1,108
Hillsborough/Pinellas	558	625	715	850	1,047
Bay	634	725	821	912	1,039
Key West	351	216	290	844	1,016
Hialeah	1,091	1,117	979	935	984
St. Petersburg	473	554	655	776	976
Pinellas County	470	451	517	729	881
Bay	516	593	654	709	807
Escambia County	510	607	664	693	787
Polk County	533	610	680	704	776
Orange	540	570	609	670	769
Dade County I	944	832	887	1,003	756
Monroe County	379	228	290	664	689
Osceola/Seminole	561	578	564	567	640
Brevard/Volusia	455	498	522	545	616
Duval County II	425	451	465	507	612
Duval County I	453	482	519	530	544
Alachua	511	511	477	469	523
Jacksonville	446	468	469	465	509
Mean	668	703	777	917	1,032
Median	560	618	697	847	980

Source: Data from PCIAA; authors' calculations.
Note: These figures do not include coverage by Citizens.

for these data was 2005, they do not reflect the most recent market changes. We would expect further average premium increases in 2006 and 2007 as insurers' approved rate changes were implemented.

An alternative approach to measuring substate differences and changes in prices is to calculate an average rate per $1,000 of coverage. This approach is less affected by differences in the amount of insurance, but still confounds other coverage terms with rates. We can employ this approach with the county-level QUASR data for Florida; our calculations for 1997 and 2006 are reflected in table 3.7. The results are quite striking and revealing, as the county with the highest rate in 2006 was Monroe, with a rate of $30.70, and the county with the lowest rate was Clay, with a rate of $2.35. Monroe also experienced the greatest increase from its rate of $18.98 in 1997. This reflects the high level of risk in Monroe County, which includes the Florida Keys.

Counties' rankings differ somewhat between the average premium and the rate per $1,000. This indicates that differences in the average amount of insurance can mask or offset differences in the price of insurance. While the rate per $1,000 of coverage controls for the amount of insurance, we would expect this rate to decline with the amount of insurance, all other things equal, because the fixed costs of writing and servicing a policy are spread over a larger amount of coverage. This likely accounts for some of the differences in counties' rates per $1,000.[10]

In sum, all of these comparisons tell a similar story: the price of homeowners' insurance is much higher in some areas of Florida than others, and the price of insurance has substantially increased, especially in the highest-risk areas. We see a similar pattern in other states, but they have experienced smaller price increases, and the differences between coastal and noncoastal areas are not as great. Of course, this is not a great surprise, but our calculations reveal the magnitude of the differences and changes and why property owners in high-risk areas have voiced strong complaints about the rising cost of insurance and are putting increasing pressure on legislators and regulators to lower rates, especially in Florida.

Availability of Coverage

The availability of insurance coverage also is an important performance outcome and an area of attention and concern to property owners, government officials, and other stakeholders. Availability is somewhat elusive to measure or quantify and can mean different things to different people. The preferred definition might be how easy or difficult it is for homeowners to obtain the coverage they want in the voluntary market from the insurers they prefer, but acquiring this information or even measuring availability so defined is difficult.

Hence, economists tend to use other availability indicators, such as the proportion of uninsured homes or the size of the residual market. However, there are problems with, and caveats to, these measures. It is difficult to obtain data on the proportion or number

Table 3.7
Homeowners' insurance rates per $1,000 by county, Florida

County	1997	2006	County	1997	2006
Monroe	$18.98	$30.70	Hamilton	$4.14	$3.78
Dade	7.23	10.57	Gadsden	3.61	3.78
Franklin	6.42	8.13	Lafayette	4.36	3.71
Gulf	4.90	7.36	Washington	3.81	3.70
Broward	5.35	7.20	Highlands	3.24	3.62
Palm Beach	4.45	6.48	Gilchrist	3.89	3.57
Walton	4.47	6.29	Liberty	4.15	3.56
Indian River	3.80	5.67	Calhoun	3.80	3.54
Martin	3.66	5.63	Volusia	2.77	3.50
Pasco	3.07	5.15	Polk	3.00	3.49
Pinellas	3.25	5.13	Union	3.78	3.48
Escambia	3.68	5.01	Suwannee	3.91	3.46
St. Lucie	3.95	4.97	Citrus	2.98	3.40
Collier	3.88	4.93	Madison	4.04	3.34
Bay	3.64	4.83	Jackson	3.64	3.30
Dixie	4.70	4.72	Putnam	3.60	3.22
Okaloosa	3.90	4.53	Bradford	3.41	3.17
Lee	3.34	4.49	Jefferson	3.86	3.11
Glades	3.96	4.48	Nassau	3.38	3.07
Charlotte	3.16	4.47	Baker	3.49	2.97
Santa Rosa	3.06	4.34	Osceola	2.67	2.97
Brevard	3.15	4.33	Columbia	3.35	2.96
Hernando	2.84	4.32	Flagler	2.76	2.95
Okeechobee	3.54	4.29	Seminole	2.53	2.92
Wakulla	4.26	4.24	Orange	2.66	2.91
Hendry	3.42	4.22	Marion	2.98	2.90
Holmes	3.89	4.20	St. Johns	2.71	2.79
Sarasota	3.30	4.14	Alachua	2.61	2.76
Hardee	3.87	4.08	Sumter	3.36	2.72
Levy	3.93	4.02	Lake	2.83	2.70
Taylor	3.76	3.97	Duval	2.76	2.67
Desoto	3.55	3.96	Leon	2.42	2.38
Manatee	3.37	3.87	Clay	2.55	2.35
Hillsborough	3.44	3.81	Total	3.87	4.73

Source: Data from FLOIR; authors' calculations.

of uninsured homes, and the lack of insurance on a home may be partly a matter of choice on the part of the homeowner. Also, a home may have insurance, but the amount or breadth of coverage may be considerably less than what the homeowner would prefer. Similarly, the number and proportion of homes and policies in the residual market are affected by a number of factors, only one of which is insurers' willingness to supply insurance. Finally, this measure can confound prices with the availability of coverage; some homeowners may choose to obtain insurance in the residual market because it costs less than what they would be required to pay in the voluntary market. This will become an increasingly important factor in Florida, where Citizens' rates and rules have been changed to make it competitive with the voluntary market.

The discussion of the residual market trends presented in chapter 2 documents their growth, especially in Florida. This is one of several indicators of the decreased availability of homeowners' insurance in coastal areas.

Distribution of Coverage Provisions

The provisions of insurance policies bought by property owners are also of interest to policymakers and other stakeholders. The various homeowners' insurance policy forms are fairly standard among insurers and insureds. The most important provision is the deductible on a policy. To better manage their catastrophe exposure and provide insureds with an option to lower their premiums, insurers have offered larger deductibles for wind or hurricane losses. These larger deductibles are typically expressed as a percentage of the dwelling (Coverage A) limit and could range up to 25 percent or more, depending on the state.

To gain some understanding of the distribution and trend of deductible levels, table 3.8 shows the distribution of HO-3 policies (house-years) by deductible levels in Florida for

Table 3.8
Distribution of wind and hurricane deductibles in Florida, 2000 and 2004

Wind or hurricane deductible	Percentage of total house-years	
	2000	2004
$1,000 hurricane	0.46%	0.10%
$2,000 hurricane	0.05	0.02
$500 hurricane	7.25	4.34
1% hurricane	1.51	0.37
1% wind/hail	0.07	0.00
2% hurricane	43.00	47.40
2% wind/hail	3.79	11.87
5% hurricane	0.34	1.11
5% wind/hail	0.01	0.04
All other	43.53	34.76

Source: Data from ISO; authors' calculations.

2000 and 2004. These data were obtained from the Insurance Services Office (ISO) and reflect information from insurers reporting statistical data to ISO (which represent approximately 50 percent of the total market). We should also note that in 2004, the highest wind or hurricane deductible allowed was 5 percent.

As is evident in this table, large wind deductibles apply to a large and growing proportion of HO-3 policies in Florida. In 2004, 47.4 percent of HO-3 policies (issued by ISO reporting companies) carried a 2 percent hurricane deductible, and another 11.9 percent carried a 2 percent wind and hail deductible, up from 43 percent and 3.8 percent in 2000, respectively. Interestingly, policies with a 5 percent wind or hurricane deductible represented a very small percentage of all policies in 2004, but this is likely changing. It would be reasonable to expect that the proportion of policies with larger deductibles has continued to grow and is currently at a higher level than indicated in the 2004 data. Property owners may prefer lower deductibles, but insurers can make these lower deductibles very expensive (in contrast with federally subsidized programs like flood insurance). Hence, a continued trend toward higher deductibles, first evident in the mid- to late 1990s, would be consistent with this market dynamic.[11]

Profitability

Firms' profitability is an important market performance outcome. In an efficient, competitive market, long-run profits would be expected to provide firms a "fair" rate of return equal to their risk-adjusted cost of capital. Profits that are too low will encourage market exit or retrenchment that could have adverse effects on consumers. But high profits over the long term would raise questions about the competitiveness of the market.[12]

The problem in insurance markets, especially in lines like homeowners' insurance, is that profits can be highly volatile from year to year. In other words, insurers can earn low or negative profits in some years and what appear to be high profits in other years. Still, over the long run, profits would be expected to average out near what would be considered a fair rate of return. This is closer to being the case in homeowners' insurance markets that are subject to normal weather-related perils, but hurricane-prone markets are subject to much greater volatility and much longer return periods. Insurers might have been prepared to handle an occasional severe hurricane (e.g., a Hurricane Andrew–level event every ten years) but not the back-to-back multiple-event years experienced in 2004 and 2005.

Even the relatively frequent occurrence of lower levels of hurricane losses in a given year, say $5 billion to $10 billion in losses, can drive insurers' state and regional results deep into the red and keep them there for some time. This generates significant concern among their owners (stockholders or member-owners for mutual companies), who do not expect the managers of these insurers to continue to subject their companies to such sustained losses in any segment of their business. For those who would question the problems created by such scenarios, one might ask whether they would be comfortable in having a substantial portion of their savings invested in insurers subject to these kinds of losses.

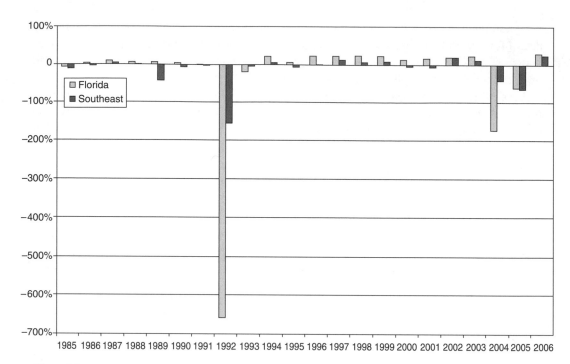

Figure 3.3
Average annual profits on homeowners' insurance transactions, Florida and the Southeast, 1985–2006. *Source:* NAIC Report on Profitability by Line by State.

Several different profit measures are used in insurance, including loss ratios, underwriting ratios, operating ratios, profits on insurance transactions, and estimates of the return on equity. We focus on *profits on insurance transactions* (PIT), a measure published by the National Association of Insurance Commissioners by line and by state, with some supplemental observations on other profit measures. This PIT measure includes incurred losses, all expenses, investment income attributable to loss reserves and unearned premium reserves (not surplus), and estimated federal taxes on the income earned (or tax credits on negative income).[13] The resulting profit (loss) is divided by direct premiums earned to produce a profit rate.

Figure 3.3 plots insurers' annual PIT rates for homeowners insurance in Florida and all Southeast states combined for the period 1985 to 2006. As can be seen from this figure, insurers earned positive profits in most of the years during this period, but had losses (negative profits) in Florida in 1992, 1993, 2004, and 2005. Insurers generated negative profits of −172.8 percent in 2004 and −62 percent in 2005. The negative profits in these four years stemmed from Hurricane Andrew and the hurricanes that struck the state in 2004 and 2005.

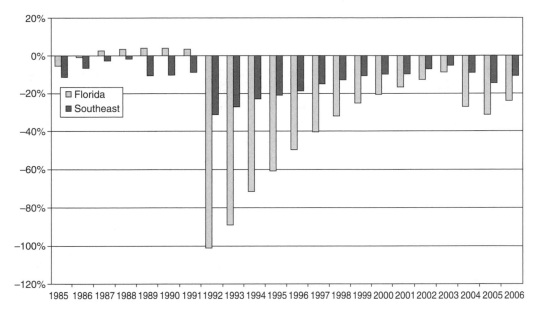

Figure 3.4
Cumulative profits on homeowners' insurance transactions, Florida and the Southeast, 1985–2006. *Source:* NAIC Report on Profitability by Line by State.

Figure 3.4 plots cumulative profits (losses) for homeowners' insurance in Florida and the Southeast for the same period, 1985–2006. Each year represents accumulated profits and losses from previous years. We can see from this figure that insurers' profits have been negative over the entire period for the Southeast and since 1992 in Florida. Cumulative losses decreased over the period until 2004. If insurers had earned positive profits in Florida in 2004 and 2005, they would have dug themselves out of the hole created by Hurricane Andrew. Even with more modest losses in 2004, they could have looked forward to eventually generating positive profits for the entire period (barring more hurricane losses), but the heavy storm seasons of 2004 and 2005 quashed any such hopes.

On a cumulative basis, as of the end of 2006, insurers were $11.4 billion in the red on their Florida's homeowners' business (representing −23.8 percent of cumulative premiums earned). Hence, insurers perceive that they are again deep in the hole with respect to their Florida and Southeast operations, and it will require a sustained period of positive profits to recoup these losses. Even if insurers were to earn $2 billion in profits each year between 2007 and 2011 in Florida, it would not be enough to erase their cumulative deficit; they earned $1.6 billion in profits in 2006. Even with a return to positive profits, future hurricanes could plunge insurers' results back into a deep hole, and this threat continues to affect insurers' caution in approaching property insurance markets in high-risk areas.

3.3 Conclusions for the Market Analysis

Our analysis of developments in Florida's and other states' homeowners' insurance markets measures the significant changes that are occurring as a result of increased hurricane risk. There has been substantial market restructuring, with leading insurers decreasing their shares of the market and other insurers retrenching or exiting from the market, especially in the highest-risk areas. Other insurers are maintaining their relative market positions, and some have entered or expanded their business. Overall, market concentration has decreased significantly at a statewide and substate level in Florida and, to a lesser degree, in the other target states.

The price of property insurance also has increased significantly, particularly in the highest-risk areas. At the same time, the availability of coverage has tightened considerably, reflected in the growing number of policies and amount of exposures insured in residual market mechanisms. Of the four states we study here, Florida has reported the greatest availability problems. Availability also has been an issue in coastal areas of South Carolina. In the aftermath of Hurricane Ike, there is some indication that the availability of insurance in coastal areas of Texas is tightening. One interesting finding is the sharp increase in prices and reduced availability of coverage in certain coastal areas outside of southern Florida. This suggests that insurers saw a greater need to make large adjustments in these other coastal areas, which had not previously experienced the magnitude of the rate increases and residual market shifts that had occurred in southern Florida prior to 2004.

Finally, it is apparent that insurers suffered substantial losses (negative profits) in Florida in 2004 and 2005 due to the hurricanes that hit the state in these years. Insurers also suffered huge losses in 2005 in Louisiana and Mississippi due to Hurricane Katrina. Prior to 2004, insurers were on the verge of earning positive cumulative profits (following Hurricane Andrew) but the 2004 and 2005 storms drove them deeper into the red. This has contributed to insurers' price and underwriting adjustments and concerns about the economic feasibility of writing homeowners' insurance in Florida and other high-risk areas under the prices and terms of coverage that preceded these storm seasons. The respite from damaging hurricanes striking the United States in 2006 and 2007 allowed insurers to improve their long-run profitability, but these gains could be wiped out by hurricane losses in 2008. Hence, hurricane risk remains high, and the potential for significant losses in future years is a substantial concern.

Clearly there is a need to increase our understanding of how property insurance markets are changing and the factors that are driving the changes. Increasing our knowledge of market conditions and changes will help us better determine what economically sound strategies might have the most beneficial effects for both insurers and property owners.

Summary

This chapter provides an updated and extended analysis of the structure and performance of property insurance markets that have been subject to varying degrees of pressure from hurricane risk. Insurance markets in high-risk coastal areas have experienced significant changes, and it is important to analyze how they have been evolving in recent years. We focus primarily on Florida and draw some comparisons with New York, South Carolina, and Texas. Florida has experienced the greatest pressures and changes in terms of insurer retrenchment, higher prices, diminished availability of coverage, and negative profits. The other states have experienced these problems to a lesser degree. This analysis continues to be a work in progress as market conditions are fluid and government and regulatory policies may change over time.

4 Come Rain or Shine: Flood Risk Financing through Public Insurance

Key Findings

The National Flood Insurance Program (NFIP) has seen a significant change in the scope of its operation since 1990. The program has grown from 2.5 million policies in 1992 to over 5.55 million at the end of 2007, an increase of 122 percent; from $800 million in premiums collected from policyholders in 1992 to $2.8 billion at the end of 2007, an increase of 250 percent; and from $237 billion in coverage in 1992 to over $1.1 trillion at the end of 2007, an increase of 364 percent. The figures for 2008 are similar to 2007. There is a huge disparity in flood insurance operations among the states. Florida alone represents nearly 40 percent of the entire NFIP portfolio.

Choice in flood coverage and its costs per dollar of coverage have changed over time. Floridians reacted to flood damage caused by the 2004 hurricanes by choosing lower deductibles and higher limits of coverage. Our analysis of several million flood insurance policies reveals that in 2005, almost 80 percent of policyholders chose the lowest possible deductible ($500). Although homeowners increased their insurance coverage between 2000 and 2005, almost three-quarters were still below the $250,000 maximum coverage limit. One reason for this large percentage is that many homes had property values below this limit. On the cost side, the average premium per policy in Florida is among the lowest in the nation. We also find that despite several major flooding episodes in 2004 in Florida, the cost of flood insurance in the state (as measured by the premium paid per $1,000 of coverage) significantly decreased in all but two counties between 2000 and 2005.

More than thirty percent of each dollar paid for flood insurance coverage goes to private insurers participating in the NFIP Write-Your-Own program. These insurers play the role of financial intermediaries between policyholders and the NFIP but do not bear any of the risk. Over the period 1968 to 2005, these private insurers received over $7.4 billion (excluding the loss adjustment expenses for which we do not have data) in fees. On the financial operation of the program, we calculate that prior to the 2005 hurricane season, which inflicted nearly $20 billion in flood claims, the NFIP had a cumulative deficit of about $3 billion after thirty-seven years of operation.

4.1 A Brief History of Flood Insurance

The National Flood Insurance Program (NFIP) grew out of a widespread opinion that flood peril was not insurable by private insurance companies.[1] Insurers in the United States claimed that floods could not be insured by the private sector because (1) only particular areas are subject to the risk, so adverse selection would be a problem; (2) the necessary premiums would be so high that no one would be willing to purchase coverage; and (3) flood losses can be catastrophic, that is, enough premiums could not be collected to cover catastrophic events.[2]

Congress established the NFIP in 1968, noting that "many factors have made it uneconomic for the private insurance industry alone to make flood insurance available to those in need of such protection on reasonable terms and conditions."[3] Congress felt that a government program could potentially be successful since it might pool risks more broadly, have funds to jump-start the program, subsidize existing homeowners while charging actuarial rates on new construction, and tie insurance to land use changes that might lower risks.[4] The government would also have the capacity to spread losses over time, due to the possibility of the program borrowing money from the federal government to cover deficits, something private insurers cannot do.

The NFIP was enacted also in response to the rising cost of taxpayer-funded disaster relief for flood victims. It was originally designed as a voluntary partnership between the federal government and communities. In exchange for enacting floodplain management regulations, property owners in participating communities would be eligible for federal flood insurance. There has not yet been a comprehensive study of the degree to which local governments comply with the required construction and development regulations, although there are some indications the regulations have reduced damages.[5]

To support local governments, the NFIP creates flood maps in participating communities, designating flood risks in different flood zones. These maps are called flood insurance rate maps (FIRMs). Buildings that were in place pre-FIRM—before the mapping of flood risk was completed in that area—are given subsidized rates. New construction, built after the risk mapping has been made public, is charged actuarial rates. The expectation was that as new construction replaced existing homes, fewer and fewer policies would be subsidized. However, around a quarter of properties are still subsidized.[6] The housing stock is turning over more slowly than predicted, due in part to renovation techniques that have extended the life of buildings longer than anticipated.[7] PricewaterhouseCoopers estimates that the number of pre-FIRM properties will decrease to 37 percent of all properties in hundred-year flood zones by 2022, down from 64 percent in 1997.[8] The Federal Emergency Management Agency (FEMA) estimates subsidized policies are 35 to 40 percent of a full-risk premium, although this is still higher than the premium homeowners would pay if they were charged actuarial rates and complied with construction standards to mitigate flooding.[9] Of particular relevance to Florida, the Congressional Budget Office found that many subsidized properties in coastal areas (23 percent from their sample of 10,000 properties) were second homes, vacation homes, or rentals.[10]

Most of this analysis is based on the risk estimates from FEMA FIRMs. There is some question about the accuracy of these maps, however. Flood risks are not stationary. Development that reduces impervious surface area can increase flooding, as can the channelization of rivers[11] and, possibly, climate change. FIRMs are not updated frequently and thus in some areas, the risk designated on the FIRMs can be a severe underestimate. For example, Temple University researchers undertook a detailed analysis of the Pennypack Creek Watershed in Pennsylvania and found that their assessment designated a larger area comprising the hundred-year flood zone than did the existing FIRM.[12]

Federal flood coverage initially was available only from insurance agents who dealt directly with the Federal Insurance Administration. In 1979, the administration was placed under FEMA, and since 1983, the direct policy program has been supplemented with a program known as the Write-Your-Own (WYO) program. The WYO program allows participating property and casualty insurers to write the standard flood insurance policy. The premium charged by the private insurer is the same as that charged by the federal government through the direct program. Nearly all flood policies issued today are written by ninety-one companies that write flood insurance through the WYO program. For example, in Florida, nearly 99 percent of all residential policies in force over the studied period 2000–2005 were WYO policies.

The WYO program is designed to be a win-win situation for the NFIP and private insurers. The NFIP benefits from the private insurance industry's marketing channels and the presence of many insurers in flood-prone areas. The WYO private insurers process flood claims as well as settle, pay, and defend all claims arising from the flood policies, while the NFIP retains responsibility for underwriting losses. In return, the private insurers participating in the WYO program receive an expense allowance (see section 4.4) and do not bear the risk. In other words, they play the role of a financial intermediary and claims manager on behalf of the federal government.

Despite this potentially synergistic effort between the NFIP and private companies, take-up rates for flood insurance have historically been low. One reason is that private insurance agents do not seem to market NFIP policies.[13] Another is that individuals are not interested in voluntarily purchasing flood insurance due to behavioral biases in evaluating low-probability risks or lack of information.[14] Tropical Storm Agnes in 1972

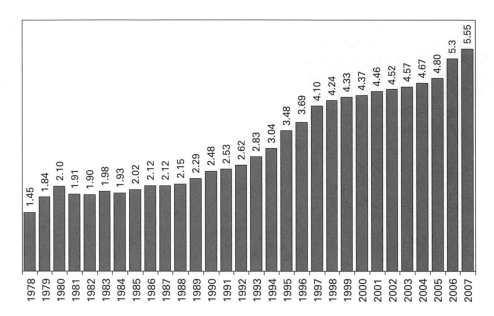

Figure 4.1
U.S. National Flood Insurance Program policies in force, 1978–2007 (millions of policies). *Sources:* Authors'
calculation; data from FEMA, Department of Homeland Security (NFIPStat, 2008).

demonstrated to Congress that very few people were participating in the NFIP, leading
to the passage of the Flood Disaster Protection Act of 1973.[15] This act limited federal
disaster assistance to nonparticipating communities and also created a mandatory purchase requirement: federally regulated lenders with mortgages must require flood insurance
for the purchase of property acquired or developed in special flood hazard areas (SFHAs),
which are defined as hundred-year flood zones. While this led to a large relative increase in
policies in force (see figure 4.1), the major 1993 floods in the Midwest revealed that the
mandatory purchase requirement was not being widely enforced, and sanctions on lenders
were tightened in 1994. The 1994 act created financial penalties for lenders that did not
comply with the mandatory purchase requirement, stated that liability is not altered by
sale or transfer of the loan, and mandated that lenders purchase insurance on behalf of
the borrower if the borrow fails to do so.

It is difficult to determine how well these regulations are working. Lack of nationwide
data on the number of properties in SFHAs makes a complete assessment somewhat difficult. Two recent studies are important in that regard. The first, published in 2004, reveals
that in a sample of coastal areas, the participation rate was 49 percent of eligible properties.[16] A 2006 RAND report also estimates that about 49 percent of properties in SFHAs
purchase NFIP flood insurance, and 1 percent of properties outside SFHAs purchase
insurance.[17]

4.2   NFIP Coverage Statistics

National Level

A noticeable effort has been made by the NFIP to increase knowledge of flood risks among the population through local and national education campaigns. FEMA launched a large-scale information campaign in 1995 called Cover America. According to FEMA, this campaign generated more than 500,000 inquiries to the NFIP. Cover America II was a new campaign launched in 1998. More recently, the NFIP launched FloodSmart, a comprehensive campaign featuring a Web site (www.floodsmart.gov) that details community risk and estimated premium rates, as well as mitigation measures, and how to enroll in the NFIP.

FEMA's increased efforts to raise awareness of the flood risk, coupled with a series of major floods in 1992–1993 significantly contributed to increasing the number of flood insurance policies issued by the NFIP.[18] By 1997, the number of policies in force reached 4 million and continued to increase in the following years. A more significant increase started in 2004 and accelerated in the aftermath of Hurricane Katrina and major floods in Louisiana. As of December 31, 2007, 5.55 million flood insurance policies were in place, 750,000 more than were in place two years before. These changes are shown in figure 4.1.

Over the same period, the total value of property insured under the NFIP has been growing rapidly, as depicted in figure 4.2. Since just 2001, the total exposure (sum of the

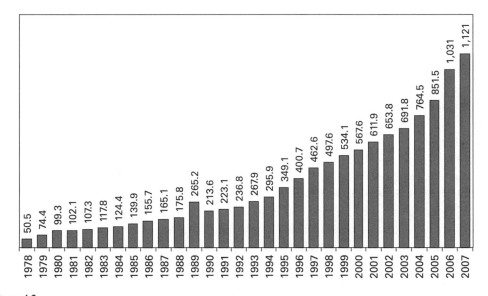

Figure 4.2
U.S. National Flood Insurance total coverage in force, 1978–2007 (billions of dollars). *Sources:* Authors' calculation; data from FEMA, Department of Homeland Security (NFIPStat, 2008).

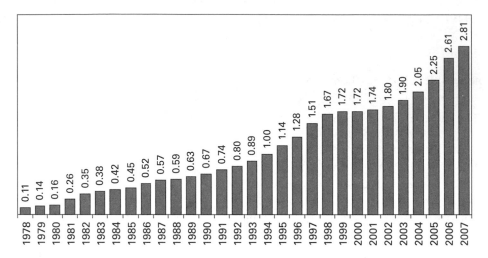

Figure 4.3
Total premiums collected by the NFIP by year, 1978–December 2007 (billions of dollars). *Sources:* Authors' calculation; data from FEMA, Department of Homeland Security (NFIPStat, 2008).

limits on all policies) has almost doubled. It was $214 billion in 1990 and $568 billion nationwide in 2000. In September 2006, it reached $1 trillion and has continued to grow; it was $1.1 trillion at the end of December 2007.

Not surprisingly, premiums collected for flood coverage have increased significantly as well, from $670 million in 1990, to $1.72 billion in 2000, to $2.81 billion at the end of December 2007 (figure 4.3). The coverage and premium figures were similar in 2008.

State Level

The NFIP does not play the same role in every state. Figure 4.4a provides the number of flood insurance policies in place for each state as of September 2006, and figure 4.4b depicts the growth rate in the number of policies in place between October 1, 2005, and September 30, 2006. The three states where the increase has been most significant are highly exposed to flood hazards, notably Mississippi (+69 percent), Texas (+30 percent), and Louisiana (+27 percent).

Table 4.1 provides a summary of the top ten states (ranked by the number of flood insurance policies in force) for several coverage and pricing measures as of December 31, 2007. We briefly discuss each of them. Note that these are average figures; they do not show the important differences within a state depending on location, exposure to risk, value of the house, and demographics of the homeowner. We discuss these variables in more detail in the next section, when we analyze the Florida market.

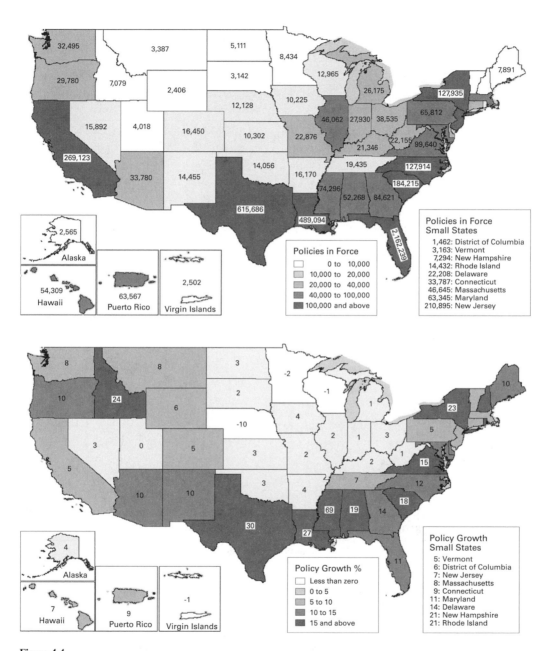

Figure 4.4
(a) Number of NFIP policies in place per state, September 30, 2006. (b) NFIP policy growth percentage change per state, October 1, 2005–September 30, 2006. *Source:* FEMA.

Table 4.1
NFIP summary statistics with a focus on the top ten states, December 31, 2007

	Number of flood policies in place	Quantity of insurance in place	Annual premiums	Average premium per policy	Average premium per $1,000 of coverage	Average quantity of insurance per policy
Nation	5,554,041	$1,120,767,708,600	$2,810,863,345	$506	$2.51	$201,793
Florida	2,189,759	454,409,776,100	901,071,362	411	1.98	207,516
% nationwide	39.43%	40.54%	32.06%			
Texas	666,920	145,170,577,200	279,895,243	420	1.93	217,673
% nationwide	12.01%	12.95%	9.96%			
Louisiana	502,085	93,608,829,200	286,015,533	570	3.06	186,440
% nationwide	9.04%	8.35%	10.18%			
California	266,171	62,041,065,600	168,952,788	635	2.72	233,087
% nationwide	4.79%	5.54%	6.01%			
New Jersey	223,650	45,945,494,500	159,123,884	711	3.46	205,435
% nationwide	4.03%	4.10%	5.66%			
Top 5 states	**3,848,585**	**801,175,742,600**	**1,795,058,810**	**466**	**2.24**	**208,174**
% nationwide	**69.29%**	**71.48%**	**63.86%**			
South Carolina	197,334	43,090,182,300	101,117,712	512	2.35	218,362
% nationwide	3.55%	3.84%	3.60%			
New York	144,253	31,598,332,600	109,182,682	757	3.46	219,048
% nationwide	2.60%	2.82%	3.88%			
North Carolina	133,955	28,618,309,100	74,043,712	553	2.59	213,641
% nationwide	2.41%	2.55%	2.63%			
Virginia	105,860	23,137,990,700	57,149,668	540	2.47	218,572
% nationwide	1.91%	2.06%	2.03%			
Georgia	88,429	19,465,735,700	49,644,456	561	2.55	220,128
% nationwide	1.59%	1.74%	1.77%			
Top 10 states	**4,518,416**	**947,086,293,000**	**2,186,197,040**	**484**	**2.31**	**209,606**
% nationwide	**81.35%**	**84.50%**	**77.78%**			

Sources: Authors' calculation from FEMA data as of December 31, 2007.

Number of Flood Insurance Policies in Place

The state of Florida represents almost 40 percent of the total number of flood insurance policies issued by the NFIP, and the top two states, Florida and Texas, represent over 50 percent of the entire NFIP portfolio. This is thus a highly concentrated market; about 70 percent of policies are located in just five states: Florida, Texas, Louisiana, California, and New Jersey.

Quantity of Insurance in Place

The distribution among the top states remains nearly the same when the dollar value of the coverage in place is used as the measure of quantity of insurance instead of the number of policies. Florida alone has $454 billion of coverage in place, over 40 percent of total coverage nationwide. The top five states account for more than $800 billion of flood coverage, or 71 percent of the national figure; the top ten states have $947 billion of flood coverage, or nearly 85 percent of total national coverage.

Total Premiums Collected over the Past Year

With more than $900 million in premiums collected, the state of Florida represents about one-third of the total $2.81 billion premiums collected by the NFIP nationwide. The top five states collected $1.8 billion, or 64 percent of the total premiums.

Average Quantity of Insurance per Policy

The average quantity of insurance coverage per policy varies somewhat by state from the national average of $202,000. In December 2007, it ranged from $186,000 in Louisiana to $233,000 in California; it was $201,000 in Florida, $217,000 in Texas, $218,000 in South Carolina, and $219,000 in New York.

Average Premium per Policy and per Dollar of Coverage

At a national level, the average premium collected per policy is $506, but there are major differences between states. Among the top ten states in table 4.1, Florida and Texas have by far the lowest average premium per policy ratio ($411 and $420, respectively). Louisiana is at $570, and the state of New York has the highest figure among these ten states, with an average of $757 per policy, almost twice that of Florida.

A somewhat better measure of the cost of insurance is the ratio of premium over quantity of insurance purchased. Despite a radical change over time in terms of new policies and total exposure of the program, the average U.S. homeowner still pays $2.50 per $1,000 of flood coverage (an implicit probability of a flood occurring every four hundred years, assuming that the price reflects exposure).[19] This average ratio varies from state to state and of course depends on the location where those who purchase flood coverage live and the characteristics of their home. On average, we find that insurance is cheaper in Florida and Texas (respectively, $1.98 and $1.93 per $1,000 of flood coverage, implying a probability of a flood that is less than 1 in 500)[20] and more expensive in New York and New Jersey ($3.46 per $1,000 of flood coverage, which is equivalent to a 1 in 300 implicit probability of flooding).[21]

4.3   Analysis of Flood Insurance in Florida

Florida represents—well above any other state—the largest portion of the NFIP portfolio. With almost 40 percent of the policies in force in the United States, Florida is a natural laboratory to study in order to better understand the functioning of the NFIP and the characteristics of homeowners who choose to buy flood coverage. Moreover, this state is also highly exposed to hurricane risks where there is a possibility of water damage that would be covered by the NFIP. It has also the highest concentration of exposed value in high-risk areas of any state in the country. Florida is thus of particular interest to many policymakers.

In this section we address four questions regarding flood insurance in Florida:

· What are the characteristics of the buyers of flood insurance in Florida?

· How much coverage do Floridians buy?

· What factors determine claims payments?

· How much does flood insurance cost in Florida? How has that cost evolved over the period 2000–2005?

Data Collected to Undertake the Study

To answer these four questions, we compiled data from several sources. The first source is a data set of over 7.5 million flood insurance policies provided to us by the NFIP.[22] It has all the policies in force in Florida for six consecutive years (2000–2005): over 1.21 million policies in 2000, 1.24 million in 2001, 1.26 million in 2002 and 2003, 1.29 million in 2004, and 1.37 million in 2005.

The data set does not include identifying information, such as household addresses (to ensure privacy), preventing us from doing a household-level analysis, but it does have the postal zone, city, and county in which the policyholder is located. The data set contains a variety of information relating to the policy, such as coverage bought, premium paid, and deductible chosen. The data also reveal the flood zone where the policy is located, the community rating system (CRS) discount (if any) (more on this below), the type of policy (single-family, commercial, and so forth), and, for some policies, structural information on the house, such as whether it has a basement or whether it is elevated.

From the NFIP, we also received a data set that contains all claims in Florida through August 31, 2006. The data set again has identifying information removed. It includes information on the claim, such as the date of the loss, the catastrophe it is associated with, the amount of damage, and how much was paid. It also contains information on the house and contents associated with the claim, such as structural features of the house and the value of the house and contents.

Finally, we drew on data from the 2000 U.S. Census. This gave us demographic information at the county level, such as median income and median value of owner-occupied

Table 4.2
Percentage of policies in force in Florida by occupancy type, 2000–2005

Occupancy type	2000	2001	2002	2003	2004	2005
Single family	81.27%	82.01%	82.51%	82.82%	83.09%	83.50%
Two- to four-family	4.94	4.81	4.69	4.66	4.58	4.45
Other residential	9.69	9.01	8.56	8.27	8.03	7.82
Nonresidential	4.11	4.18	4.24	4.26	4.29	4.22

housing. While these figures have certainly evolved since 2000, these are the most recently available census data. Measures such as these were used to better understand the factors driving the decision to purchase insurance.

Characteristics of the Buyers of Flood Insurance in Florida

As shown in table 4.2, the majority of flood policies in Florida (over 80 percent) are for single-family residential properties. The remaining policies are either multiple-family homes or other residential coverage (e.g., mobile homes). About 4 percent of policies in force are nonresidential (e.g., commercial). For that reason, most of the analyses in the rest of the chapter focus on single-family residential properties, which represented over 1.15 million policies in Florida in 2005.

The highest absolute numbers of single-family policies in force in Florida in 2005 were in Broward (254,497 policies), Miami-Dade (197,078 policies), Palm Beach (82,408 policies), Lee (79,330 policies), and Pinellas (68,048 policies) counties. These five counties account for nearly two-thirds of all single-family policies in force in the state in 2005. The five counties with the fewest absolute numbers of policies in force are Liberty (23 policies), Union (38 policies), Hamilton (56 policies), Jefferson (60 policies), and Madison (73 policies). Not surprisingly, given the hurricane risk in Florida, the counties with more policies in force on are on the coast, while those with fewer policies tend to be inland.

If instead of absolute numbers, the percentage of policies in force is examined (using an estimate of number of households from the 2000 Census), it provides a measure of market penetration. The counties with the highest percentage of policies in force per household in 2005 are Franklin (67 percent), Monroe (66 percent), Charlotte (41 percent), Lee (39 percent) and Broward (39 percent) Counties (see figure 4.5). The counties with the fewest policies per household are Gadsden (0.005 percent), Liberty (0.005 percent), Jackson (0.006 percent), Madison (0.01 percent) and Washington (0.01 percent). Again, the counties with the highest percentages are, not surprisingly, located on the coast.

One can also examine the rankings of counties using the total value at risk for the NFIP. The counties with the highest total amount of coverage in force (building plus contents; that is, NFIP's exposure) for single-family policies in 2005 are Broward ($53.6 billion), Miami-Dade ($36.6 billion), Palm Beach ($18.5 billion), Lee ($14.7 billion), and Pinellas

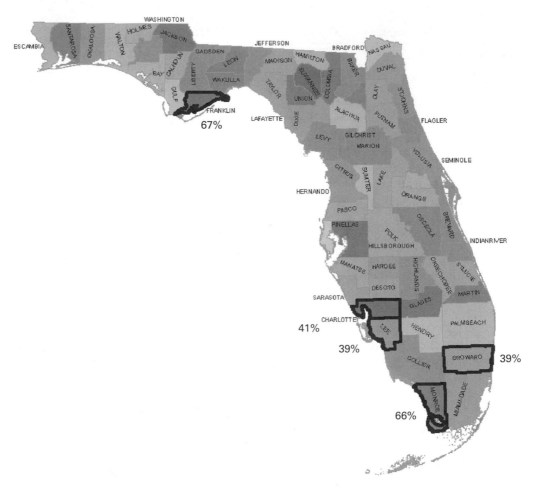

Figure 4.5
Top five Floridian counties in terms of market penetration, 2005

($11.6 billion). The counties with the highest number of policies in force are the same counties with the highest amount of total coverage. They are not, however, the counties with the highest market penetration, which are, as discussed above and as shown in figure 4.5, Franklin (67 percent), Charlotte (41 percent), Lee (39 percent), Monroe (66 percent), and Broward (39 percent). The five counties with the lowest amounts of total coverage are Liberty ($962,900), Union ($3.38 million), Hamilton ($4.51 million), Jefferson ($5.14 million), and Madison ($7.26 million).

It is also important to consider how the number of policies in force varies by risk level (at least as defined by FEMA). FEMA has mapped the flood risk of communities partici-

Table 4.3
Percentage of single-family residential policies in force in Florida, by flood zone, 2000–2005

Flood zone	2000	2001	2002	2003	2004	2005
X	15.40%	15.62%	15.33%	14.89%	15.15%	17.9%
A-A99	21.70	20.9	20.3	19.64	18.74	17.36
AE	31.80	31.56	31.77	32.3	32.8	32.22
AHB	19.77	20.07	20.13	18.34	22.99	22.17
AO, AOB, AH	2.65	3.52	4.3	6.81	2.55	2.26
V-VE	1.23	1.16	1.12	1.09	1.04	0.94
B, C, D	7.45	7.17	7.05	6.93	6.73	7.15
Total	100	100	100	100	100	100

Note: The flood zones are detailed in appendix 4A.

pating in the NFIP. The risk is differentiated by flood zones. In reporting on flood zones here, we are not making any judgment on the quality of this risk assessment.[23] Ideally, we would like to be able to look at take-up rate by flood zone. Unfortunately, there is no comprehensive data set of the number of households in each flood zone by county for Florida. From our data, however, we do have the number of policies in force in each flood zone. A summary is presented in table 4.3. Definitions of NFIP flood zones are detailed in appendix 4A.

Flood zone X comprises areas that are determined to be outside the hundred-year and five-hundred-year floodplains, thus designating minimal flood risk.[24] Flood insurance is not required for this zone. Interestingly, despite no insurance requirement and minimal risk, about 15 percent of all residential single-family policies in force since 2000 have been in this zone, increasing to about 18 percent in 2005.

Zone B designates moderate flood risk, and zone C designates minimal flood risk. Both areas are outside the hundred-year floodplain. Zone D areas have possible flood risks, but no analysis has been completed on them. These three zones represent only a small percentage of policies in Florida.

The A zones are FEMA-designated hundred-year floodplains, and NFIP insurance is mandatory. The subcategories within the A designations (A-A99; AE; AHB; AO, AOB, AH) refer to whether a detailed hydraulic analysis has been done, and if so, the nature of the flooding. Not surprisingly, about 75 percent of all single-family policies in Florida are located in these hundred-year floodplains.

Finally, the V and VE zones correspond to coastal hundred-year floodplains that have associated with them risk of storm surges. Quite surprisingly to us, given that Florida is highly exposed to hurricane risk, very few policies are in the V and VE zones.

The NFIP also maintains a community rating system (CRS), which is a voluntary program that rewards communities that undertake mitigating activities by lowering their premiums (to reflect the now lower risk). The deduction in premiums can range from 0 to 45

Table 4.4
Percentage of residential policies in force in Florida by CRS class

CRS discount	2000	2001	2002	2003	2004	2005
0%	22.20%	23.08%	23.03%	22.97%	23.15%	26.36%
5%	17.50	13.84	10.01	7.67	6.83	5.09
10%	35.81	33.10	31.62	28.15	27.57	25.24
15%	23.90	25.64	17.41	19.68	20.52	21.68
20%	.09	3.79	17.21	18.30	8.64	8.22
25%	.50	.55	.72	3.23	13.29	13.41
More than 25%[a]	0	0	0	0	0	0

[a] Only a few policies in the data set are in CRS classes that provide a discount higher than 25 percent: one policy (with a 50 percent discount) in 2004, one in 2002 (with a 30 percent discount), thirty-five in 2000 (with a 75 percent discount), and none with over a 25 percent discount in 2001, 2003, and 2005.

percent of the full actuarial rate (as determined by FEMA), depending on the actions taken. Table 4.4 shows how policies in force break down by CRS class. In 2005, about a quarter of residential policies in force were in communities with no CRS discount. The remaining three-quarters of policies benefit from some type of price discount, ranging from 5 to 25 percent. Virtually no policies receive a discount higher than 25 percent.

Table 4.4 also shows how these percentages varied between 2000 and 2005. Over the time period, an increasing percentage of policies has received no discount, but a higher number has received the 25 percent discount. For instance, from 2000 to 2003, less than 1 percent of the policies were located in communities that received a 25 percent discount on the actuarially based price (as defined by FEMA). That proportion significantly increased in the following two years; more than 13 percent of the policies had such a discount in 2005. Since we cannot follow one specific policy over time, it is not possible to draw any conclusions from our data set as to whether these changes are due to new policies or existing policies located in communities that have become much more active in mitigating flood risk.

In conclusion, a more granular analysis of the state reveals important differences among counties. Like the country overall, the NFIP market in Florida is highly concentrated, with just a few counties responsible for the majority of policies and coverage. Most of these policies are for single-family homes, and naturally, most of the coverage in force is located along the coasts and in SFHAs. That said, almost 20 percent of homeowners are buying insurance outside the mandatory purchase areas.

Amount of Coverage Floridians Buy

The second question focuses more specifically on the design of the flood insurance contract that Floridians purchase. Here, we analyze the demand side of flood insurance by determining policyholders' choice on the contract: what deductible and what limit they select.

Table 4.5
NFIP single-family, residential coverage limits by policy (nominal dollars)

Year	Structure limit	Contents limit
1994	$250,000	$100,000
1977[a]	150,000	50,000
1973	35,000	10,000
1968	17,500	5,000

Source: 42 U.S.C. 4013 (as amended).
[a] Since 1977, limits are the same for single-family dwelling and multifamily dwellings.

Limit on Coverage

The amount of insurance homeowners can purchase from the NFIP has evolved. The NFIP has always had a maximum coverage limit (a policy has, in fact, two maximum limits: one for the structure and one for the contents). These limits have increased over time but remained the same between 1994 and December 2007 (see table 4.5).[25] A minimum amount was established with the enactment of the mandatory purchase requirements for properties affected by the requirements. This minimum is the principal remaining on the outstanding mortgage (unless this amount is above the maximum coverage limit) with purchase being required for the life of the loan.

In order to compare the evolution of the real value of this maximum, we compiled data by indexing this limit to 2008 prices (total maximum limit of $350,000 in 2008). Figure 4.6 depicts this 2008: index total policy limit over the period 1968–2008 using the official U.S. inflation rate for each year over this forty-year period. This index was computed on January 1, 2008. In real price, the maximum limit on a flood policy in 2008 is about the same as it was twenty years earlier, despite significant inflation over this period (not to mention that in many places, real estate prices have actually increased at a much higher rate than just the inflation).

Over the years, many have argued that the $250,000 coverage limit is a problem for many homeowners. This concern was raised again following Hurricane Katrina. Given our data on the over 7 million flood insurance policies issued in Florida between 2000 and 2005, it is possible for us to measure whether that $250,000 threshold really constitutes a limitation on the demand side.

Our conclusion, looking at all policies in force in the state of Florida in 2005, is that this limit is not binding for the majority of homeowners. More specifically, we find that about 73 percent of single-family homes had building coverage below the $250,000 limit in 2005. Given that the median value of owner-occupied housing units in Florida reported in the 2000 Census was only $105,000, this result should not be surprising. While much media attention has been paid to the multimillion-dollar houses located on the beach, the large majority of residences in Florida are valued at less than the NFIP building coverage limit for residential properties.

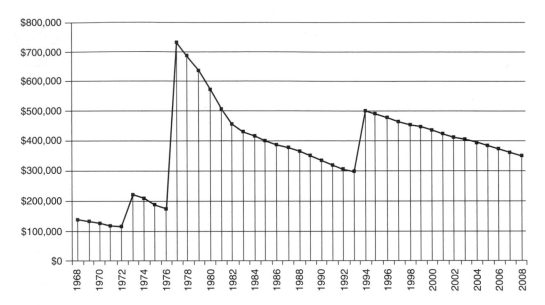

Figure 4.6
Maximum flood coverage limit by year (structure plus contents), 1968–2008. *Note:* Indexed to dollars as of January 1, 2008. *Source:* Authors' calculation.

Figure 4.7 depicts the percentage of the 1.14 million flood policyholders in 2005 that selected a given limit for building and contents coverage. As seen in the figure, about 27 percent of homeowners purchased building coverage at the insurance limit. Presumably many of these policyholders would welcome the option of choosing a higher limit.[26]

The pattern for contents coverage is also shown in figure 4.7. About 23 percent of single-family policies in Florida in 2005 were at the $100,000 limit for contents coverage—very close to the 27 percent at the building coverage limit. Of the 1.14 million single-family policies in force in 2005, however, roughly 12.5 percent had no contents coverage. This number has been declining slowly since 2000, however, while the number at the coverage limit rose substantially over this time from 7.5 percent in 2000 to almost 23 percent in 2005.

Similarly, the number and proportion of policyholders who have purchased the $250,000 limit has been growing steadily. In 2000, only around 10 percent of single-family policyholders were at the maximum coverage limit. In 2003, there were 17 percent, and 27 percent in 2005. In part, this reflects the growth of Florida's population over this period and the increased value of the real estate.

As expected, those with higher building coverage tend to have higher contents coverage. Our analysis of the data shows that on average over the entire state, there is approximately a 70 percent chance a policyholder will buy the maximum limit of contents coverage if she has bought the maximum limit of building coverage.

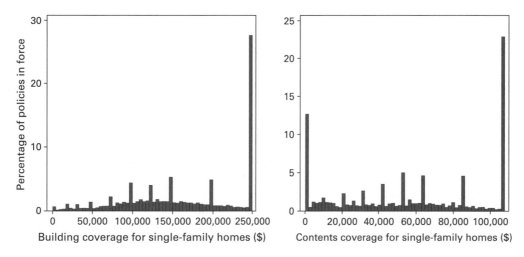

Figure 4.7
Distribution of building and contents coverage for single-family homes in the state of Florida for 2005

These state averages mask considerable county-level variability in whether policyholders are up against the maximum coverage limit. In 2005, there were some counties with virtually no policyholders at the limit, such as Liberty and Lafayette, and some counties with half or more policyholders at the limit, such as Walton, Nassau, Collier, and Martin. As mentioned, over time, more counties are finding more policyholders at the coverage limit. In 2000, the counties with the highest percentages of policies at the limit had only about 25 percent at the limit (these were Indian River, Walton, and Martin counties), whereas in 2005, the highest percentages were over 50 percent.

As expected, the percentage of policyholders at the limit is positively correlated with income measures from the 2000 census, such as the median value of owner-occupied housing and median income. We calculated that the correlation coefficient is approximately .6 for both measures. The higher the value of the home or the higher the income of the policyholder, the more likely homeowners are to be at the coverage limit. Both the median value of owner-occupied housing and median income are significant predictors in county-level regressions, with the percentage of policies at the coverage limit as the dependent variable (not provided here due to space limitations). Also, as expected, as the cost of insurance increases, the amount of coverage purchased declines.

Policyholders' Choice of Low Deductible
The second element of the contract we analyze is the choice of the deductible. The NFIP offers policyholders a choice of six deductibles for building coverage under which policyholders retain the full loss: $500, $1,000, $2,000, $3,000, $4,000, and $5,000.

We find that the majority of homeowners prefer a lower deductible. Our findings reinforce results previously published in the literature on decision making and insurance.

Eldred (1980) examined decisions with respect to homeowners and automobile insurance in South Carolina. He found that 20 percent of the 657 respondents who were interviewed had chosen the lowest possible deductible for automobile insurance and 57 percent for homeowners insurance. More recently, Sydnor (2006) studied deductible choices by 50,000 homeowners using a data set provided by an insurance company and found that 83 percent of customers chose a deductible lower than the maximum available one. Cutler and Zeckhauser (2004) examined decisions with respect to auto insurance (in Boston and Miami) and homeowners' insurance (in Philadelphia and Orlando). They found that 60 to 90 percent of the individuals in each of these cities selected the minimal $500 deductible.

Also, in an earlier study, Schoemaker and Kunreuther (1979) reported that 36 percent of subjects sampled from a population of insurance agency clients would rather pay a $90 premium for a zero-deductible insurance policy than $20 for a policy with a $500 deductible to protect themselves from a .01 probability of losing an amount between $10,000 and $30,000. For rational economists, this finding is somewhat counterintuitive. Indeed, it means that more than one-third of these people were apparently willing to pay $70 more (the difference between the $90 premium with no deductible and the $20 premium with a $500 deductible) to protect themselves against a loss of $5 (expected loss: .01 probability of losing $500).[27]

Our results, based on a very large sample of policies, are even more pronounced than the findings of these previous studies. We find that of the 1.14 million flood insurance policies in force in 2005, 98.3 percent of customers chose a deductible lower than the maximum available one. We also find that almost 80 percent of policyholders chose the lowest possible building deductible ($500), and around 18 percent chose the second-lowest deductible available, $1,000. These percentages are largely constant over the time period we studied (2000–2005).

There might be several explanations for the choice of a low deductible, but in the absence of interviews of buyers of flood coverage, we are unable to tease apart these competing explanations. First, consumers might want to cover as much as possible whatever happens (risk aversion). They do not act on a rational basis by evaluating expected loss, but rather assess risk in a binary way: "I suffer a loss or I don't; but if I do, I want to be sure my investment in insurance protection gets me as much as possible back." Second, some homeowners might not be aware of the existence of the different levels of deductible insurance. Third, for some customers who are forced to buy flood insurance by law or by lenders, a low deductible means that the insurer will indeed make payments to customers more often. Although such payments may not be a valid indication of a company's reliability, they may at least increase confidence in the company's promise of protection against unlikely large losses. Small claims might help make the payment of required insurance more tangible. Fourth, some individuals see insurance more as an investment, and they want to collect something back from their policy. The lowest possible deductible guarantees that in case of a loss, they will collect as much as possible.[28]

Table 4.6
Percentage of policyholders choosing the given deductible for varying amounts of building coverage, 2005

Building coverage deductible	0–$50,000	$50,000– $99,999	$100,00– $149,999	$150,00– $199,999	$200,00– $249,999	$250,000	Total policies
$500	72.5%	72.8%	79.9%	80.9%	82.1%	81.2%	909,077
$1,000	25.6%	24.3%	17.9%	16.5%	15.1%	14.8%	202,714
$5,000	1.2%	1.9%	1.4%	1.5%	1.6%	2.4%	20,417
Number of policies	58,099	153,036	270,668	209,988	138,796	313,257	1,143,844

One hypothesis we wanted to test was that people with the highest limit would also tend to have a higher deductible on their policy.[29] This would be consistent with individuals choosing to insure against catastrophic losses but not small losses. However, the analysis reveals that is not the case. To the contrary, we find that proportionally more people who bought the highest limit on their coverage are likely to take the lowest possible deductible: nearly 81 percent of policyholders with the maximum $250,000 limit also have the lowest possible deductible, versus nearly 73 percent for a policy with a limit lower than $100,000 for building coverage. Table 4.6 presents the number of policyholders choosing a given deductible stratified by the amount of building coverage purchased in 2005 (results for previous years are very similar). This suggests that individuals are trying to receive the maximum payout from their insurance or cover both small losses and catastrophic ones.

For contents coverage (full results not provided here), the deductibles were similar, with about 83 percent of single-family policies having a deductible of $500 and 15 percent having a deductible of $1,000. Again, these percentages are fairly consistent from 2000 to 2005 and the number and proportion choosing the $500 deductible increased with higher amounts of contents coverage.

Impact of Catastrophes on Consumers' Choice

It is also interesting to contrast our analysis for 2005 with the distribution of choices (deductible; limit) in 2000. Keeping in mind that Florida went through several flooding episodes in 2004, one would expect more people to buy flood insurance as a reaction to these catastrophes and that people who were already insured would want to be more fully covered if the differential in price is not too high. As we discuss below, the NFIP does not react to any specific local episode by increasing its rates there to reflect an updated view of the risk exposure, but rather defines its rates at a national level. As a result, the cost of flood insurance has remained virtually the same in Florida between 2000 and 2005 (see our analysis of the fourth question).

In that context, our results are not surprising. First, there were 973,444 flood insurance policies in place for single-family homes in 2000 versus 1,143,844 in 2005 (a 17 percent increase). Second, in most building coverage limit brackets, many more insureds selected the lowest possible deductible in 2005 than they had in 2000. For instance, taking into account all single-family flood insurance policies in Florida, in the lowest limit bracket ([$0; $50,000]), 58 percent of the insureds selected the $500 deductible in 2000; this increased to 72.5 percent in 2005. In the two counties that suffered significantly from the 2004 hurricane season in Florida (Santa Rosa and Escambia), 73 and 76 percent of the insureds in this low bracket, respectively, selected the $500 deductible in 2000; the year following the floods, this proportion increased to 87 percent and 92 percent, respectively. We noticed that effect even for those who had selected the highest possible limit on their policy ($250,000). In Santa Rosa County, for instance, 85 percent of them selected the $500 deductible in 2000; this number increased to 92 percent in 2005.

Third, the distribution of limit choice has evolved as well. While 70 percent of the flood policies in Florida in 2000 had a limit lower or equal to $150,000, only 40 percent of the increased number of total policies in the state had a limit below that threshold in 2005. Also, 10 percent of the 973,444 flood insurance policies in force for single-family homes had a $250,000 limit in their contract in 2000; in 2005, more than 27 percent of the 1,143,844 flood insurance policies had selected that maximum limit.

There might be several explanations for these changes: people living in devastated areas and who had coverage wished they had purchased the largest possible coverage before being flooded (regret); the floods were a vivid experience not only for those affected but also their neighbors and family, and they revised their beliefs that a flood is actually more likely to happen to them than they had thought before; the decision to buy more insurance also becomes more appealing because it is viewed as a sound financial investment.

Factors That Determine Claims Payments

The NFIP does not cover wind damage (this coverage is provided by private insurers through homeowners policies), but major hurricanes in coastal states typically induce significant flood losses due to storm surge pushing water inland, which is covered by the NFIP. In addition, as hurricanes move inland, the torrential rains can lead to substantial inland flood damage. For these reasons, hurricanes are responsible for the majority of claims in Florida.

In 2004, 15 percent of NFIP claims in Florida were attributable to Hurricane Charley, 17 percent to Hurricane Frances, 36 percent to Hurricane Ivan, and 18 percent to Hurricane Jeanne—a total of 86 percent of flood claims. In 2005, over 50 percent of all claims payments for covered households in Florida were associated with Hurricane Wilma, and just under a quarter were associated with Hurricane Katrina.[30] Another 13 percent of claims were due to Hurricane Dennis[31]—a total of 88 percent of the claims for that year. This likely explains the fact that the mean claim payment in Florida is significantly higher for V flood zones—floodplains associated with wave action—than for other flood zones.

It is also interesting to take a closer look at the counties that have generated the largest amount of flood insurance claims over the six-year period we studied (2000–2005). Santa Rosa and Escambia counties, located in the far northwest of Florida (see figure 4.5), suffered severe losses from the 2004 hurricane season. Flood claims for Santa Rosa were about $350 million, or about 30 percent of the total flood coverage in the county; Escambia claims were $260 million, or 25 percent of its entire coverage.

Rather than looking at the total value of these reimbursements (a county with many more policies will receive more payments, all thing being equal), we use the average insurance claims per policy in each county as a measure of quantity. For certain counties, this figure is quite high indeed: $44,017 for Santa Rosa, $34,954 for Escambia, and $10,259 for Monroe.[32] The other seven counties in the top ten are as follows: Wakulla ($8,868), Okaloosa ($7,366), Franklin ($5,481), Baker ($3,499), Gilchrist ($3,083), De Soto ($3,035), and Walton ($2,640).[33] This raises the question: What are the main drivers of these claims?

Determinants of Claims Payments

To examine claim payments in Florida, we received a data set from the NFIP that contained all claims for the state through August 31, 2006. Although identifying information was removed, it still allows us to examine general patterns. In order to determine the main drivers of flood claims in Florida, we ran a simple ordinary-least-squares (OLS) regression for residential properties.[34] The dependent variable is the log of the total claims paid (building plus contents). The explanatory variables we include are dummy variables as to whether the property is in a special flood hazard areas (SFHA),[35] if the property is elevated, and if it is the owner's principal residence. Variables are also included for the value of the building and the contents before damage, the number of floors in the house, and a code for the type of basement (e.g., if there is a basement, if it is finished), as well as county fixed effects, the date of the loss, and fixed effects for each catastrophe.

The specification is given by:

$$\mathrm{Ln}(total\ claims\ paid) = \beta_0 + \beta_1(SFHA\ dummy) + \beta_2(Elevated\ dummy)$$
$$+ \beta_3(value\ of\ building) + \beta_4(value\ of\ contents)$$
$$+ \beta_5(number\ of\ floors) + \beta_6(basement\ code) + \beta_7(date\ of\ loss)$$
$$+ \beta_8(principal\ residence\ dummy) + \lambda_1(county\ FE)$$
$$+ \lambda_2(catastrophe\ FE) + \underline{\varepsilon}.$$

Results of this regression are presented in table 4.7. While the R^2 is somewhat small, the regression does confirm some intuitive notions about what drives claim amounts. Properties in the hundred-year floodplain—SFHAs—have higher claims paid (coefficient +0.12453). This makes sense since the risk for these properties is higher. If a building is elevated, paid claims are less (the coefficient is −0.77518),[36] which is expected, since the risk of being flooded should be lower. If the building is a principal residence, claims paid are higher. This may be because second homes are less valuable, they contain less valuable contents, or they have lower levels of coverage.

Table 4.7
Results of the OLS regression explaining total paid claims to flooded NFIP-covered residential properties in Florida

Variable	Coefficient estimate
Constant	4.6655*** (.43181)
Dummy equal to 1 if property is in a SFHA	.12453*** (.02070)
Dummy equal to 1 if building is elevated	−.77518*** (.01953)
Value of building	−1.05e-06 (8.21e-07)
Value of contents	.00001*** (2.53e-06)
Number of floors	−.10349*** (.00634)
Basement code	−.08490*** (.01591)
Date of loss	.00030*** (.00002)
Dummy equal to one if building is principal residence of owners	.14372*** (.01709)
County fixed effects	Y
Catastrophe fixed effects	Y
R-squared	0.2832
N (number of claims studied)	45,374

Note: The dependent variable is a natural log of the total amount paid (building plus contents) for a given claim. Robust standard errors are given in parentheses. Coefficients significant at the 10 percent level are marked with *, those significant at the 5 percent level are marked with **, and those significant at the 1 percent level are designated by ***.

The coefficients on the value of the building and value of the contents are essentially zero, implying that flood claims do not disproportionably affect high- or low-valued homes. That result is somewhat puzzling, as one might expect a house with higher contents and building values to suffer a larger loss (all things being equal). One possible explanation is that these more costly houses are also more protected against flooding (for instance, because the owners are wealthier and willing to invest more in mitigation).

Evolution of the Cost of Flood Insurance in Florida, 2000–2005

We turn to our last question to determine the cost of flood insurance in different parts of the state. We also discuss how flood insurance pricing has evolved in the aftermath of the major flooding that occurred during the period of our analysis to conclude that while the average premium per policy has slightly increased, the cost of insurance (measured as premium per $1,000 of coverage) has significantly decreased.

Cost of Flood Coverage in Florida Counties

As we discussed in section 4.2, among the top ten states that make up the largest portion of the NFIP's portfolio, Florida has, on average, one of the lowest cost of flood insurance per $1,000 of coverage. Table 4.8 depicts for each of the sixty-seven Florida counties the average premium paid per $1,000 of flood coverage, the average premium per policy (we use nominal dollars here), and the percentage of policies in SFHAs in 2000 and 2005.

Looking at the first measure of insurance cost, among the sixty-seven counties we analyze, in 2005 cost ranges from $1.30 in Flagler County to $7.46 in Dixie County, with an average of $2.79 and a median of $2.50. While data confirm that the proportion of policies in a hundred-year flood zone is an indicator of the average cost of flood insurance in the county, we notice that the relationship is not always clear. For instance, the counties in which insurance is the most expensive are not necessarily those with the highest proportion of policies in SFHAs: Palm Beach, Broward, and Santa Rosa counties all have over 50 percent of their policies in these high-risk zones but are among the counties with the lowest average cost of flood insurance. At the extreme, over 90 percent of flood policies in Miami–Dade County are located in SFHAs, where the probability of a flood is expected to be at least one in a hundred, but the cost there is less than $2 per $1,000 of coverage—an implicit probability of a flood occurring only once every five hundred years. Only the monitoring of flood claims over a much longer period of time than given by our data set would allow some evaluation of this rating (e.g., fifty years).

Another way to measure the cost of insurance is to determine the average premium per policy. We find that in 2005, premiums ranged from $299 in Okeechobee County to $985 in Franklin County, with an average of $450 and a median of $395.

Private versus Public Insurance: Difference in Price Adjustment
NFIP rates are established at a national level, and it appears that the 2004 hurricane information was not incorporated into rate changes. In table 4.8 we generated for each county the evolution of the cost of insurance (using the same two measures) between 2000 and 2005. We find that not only has the cost of insurance not increased, but it has significantly decreased in all but two of the sixty-seven counties in Florida (Franklin and Liberty). The situation is especially extreme in Santa Rosa and Escambia counties. These counties suffered the largest flood loss in 2004. Moreover, they had a significant increase in the proportion of flood policies located in high-risk areas (SFHAs). Nevertheless, the average cost of flood insurance in Santa Rosa decreased from $2.27 per $1,000 of flood coverage in 2000 to $1.60 in 2005 (a 29 percent decrease); in Escambia, the cost decreased from $2.85 per $1,000 of flood coverage in 2000 to $1.91 in 2005 (a 33 percent decrease).[37]

There is some concern that FEMA's flood zone designations are not updated frequently enough and are not at a fine enough resolution. Furthermore, the operation of the NFIP is such that rates are set nationally by zone and are not typically modified locally as the result of a flood episode. NFIP rates are revised every May. By law, any yearly increase in premiums cannot exceed 10 percent overall. Still, some might have expected in the aftermath of the 2004 and 2005 flood claims that the NFIP would have revised its cost of flood insurance. The 2004 *Actuarial Rate Review*, however, recommended no change in premiums for V zones—those associated with wave action—and only a 1.4 percent total increase in premiums across other zones. The federal view is that the ultimate goal of the program is to guarantee a financial balance over time at a national level rather than being

Table 4.8
Flood insurance rates per $1,000 and per policy by county in Florida for single-family, residential policies only and percentage of policies in SFHAs, 2000 and 2005

County	Average premium per $1,000 of coverage		Average premium per policy (nominal value)		Percentage of policies in SFHAs	
	2005	2000	2005	2000	2005	2000
Alachua	$2.02 (−26%)	$2.75	$339	$337	45%	31%
Baker	2.50 (−28)	3.48	353	337	47	43
Bay	1.72 (−19)	2.13	382	326	34	36
Bradford	3.07 (−21)	3.90	406	346	74	74
Brevard	1.46 (−25)	1.95	322	294	37	35
Broward	1.62 (−16)	1.94	372	328	95	96
Calhoun	4.73 (−14)	5.49	478	328	81	82
Charlotte	2.62 (−30)	3.76	523	499	94	88
Citrus	3.64 (−27)	4.97	527	487	91	87
Clay	1.64 (−22)	2.09	369	338	46	38
Collier	2.35 (−15)	2.75	590	528	78	73
Columbia	2.99 (−35)	4.62	401	385	79	55
Desoto	2.71 (−15)	3.20	417	328	55	56
Dixie	7.46 (−11)	8.38	734	506	88	88
Duval	1.38 (−22)	1.76	334	305	23	23
Escambia	1.91 (−33)	2.85	443	478	64	40
Flagler	1.30 (−28)	1.80	317	288	20	17
Franklin	4.50 (+2)	4.40	985	702	93	92
Gadsden	2.29 (−23)	2.97	356	277	41	49
Gilchrist	3.65 (−35)	5.61	451	428	82	72
Glades	3.34 (−16)	3.98	363	300	91	92
Gulf	3.01 (−4)	3.15	557	398	61	62
Hamilton	3.72 (−15)	4.39	405	323	77	75
Hardee	3.01 (−9)	3.29	396	295	43	52
Hendry	3.73 (−12)	4.23	388	337	72	83
Hernando	3.99 (−35)	4.57	683	517	74	63
Highlands	1.93 (−21)	2.45	318	266	55	58
Hillsborough	2.58 (−21)	3.28	517	475	80	69
Holmes	3.02 (−39)	4.94	358	329	71	63
Indian River	1.80 (−18)	2.21	440	433	58	66
Jackson	2.46 (−25)	3.28	331	386	50	44
Jefferson	3.17 (−16)	3.76	360	308	72	77
Lafayette	5.08 (−18)	6.19	494	377	91	95
Lake	1.94 (−24)	2.57	340	308	63	58
Lee	2.53 (−18)	3.08	548	478	85	84
Leon	2.26 (−20)	2.82	384	319	69	57

Table 4.8
(continued)

County	Average premium per $1,000 of coverage		Average premium per policy (nominal value)		Percentage of policies in SFHAs	
	2005	2000	2005	2000	2005	2000
Levy	6.10 (−7)	6.53	808	573	92	88
Liberty	5.97 (+1)	5.90	440	275	87	70
Madison	3.19 (−29)	4.48	391	452	60	58
Manatee	2.75 (−22)	3.52	569	501	75	70
Marion	1.95 (−29)	2.76	314	289	37	31
Martin	1.70 (−22)	2.19	447	441	43	43
Miami-Dade	1.89 (−19)	2.33	395	355	93	93
Monroe	3.72 (−7)	3.99	760	594	93	94
Nassau	1.48 (−19)	1.82	396	361	35	33
Okaloosa	1.66 (−20)	2.08	415	375	30	28
Okeechobee	2.30 (−20)	2.87	299	273	75	77
Orange	1.73 (−21)	2.18	342	301	50	53
Osceola	1.78 (−25)	2.39	325	276	65	68
Palm Beach	1.42 (−22)	1.82	368	364	51	48
Pasco	3.59 (−24)	4.70	549	477	82	76
Pinellas	3.49 (−10)	3.89	686	560	78	76
Polk	2.10 (−25)	2.80	335	298	62	60
Putnam	2.88 (−25)	3.81	396	366	82	79
Santa Rosa	1.60 (−29)	2.27	411	406	53	35
Sarasota	2.41 (−22)	3.10	524	480	62	58
Seminole	1.52 (−21)	1.93	335	299	40	39
St. Johns	1.62 (−19)	2.01	417	395	53	54
St. Lucie	1.72 (−32)	2.54	339	303	61	52
Sumter	1.95 (−38)	3.14	326	283	58	39
Suwannee	3.24 (−33)	4.87	355	352	76	75
Taylor	6.36 (−3)	6.54	759	517	89	87
Union	3.30 (−27)	4.51	354	377	59	53
Volusia	1.83 (−22)	2.36	358	308	41	46
Wakulla	6.23 (−2)	6.38	961	628	94	89
Walton	1.76 (−22)	2.25	476	444	29	40
Washington	2.63 (−48)	5.12	330	276	70	45

Source: Authors' calculation.

accurate everywhere at a microlevel (and then compensating negative results in certain areas with positive ones in others). Our analysis of the financial balance of the program in the next section reveals that such a goal had been more or less reached over the operation of the NFIP until Hurricane Katrina.

4.4   Financial Performance of the NFIP over the Years

In the aftermath of Hurricane Katrina and the flooding of New Orleans, the NFIP has been under severe criticism because its reserve was far below its claims payments, and so it was forced to borrow over $20 billion from the federal government. We first analyze the balance of the system since its creation in 1968 and determine the main sources of spending beyond the payment of flood claims.

Premiums collected from NFIP policies, plus a small policy fee, are deposited in the National Flood Insurance Fund, from which losses and administrative costs are paid. The NFIP also has borrowing authority from the U.S. Treasury. Borrowing authority started at $1 billion and was increased to $1.5 billion in 1996. Due to the catastrophic nature of flooding and the desire to keep premiums affordable, as well as the subsidization of many properties, the fund was not large enough to make payouts for the 2005 hurricane season. In the aftermath of Hurricane Katrina and the levee breaches in New Orleans, borrowing authority was increased to over $20 billion to pay claims from 2005.[38] While this obviously raises major issues regarding the long-term financial stability of the program, it is worthwhile to look at previous years to judge how the program has performed over time.

Premiums versus Claims

Figure 4.8 shows total premiums collected by the NFIP minus total claims paid by the NFIP for each year (not cumulative) from 1978 to 2006. As this figure shows, until the hurricanes in 2004 and 2005, the program had generally been collecting enough premiums each year to cover policyholders' claims.[39] Note that figure 4.8 does not include management costs or payments NFIP makes to WYO insurers. It is thus an overly optimistic depiction of the financial situation of the program in each year. In order to provide a more realistic description of the balance sheet of the program over time, we must look at the financial records of the NFIP since its inception in 1968 up to the most recent information available (year closing September 30, 2006).[40] While there are typically many elements to integrate into the calculation of the NFIP's financial performance, several budget lines are particularly critical.

On the earning side, the main income outside of the earned premiums is provided by the $30 policy fee levied against all NFIP flood policyholders, which typically accounts for an additional 6 or 7 percent of the earned premiums. The NFIP also had some investment revenue. Overall, for the period 1968 to September 2005 (before Hurricane Katrina and

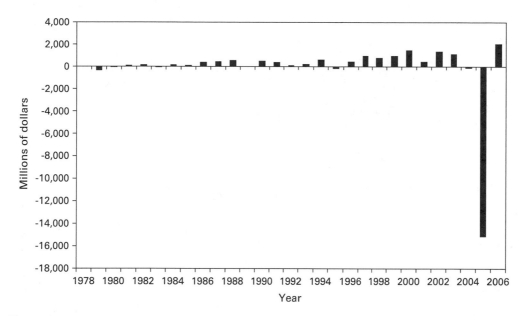

Figure 4.8
NFIP premiums minus claims by year, 1978–2006. *Sources:* Authors' calculation; data from FEMA, Department of Homeland Security.

the flooding of New Orleans), the NFIP collected $22.15 billion in premiums, $1.16 billion in federal policy fees, and $0.258 billion in investment revenue. It also received federal appropriations of $1.2 billion in the early 1980s to repay borrowed funds from the early years of the program, as no funds had been given to capitalize the program initially.[41]

On the expense side, the major source of spending, after the payment of claims, is the payment to the insurers and agents participating in the WYO program on behalf of the federal government. The program pays them an expense load based on the average costs for underwriting, policy writing, and advertising, as well as taxes and general expenses. On average, that represents about 15.6 percent of earned premiums. In addition, insurers receive a 15 percent commission allowance, paid to them regardless of whether an agent or broker receives a commission. Another payment is made to the WYO companies by the NFIP (up to 2 percent of earned premiums if the WYO insurer meets "production" goals).

In addition, following a flooding episode, FEMA pays WYO insurance companies for claims adjustment expenses (e.g., attorney fees and adjuster fees) and an allowance of 3.3 percent of each claim settlement amount to pay for their processing expenses. For example, the amount FEMA paid WYO insurance companies for Katrina's claims processing expenses increased more than tenfold, from $30 million in fiscal year 2004 to about $385 million in fiscal year 2005.[42] Figure 4.9 provides an overview of this spending as a percentage of the premiums collected by the program over time.

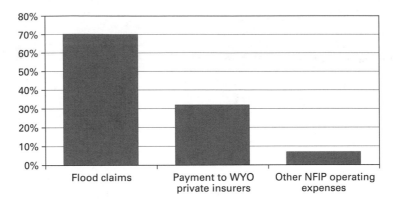

Figure 4.9
NFIP main expenditures as a percentage of premiums collected, 1968–September 2005. *Note:* Percentages add up to more than 100 percent since the program runs a deficit.

Overall, more than 30 percent of the total earned premiums go to WYO participating companies, which do not bear any of the risk.[43] In 2006, that proportion was higher due to additional costs incurred to process a historic number of claims due to Katrina, Rita, and Wilma. Over the period 1968 to 2005, participating insurers collected over $7.4 billion (excluding the loss adjustment expenses for which we do not have data). Whether these fees are too high is an open question. On the one hand, unless there is a better understanding of the true cost incurred by the private insurers to manage flood policies as intermediaries, it is difficult to put a price tag on it. On the other hand, one may also ask how much it would cost the federal government to establish and maintain a public structure capable of managing over 5 million insurance policies. Other expenses include NFIP operating expenses and floodplain management costs (flood studies and surveys, mitigation grants, community rating system operation costs).[44] That represents about 7 percent of the earned premiums. Over the period 1968 to 2005, these other program expenses accounted for $2.2 billion.[45]

The findings of our analysis, undertaken during the summer of 2007, are very much aligned with those of the U.S. Government Accountability Office (GAO), published in September 2007. In its report to congressional committees, GAO specifically points out that aspect of the program and recommends that "FEMA take steps to ensure that it has a reasonable estimate of actual expenses WYO companies incur to help determine payments for services and that financial audits are performed. The Department of Homeland Security reviewed a draft of this report and generally agreed with our recommendations."[46]

To summarize, from 1968 to 2005, NFIP's revenue was $23.6 billion, and its total insurance expenses were $24.3 billion (including $16.5 billion of claims paid to insured victims of flood and $7.4 billion paid to companies participating in the WYO program). In addition, the program spent $2.2 billion for administrative expenses. After thirty-seven years of operation, the cumulative operating result was a deficit of about $3 billion.

NFIP could have balanced its current deficit by doing either of two simple things, or a combination of the two: increasing the federal policy fee from $25 to $100, and increasing the premium charged against policyholders by 15 percent. A combination of these changes could have ended up being a smoother decision: if the federal policy fee had been $50 instead of $25, the premiums had been increased by 5 percent, and payments to insured reduced by 10 percent (if financial audits reveal the current levels were too high given the real spending of the insurers), the NFIP would have had a balanced budget before being hit by the most devastating natural disaster in the history of the country.

It becomes clear from this analysis that right before the tragedy of Katrina, the program had been relatively balanced (or could have been by slightly modifying the terms of the flood premiums or payments to insurers participating into the program), even though millions of new policies were added to its national coverage over the years.

The Impact of Truly Extreme Events

The 2005 hurricane season radically changed the balance sheet of the NFIP. This raises at least two important questions: How did the program manage the very large number of claims it received from flood victims? Should the NFIP build up enough reserve to face such a truly large-scale catastrophe, or is it better to finance truly exceptional losses through federal funding after the event?

On the claims management side, despite the scale of the catastrophe, collaboration between participating insurers and FEMA enabled a large portion of the loss to be settled in the months following Hurricane Katrina. As of May 2006, with over 95 percent of the claims reported by FEMA settled, the NFIP had paid claims for about 162,000 losses for flood damage from Hurricane Katrina in Alabama, Florida, Louisiana, and Mississippi. As a point of comparison, the program processed about 30,000 claims in each of the two largest single flood events prior to Hurricane Katrina: the 1995 Louisiana flood and Tropical Storm Allison in 2001. The average amount paid per claim for Hurricane Katrina flood damages, $94,800, was about three times the average paid per claim in the previous record year, 2004.[47]

On the financial side, the magnitude and severity of losses from Hurricane Katrina and other 2004 and 2005 hurricanes required the NFIP to obtain borrowing authority of $20.8 billion from the Treasury. Many believe that this is a level of deficit that the program is unlikely to be able to repay with its current annual premium income of about $2.8 billion.[48] This calls into question the structure of the program and whether it can, and should, be designed to handle catastrophes of this magnitude.

The policy question is whether the program should be in a position to build up a significant reserve in order to be able to face future catastrophic disasters or whether such extreme events should be financed by the U.S. Treasury—essentially general taxpayers. If one relies solely on the resources of the NFIP, then residents in flood-prone areas would have to pay much more to insure their homes against water damage from flooding. After several years without a major loss, many are likely to question FEMA, which would then be sitting on a multibillion-dollar reserve. It was known prior to the NFIP's inception that it would not be able to handle very large catastrophes even if the premiums that are subsidized (25 percent of all flood policies) were charged the full actuarial rate. A private insurance representative is reported to have said during early discussions of the NFIP, "It will be a damage-reimbursement program that will hit the Treasury whenever you have a serious disaster."[49]

The question of whether the NFIP should be able to cover the costs of catastrophes must be addressed in the context of the program's goals. These are to decrease the risk of future flood losses, reduce the costs of flooding, reduce the demand for disaster assistance after floods, and preserve and restore the natural value of floodplains.[50] Another implicit goal is political feasibility. For instance, the decision was made at the NFIP's inception to subsidize existing structures to improve political feasibility and maintain property values,[51] although at the expense of developing a financially independent insurance program. In 1981, a goal was set to make the program self-supporting for the average loss year. Pasterick (1998) points out that this is not the same as being actuarially sound. A current question is whether the NFIP should be actuarially sound and what time horizon policymakers should consider.

There are many steps that could be taken both to reduce costs and increase revenue for the NFIP. After NFIP's almost forty years in existence, the subsidies for pre-FIRM properties could be reduced or eliminated. More efforts could be made to enforce the mandatory purchase requirement. Currently properties located behind levees can petition to be removed from SFHAs and thus made exempt from the mandatory purchase requirement. As seen in New Orleans, properties behind levees are not safe and perhaps should not be given this exemption. The tragedy of New Orleans was that the levee system gave inhabitants the feeling they were fully protected when they were not. In addition, if a property is elevated above the base-flood level, due to either topography or fill, the owners can request to be exempted from insurance requirements. Finally, the NFIP could work on improving the connection between insurance and mitigation and land use regulation. While at least 6,000 acres of previously developed floodplain have been returned to open space, most areas at risk from flooding are still subject to development.[52]

Summary

This chapter describes the evolution of the program since its inception in 1968 by focusing on three key elements: number of policies in place, premiums collected, and value at risk at a state and national level. We specifically discuss these variables, along with several measures of price, for the top ten states (ranked by proportion of the NFIP portfolio).

Florida alone represents nearly 40 percent of the entire NFIP portfolio; the second part of this chapter provides a detailed analysis of flood insurance in Florida. We ask and answer four questions using the entire NFIP data set for Florida over the period 2000 to 2005, as well as U.S. Census data.

· What are the characteristics of the buyers of flood insurance in Florida?

· How much coverage do Floridians buy?

· What factors determine claims payments?

· How much does flood insurance cost in Florida? How has that cost evolved over the period 2000–2005?

The chapter then analyzes the financial stability of the NFIP since 1968 and how flood insurance premiums are spent. We find that private insurers collect on average one-third of the total flood insurance premiums just to administer the program on behalf of the federal government, even though they bear no risk.

APPENDIX 4A: DEFINITIONS OF THE NFIP FLOOD ZONES

Zone A   The flood insurance rate zone that corresponds to the 1 percent annual chance floodplains that are determined in the Flood Insurance Study by approximate methods of analysis.[53] Because detailed hydraulic analyses are not performed for such areas, no Base Flood Elevations or depths are shown within this zone. Mandatory flood insurance purchase requirements apply.

Zones AE and A1–A30   The flood insurance rate zones that correspond to the 1 percent annual chance floodplains that are determined in the Flood Insurance Study by detailed methods of analysis. In most instances, Base Flood Elevations derived from the detailed hydraulic analyses are shown at selected intervals within this zone. Mandatory flood insurance purchase requirements apply.

Zone AH   The flood insurance rate zone that corresponds to the areas of 1 percent annual chance shallow flooding with a constant water-surface elevation (usually areas of ponding) where average depths are between 1 and 3 feet. The Base Flood Elevations derived from the detailed hydraulic analyses are shown at selected intervals within this zone. Mandatory flood insurance purchase requirements apply.

Zone AO   The flood insurance rate zone that corresponds to the areas of 1 percent shallow flooding (usually sheet flow on sloping terrain) where average depths are between 1 and 3 feet. Average flood depths derived from the detailed hydraulic analyses are shown within this zone. In addition, alluvial fan flood hazards are shown as Zone AO on the Flood Insurance Rate Map. Mandatory flood insurance purchase requirements apply.

Zone AR   The flood insurance rate zone used to depict areas protected from flood hazards by flood control structures, such as a levee, that are being restored. FEMA will consider using the Zone AR designation for a community if the flood protection system has been deemed restorable by a federal agency in consultation with a local project sponsor, a minimum level of flood protection is still provided to the community by the system, and restoration of the flood protection system is scheduled to begin within a designated time period and in accordance with a progress plan negotiated between the community and FEMA. Mandatory purchase requirements for flood insurance will apply in Zone AR, but the rate will not exceed that for an unnumbered Zone A if the structure is built in compliance with Zone AR floodplain management regulations.

For floodplain management in Zone AR areas, the property owner is not required to elevate an existing structure when making improvements to the structure. However, for new construction, the structure must be elevated (or floodproofed for nonresidential structures) so that the lowest floor, including basement, is a minimum of three feet above the highest adjacent existing grade, if the depth of the Base Flood Elevation (BFE) does not exceed five feet at the proposed development site. For infill sites, rehabilitation of existing structures, or redevelopment of previously developed areas, there is a three-foot elevation requirement regardless of the depth of the BFE at the project site.

The Zone AR designation will be removed and the restored flood control system will be shown as providing protection from the 1 percent annual chance flood on the National Flood Insurance Program map on completion of the restoration project and submittal of all the necessary data to FEMA.

Zone A99   The flood insurance rate zone that corresponds to areas within the 1 percent annual chance floodplain that will be protected by a federal flood protection system where construction has reached specified statutory milestones. No Base Flood Elevations or depths are shown within this zone. Mandatory flood insurance purchase requirements apply.

Zone D   Areas where there are possible but undetermined flood hazards. In areas designated as Zone D, no analysis of flood hazards has been conducted. Mandatory flood insurance purchase requirements do not apply, but coverage is available. The flood insurance rates for properties in Zone D are commensurate with the uncertainty of the flood risk.

Zone V   The flood insurance rate zone that corresponds to areas within the 1 percent annual chance coastal floodplains that have additional hazards associated with storm waves. Because approximate hydraulic analyses are performed for such areas, no Base Flood Elevations are shown within this zone. Mandatory flood insurance purchase requirements apply.

Zone VE   The flood insurance rate zone that corresponds to areas within the 1 percent annual chance coastal floodplain that have additional hazards associated with storm waves. Base flood elevations derived from the detailed hydraulic analyses are shown at selected intervals within this zone. Mandatory flood insurance purchase requirements apply.

Zones B, C, and X   The flood insurance rate zones that correspond to areas outside the 1 percent annual chance floodplain, areas of 1 percent annual chance sheet flow flooding where average depths are less than one foot, areas of 1 percent annual chance stream flooding where the contributing drainage area is less than 1 square mile, or areas protected from the 1 percent annual chance flood by levees. No Base Flood Elevations or depths are shown within this zone. Insurance purchase is not required in these zones.

APPENDIX 4B: RESIDENTIAL POLICIES IN FORCE, FLORIDA COUNTIES, 2005

This list shows the percentage of residential policies in force, including single-family residences, located in SFHAs in each Florida county in 2005 in the hundred-year floodplains, where insurance is mandatory.

County	%	County	%	County	%
Flagler	17.42	Union	52.63	Suwannee	74.81
Duval	23.25	Orange	53.09	Hamilton	75.00
Okaloosa	27.59	St. Johns	54.41	Pinellas	75.92
Marion	31.18	Columbia	55.45	Pasco	76.49
Alachua	31.19	Desoto	55.53	Jefferson	76.67
Nassau	33.30	Leon	56.81	Okeechobee	77.24
Santa Rosa	34.82	Madison	57.53	Putnam	78.79
Brevard	35.44	Highlands	57.63	Calhoun	81.94
Bay	36.04	Lake	57.88	Hendry	82.72
Clay	37.96	Sarasota	58.49	Lee	83.81
Sumter	39.43	Polk	59.63	Taylor	87.26
Seminole	39.49	Gulf	61.54	Citrus	87.34
Walton	39.54	Holmes	63.16	Dixie	88.07
Escambia	39.80	Hernando	63.19	Levy	88.15
Martin	42.69	Indian River	65.65	Charlotte	88.35
Baker	43.43	Osceola	67.68	Wakulla	89.21
Jackson	44.44	Hillsborough	68.56	Glades	91.55
Washington	45.00	Liberty	69.57	Franklin	92.29
Volusia	46.35	Manatee	70.18	Miami-Dade	93.43
Palm Beach	48.12	Gilchrist	72.20	Monroe	93.67
Gadsden	49.38	Collier	73.40	Lafayette	94.81
Hardee	51.69	Bradford	74.43	Broward	96.15
St. Lucie	52.07				

II UNDERSTANDING THE DEMAND AND SUPPLY OF DISASTER INSURANCE

5 Homeowners' Decision Making for Purchasing Insurance Coverage

Key Findings

Empirical evidence reveals that most individuals do not make cost-benefit trade-offs in their insurance purchase decisions. Many people may correctly think about risk and have adequate insurance coverage, but others do not. A key factor that explains their decisions not to purchase insurance or not to buy adequate levels of coverage is underestimation of the risk. In fact, some homeowners in hazard-prone areas believe that the disaster will not happen to them. Some families also face budget constraints that limit their interest or ability to voluntarily purchase adequate insurance to cover replacement costs should they suffer a major loss. This behavior is especially likely in areas where property values have increased rapidly.

The number of presidential disaster declarations has dramatically increased since 1965. There were 162 presidential disaster declarations during the period 1955–1965 and 545 declarations during the years 1996–2005, with notable spikes during election years. Despite this upward trend, there is no empirical evidence indicating that individuals are uninsured or underinsured because they expect to receive federal disaster relief following a disaster.

Homeowners' decisions related to the purchase of insurance are driven by a variety of goals other than financial protection. These may include reduction of anxiety (obtaining peace of mind), satisfying mortgage requirements, and satisfying social norms (e.g., purchasing insurance because one's friends and neighbors have coverage).

This chapter shows that a normative theory of decision making for purchasing insurance based on expected utility theory does not incorporate descriptive aspects of behavior.[1] We provide an illustrative example as to how a typical homeowner would determine how much insurance (if any) to purchase against losses from a natural disaster by trying to maximize expected utility.

While this model does have some predictive power, there are other subtleties to actual decision making that need to be addressed. People do not have access to perfect data, and even if they did, they may process information in somewhat different ways. We review empirical evidence on how these behavioral and informational factors are likely to affect insurance buying.

5.1 Normative Model of Choice: Expected Utility Theory

The Waterman family, a hypothetical family in New Orleans, owns their house outright and has wealth (W). They are considering how much insurance coverage (I) to purchase next year against water damage to their house from a future hurricane. To keep the analysis simple and without loss of generality, we assume only two states of nature—flood or no flood—with annual probabilities p and $1 - p$, respectively. If a flood occurs, the damage to the Waterman house will be L dollars. The cost of insurance per dollar coverage is c.

We assume that there are no moral hazard problems so that the Waterman family will not take advantage of purchasing insurance by either being more careless or putting objects in harm's way (e.g., moving unwanted furniture to the basement). Furthermore, we assume that the insurer has the same information about risk as the Waterman family and charges premiums that reflect risk so that it will not lose money in the long run.

The optimal amount of insurance will be determined by maximizing the Watermans' expected utility $E[U(I)]$ where:

$$E[U(I)] = p \cdot U[W - L + I(1 - c)] + (1 - p)U(W - cI)$$

where $0 \leq I \leq L$

According to this model, the Watermans should determine the amount of insurance to purchase based on the premium per dollar (c). If c equals the likelihood of a flood (p), the family should buy full insurance, covering all losses up to the value of their property with no deductible. This premium is unrealistic. With a more realistic premium loading built in, the family should scale down its coverage.

Government intervention can reshape insurance buying patterns. According to federal income tax laws, any uninsured loss from a natural disaster can be mostly written off the family's federal income taxes at the marginal tax rate t, based on the Watermans' current income. $D(I, L)$ is the amount of disaster assistance the family will receive should they have I dollars of insurance coverage and L dollars of losses.[2] The new utility function would now look as follows:

$$E[U(I)] = p \cdot U[W - L + I(1 - c) + t(L - I) + D(I, L)] + (1 - p)U(W - cI)].$$

The combined effect of a tax write-off and expectation of disaster relief may dampen the demand for insurance—perhaps to the point where some homeowners decide not to purchase any coverage.

5.2 Factors Influencing Insurance Purchasing Decisions

In this section, we examine empirical evidence on several factors that may influence the purchase of insurance if individuals use an expected utility model.

Misperception of the Risk

Individuals normally purchase insurance on an annual basis and thus must decide each year whether to renew or cancel their policy, assuming they have the discretion to do so. In the case of residents of hazard-prone areas, the annual probability of a disaster damaging their structure is not high; it is within the range of one in fifty to one in five hundred. So while the financial losses could be significant should such an event occur, the great majority of people will not have observed an event close at hand recently. The evidence on decision making under uncertainty in these low-probability cases suggests that many individuals do not use an expected utility model such as the one characterized above to determine how much insurance coverage to purchase.

For one thing, people have difficulty dealing with probabilities for infrequent events because they need a context in which to evaluate the data. In one study, individuals were presented with a probability or an actuarially fair insurance premium characterizing the risks associated with the discharge of a hypothetical toxic chemical, Syntox.[3] The chemical had the potential for causing fatalities to individuals living near the fictitious ABC chemical plant located on the outskirts of an urban center in New Jersey. To give some reference points, respondents were also provided with the probability of death from a car accident. Finally, the participants were asked a set of questions regarding how risky they perceived the facility to be.

People were not able to distinguish between probabilities that ranged from 1 in 10,000 to 1 in 1 million in judging the riskiness of the facility. Surprisingly, the study also found that subjects did not respond to insurance premiums as a signal of risk. While individuals may not be able to think meaningfully about what a 1 in 100,000 chance of death implies, they should understand what a \$15 premium means. Yet individuals distinguished no difference between the perceived risks of the ABC chemical plant, whether the annual premiums paid for coverage against fatalities from the release of Syntox were \$15.00, \$1.50, or 15 cents.

With respect to obtaining such data on their own, many potential victims of disaster perceive the costs of getting information about the hazard and costs of protection to be so high relative to the expected benefits that they do not even consider purchasing insurance.[4] Research shows that decision makers use threshold models: if the probability of a disaster is below some prespecified level, they do not think about the event.[5] In a laboratory experiment on purchasing insurance, many individuals bid zero for coverage, apparently viewing the probability of a loss as sufficiently small that they were not interested in protecting themselves against it.[6]

Affordability Issues

This reluctance to invest in protection voluntarily is compounded by issues of affordability. For some homeowners with relatively low incomes, disaster insurance is considered a discretionary expense that should be incurred only if residual funds are available after taking care of what individuals or families consider to be the necessities of life. In focus groups on the topic, a typical response of a homeowner living in a hazard-prone area to the question, "Why don't you have flood or earthquake insurance?" is, "I live from payday to payday."[7] This response implies that an increase in premiums will cause people to buy less insurance because of limited funds for discretionary expenditures. In addition, other factors may discourage purchasing coverage, such as uncertainty of the loss, the fact that economic benefits from insurance occur in the future, and personal financial protection should a homeowner declare bankruptcy.

Role of Disaster Relief

One of the arguments that has been advanced as to why individuals do not adopt protective measures prior to a disaster is that they assume that liberal aid from the government will be forthcoming should they suffer losses from an earthquake, hurricane, or flood. Federal disaster assistance may create a type of Samaritan's dilemma: providing assistance after a disaster reduces parties' incentives to undertaking loss reduction measures prior to a disaster.[8] In the context of insurance purchases, if a family expects to receive government assistance after a loss, it will have less economic incentive to purchase coverage prior to a disaster. The increased loss due to the lack of protection by residents in hazard-prone areas then amplifies the pressure on government to provide assistance to disaster victims.

The empirical evidence on the role of disaster relief suggests, however, that individuals or communities have not based their protective decisions in advance of a disaster by focusing on the expectation of government assistance. Kunreuther et al. (1978) found that most homeowners in earthquake- and hurricane-prone areas did not expect to receive aid from the federal government following a disaster. Burby et al. (1991) found that local governments that received disaster relief undertook more efforts to reduce losses from future disasters than those that did not. This behavior seems counterintuitive, and the reasons for it are not fully understood. In fact, one concern would be that homeowners in hazard-prone areas expect to receive more assistance from a disaster than they would actually obtain should they suffer losses.

Whether or not individuals incorporate an expectation of government relief in their pre-disaster planning process, the driving force in the provision of government assistance, is the occurrence of large-scale losses.[9] Under the current system of disaster assistance, the governor of the state can request that the president declare a "major disaster" and offer special assistance if the damage is severe enough. Although the president does not specify the amount of aid (the House and Senate determine this), he is responsible for a crucial step in the process. As discussed briefly in chapter 1, this obviously raises questions as to the key drivers of such a decision and whether some states are more likely to benefit from such a situation than others, and if so, when this occurs.

Recent research has shown that disaster assistance is more prevalent in presidential election years, all other things being equal. Three salient examples are the Alaska earthquake of March 1964, Tropical Storm Agnes in June 1972, and Hurricane Andrew in September 1992. These three disasters occurred during presidential election years and led to special legislation by the U.S. Congress in the form of liberal disaster assistance. For example, following the Alaska earthquake in 1964, where relatively few homes and businesses had insurance protection, the U.S. Small Business Administration provided 1 percent loans for rebuilding structures and refinancing mortgages through its disaster loan program. In fact, the uninsured victims in Alaska were financially better off after the earthquake than their insured counterparts were.[10] More recently, a battleground state with twenty electoral votes received more than twice as many presidential disaster declarations as a state with only three electoral votes.[11]

Overall, the number of presidential declarations has dramatically increased since 1965: there were 162 during the period 1955–1965, 282 during the period 1966–1975, 319 during the period 1986–1995, and 545 during the period 1996–2005.[12] Figure 5.1 depicts the evolution of the number of these declarations between 1955 and 2007. It also highlights the peak years, which often correspond to presidential election years. There were 75 such declarations in 2008, the largest number ever since 1996, also a presidential election year.

In the case of Hurricane Katrina, Governor Kathleen Blanco declared a state of emergency on August 26, 2005, and requested disaster relief from the federal government on

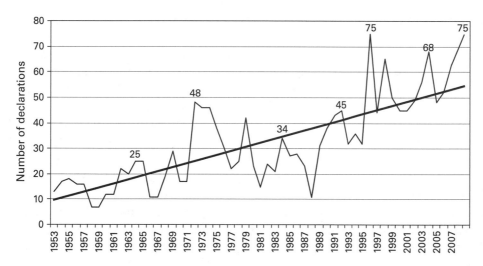

Figure 5.1
U.S. presidential disaster declarations per year, 1953–2008. *Source:* Data from FEMA.

August 28. President Bush declared a state of emergency that day, an action that freed federal government funds but caps them at \$5 million and puts emergency response activities, debris removal, and individual assistance and housing programs under federal control.[13]

On August 29 in response to Governor Blanco's request, President Bush declared a "major disaster," allotting more federal funds to aid in rescue and recovery. By September 8, Congress had approved \$52 billion in aid to victims of Hurricane Katrina. Two years after the catastrophe, the total federal relief allocated by Congress for the reconstruction of the areas devastated by the 2005 hurricane season was nearly \$125 billion.

5.3   Role of Goals and Plans in Insurance Decision Making

The expected utility model assumes that financial considerations determine one's decision on whether to purchase insurance.[14] In practice, individuals make insurance decisions by constructing or selecting plans designed to achieve multiple goals. For example, a plan to purchase homeowners' insurance may satisfy as many as seven goals simultaneously: (1) reducing the chances of a catastrophic loss, (2) reducing anxiety about risks of fire and theft, (3) avoiding regret or providing consolation in case a loss occurs, (4) satisfying conditions required by a bank, (5) presenting the appearance of prudence to others who will learn about the insurance purchase, (6) maintaining one's relationship with an insurance agent, and (7) avoiding highly burdensome insurance premium payments.

The importance of these goals obviously varies with the decision maker but may also be affected by contextual variables that change over time. When reflecting on paying monthly bills, an insurance purchaser may focus primarily on the goals of satisfying the requirements of the bank that holds the mortgage loan (goal 4) and minimizing the cost of insurance (goal 7). When that same person reflects on her valuable works of art, she may think about reducing anxiety (goal 2) and avoiding regret (goal 3).

The plan and goal representation appears to capture the insurance decision-making process, as illustrated by the following example based on empirical data. People often purchase flood insurance only after suffering damage in a flood, but many cancel their policies when several consecutive years pass with no flood.[15] In the case of flood insurance, this finding is particularly striking since the National Flood Insurance Program (NFIP) requires that homes located in special flood hazard areas (SFHAs) purchase insurance as a condition for federally backed mortgages. To determine the extent to which residents in hazard-prone areas adhere to the law, FEMA examined applications for disaster assistance from 1,549 victims of a flood in August 1998 in northern Vermont and found that 84 percent of applicants in SFHAs did not have insurance, 45 percent of whom were required to purchase it.[16] A simple explanation is that following flood damage, anxiety is high, and reducing it is a salient goal; it is also easy to justify buying the insurance, since a flood has just occurred.

Thus, insurance is purchased based strongly on the desire to feel justified and avoid anxiety. After several years, many people may find that the prospect of a flood no longer troubles their peace of mind, so anxiety avoidance (goal 2) now has low value. Meanwhile, insured individuals do not feel justified in continuing to pay premiums and not collecting on their policy; the goal of feeling justified is unfulfilled and becomes more salient. The differential weighting of these two goals can lead a homeowner to decide not to purchase insurance, and cancel his or her existing policy.

Note that this theory predicts that a decision maker who puts heavy weight on the goals of avoiding catastrophic loss and avoiding regret will likely continue to purchase flood insurance year after year if the cost is modest. A decision advisor confronting such a view might well ask the individual about the importance of having good justification for purchasing insurance and whether protection against catastrophic losses might justify paying the premium.

We now discuss four main goals satisfied by purchasing insurance: sharing financial risk, emotion-related goals (either worry or regret), satisfying legal or other official requirements, and satisfying social or cognitive norms. (Maintaining a relationship with a trusted agent or advisor and affording premiums are self-explanatory).

Financial Protection

Individuals can purchase insurance at relatively low cost and be financially protected against a catastrophic loss if the negative event in question has a low probability of occurrence, if there are many at risk, and if occurrences of the event are statistically independent. For low-probability, high-impact events, one benefit of purchasing insurance is being protected against the risk of a large financial loss.

Emotion-Related Goals

There is a growing literature on how affect and emotional goals influence individuals' decision making under risk.[17] Three goals in this category with respect to insurance are reduction of anxiety (peace of mind), avoidance of anticipated regret,[18] and disappointment.[19] One might also expect individuals to pay more for insurance if they feared a specific event (e.g., their car or painting being stolen; their house being damaged by a hurricane) than if they were not very concerned about the event occurring. With respect to negative feelings about a situation, experimental findings indicate that people focus on the unpleasantness of the outcome rather than on its probability when they have strong emotional feelings attached to the event.[20]

Individuals may also purchase insurance as a form of consolation should they suffer a loss. In particular, if one has special affection for an item, such as a piece of art, then the knowledge that one can make a claim should the item be destroyed or stolen may give special comfort to the person. Hsee and Kunreuther (2000) attribute the need for consolation as the reason that individuals are willing to pay higher premiums for the same amount of coverage for objects they love than for those where they do not have special feeling. This behavior is consistent with Adam Smith's observation about human nature in *The Theory of Moral Sentiments:*

A man grows fond of a snuff-box, of a pen-knife, of a staff which he has long made use of, and conceives something like real love and affection for them. If he breaks or loses them, he is vexed all out of proportion to the value of the damage. The house which we have long lived in, the tree whose verdure and shade we have long enjoyed, are both looked upon with a sort of respect that seems due to such benefactors. The decay of the one, or the ruin of the other, affects us with a kind of melancholy though we should sustain no loss by it. (Adam Smith, 1759)

Satisfying Requirements

Insurance coverage is often mandatory. Homeowners' insurance is normally required by mortgage lenders, and flood insurance must be purchased as a condition for a federally insured mortgage in SFHAs. In these cases, the purchase of insurance may be viewed as a subgoal for meeting end goals such as owning a car or a home or practicing one's profession.

Satisfying Social and Cognitive Norms

Many insurance decisions are based on what other people are doing or think is an appropriate action to take. There is also empirical evidence that the purchase of insurance, like buying new products, is based on knowledge of what friends and neighbors have done. An illustration of this behavior came from a pretest interview of an earthquake questionnaire when a homeowner, hearing that his neighbor had purchased earthquake insurance, indicated that he would want to buy such coverage himself without changing his beliefs about the risk he was facing or knowing about the actual cost of coverage.[21]

In the discussion of flood insurance, we introduced feeling justified as one of several important goals. Someone who purchases flood insurance soon after suffering damage from such a disaster may do so in part because it is easy to justify the expenditure by pointing to the flood that just occurred. Canceling insurance after some years of coverage may result from the social norm that it is hard to justify an expenditure that has not paid off. In fact, people are concerned with justifying their decisions to themselves and others.[22] In the process, they often use arguments that have little to do with the trade-offs between the cost of insurance and the expected loss that forms the basis of economic analyses of insurance or warranty transactions.[23]

5.4   Conclusion

The empirical evidence suggests that individuals do not make trade-offs regarding the expected benefits and costs of purchasing insurance as economic theory based on expected utility maximization would predict. In fact, many of the individuals who do not buy coverage voluntarily decline to do so because they underestimate the risk and face budget constraints. Those who do buy homeowners' coverage are normally required to have this insurance as a condition for a mortgage. Others may buy protection to reduce their anxiety and sleep better at night. One question explored in chapter 14 is the design of alternative programs for better providing insurance coverage for those residing in hazard-prone areas so as to avoid the liberal governmental disaster relief that normally is provided following a large-scale disaster.

Summary

Expected utility theory is the normative model of choice for characterizing how homeowners should make insurance purchase decisions. This model does not characterize the behavior of most individuals, who do not engage in cost-benefit analysis in the way that the theory suggests they should.

In reality, many individuals misperceive risks and believe that the disaster will not happen to them until after the hurricane, flood, or earthquake occurs. Only then do they consider purchasing insurance coverage. A significant number of individuals will cancel their coverage if a disaster does not occur within the coming few years. Some homeowners are likely to face budget constraints, which limit their interest or ability, or both, to voluntarily purchase coverage.

Our findings show that individuals seem to make their insurance decisions by focusing on how well they satisfy a set of goals. These include financial protection, emotion-related goals (either worry or regret), satisfying legal or other official requirements, and satisfying social or cognitive norms (friends, family, neighbors).

6 Private Insurers' Decision Making for Supplying Coverage

Key Findings

Insurers are likely to charge higher premiums if there is ambiguity associated with estimating the likelihood and consequences of a risk. A recent survey of actuaries and underwriters undertaken by the Wharton Risk Management Center as part of this project revealed that the premiums for ambiguous risks are 25 percent higher than when risks are unambiguous.

Due to the unpredictability and sizable losses associated with catastrophes, insurers need to allocate more capital to cover the losses in the tail of the probability distribution. The need to secure an adequate rate of return on capital is not sufficiently understood. In particular, the prices charged for catastrophe insurance must be sufficiently high not only to cover the expected claims costs and other expenses, but also the costs of allocating capital to underwrite this risk. For truly extreme risks, the resulting premium can be as much as five to ten times higher than the expected loss (probability multiplied by consequence) to provide investors with a fair return on equity and also maintain the insurer's credit rating. Following the 2004 and 2005 hurricanes in the United States, rating agencies instituted more stringent criteria for providing protection against catastrophic risk. This led insurers to allocate even more capital than they had previously to cover the tail of the distribution.

While catastrophes are often characterized as low-probability, high-consequence events, the data suggest that they are expected to occur with a much higher frequency than in the past. Catastrophe models and exceedance probability (EP) curves have been used in recent years by insurers to estimate their risks from natural disasters and manage their portfolios. Working with the risk modeling firm Risk Management Solutions, we determined aggregate residential losses for our four focus states. Using Florida as an illustrative example, we specified an EP curve that revealed a 15 percent annual probability of an insured loss in the state of at least $10 billion and a 5 percent annual probability that insured losses will exceed $25 billion.

To evaluate the cost of capital required by insurers and reinsurers to cover these catastrophes, it is critical to examine the expected loss and standard deviation of the risk. We compared the insured losses from hurricanes in the postal codes within Miami-Dade County with forty-six counties in the northern part of Florida. Taken together, these forty-six counties have the same expected annual insured losses as Miami-Dade County; however, the standard deviation of losses for Miami-Dade is $4.2 billion, and for the forty-six northern counties it is $2.8 billion. The cost of capital in Miami-Dade County to cover losses should then lead to higher premiums than in portions of northern Florida that have the same expected loss but a much lower standard deviation, if insurers had the freedom to charge premiums reflecting risk.

6.1   The Concept of Insurability

In this chapter and the next, we analyze how insurers and reinsurers decide whether to cover a risk and also what premiums to charge. As a result of the recent catastrophes, insurers and reinsurers are reexamining their ability to provide protection against wind damage from hurricanes and are asking whether these events are insurable.

To understand the concept of insurability, consider a standard policy whereby premiums are paid at the start of a given time period to cover losses during this interval (usually a year). Two conditions must be met before insurance providers are willing to offer coverage against an uncertain event. The first is the ability to identify and quantify, or estimate at least partially, the chances of the event occurring and the extent of losses likely to be incurred. The second condition is the ability to set premiums for each potential customer or class of customers at prices that provide a competitive return at the assumed level of risk.

If both conditions are satisfied, a risk is considered to be insurable. But it still may not be profitable. In other words, it may be impossible to specify a premium for which there is sufficient demand and incoming revenue to cover the costs of development, marketing, operating, cost of holding capital, and claims processing costs of the insurer and yield a net positive profit over a prespecified time horizon. In such cases, the insurer will not want to offer coverage against this risk.

6.2   Determining Whether to Provide Coverage

Based on their knowledge of likelihood and outcome, insurers must make a decision as to whether to cover the risk unless they are required to do so by law (see chapters 2 and 3). In his study on insurers' decision making as to when they would market coverage for a specific risk, Stone (1973) develops a model whereby firms maximize expected profits subject to satisfying a constraint related to the survival of the firm.[1] An insurer satisfies its survival constraint by choosing a portfolio of risks that has a likelihood of experiencing total claim payments greater than some predetermined amount (L^*) that is less than some threshold probability p_1.

The value of L^* is determined by an insurer's concern with insolvency or a sufficiently large loss in surplus that will lead a rating agency to downgrade its credit rating. The threshold probability reflects the trade-off between the expected benefits of issuing another insurance policy and the costs to the firm of a catastrophic loss that reduces the insurer's surplus by L^* or more.

A simple example illustrates how an insurer would use its survival constraint to determine whether a particular portfolio of risks is insurable with respect to hurricanes. Assume that all homes in a hurricane-prone area are identical and equally resistant to damage such that the total insurance premium, P, is the same for each structure. Furthermore, assume that an insurer has S dollars in current surplus and wants to determine the number of policies it can write and still satisfy its survival constraint. Then the maximum number of policies, n, satisfying the survival constraint is given by equation 6.1:

$$\text{Probability } L^* > (n \cdot P + S)] < p_1 \tag{6.1}$$

The insurer will use the survival constraint to determine the maximum number of policies it is willing to offer. Naturally it can issue more policies by reducing the amount of coverage per policy or transferring some of its risk to others in the private sector (e.g., reinsurers or capital markets). It may also rely on state or federal programs to cover its catastrophic losses.

Following the series of natural disasters that occurred at the end of the 1980s and in the 1990s, many insurers focused on the survival constraint to determine the amount of catastrophe coverage they were willing to provide because they were concerned that their aggregate exposure to a particular risk must not exceed a certain level. Rating agencies, such as A.M. Best, focused on insurers' exposure to catastrophic losses as one element in determining credit ratings.

6.3 Setting Premiums

If the insurer decides to offer coverage, it needs to determine a premium rate that yields a profit and satisfies its survival constraint given by equation 6.1. As discussed in chapter 2, state regulations often limit insurers in their premium-setting process. Competition can play a role as well in determining what premium can be charged in a given marketplace. Even in the absence of these influences, an insurer must consider problems associated with the ambiguity of the risk, asymmetry of information (adverse selection and moral hazard), and degree of correlation of the risks in determining what premium to charge. We briefly examine each of these factors.

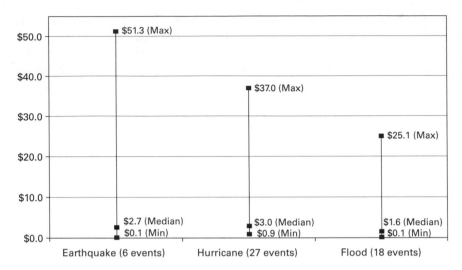

Figure 6.1
Historical economic losses versus type of significant U.S. natural disasters, 1950–2000 (billions of dollars). *Source:* American Re (2002). Reprinted in Grossi and Kunreuther (2005).

Ambiguity of the Risk

Figure 6.1 illustrates the total number of loss events from 1950 to 2000 in the United States for three types of natural disasters: earthquakes, hurricanes, and floods. Events were selected that had at least $1 billion of economic damage or over fifty deaths. Across all the disasters of a particular type (earthquake, hurricane, or flood) for this fifty-year period, the median loss is low while the maximum loss is very high. Given this wide variation in loss distribution, it is not surprising that insurers are concerned about the uncertainty of the loss in determining premiums or even providing any coverage in certain hazard-prone areas.

The 2004 and 2005 seasons dramatically changed the upper limits in figure 6.1. Hurricane Katrina is estimated to have caused between $150 billion and $170 billion in economic losses, more than four times the most costly hurricane between 1950 and 2000. But despite predictions of higher-than-normal hurricane activity in 2006 and 2007, the only hurricane to make landfall in the United States during these two years was a Category 1 hurricane. However, 2008 brought devastating hurricanes that hit the Gulf Coast.

The infrequency of major catastrophes in a single location implies that the loss distribution is not well specified. The ambiguities associated with both the probability of an extreme event occurring and the outcomes of such an event raise a number of challenges for insurers with respect to pricing their policies. As shown by a series of empirical studies stimulated by the classic study on ambiguity by Ellsberg (1961), actuaries and underwriters are averse to ambiguity and want to charge much higher premiums when the likelihood

Table 6.1
Scenarios of three risky situations

No ambiguity: Precise probability	Source of the ambiguity: Imprecise probability	Source of the ambiguity: Conflicting probability
Both modeling firms estimate that there is 1 in a 100 chance that a flood will severely damage homes in this area this year (the annual probability is 1 percent). Both are confident of their estimate.	Both modeling firms recognize that it is difficult to provide a precise probability estimate. The two modeling firms agree that the probability that a hurricane will severely damage homes in this area this year ranges somewhere between a 1 in 200 chance and 1 in 50 chance.	One modeling firm confidently estimates a 1 in 200 chance that a fire will severely damage homes in this area this year (the annual probability is 0.5 percent). The other firm confidently estimates that the chance that a fire will severely damage homes in this area this year is much higher: 1 in 50 chance (the annual probability is 2 percent).

or consequences of a risk are highly uncertain than if these components of risk are well specified.[2]

Because of our limited scientific knowledge of most catastrophic risks, insurers are left with imprecise estimates of the probability of a specific risk, such as a range of probabilities ($p \in [p_{low}; p_{high}]$). In some cases, experts strongly disagree on the estimate of this probability. For instance, one group of experts could confidently estimate that the probability of the risk is p_{low}, and another group could confidently estimate it to be p_{high}.

Fueled with such estimates, how would insurers react? How do they aggregate the probability estimates that the risk modeling firms have provided them? In the case of conflicting estimates, would they take the arithmetic mean of the two estimates or some other linear combination? What is the effect of controversies on the estimate of the probability of a risk on insurance premiums?

Recent research shows that insurers are also sensitive to the type of ambiguity. In a survey of seventy-eight actuaries in France, Cabantous (2007) showed that actuaries would charge a much higher premium when ambiguity came from conflict and disagreement regarding the probability of a loss than when the ambiguity came from an imprecise forecast. On average, the annual mean premium was 32 percent higher when the ambiguity came from an imprecise forecast than when the risk was well known, and it was 40 percent higher when ambiguity came from conflict. The survey also showed that the source of ambiguity matters. (See table 6.1 for details of the scenarios.)

For this study, the Wharton Risk Management Center launched a Web-based survey of U.S. actuaries and underwriters' decision making under risk, uncertainty without conflict, and uncertainty with conflicting information on risk estimates.

In this survey, nine scenarios were developed by crossing three different types of natural hazards (fire, flood, and hurricane) with three types of information about the probability of a disaster (precise probability, imprecise probability, and conflicting probability) with a loss of $100,000, using the same type of questions as in the survey of actuaries in France

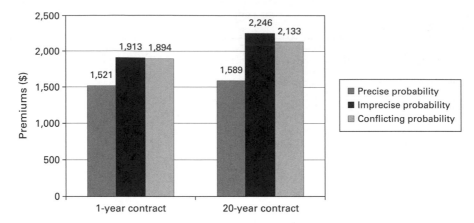

Figure 6.2
Mean annual premiums in dollars, across natural hazards ($N = 78$)

as described in table 6.1 Participants were asked to determine the annual premium they would charge to cover a homeowner against a risk, assuming a one-year contract. We are also interested in how insurers would behave if they had the opportunity to offer a long-term insurance contract (e.g., twenty years) with a fixed premium, tied to the homeowner's mortgage.[3]

When there was no ambiguity, the annual probability of the loss was 1 in 100 so the expected loss is $1,000. In the two ambiguous cases, 1 in 200 and 1 in 50 were the minimum and maximum estimates of the annual probability of the loss—the geometric mean of the probability equals 1 in 100. The expected loss for the two ambiguous cases was $500 and $2,000 respectively, a geometric mean of $1,000.

The type of hazard does not have a significant effect on mean premiums. However, the results shown in figure 6.2 reveal that the quality of the probabilistic information can change the premium significantly.

Under a one-year contract, insurers would charge on average $1,521, which reflects their estimate of the expected loss plus a loading factor (administrative cost and cost of capital). Under the same one-year contract, mean annual premiums when the probability is ambiguous are 25 percent higher than when it is given precisely. The source of uncertainty, however, does not affect insurers, and premiums under conflict are not significantly different from premiums under imprecision. Contrary to results by Cabantous (2007), in this population of U.S. insurers, imprecision is of only slightly greater concern than conflict. The mean annual premium under imprecision is 5 percent higher than the mean premium under conflict.

Under the twenty-year contract, the premium with precise probability is $1,589 (or about 5 percent above $1,521, the amount which insurers would charge for a one-year contract with precise probability). But aversion to ambiguity increases significantly as the length of the contract increases. Depending on whether the probability is imprecise or there are conflicting probability estimates, mean annual premiums are 41 percent and 34 percent higher, respectively, than when there is no ambiguity ($2,246 and $2,133). When probabilities are precise, the annual premium charged for the twenty-year contract is only slightly higher than for a one-year contract.

Adverse Selection

If the insurer cannot differentiate the risks facing two groups of potential insurance buyers and all buyers know their own risk, then the insurer is likely to suffer losses if it sets the same premium for both groups by using the entire population as a basis for this estimate. If only the highest-risk group is likely to purchase coverage for that hazard and the premium is below its expected loss, the insurer will have a portfolio of bad risks. This situation, referred to in economics as *adverse selection*, can be rectified by the insurer's charging a high enough premium to cover the losses from the bad risks. In so doing, the good risks might purchase only partial protection or no insurance at all, because they consider the price of coverage to be too expensive relative to their risk.[4]

This was one of the arguments made by private insurers regarding the noninsurability of flood risk that led to the creation of the National Flood Insurance Program (NFIP) in 1968 (see chapter 4). Indeed, insurers thought that families who had lived in a specific flood-prone area for many years had a much better knowledge of the risk than any insurer would have gained unless it undertook costly risk assessments.

In the context of hurricanes, however, it is not clear whether there is any adverse selection. Indeed, there is no evidence that those at risk have an informational advantage over the insurer. In fact, the opposite might be true: if insurance companies spend a lot of resources estimating the risk (which they do today), they might gain an informational advantage over their policyholders who cannot afford the time or costs of obtaining these data. In recent years, there has been a growing literature on the impact of insurers' being more knowledgeable about the risks than the insureds themselves. Research in this field reveals that insurers might want to exploit this reverse information asymmetry, which results in low-risk individuals being optimally covered, while high-risk individuals are not.[5]

Moral Hazard

Moral hazard refers to an increase in the expected loss (probability or amount of loss conditional on an event occurring) as a result of purchasing insurance coverage. Having insurance protection may lead the policyholder to alter his or her behavior in ways that increase the expected loss relative to what it would have been without coverage. If the insurer cannot predict this behavior and relies on past loss data from uninsured individuals to estimate the distribution of claim payments, the resulting premium is likely to be too low to cover expected losses. The introduction of deductibles, coinsurance, or upper limits on coverage can be useful tools in reducing moral hazard by encouraging insureds to engage in less risky behavior because they know they will incur part of the losses from an adverse event.

Correlated Risks

For extreme events, the potential for high correlation between the risks will have an impact on the tail of the distribution. In other words, at a predefined probability p_i, this region is likely to expand for higher correlated risks covered by insurers. This requires additional capital for the insurer to protect itself against large losses. Insurers normally face spatially correlated losses from large-scale natural disasters. State Farm and Allstate paid $3.6 billion and $2.3 billion in claims, respectively, in the wake of Hurricane Andrew in 1992 due to their high concentration of homeowners' policies in the Miami–Dade County area of Florida. Given this unexpectedly high loss, both companies began to reassess their strategies of providing coverage against wind damage in hurricane-prone areas.[6]

Hurricanes Katrina and Rita, which devastated the U.S. Gulf Coast in August and September 2005, had dramatic impacts on several lines of insurance, notably property damage and business interruption. Edward Liddy, chairman of Allstate, which provided insurance coverage to 350,000 homeowners in Louisiana, Mississippi, and Alabama, was quoted in the *Wall Street Journal* shortly after Katrina, saying that "extensive flooding has complicated disaster planning ... and the higher water has essentially altered efforts to assess damage. We now have 1,100 adjusters on the ground. We have another 500 who are ready to go as soon as we can get into some of the most-devastated areas. It will be many weeks, probably months, before there is anything approaching reliable estimates."[7]

6.4   Importance of the Cost of Capital

The importance of capital for securing an adequate rate of return is often not sufficiently understood.[8] In particular, the prices charged for catastrophe insurance must be sufficiently high to cover the expected claims costs and other expenses, but also must cover the costs of allocating risk capital to underwrite this risk. Moreover, because large amounts of risk capital are needed to underwrite catastrophe risk relative to the expected liability, the resulting premium is high relative to its loss expenses simply to earn a fair rate of return on equity and thereby maintain the insurer's credit rating.

There is indeed a temptation for parties to imbue the notion of a fair premium to serve their own interests. For example, the term *actuarially fair premiums* has a precise definition: the premium is equal to the expected loss. Much of the public debate surrounding a fair price of catastrophe insurance implicitly uses the concept of actuarially fair premium because it is simple and results in a low cost to the policyholder. However, while *actuarially fair* is a useful statistical concept, the implied premiums are not economically sustainable; insurers must cover their fixed costs and marketing expenses in addition to their expected claims in order to survive and attract capital.

An expanded notion of fair premiums derives from the notion of a *fair rate of return on capital*. A fair return is one that offers investors a competitive return on capital so that they will want to place their funds with the insurer rather than elsewhere. A fair premium would then be one that just offered the investor a fair rate of return. To offer a fair return, the premium would have to cover all costs (expected claims, expenses of various sorts, and taxes), and then produce an expected return to the investor equal to the cost of capital or fair return. The premium would yield some profit, but only the normal level of profit necessary to attract and maintain the insurer's capital base.

While a sustainable premium must offer a return consistent with the cost of capital, we also need to pay attention to how much capital the insurer will want to have so that it can promise to pay claims with an acceptably low probability of default. The amount of capital necessary to do so will depend on the risk characteristics of its liability portfolio, its asset portfolio, and the effectiveness of its risk management strategy. What is an acceptably low risk will be interpreted differently by prospective policyholders, regulators, and rating agencies that impose standards ostensibly on behalf of such policyholders. For current purposes, we can think of the economic capital as that required to maintain the insurer's credit rating or the capital needed to satisfy regulatory requirements if this is higher than the rating agency's requirements.

Each policy the insurer sells imposes its own capital burden. If an additional policy were sold without adding to the insurer's overall capital, there would normally be a small increase in the likelihood that the insurer would default. Just how much of a change would depend on the riskiness of the policy and its covariance with other policies and assets held by the insurer. The appropriate allocation of capital to a policy would be that amount required to maintain the insurer's credit status; the addition of the policy and the accompanying capital would leave the insurer with the same credit status as before.

We thus define a fair price for insurance as a premium that provides a fair rate of return on invested equity. To illustrate, we construct a somewhat conservative hypothetical example that ignores taxes and regulatory constraints. Consider a portfolio that has $1,000 in expected losses, $E(L)$. Let k be the ratio of capital to expected losses for the insurer to maintain its credit rating. For this example, $k = 1$, a value many property liability insurers use for their combined book of business.[9]

In addition to paying claims, the insurer is assumed to set aside capital for covering additional expenses (X) in the form of commissions to agents and brokers and for underwriting and claims assessment expenses. For this example, $X = \$200$. Given the risk characteristics of the portfolio, investors require a return on equity (ROE) of 15 percent to compensate for risk. The insurer invests its funds in lower-risk vehicles that yield an expected return, r, of 5 percent. What premium π would the insurer have to charge its policyholders to cover them against natural disasters and secure a return of 15 percent for its investors?

The formula is given by:

$$\pi = \frac{E(L) + X(1 + r)}{(1 + r) - k(ROE - r)},$$

which yields a value of $\pi = \$1,274$ for this hypothetical example. We can think of this premium now as the expected loss of $1,000 plus a proportionate loading factor, λ, of 0.274. Thus, the premium is

$$(1 + \lambda)E(L) = (1 + 0.274)\$1,000 = \$1,274.$$

This calculation is very sensitive to the ratio of capital to expected liability, k, needed to preserve credit. In the example, the ratio was one dollar of capital for one dollar of expected liability. This ratio is in the ballpark for the combined books of business of many property liability insurers. However, for catastrophic risk, with its very large tail risk (which severely affects the insurer's credit risk), the capital-to-liability ratio needs to be higher. Indeed, this ratio depends on the volatility of the catastrophe liability and its correlation with the insurer's remaining portfolio. For the catastrophe risk premium for individual homeowners, this may translate into a loading cost, λ, that approximates 0.5. Thus, the premium would be 150 percent of the expected loss. This does not reflect undue profitability, simply that insurers need considerable capital to supply this insurance, and the cost of that capital is included in the premium.

When it comes to reinsurance of catastrophic risk, the relative capital cost is much higher. For higher layers of catastrophe reinsurance, the expected loss is often quite low and the volatility very high. At these layers, the required capital-to-liability ratio can be considerably greater than the one-to-one used in the example. An increase in this ratio will increase the premium required to generate a fair return on equity.

A second issue with respect to catastrophic risk is that it can be expensive to underwrite since it requires extensive modeling. Many companies buy commercial models or use their own in-house modeling capability. We recalculate the premium formula with $X = \$600$ and $k = 5$. The required premium is now $2,965, more than twice the value of π computed above and now nearly three times the expected loss. Notice this translates into a loading factor, λ, of 1.965, so the premium is

$$(1 + \lambda)E(L) = (1 + 1.965)\$1,000 = \$2,965.$$

There are other considerations that can dramatically increase the capital cost, notably the impact of double taxation. Harrington and Niehaus (2001) have simulated the tax burden over many parameters and show that tax costs alone can reasonably be as much as the claim cost and lead to further increases in premiums. When we account for all these factors (high capital inputs, transaction costs, and taxes), catastrophe insurance premiums often are several multiples of expected claims costs.

6.5 The Role of Rating Agencies

During the past few years, rating agencies have paid increasing attention to the impact that natural disasters will have on the financial stability of insurers and reinsurers. The rating given to a company will affect its ability to attract business and, hence, its pricing and coverage decisions.

To illustrate how ratings are determined, consider the rating agency A.M. Best, which undertakes a quantitative analysis of an insurer's balance sheet strength, operating performance, and business profile. Evaluation of catastrophe exposure plays a significant role in the determination of ratings, as these are events that could threaten the solvency of a company. Projected losses from disasters occurring at specified return periods (a 100-year windstorm or hurricane or a 250-year earthquake) and the associated reinsurance programs to cover them are two important components of the rating questionnaires that insurers are required to complete.

For several years, A.M. Best has been requesting such information for natural disasters. Its approach has been an important step forward in the incorporation of catastrophic risk into an insurer's capital adequacy requirements. Until recently, the rating agency has been including probable maximum loss (PML) for only one of these severe events (100-year windstorm or 250-year earthquake, depending on the nature of the risk the insurer was mainly exposed to) in its calculation of a company's risk-adjusted capitalization. In 2006, A.M. Best introduced a second event as an additional stress test. The PML used for the second event is the same as the first event in the case of hurricane (a 1-in-100-year event; the occurrence of one hurricane is considered to be independent of the other one). If the main exposure facing the insurer is an earthquake, the second event is reduced from a 1-in-250-year event to a 1-in-100-year event.[10] These new requirements have increased the amount of risk capital that insurers have been forced to allocate to underwrite this risk and have made them more reluctant to provide this coverage unless they are able to increase premiums sufficiently to reflect these additional costs.

Standard and Poor's, another rating agency, has also revised criteria for measuring catastrophic risk, which traditionally has been based on premium charges. But the new criteria measure catastrophic risk based on exposure of the insurer. In the past, only reinsurers received a specific catastrophe charge. This includes an exposure-based capital charge for insurers similar to what it does for reinsurers based on net expected annual aggregate property losses for all perils at 1-in-250-year return period.[11] And Moody's has adjusted the industry loss exceedance curves used in its risk-adjusted capital model for U.S. companies to reflect the recent storm activity.[12] Appendix 6A provides a summary table of recent changes in rating agencies' requirements.

The changes in risk estimates and the new requirements by rating agencies have significantly affected the way insurers are managing their exposure. As a graphic example, figure 6.3 depicts two hypothetical distributions of probability. The x-axis measures losses in a

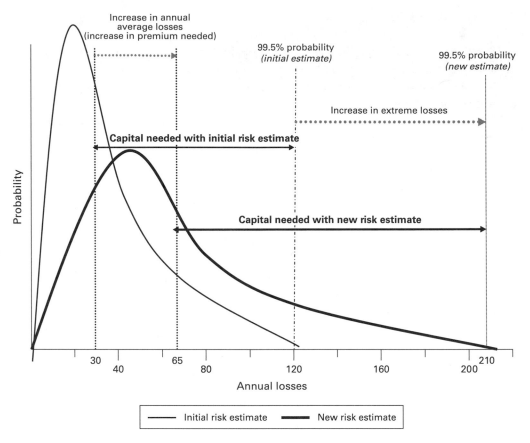

Figure 6.3
Demand for capital when risk estimate increases

given unit of capital. The first corresponds to insurer A's portfolio prior to the 2004 and 2005 hurricane seasons and before rating agencies asked for more stringent stress tests for extreme events. On average, the insurer needs to collect 30 units of capital in premiums per year to cover its claims and other administrative costs (half of the area below the curve). But the insurer also realizes a possibility that it will suffer more claims. For that reason, it needs to be in a position to access additional capital (internal or external) to pay all its claims. In the figure, we show that it would need 120 units of capital to have 99.5 probability of paying all its claims in a very bad year.

If there is a shift to the right in the probability distribution, two things occur. First, the insurer needs to charge much higher premiums to cover the higher average annual claims (65 in figure 6.3). Second, since this new distribution has a much fatter tail than the previous one, the insurer needs to access much more capital than before. In this example, the insurer needs 210 units of capital to pay 99.5 percent of its claims when there is a very bad year, whereas it required only 120 to meet this criterion for the initial probability distribution of losses prior to the 2004 and 2005 hurricane seasons.

6.6   Measuring Exposure to Natural Disasters: The Role of Catastrophe Models

In order to adequately manage their portfolios, insurers must undertake a systematic analysis of the damage that can be caused by hurricanes of different magnitudes and intensities and the likelihood that these events will occur in specific parts of the country.[13]

History of Catastrophe Modeling

Catastrophe modeling is not rooted in one field or discipline. The science of assessing and managing catastrophic risk originates in the fields of property insurance and the science of natural hazards. In the 1800s, residential insurers managed their risk by mapping the structures that they covered. They used tacks on a wall map to indicate their concentration of exposure. This crude technique served insurers well and limited their risk. Widespread use of mapping ended in the 1960s when it became too cumbersome and time-consuming to execute.[14]

Measuring an earthquake's magnitude and a hurricane's intensity is one of the key elements in state-of-the-art catastrophe modeling. A standard set of metrics for a given hazard must be established so that risks can be assessed and managed. This measurement began in the 1800s when the first modern seismograph (measuring earthquake ground motion) was invented and modern versions of the anemometer (measuring wind speed) gained widespread use.

In the first part of the twentieth century, scientific measures of natural hazards advanced rapidly. Two separate developments, mapping risk and measuring hazard, came together in a definitive way in the late 1980s and early 1990s through catastrophe modeling as shown in figure 6.4. Computer-based models for measuring catastrophic loss potential were developed by linking scientific studies of natural hazards' measures and historical occurrences with advances in information technology and geographic information systems (GIS). The models provided estimates of catastrophic losses by overlaying the properties at risk with the potential natural hazard sources in the geographic area. With the ability to store and manage vast amounts of spatially referenced information, GIS became an ideal environment for conducting future hazard and loss studies more easily and cost-effectively.

Around the same time, several new companies developed computer software for analyzing the implications of natural hazard risk. Three major modeling firms emerged: AIR Worldwide Corporation was founded in 1987 in Boston, Risk Management Solutions (RMS) was formed in 1988 at Stanford University, and EQECAT began in San Francisco in 1994 as a subsidiary of EQE International. In 2001, EQE International became a part of ABS Consulting.

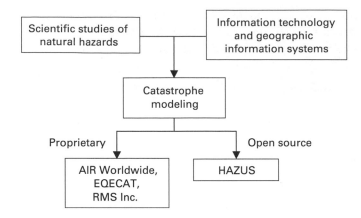

Figure 6.4
Development of catastrophe modeling

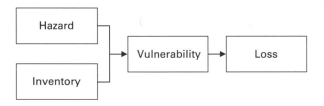

Figure 6.5
Structure of catastrophe models

Nature of Catastrophe Models

Catastrophe risk assessment often relies on estimates based on past data (e.g., loss history in a specific region) coupled with data on what experts know about a particular risk through the use of catastrophe models. The four basic components of a catastrophe model are hazard, inventory, vulnerability, and loss, as depicted in figure 6.5 and are illustrated for a natural hazard such as a hurricane. First, the model determines the risk of the hazard phenomenon, which in the case of a hurricane is characterized by its projected path and wind speed. Next, the model characterizes the inventory (or portfolio) of properties at risk as accurately as possible. This is done by assigning geographic coordinates to a property and then determining how many structures in the insurer's portfolio are at risk from hurricanes of different wind speeds and projected paths. For each property's location in spatial terms, other factors that characterize the inventory at risk are construction type, number of stories in the structure, and its age.

The hazard and inventory modules enable one to calculate the vulnerability or suscepti-bility to damage of the structures at risk. In essence, this step in the catastrophe model quantifies the physical impact of the natural hazard phenomenon on the property at risk. How this vulnerability is quantified differs from model to model. Based on this measure of vulnerability, the loss to the property inventory is evaluated. In a catastrophe model, loss is characterized as direct or indirect in nature. Direct losses include the cost to repair or replace a structure, which has to anticipate the increase in cost of material and workforce due to the demand surge in the aftermath of a major disaster. Indirect losses include business interruption impacts and relocation costs of residents forced to evacuate their homes.

Constructing Exceedance Probability Curves

Based on the outputs of a catastrophe model, the insurer can construct an exceedance probability (EP) curve that specifies the probabilities that a certain level of losses will be exceeded in a specific location (or its entire portfolio) over a specific period of time (e.g., one year, ten years).[15] These losses can be measured in terms of dollars of damage, fatalities, illness, or some other unit of analysis.

Suppose one were interested in constructing an EP curve for an insurer with a given portfolio of policies covering wind damage from hurricanes in Miami-Dade County, Florida. By combining the set of events that could produce a given dollar loss, one can determine the resulting probabilities of exceeding losses of different dollar magnitudes. In the hypothetical mean EP curve of figure 6.6, the x-axis measures the loss to insurer in dollars and the y-axis depicts the probability that losses will exceed a particular level. Suppose the insurer focuses on a specific loss L_i. The likelihood that insured losses will exceed this L_i is given by p_i.

An insurer uses its EP curve for determining how many structures it will want to include in its portfolio, given that there is some chance of hurricanes causing damage to some

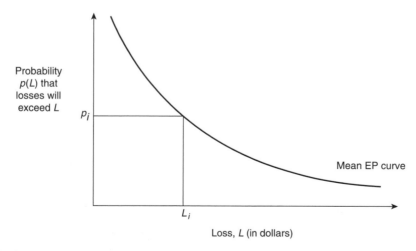

Figure 6.6
Hypothetical mean exceedance probability curve

subset of its policies during a given year. The uncertainty associated with the probability of an event occurring and the magnitude of dollar losses of an EP curve can be reflected in confidence intervals surrounding the mean EP curve.

The EP curve serves as an important element for evaluating risk management tools. It puts pressure on experts to make explicit the assumptions on which they are basing their estimates of the likelihood of certain events occurring and the resulting consequences. A key question that needs to be addressed in constructing an EP curve is the degree of uncertainty regarding probability and outcomes. There will be considerably more uncertainty facing an insurer that constructs an EP curve reflecting losses to a specific region (e.g., Miami-Dade County) than for a wider area (e.g., Florida).

Application to Florida: Focus on Hurricane Risks

Risk Management Solutions has provided us with an analysis of the data from the Florida Hurricane Catastrophe Fund (FHCF) book of business as of 2005.[16] Since the FHCF is a state mandatory reinsurance program (see chapter 2 for more details), it has every residential insurance policy written in the state by private insurers as well as the state-run insurer, Citizens Property Insurance Corporation. Data collected for this simulation include all lines of coverage of the FHCF. Total insured value (TIV) by the fund at the end of 2005 was estimated to be $1.7 trillion for the entire state of Florida. We focus on wind coverage only.[17]

Table 6.2 provides estimates of the annual probability that insured wind losses from hurricanes will equal or exceed different magnitudes for eighteen thresholds ranging from

Table 6.2
Exceedance probability of insured residential losses in Florida (in $ billion)

$1 bn	42.5%
$2 bn	35.9%
$5 bn	24.5%
$10 bn	15.0%
$15 bn	10.1%
$20 bn	6.9%
$25 bn	5.0%
$30 bn	3.9%
$40 bn	2.5%
$50 bn	1.7%
$60 bn	1.3%
$75 bn	0.81%
$100 bn	0.41%
$125 bn	0.22%
$150 bn	0.11%
$200 bn	0.028%
$250 bn	0.005%
$350 bn	0.00012%

Sources: Wharton Risk Center, FHCF Data 2005; simulation by RMS.

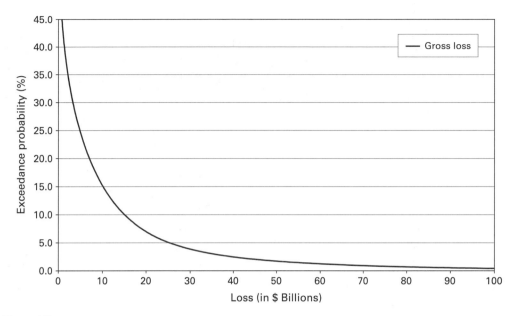

Figure 6.7
Exceedance probability curve for Florida (entire FHCF portfolio) for insured losses from hurricanes up to $100 billion. *Sources:* Wharton Risk Management Center, FHCF Data, 2005; simulation by RMS.

$1 billion to $350 billion. Specifically, there is a 42.5 percent chance that there will be at least $1 billion of insured residential losses in Florida next year. The probability that hurricanes will inflict at least $10 billion of insured residential losses in Florida next year is 15 percent, and there is a 0.81 percent chance that insured losses will be at least $75 billion.

The probability decreases significantly as the threshold level of losses increases. For very high levels of insured losses ($100 billion and greater), the exceedance probability is less than 0.5 percent. This translates into a hurricane that occurs less than once in every two hundred years. Of course, such an unlikely catastrophic event could occur during the next hurricane season. By undertaking this analysis for all possible levels of insured hurricane losses, one can generate the entire exceedance probability curve for the FHCF. Figure 6.7 provides this curve for losses up to $100 billion.

Measuring the uncertainty surrounding these estimates requires data on the average annual expected losses and the standard deviation for each postal code in the state. For all postal codes combined, the average annual expected loss for Florida residential insurance is $5.4 billion, and the standard deviation is $13.9 billion (a 2.55 coefficient of variation).[18] Even if the average expected loss is identical in two regions, their standard deviations can differ significantly. To illustrate this point, we compared the insured losses from hurricanes in postal codes within Miami-Dade County with forty-six counties in the northern part of Florida, depicted in figure 6.8. These counties taken together had the same expected

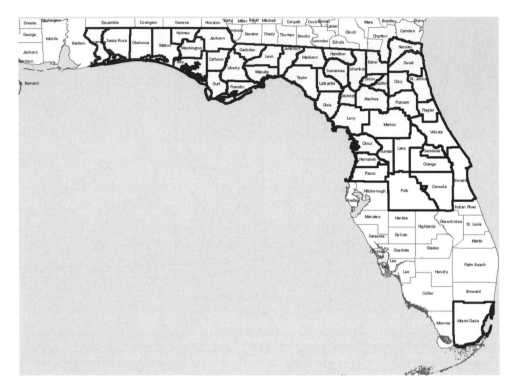

Figure 6.8
Counties whose combined annual expected loss equals Miami-Dade's alone

annual insured losses as Miami-Dade County. Figure 6.9 depicts the two EP curves for these two regions. Although the EP curves between the two regions look similar, their standard deviations are quite different. For both Miami-Dade County and the forty-six northern counties in Florida, the average annual expected loss is approximately $900 million. The standard deviation of losses for Miami-Dade is $4.2 billion (a coefficient of variation of nearly 5), and for the forty-six northern counties it is $2.8 billion (a coefficient of variation of approximately 3). This uncertainty in losses poses serious insurability problems for insurers as well as reinsurers, to which we now turn.

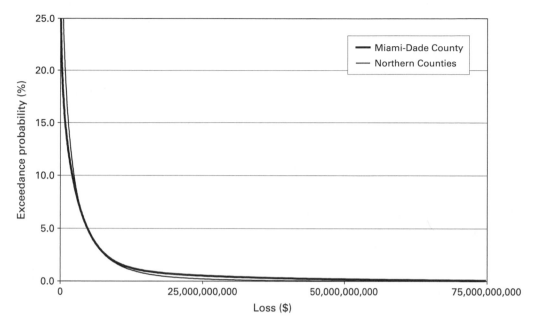

Figure 6.9
EP Curves of the two areas

Summary

Given the new era of catastrophes we have entered, insurers are reexamining their ability to provide protection against wind damage from hurricanes and are asking whether these events are insurable. A risk is considered to be insurable if one has the ability to identify and quantify it and set premiums at a price that yields a competitive rate of return.

To determine whether to offer coverage against a specific risk, insurers look to maximize their expected profits subject to satisfying constraints related to the survival of the firm. The premium that the insurer would like to charge reflects not only the expected loss but how uncertain the risk is, whether there are potential problems of adverse selection and moral hazard, and how correlated the losses are likely to be in the event of a severe disaster. The prices charged for catastrophe insurance must be sufficiently high to cover not only the expected claims costs and other expenses, but also the costs of allocating capital so that investors obtain a fair rate of return. Because large amounts of capital are needed to underwrite catastrophe risk relative to the insurer's expected liability, the capital cost built into the premium is high.

In recent years, rating agencies have put more emphasis on the impact that catastrophic risks will have on the financial stability of insurers. Insurers have thus focused their attention on the amount of coverage that they are willing to provide against wind losses from hurricanes and damage from earthquakes, given the need to allocate more capital to underwrite this risk.

The last part of the chapter shows how catastrophe models help insurers and reinsurers assess risk. Catastrophe models help measure exposure to natural disasters. Using a complete data set of residential coverage in the state of Florida provided by the Florida Hurricane Catastrophe Fund, Risk Management Solutions developed an exceedance probability curve for insured losses from hurricanes in the state. Comparisons are then made between exceedance probability curves for Miami-Dade County and forty-six counties in northern Florida with the same combined annual expected insured losses from hurricane damage. The coefficient of variation for the Miami-Dade County area is about 5, compared to a coefficient of about 3 for the forty-six counties. This implies that Miami-Dade is much more likely to suffer catastrophic losses from hurricanes in the future than are these forty-six counties in northern Florida.

APPENDIX 6A: TREATMENT OF NATURAL CATASTROPHIC RISK BY THE RATING AGENCIES

Category	AM Best[a,g]	Standard & Poor's[b,c,g]	Fitch[d,e,g]	Moody's[f,g]
Adjustment to capital	Adjusted actual capital reduced for the higher of the 1/100 wind or the 1/250 earthquake net PML (occurrence basis)	Target capital increased for net 1/250 net PML (aggregate basis), net of one year's catastrophe premiums written less 30% for expenses	Target capital include an amount based on tail value at risk (TVaR) from the catastrophe aggregate loss exceedance curve. The TVaR thresholds have not yet been determined.	Target capital in simulation iterations includes amounts generated from random draws of exceedance curves for seven U.S. catastrophes
Catastrophe model assumptions	Five-year horizon (medium or near term depending on catastrophe modeler)	Five-year horizon (medium or near term depending on catastrophe modeler)	Not yet determined	Five-year horizon (medium or near term depending on catastrophe modeler)
Coverages	Property structure and contents, additional living expenses, business Interruption, flood, auto/motor physical damage, workers' compensation, energy, ocean marine, inland marine and crop	Global property	Property	Property (including workers' compensation for earthquake)
Perils	Hurricane, earthquake, tornado, hail	All	Hurricane (wind) and earthquake	Hurricane (wind) and earthquake
Components of loss	Demand surge, storm surge, fire following earthquake, secondary uncertainty and loss adjustment expenses	Demand surge, storm surge, fire following earthquake, sprinkler leakage, and secondary uncertainty	All switches are turned on (demand surge, storm surge, secondary uncertainty and fire following)	All switches are turned on (demand surge, storm surge, secondary uncertainty and fire following)
Reinsurance	Net of reinsurance, plus reinstatements and coparticipations	Net of reinsurance, plus reinstatements and coparticipations	Net of generic or company-specific reinsurance (if companies provide information)	Assumes 90% cession for losses between the 1/25 to 1/100 level
Tax	Posttax	Pretax	Modeled pretax with later scope for adjustment	Pretax

Category	AM Best[a,g]	Standard & Poor's[b,c,g]	Fitch[d,e,g]	Moody's[f,g]
Credit risk	Stress test adds credit risk charge by applying the credit factor to 80% of ceded reserves from first event and by assuming one level downgrade	Potential material increases in reinsurance recoverables added to reinsurance risk taken into account (analyst discretion)	Under development	Ceded losses are considered reinsurance recoverables and added to the reinsurance risk
Second event stress test	Calculate a stressed BCAR including a second net catastrophe PML at the higher of the 1/100 wind or the 1/100 earthquake	Not applicable	Not applicable	Adds randomly generated catastrophes from the seven areas, so this includes multiple events, but not necessarily second event in same region or peril

[a] AM Best, *Catastrophe Analysis in AM Best Ratings*, November 2005, Revised April 2006.
[b] Standard and Poor's, *Insurance Criteria: Catastrophe-Specific Capital Charges to Be Extended to Primary Insurers, But Reinsurance Criteria Unchanged*, November 7, 2005.
[c] Standard and Poor's, *Reinsurer Criteria: Larger Losses and Better Modeling Prompt Changes to Property Catastrophe Criteria*, June 27, 2005.
[d] Fitch Ratings, *Special Report: New Thinking on Catastrophic Risk and Capital Requirements*, November 9, 2005.
[e] Fitch, *Criteria Report, Exposure Draft: Capital Assessment Methodology and Model (Prism)—Executive Summary*, June 2006.
[f] Moody's, *Rating Methodology: Risk Adjusted Capital Model for Property and Casualty Insurers*, September 2004.
[g] Conversations with the rating agency.
Sources: The Review Pedant's Guide to Renewals 2006

7 Private Reinsurers' Decision Making for Supplying Coverage

Key Findings

Reinsurers consider both the expected loss and the variance of losses in their portfolio when pricing different layers of coverage. The prices are typically much higher in a hard market than in a soft market, reflecting the different weights placed on the variance dimension to reflect the cost of capital. An analysis of different layers of reinsurance for a constructed portfolio of homeowners' policies in Florida reveals that the average annual loss decreases with higher layers but the variance of the losses increases. Using that portfolio, we calculate that the average annual loss (in billions) for the [$10 bn; $20 bn] layer is $1.35; for the [$20 bn; $40 bn] layer it is $0.99; and for the [$40 bn; $80 bn] layer it is $0.63. The standard deviation (in billions) for the first layer is $4.52, $5.37 for the second and $5.65 for the third.

Due to the severe hurricanes in 2004 and 2005, the reinsurance market hardened in 2006 and premiums measured by rate on line rose on average 76 percent between July 1, 2005, and June 30, 2006. The premium increase was much higher for Florida-only insurers. The large increase in premiums attracted new major entrants into the market and $26 billion to $27 billion of new capital during this period.

Between July 1, 2006, and June 30, 2007, prices fell slightly but were still considerably higher than during 2005. Prices continued to fall at the January 2008 renewal, but increased by 8 percent at the January 2009 renewal. Retention and limits on reinsurance programs continued to increase in 2007 and 2008.

7.1 Nature of Reinsurance

Reinsurers provide protection to private insurers in much the same way that insurers provide coverage to their policyholders. They offer coverage against the catastrophic portion

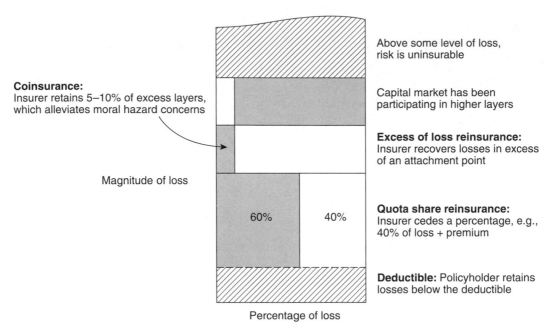

Figure 7.1
Overview of transfer risk: Policyholder, insurer, reinsurer, and capital market. *Source:* Lalonde (2005).

of a loss for which insurers do not want to be financially responsible. In this type of arrangement, the reinsurer charges a premium to indemnify an insurance company against a layer of the catastrophic losses that the insurer would otherwise be responsible for covering.

There are two main types of reinsurance: *pro rata* (coinsurance or quota-share) reinsurance, in which premium and loss are shared on a proportional basis, and *excess of loss* reinsurance, for which a premium is paid to cover losses between two attachment points. For example, a contract that specifies $200 million in excess of $500 million for hurricane losses in Texas means that an insurer who purchased reinsurance to cover losses of $200–$500 million would cede its exposure for claims from Texas hurricanes in the $500 million to $700 million layer. The reinsurer needs to determine whether it wants to add this layer to its portfolio. Figure 7.1 illustrates how these types of reinsurance contracts relate to the entire risk transfer process. Although a certain amount of pro rata reinsurance is used for catastrophe protection, excess of loss reinsurance is the predominant form.

7.2   How Reinsurers Determine Coverage and Set Premiums

Since reinsurance price is not regulated (as insurance price is), there is no systematic data collection publicly available on the reinsurance market. However, based on discussions with brokers, reinsurers and insurers, we have a clearer understanding of how capital is allocated by the reinsurer for providing coverage against catastrophic risks and how prices are determined.

Determining Whether to Offer Coverage

Reinsurers are concerned about having a high concentration of risk in any region for the same reason that insurers limit their coverage: they want to avoid a large decrease in their surplus from a catastrophic loss. They thus restrict their exposure in hazard-prone areas so as to keep the chances of severe losses at an acceptable level.

Consider a reinsurer who has S dollars in current surplus that reflects the amount of its internal capital and the amount of capital it can raise from investors. The value of S includes premiums received by the reinsurer on the risks in its current portfolio. The insurer wants to determine whether to cede a layer of excess of loss coverage (Δ) to a reinsurer against hurricane-related losses in coastal regions of Texas. The reinsurer needs to determine whether it will take on this layer, and, if so, what price it should charge the insurer for accepting this risk. The reinsurer will make this decision based on the following considerations:

- The likelihood (p) of having to pay claims for this layer
- The distribution of the claim payments should this layer be affected by a hurricane
- The expected loss associated with the layer $E(L)$
- The incremental impact of the layer on the variance of losses in the reinsurer's portfolio as (σ_Δ^2)
- The premium (P_Δ) the reinsurer would want to charge to the insurer should it decide to offer coverage
- The minimum return on equity required by investors (ROE^*) so they will provide capital to the reinsurer

Based on these considerations, the reinsurer will make a decision as to whether it reinsures this layer Δ by first determining what the rate of return on equity (ROE_Δ) will be. If $ROE_\Delta > ROE^*$, then the reinsurer will want to provide this coverage as long as it has met a survival constraint similar to that faced by the insurer in determining whether it wants to offer additional coverage. More specifically, based on its current portfolio of risks, the reinsurer computes the distribution of total claim payments if it incorporates this layer in its book of business, thus adding P_Δ to its current surplus (S) and determines whether:

Probability [*Total claims payments* $> z(P_\Delta + S)$] $< p_1$ (7.1)

The value of z reflects the fraction of surplus that the reinsurer considers to be critical to its continued operation where $0 < z \leq 1$. If $z = 1$ then the critical value ($P_\Delta + S$) is where the reinsurer would become insolvent and equation 7.1 is equivalent to a survival constraint used by insurers in determining whether or not to offer coverage (see equation 6.1 in chapter 6). The threshold probability, p_1, plays a similar role for the reinsurer as it does for the insurer. It reflects the trade-off between obtaining a ROE$_\Delta$ should the reinsurer add Δ to its portfolio and the costs to the firm of a catastrophic loss that reduces the insurer's surplus below a critical level. Reinsurers' decisions on how much coverage to offer are also based on a stability constraint. They are concerned that if their surplus falls below a critical level given by $z(P_\Delta + S)$, rating agencies are likely to downgrade them. Should this occur, the reinsurer will be forced to offer a higher return on investment to attract new capital. It will also have to charge a lower premium to insurers for the same layer of coverage.[1]

It should be clear from this simplified descriptive model that the composition of a reinsurer's existing book of business plays a key role in whether to accept a certain contract and what price to charge for it. A layer that is not highly correlated with the existing book of business will be viewed as much more attractive than a layer in a hazard-prone region where the reinsurer already has a large amount of surplus at risk.

In summary, the decision to offer coverage against catastrophic risk depends on the following three factors:

• Current portfolio and volatility of the layer (Δ) under consideration. Hurricane losses are more volatile than fire or wind. The higher the volatility of Δ, the less attractive it will be to the reinsurer at a given price.

• The minimum required rate of return (ROE^*) for an investor to want to provide capital to the reinsurer.

• Price of coverage (P_Δ). The higher the price for providing Δ, the greater the ROE_Δ and the more likely the reinsurer will accept this layer of coverage.[2]

• The amount of capital available to the reinsurer from either internal or external sources.

Setting Premiums for a Given Layer

The pricing of a layer of reinsurance needs to cover the expected claims $[E(L)]$ as well as marketing, brokerage, and claims processing expenses, while at the same time ensuring that the coverage earns a high enough expected return on equity (ROE) so that it is attractive to investors.[3] The reinsurer is also concerned with the impact of the policy on the variance of its portfolio, since this has an impact on the survival constraint given by equation 7.1. Hence, it will charge a higher price for a given layer, the greater its variance as well as the more highly correlated this layer is with the reinsurer's existing book of business.[4] For a prespecified layer Δ, we denote the incremental impact of the policy on the standard deviation of the portfolio as σ_Δ.

The model most reinsurers use for determining the premium (P_Δ) for a specific layer of excess loss coverage (Δ) that captures these concerns is given by the following simple formula:

$$P_\Delta = E(L_\Delta)(1 + \lambda) + c \cdot \sigma_\Delta \tag{7.2}$$

where λ = the loading factor and c = the degree of risk aversion of the reinsurer.

The higher the value of σ_Δ, the more the reinsurer will want to charge for providing Δ. A reinsurer who is highly risk averse will specify a higher value of c reflecting its concern with taking on any new book of business.[5]

7.3 The Use of Catastrophe Modeling to Price Reinsurance: Application to Florida

To illustrate how reinsurers would price coverage in a competitive market, Risk Management Solutions (RMS) provided us with an analysis of the data from the Florida Hurricane Catastrophe Fund (FHCF) book of business as of 2005 (that is, all policies issued in the state that year) to determine the price of different layers of reinsurance for wind coverage.[6] Here we assume that this portfolio is managed by a single entity concentrating exclusively on Florida that would like to determine how much it will have to pay for different amounts of reinsurance coverage for two different regions of Florida that have the same expected loss but different concentrations of exposure: Miami-Dade County (highly concentrated exposure) and 46 northern counties in Florida (diffuse exposure).

Based on the characterization of reinsurance pricing detailed in section 7.2, we can analyze what the prices of reinsurance would be under two separate pricing structures. For the sake of simplicity, we assume $\lambda = 0$. In the first pricing structure, reinsurance coverage costs less (i.e., $c = 0.4$), as it is more readily available (i.e., there is a "soft" market condition). In the second pricing structure, coverage costs more (i.e., $c = 0.7$), as reinsurance is hard to get (i.e., there is a "hard" market condition). The choices of values for "c" were designed to reflect the difference between soft and hard market conditions and reflect the degree of risk aversion of the reinsurer.

There are two driving principles for this exercise. First, relative to the expected loss, higher reinsurance layers cost more than lower reinsurance layers due to their higher volatility. Second, for two regions with the same expected loss, the area with the more concentrated exposure will have greater impacts on higher reinsurance layers than the region with more diffuse exposure.

In reality, reinsurers provide coverage in many regions of the world, so they have to estimate the correlation between different types of risk such as a hurricane in Florida, a hurricane in New York, an earthquake in Japan, and an earthquake in California in making their pricing decisions.

The following method was used by RMS in completing this reinsurance analysis.[7] First, four reinsurance layers were defined for the FHCF portfolio, which define the attachment and exhaustion points of coverage along the exceedance probability curve. In this example, we use $5 billion to $10 billion for layer 1, $10 billion to $20 billion for layer 2, $20 billion to $40 billion for layer 3, and $40 billion to $80 billion for layer 4. With these defined

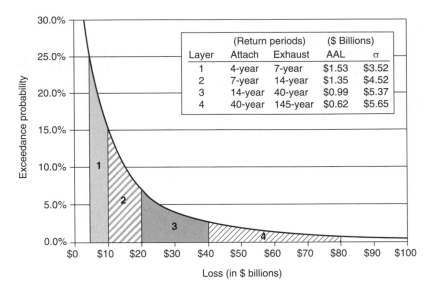

Figure 7.2
Technical risk (AAL) and uncertainty (σ_Δ) associated with each layer of reinsurance. *Source:* Simulation by RMS.

layers, the RMS U.S. Hurricane Model was run against the FHCF portfolio to determine the expected loss (E(L)) or average annual loss (AAL) for each layer, along with the uncertainty of the loss. The return periods associated with the attachment and exhaustion points, as well as the average annual loss and its standard deviation for each layer, are illustrated in figure 7.2. For example, layer 4, covering losses from $40 billion to $80 billion ($40 billion in excess of $40 billion) has an attachment point with an annual probability of 1 in 40 and an exhaustion point of 1 in 145 years. Since it is much less likely that this layer is triggered annually than layer 1, the AAL is much lower ($0.62 billion), but σ_Δ is higher ($5.65 billion).

We can now apply a pricing scheme for each of the 4 layers. For each layer, we use $P_\Delta = E(L_\Delta)(1+\lambda) + c \cdot \sigma_\Delta$. Here, we are interested in the true risk financing cost. We thus assume that there is no loading factor to cover administrative cost ($\lambda = 0$) so $P_\Delta = AAL + c \cdot \sigma_\Delta$. As previously mentioned, we will study two market conditions: a soft market, with $P_\Delta = AAL + 0.4 \cdot \sigma_\Delta$, and a hard market, with $P_\Delta = AAL + 0.7 \cdot \sigma$. Table 7.1 summarizes the price of reinsurance for different layers under these two market conditions.

It is also possible to compute the ratio $c \cdot \sigma_\Delta / AAL$ to measure the effect of volatility on reinsurance prices. As table 7.2 illustrates, as expected, higher reinsurance layers cost more than lower reinsurance layers relative to the expected loss due to their higher volatility.

Next, in order to determine the cost of reinsurance in each postal code by layer, the proportion of total average annual loss must be assigned to each layer within the state of Florida for the FHCF portfolio. For example, the proportion of AAL losses in a given postal

Table 7.1
Price of reinsurance under soft and hard markets $P_\Delta = AAL + c \cdot \sigma_\Delta$ (in $ billion)

	Layer 1 [$5; $10]	Layer 2 [$10; $20]	Layer 3 [$20; $40]	Layer 4 [$40; $80]
Soft market ($c = 0.4$)	$2.94	$3.16	$3.14	$2.88
Hard market ($c = 0.7$)	4.00	4.51	4.75	4.57

Table 7.2
Changes in ($c \cdot \sigma_\Delta$/AAL) ratio for different reinsurance layers (in $ billion)

	Layer 1 [$5; $10]	Layer 2 [$10; $20]	Layer 3 [$20; $40]	Layer 4 [$40; $80]
Soft market ($c = 0.4$)	$0.92	$1.34	$2.17	$3.65
Hard market ($c = 0.7$)	1.61	2.34	3.80	6.38

code that contribute to an industry-wide loss greater than $5 billion and less than $10 billion is assigned to layer 1.

These results are shown in the maps in figure 7.3. The darker the color, the higher the AAL for the postal code assigned to that layer. Not surprisingly, for the first layer, there are several dark areas where the loss is concentrated, as many events in the probabilistic hurricane model can impact this lower layer. These dark areas concentrate themselves in the highest risk areas and highest exposure regions as losses impact the higher layers (i.e., as we move to the tail of the EP curve—from layer 1 to layer 4).

For the remaining losses above and below the four reinsurance layers (i.e., below $5 billion and above $80 billion), the losses are assigned to each postal code as appropriate. In this way, the total loss along the EP curve (e.g., the AAL is the area under the EP curve) is assigned across all postal codes in Florida.

The final step is the calculation of each postal code's contribution to the overall reinsurance cost under a soft and hard market condition. This is illustrated using one specific postal code. Assume that the contribution of the chosen postal code for losses below layer 1, where there is no reinsurance, is $25.9 million. For the first layer of reinsurance, the AAL contribution of that postal code is $14.6 million. Given that $c \cdot \sigma_\Delta/AAL = 0.92$ for layer 1 under the soft market, the postal code will contribute to $13.1 million of the reinsurance cost for that layer. Table 7.3 provides results for this illustrative example.

By repeating this exercise for each layer, we can determine the contribution of that postal code to the reinsurance cost, including the retention portion of it below layer 1 and above layer 4: it is $208.2 million under the soft market and $331.3 million under the hard market. Under the soft market, the ratio of total reinsurance cost to average annual loss is $208.2/119.3 = 1.75$. Under the hard market, the ratio is $331.3/119.3 = 2.78$. This represents a 59 percent increase in pricing ratio between these two market conditions.

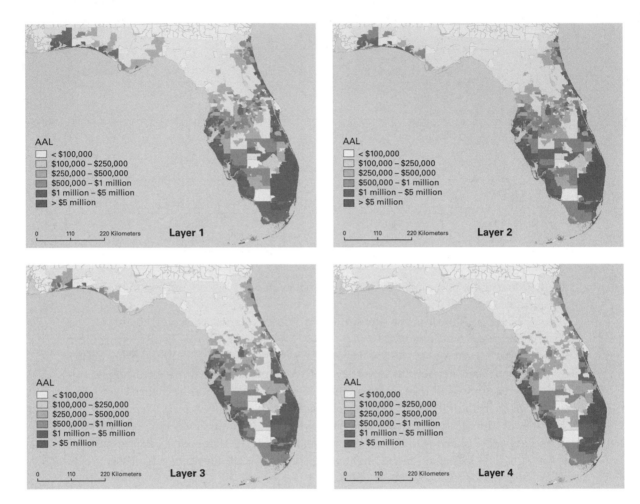

Figure 7.3
Postal codes' AAL for each of the four reinsurance layers

This exercise is repeated for each postal code in the state. Figure 7.4 depicts the results. As figure 7.4 illustrates, the market environment plays a critical role in the availability and cost of reinsurance. The simulation reveals that the typical ratios of risk financing over AAL for the soft market are between 1.03 and 1.78, with higher ratios between 1.16 and 2.88 for the hard market. We also find that the nature of the reinsurance market has its greatest impact where exposure is most concentrated, where the postal codes with the highest sensitivity to pricing are in southern Florida. This example illustrates the challenges faced by the FHCF and the extreme risk associated with hurricanes along Florida's coastline, the highest anywhere in the world.

Table 7.3
Contribution of a given postal code to the price of reinsurance (in $ million)

	AAL	Soft market	Hard market
Below layer 1	$25.9	$25.9	$25.9
Layer 1	$14.6	$31.1	$23.5
Layer 2	$19.1	$25.6	$44.7
Layer 3	$16.9	$36.7	$64.2
Layer 4	$24.2	$88.3	$154.4
Above layer 4	$18.6	$18.6	$18.6
Total	$119.3	$208.2	$331.3

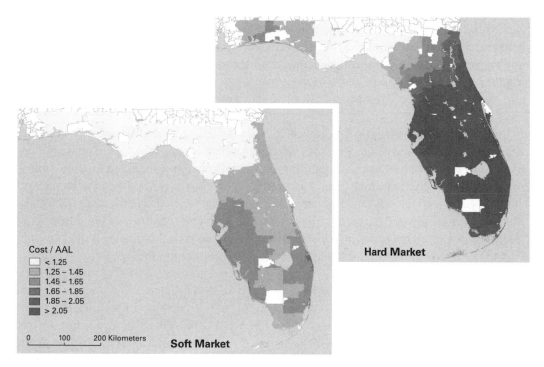

Figure 7.4
Ratio true cost of risk financing over AAL for soft and hard markets. *Source:* Simulation by RMS.

7.4   Broader Empirical Data on Reinsurance Contracts

Empirical evidence supporting the above reinsurer's pricing model comes from a detailed analysis by Froot and O'Connell (1999) of Guy Carpenter's reinsurance contracts for catastrophic risks over the period 1970 to 1994. Guy Carpenter is a leading reinsurance broker. The contracts covered a wide variety of natural hazards including earthquake, fire, winter storm, and hurricane. Specifically, they examined the prices and quantities offered for excess of loss reinsurance contracts.

In their analyses of these data, Froot and O'Connell (1999) found that following a $10 billion loss in a particular region, there is a decline in quantity of 5.2 percent in surplus on average over the next year. This decline in quantity leads to an average price increase of 19 percent across all reinsurance contracts. This price increase is independent of whether the reinsurer had contracts that were affected by the disaster, although there was an additional increase in prices by reinsurers who had higher exposure in the affected region. This price behavior implies that surplus is not instantly replaced after suffering catastrophic losses and suggests that reinsurers are concerned with the survival constraint when determining whether to offer new excess loss coverage for catastrophic risks. This post-loss phenomenon is known as the *capacity constraint theory* and is examined in detail in the next chapter.

More generally, Froot and O'Connell found that reinsurance premiums at that time were considerably above the expected loss, sometimes as much as seven times higher. Moreover, the higher attachment point for a layer with the same expected loss, the higher, on average, the premium multiple. These results reflect the cost associated with the very large levels of capital needed to underwrite reinsurance for catastrophic risks. They also found that a 10 percent increase in the variance of reinsurer exposure increased prices by about 6.8 percent. This behavior is also consistent with the premium-setting model given by equation 7.2, where the risk load plays a key role in determining the price of reinsurance.

The elasticity of supply for catastrophe reinsurance contracts that Froot and O'Connell analyzed was on the order of 7. This implies that a 10 percent increase in premiums above the expected losses increases reinsurance capacity by 70 percent. Froot and O'Connell point out that this is a very small increase from what capital markets could be expected to provide for liquid instruments. This behavior suggests the importance of a survival constraint given by equation 7.1 in determining the amount of excess loss coverage that a reinsurer will provide against catastrophic risks. The authors conclude that capital market imperfections impede the flow of capital into the reinsurance sector, leading to price increases and supply contractions following severe disaster losses.

As noted in chapter 1, the catastrophic risk environment has radically changed in the past ten years, with extreme events hitting the United States at an increasing rate and with severe effects. Our discussions with reinsurers, coupled with the recent data from the reinsurance market presented in the next section, suggest additional pressures being placed on capital allocation in general, and on reinsurers in particular, by rating agencies that may restrict the supply of their coverage for catastrophic losses even more than during the period that Froot and O'Connell studies.

We next discuss the evolution of the reinsurance market in reaction to the 2005 hurricane season, the revisions in the catastrophe models, and the increased concern by rating agencies with respect to catastrophe exposure management. We then turn to a comparison of the reinsurance market of January 1, 2005, and over the period 2006–2008.

7.5 Reinsurance Market in 2005–2006

According to a report on the nature of the world reinsurance market during the period July 1, 2005, through June 30, 2006 prepared by Guy Carpenter (2006), reinsurers behaved during this period of time in a manner that appears to be consistent with the model of section 7.2 characterizing reinsurers' decisions regarding coverage and premiums. The Guy Carpenter report is based on a sample of more than 200 layers of catastrophe data within Guy Carpenter's catastrophe analysis database that was tracked consistently from 1989 to 2006. We discuss some of the key findings from this report and related studies.

Impact of Reinsurer Losses on Pricing, Coverage Availability, and Profitability

The storms of 2005 placed a disproportionate burden on the reinsurance industry. Reinsurers estimated their losses for 2005 to be $40 billion, approximately half due to Hurricane Katrina. This immediately changed the market to a hard market. As a direct application of the pricing process described in section 7.3, reinsurance premiums as measured by rate on line (ROL; the premium charged for a layer of coverage over the amount of coverage) increased significantly in the United States, rising 76 percent between July 1, 2005, and June 30, 2006, as depicted in figure 7.5.

The large increase in premiums attracted new capital into the market with eight new major entrants. The Guy Carpenter (2006) report points out that "many investors viewed the anticipated reinsurance price increases and capacity shortages as compelling motivators to enter the market." An estimated $26 billion to $27 billion of capital flowed into existing reinsurance companies through new start-ups and other alternative risk transfer instruments between Hurricane Katrina and June 30, 2006.[8] Despite the influx of new capital in the market, regions with high exposure to windstorm, notably Florida and the Gulf Coast, experienced a much harder market for catastrophe reinsurance, which has led to significant increases in ROL premiums. Private U.S. insurers thus increased their retention limits in 2006 by 40 percent on average from the previous year, as shown in figure 7.6, which is based on a select group of companies tracked consistently between 1989 and 2006.

These same insurers also increased the average limit of reinsurance coverage by 11.4 percent. This increase reflects their concern with the possibility of increased catastrophic losses

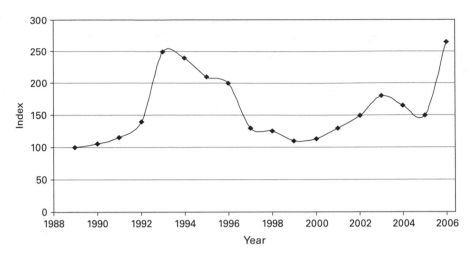

Figure 7.5
Catastrophe property rate-on-line index for the United States, 1989–2006.
Source: Data from Guy Carpenter. *Note:* Indexed to 1989.

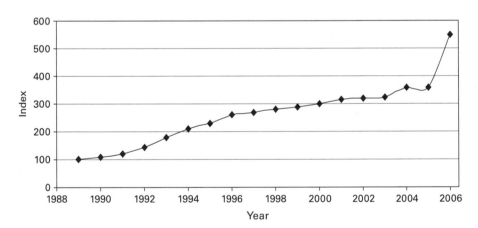

Figure 7.6
Average retention per program index for United States, 1989–2006.
Source: Data from Guy Carpenter. *Note:* Indexed to 1989.

as indicated by the modeling companies, as well as continued pressure from rating agencies on capital adequacy and the management of catastrophe exposures (see section 6.5 for a more detailed discussion of these points). In addition, the increased population growth in hazard-prone areas and the large hurricane losses in 2004 and 2005 heightened insurers' awareness of their catastrophe loss potential. The Guy Carpenter report also projects that the increased limits in reinsurance coverage would have been considerably higher if the ROL for catastrophe coverage had not increased dramatically and capacity had been more plentiful.

An indication of the scarcity of reinsurance for catastrophe coverage in these high-risk regions of the United States is highlighted, for a given reinsurance program, by an increase in attachment points, the reduction in expected loss, and the higher premiums and risk loads between 2005 and 2006 for national companies, regional companies, and insurers that write only in Florida, as depicted in figures 7.7 to 7.9. The figures show that catastrophe reinsurance premiums increased significantly for all insurers between 2005 and 2006 but were noticeably higher for stand-alone Florida companies. The risk loads were also substantially higher than in the previous year. This reflects the reinsurers' perception that the hurricane risk is now higher, as indicated by the modeling companies' upward revisions in their estimates of frequency of hurricanes and the more stringent requirements by rating agencies. As a result, reinsurers might be less exposed today (lower expected loss) because they are providing less coverage in these high-risk areas.

Determining the expected profitability of reinsurers for different layers of coverage for any given period requires computing several different measures:

• *Rate on line* (ROL_J) *for each layer J.* This is the ratio of the premium charged for this layer of coverage over the amount of coverage.

• *Loss on Line* (LOL_J) *for each layer J.* This is the ratio of the expected loss over the amount of coverage for this layer of coverage. The expected loss for layer J is determined by multiplying the probability (p_{iJ}) of each loss (L_{iJ}) within a given layer J. $LOL_J = \sum_i p_{iJ} L_{iJ}$

• *Expected underwriting profitability for each layer J.* $E(\Pi_J) = ROL_J - LOL_J$

The higher the attachment point, the lower the LOL for a fixed layer of coverage because of the lower frequency at the higher attachment points. To illustrate this, if one provides excess loss reinsurance coverage to a given insurer for $50 million in excess of $100 million (losses between $100 million and $150 million), one has to recognize that there is a higher LOL for this layer than for $50 million in excess of $500 million.

Figure 7.10 indicates that the ROL (*y*-axis) for 2006 (upper line) was considerably higher than for 2005 (lower line) for all layers of reinsurance as reflected in the LOL (*x*-axis). The lines between the two years are approximately parallel, indicating that the increases in ROL for 2006 were proportionately higher at lower LOL, which corresponds

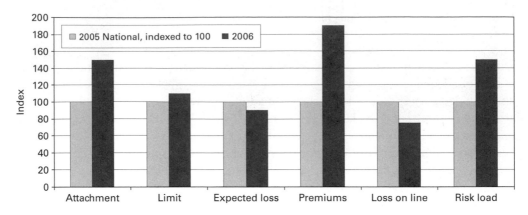

Figure 7.7
Comparison of key renewal statistics for national companies, 2005–2006

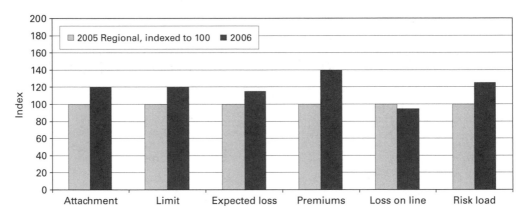

Figure 7.8
Comparison of key renewal statistics for regional companies, 2005–2006.

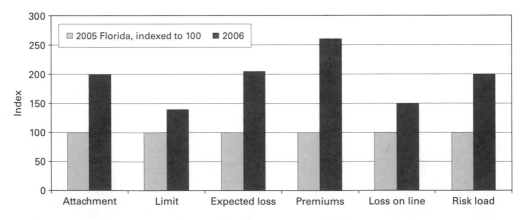

Figure 7.9
Comparison of key renewal statistics for Florida-only companies, 2005–2006. *Source:* Data from Guy Carpenter.

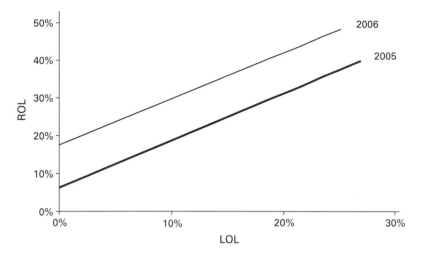

Figure 7.10
Rate on line as a function of loss on line, 2005 and 2006. *Source:* Guy Carpenter (2006).

to higher reinsurance attachment levels, suggesting that reinsurers expected profits for a fixed layer of coverage increases as the attachment point increases. There may be several explanations for this behavior:

• The LOL values in figure 7.10 may not reflect the current estimates of expected loss based on the modeling companies' upward revisions in the spring of 2006.

• Reinsurers are now more conservative because of more stringent rating agency requirements and the higher capital costs associated with holding more surplus to protect themselves against catastrophic losses.

• The expected profitability of a given layer is overstated if one defines it as $E(\Pi_J) = ROL_J - LOL_J$. There are other expenses (e.g., capital costs) that need to be incorporated in determining $E(\Pi_J)$.

Reinsurance Capacity for Covering Catastrophic Natural Disaster Losses

One issue that is somewhat controversial is the available capacity of the reinsurance industry to cover catastrophic losses from natural disasters. After considerable discussion on this point with large reinsurers as well as several large brokers, we have concluded that it is difficult to pinpoint any specific figure that could be used as a magic number in the current policy debate regarding the role of the private and public sectors in providing coverage for high layers of catastrophe exposure. Even providing a range of values might be misleading for the following reasons:

• The amount of reinsurance provided by any company is partially determined by the premium that it can obtain for coverage. The higher the premium for a given layer, the more reinsurance that will be provided. In other words, the amount of available reinsurance depends on the insurer's willingness to pay for coverage for a given exposure to loss.

• The U.S. market is only one of the markets where reinsurers operate. It is important to keep in mind the international aspect of insurance and reinsurance markets. Indeed, the way a reinsurer will allocate its limited capacity between risks in different regions (e.g., earthquakes in the United States or in Japan, storms in Europe, hurricanes in the United States, typhoons in Asia) and increase or decrease capacity in some of these regions depends on many factors related to the specificities of its portfolio, the relative likelihood of these catastrophic risks, the demand for coverage in these different regions, and the availability and price of other sources of capital to expand its capacity.

• The amount of capacity of a reinsurer will also depend on its loss experience and the amount of surplus it has available. For example, the absence of hurricanes hitting the United States during the 2006 season implies a larger surplus on hand to allocate for natural disaster risks in 2007; hence, capacity was expanded.

• The modelers' upward estimates of expected losses coupled with more stringent rating agency criteria for dealing with catastrophe risks may make reinsurers more conservative in their willingness to provide certain layers of coverage against such losses.

• There is no standard for defining and measuring capacity, so the definition also varies across reinsurers.

Florida Reinsurance Market in 2006

The Florida property insurance market relies heavily on the Florida Hurricane Catastrophe Fund (FHCF) and the private reinsurance market for protection. Approximately 50 percent of primary residential insurance premiums are typically ceded to reinsurers in comparison with the national average of approximately 33 percent.[9] According to V. J. Dowling (2006a), total direct premiums written (DPW) in the private insurance market for Florida were $5.6 billion, of which $4.1 billion was written by insurance carriers writing only in Florida. A comparison of figures 7.7 to 7.9 reveals that the Florida-only companies experienced the sharpest increase in cat reinsurance premiums (about 150 percent). Many were unable to find capacity or decided not to buy at the elevated prices. Hence, they are exposed to more risk today. It is unclear how they will fare should another severe hurricane hit Florida in the coming years.

One of the key issues that we have been exploring is what is required for premiums to reflect risk. According to Dowling (2006b), Florida gross premiums need to reach $10.6 billion, or 56 percent above prerate approval base, to generate a 12 percent return on equity (ROE). In other words, if insurers are forced to provide coverage in high-risk areas of Florida at the current regulated premiums, their ROE will be less than what they could earn on other coverage they provide. Assuming all pending rate increases are approved in their entirety, Dowling estimated that the rates need to rise another 22 percent from their levels in October 2006.

We also obtained data on the reinsurance programs of Florida's Citizens, so it is possible to compare the programs for 2005 and 2006. Citizens elected in the spring of 2006 to forgo $500 million of private reinsurance should its losses exceed $5 billion because of the relatively high cost for this coverage ($137 million) (the rate on line is $137 million/ $500 million = 27.4 percent). Instead, Citizens purchased $5 billion of coverage in excess of $1.35 billion for only $250 million from the Florida Hurricane Catastrophe Fund (FHCF) (ROL: $250 million/$5 billion = 5 percent, or six times lower than what was available from the private market as of June 2006).[10]

Legislation passed in Florida in 2007 (see chapter 3) is likely to have a considerable impact on the state's private reinsurance market. An important feature of this legislation is the significant expansion of reinsurance coverage provided to insurers by the FHCF. The FHCF will charge insurers reinsurance prices based on average long-term annual loss. These prices are therefore likely to be lower than current rates charged by private reinsurers. Nevertheless, at the July 2007 renewal, private reinsurers had not significantly reduced their premiums (compared to January 2007).

Profitability of the Reinsurance Industry in 2006

The absence of major catastrophic losses combined with better catastrophe exposure management and a significant increase in reinsurance prices contributed to a record profit year for reinsurers in 2006. According to Guy Carpenter, "This has helped quickly replenish whatever capital was extracted from the market in 2004 and 2005."[11] In addition, $17 billion in new capital that entered the reinsurance market in 2006 bolstered capacity in the marketplace. Coupled with the $25 billion of new capital in the fall of 2005 (see chapter 8), the reinsurance industry has had an infusion of approximately $40 billion since Hurricane Katrina.

7.6 Reinsurance Market at 2007 and 2008 Renewals

Data supplied by reinsurance brokers provide a picture of the changes in the market between January 1, 2006, and July 1, 2007. According to a report by Benfield (2007), January 1, 2007, pricing for national and multiregional companies was slightly below July 1, 2006, but still remained 30 to 50 percent higher than for the January 1, 2006, renewals and significantly higher than January 1, 2005, prices. A Guy Carpenter report published in September 2007 depicts the evolution of pricing (rates on line) for lower and higher

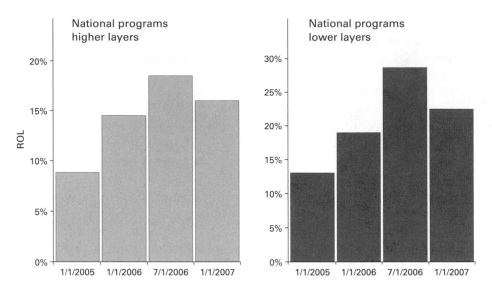

Figure 7.11
Comparison of rate on line for national companies, January 2005–January 2007. *Sources:* Guy Carpenter (2007a).

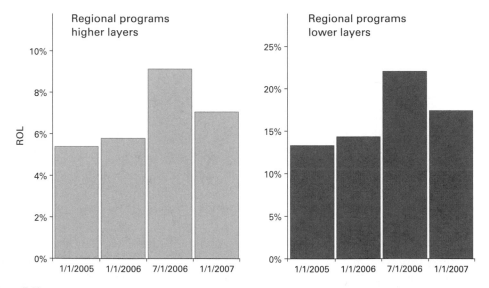

Figure 7.12
Comparison of rate on line for regional companies, January 2005–January 2007. *Sources:* Guy Carpenter (2007a).

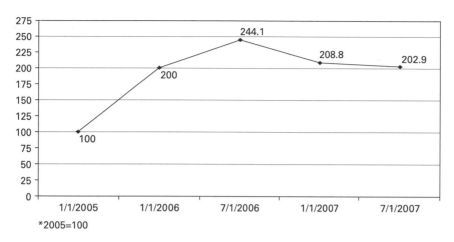

Figure 7.13
Catastrophe reinsurance pricing index in the United States: Rate on line benchmark pricing for loss on line of 1 percent, January 1, 2005–July 1, 2007. *Note:* Index 100: 01/2005. *Source:* Data from Guy Carpenter.

layers of reinsurance programs for national and regional companies (excluding Florida-only accounts) between January 1, 2005, and January 1, 2007.

Figure 7.11 shows that national companies saw prices for lower layers of reinsurance programs decrease by 17 percent and prices for higher layers by 14 percent from July 1, 2006, to January 1, 2007. Still, the January 1, 2007, prices represent a 28 percent increase for lower layers (9 percent for higher layers) when compared to January 1, 2006, pricing of coverage. The figure also reveals that January 1, 2007, prices were more than twice as high as they were at the January 1, 2005, renewals for both the lower and higher layers for national companies. As shown in figure 7.12, regional companies followed a similar path between January 2006, July 2006, and January 2007.

To provide some perspective on the price movements in the catastrophe reinsurance market over the past twenty-four months, Guy Carpenter used the benchmark of a 1 percent loss on line (LOL) (tranches of reinsurance with a 1-in-100-year chance to be triggered). Figure 7.13 depicts the evolution of prices between January 1, 2005, renewals and those of July 1, 2007. Rates for these 1 percent LOL layers had then returned to approximately the level of January 2006, which is still twice what they were at the beginning of 2005.

In 2007, the U.S. reinsurance market continued to soften. At the January 1, 2008, renewals, reinsurance prices had decreased about 10 percent compared to what they were on July 1, 2007.[12] According to a release by Guy Carpenter (2009), high catastrophe losses in 2008 and the international credit crisis pushed property catastrophe rates up by 8 percent at the January 2009 reinsurances renewal period. Despite the slight decrease in price, reten-

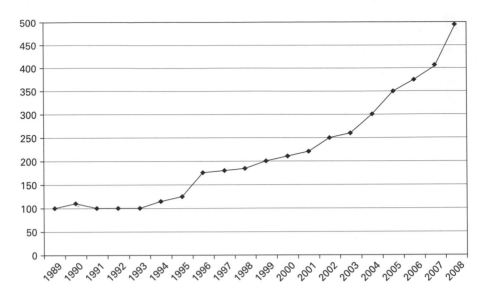

Figure 7.14
Average limit per program index in the United States, 1989–2008. *Note:* Index 100: 1989.

tions and limits on reinsurance programs continued to increase in 2007, but at a much slower pace than in the previous year. More specifically, after a 40 percent jump in 2006 (figure 7.6), retentions increased approximately 5.6 percent in 2007 (from roughly 540 to 570 on the 1989 index). Reinsurance programs on average are attaching at around the fifteen-year return period level. As depicted in figure 7.14, average reinsurance limits continued to increase in 2007 and 2008.[13]

Summary

This chapter focuses on the role of reinsurance in providing financial protection to insurers against catastrophic losses from natural disasters. We first develop models for characterizing reinsurers' decisions on what coverage to offer and how to price specific layers of protection. The pricing of a layer of reinsurance needs to cover the expected claims as well as marketing, brokerage, and claims processing expenses while at the same time ensuring that the coverage earns a high enough expected return on equity so that it is attractive to investors. The reinsurer is also concerned with the impact of the variance of its portfolio under soft and hard market environments, given the cost of capital.

The 2005 hurricane season created a hard market that had similar features to the post–Hurricane Andrew environment in 1992–1993. The data collected by Guy Carpenter, a large insurance and reinsurance broker, revealed significant increases in price in Florida (in the 50 to 100 percent range) as well as other parts of the United States in 2006, even though $26 billion to $27 billion of new capital entered the market. Between July 1, 2006, and January 2008, prices fell slightly but increased again at the January 2009 renewals; they remain considerably higher than in January 2005. Retentions and limits on reinsurance programs continued to increase in 2007 and 2008.

8 Innovative Insurance-Linked Securities for Financing Extreme Events

Key Findings

The significant increase in reinsurance prices after the 2005 hurricane season in the United States, along with more stringent criteria by rating agencies for providing protection against catastrophic risk, has led to a significant expansion of the insurance-linked securities (ILS) market. Securitization still represents a small proportion of the capital in the global insurance market today.

Benchmark: Credit and weather derivatives. There is an opportunity to make the ILS market more significant in comparison to other instruments created in the past ten years, such as global credit derivatives and global weather derivatives.

Looking forward: Financial innovations. Tranching (several distinct risks pooled together with the resulting portfolio divided into multiple layers with different expected returns) constitutes a natural way to expand the market by reaching investors other than the traditional hedge and cat funds. Standardized index-based derivatives, like catastrophe-related futures and options introduced in 2007 on the New York Mercantile Exchange and the Chicago Mercantile Exchange, present attractive features for investors as well. The concept of equity volatility dispersion using swaps (covering both underwriting and asset management volatility) may also be a way of providing protection against catastrophic risks, especially in the aftermath of the 2008 financial crisis.

8.1 The Emergence of Alternative Risk Transfer Instruments

As discussed in the previous chapter, there was a significant increase in reinsurance prices for catastrophic risks in the United States in the aftermath of the 2005 hurricane season.[1] In particular, the fact that the size of the retrocession market (reinsurance for reinsurers) was dramatically reduced caused greater uncertainty among reinsurers as to whether such coverage would be available to them in the long term.

These developments provided an impetus for the expansion of alternative risk transfer (ART) instruments that complement traditional insurance and reinsurance. The field of ART grew out of a series of insurance capacity crises in the 1970s through 1990s that led purchasers of traditional reinsurance coverage to seek more robust ways to buy protection. While ART instruments can comprise a wide range of alternative solutions (including the creation of captives or risk-retention groups), we focus on instruments that transfer part of the exposure to catastrophic losses to investors in the financial markets. Most of these risk-transfer techniques permit investors in the capital markets to play a more direct role in providing insurance and reinsurance protection. Investors see these products as a way of enhancing their returns by allocating funds to instruments that are not highly correlated with other financial risks (e.g., fluctuations in interest rates).

We are interested in the role that insurance-linked securities (ILS) can play in the securitization markets for catastrophes. How has the market for industry loss warranties and catastrophe bonds (cat bonds) evolved as a result of the unprecedented 2004 and 2005 hurricane seasons? What are some recent innovations in the ILS market? What has been the impact of the respite from major hurricanes in the United States in 2006 and 2007?

Since their inception more than a decade ago, insurance-linked securities have often been presented as a promising solution to address the capital needs of companies exposed to potential catastrophic risk. In a relative sense, the 2005–2007 period has been a clarion call for new investment opportunities,[2] and we have witnessed historic records in cat bond issuance and the development of a multibillion dollar market for other innovative instruments. In absolute terms, however, this market remains a tiny niche. Securitization represents only a small proportion of the capital in the global insurance market today.

The recent evolution of ART instruments is promising, though. Can the period 2005 to 2007 be considered a tipping point for this market? In other words, have we reached a critical mass in issuances to trigger enough interest from investors and potential risk hedgers (all types of companies, including—but not limited to—insurers and reinsurers)? If not, what are the necessary conditions so that the insurance-linked securities will become a much larger market on its own? This chapter suggests ways to address some of the limitations and also innovative approaches to expand this market.

8.2   Financial Capacity Provided by Insurance-Linked Securities: Past and Present

In this section we discuss three types of insurance-linked securities instruments provided by the capital markets: industry loss warranties, catastrophe bonds, and sidecars.[3] The first two are similar to excess-of-loss reinsurance, whereas sidecars are more often quota-share-like coverage and therefore similar to pro rata reinsurance. (See chapter 7.)

Industry Loss Warranties

The first ILWs were issued in the 1980s to cover airline industry losses and then developed in the property and casualty insurance industry in the aftermath of major natural disasters that have occurred since the early 1990s. As the name indicates, an industry loss warranty (ILW) (also known as original loss warranty) is a financial instrument designed to protect insurers and reinsurers from severe losses due to extreme events such as natural disasters. The ILW market today focuses almost exclusively on catastrophic risks and increased significantly after Hurricanes Katrina, Wilma and Rita.

ILWs operate as follows. The buyer who wants to hedge risk pays the seller a premium at the inception of the contract. In return, the buyer can make a claim in the event of a major industry loss. The payout of an ILW can be structured in a simplified way such that the buyer can make a claim equal to the limit (L) of the ILW if a predefined industry loss index (IL) exceeds a threshold known as the trigger (T) for a particular state or region, regardless of the buyer's actual amount of incurred loss:[4]

Claims $= L$ if $IL \geq T$

Claims $= 0$ if $IL < T$

For example, the buyer of a \$200 million limit U.S. wind ILW in New York in 2009 attached at \$20 billion will pay a premium to a protection writer (e.g., a hedge fund acting as a reinsurer) and in return will receive \$200 million if total losses to the insurance industry from a single U.S. hurricane in New York in 2009 exceed \$20 billion.

In this sense, ILWs are similar to excess-of-loss reinsurance, but where the insurer now has some basis risk: the covered loss of the insured's book of business does not necessarily correlate perfectly with the amount of claim collected from the index-based contracts.[5] Note that because an ILW is similar to a nonindemnity cat bond, it presents the same basis risk issues. To date, most ILW buyers have been large companies that see these instruments as another way to spread their exposure. For those that write a large portion of market share, the basis risk might be reduced as well because their losses are likely to be representative of the industry losses in the aftermath of a major natural disaster. ILWs are particularly attractive for single state insurers and reinsurers or companies with a higher concentration of business in a limited number of locations, thus enabling them to take on larger books of business in their primary area of operation.

Estimating industry losses after a disaster is thus critical. In the United States, the Insurance Services Office (ISO) is the organization that measures the total amount of industry insurance losses in the aftermath of a catastrophe to be used as the reference index. In Europe, however, there is no centralized structure that estimates industry losses. Recently there have been calls to create such a European organization in order to provide both hedgers and investors with more clarity, and then foster this market.

Table 8.1
Evolution of ILW premiums in April 2006 compared to pre-Katrina, 2005

ILW trigger	Florida wind	All U.S. natural perils	California earthquake
$5.0	54%	NA	43%
$10.0	83	85%	75
$12.5	87	105	76
$15.0	92	111	81
$20.0	132	133	100
$25.0	164	124	89
$30.0	176	130	49
$40.0	178	157	44
$50.0	113	160	42
Average	120	126	66

Source: Lane Financial (2006).

One of the main advantages of ILWs is that they have relatively low transaction costs for both buyers (insurers or reinsurers) and sellers (e.g., hedge funds). The sellers do not have to evaluate the expected loss to the (re)insured portfolio of a specific company from the trigger event, only the exceedance probability curve of the entire industry, which typically reduces the uncertainty, and hence, the cost associated with a higher level of volatility.

In spring 2006, Lane Financial published an analysis of the evolution of ILW premiums between 2005 (pre-Katrina) and April 1, 2006, for different trigger levels (from $5 billion up to $50 billion insurance industry losses) and different types of risk (wind in Florida, wind nationwide, earthquake in California). The study was based on information obtained from specialist dealers between 2001 and 2006. Although this information is not exhaustive, table 8.1 provides a reasonably accurate picture of the nature of those changes.[6]

As table 8.1 indicates, for a $5 billion trigger, estimated prices increased by 54 percent, and for a $50 billion trigger, by 113 percent due to a major hurricane in Florida, compared with prices prior to Hurricane Katrina. Despite this increase, the market grew significantly in the aftermath of Katrina, which indicates a strong appetite from insurers and reinsurers for access to other sources of capital than traditional reinsurance or retrocession. It is estimated that nearly $4 billion in ILWs were issued between September 2005 and September 2006.[7] The ILW volume in 2008 was about $5 billion. Because most of these transactions were done company-to-company, though, it is difficult to precisely know the aggregate volume and prices.

Catastrophe Bonds

Catastrophe bonds enable an insurer or reinsurer to access funds if a severe disaster produces large-scale damage, in a manner similar to ILWs. Cat bonds typically cover narrowly defined risks on an excess-of-loss basis. They are issued in the form of debt with high coupons.

To illustrate how cat bonds work, consider an insurer or reinsurer, SafeCompany, which would like to cover part of its exposure against catastrophic losses. In order to do so, it creates a new company, BigCat, whose only purpose is to cover SafeCompany. In that sense, BigCat is a single-purpose reinsurer (also called special-purpose vehicle, SPV). When the reinsurance contract is signed, the sponsor (SafeCompany) pays premiums to BigCat. On the other side, investors place their funds with the SPV BigCat; these funds constitute the initial principal for the bond to be issued by BigCat. Reinsurance premiums collected from SafeCompany will be used to provide the investors with a high enough interest rate to compensate for a possible loss should a disaster occur.

Suppose the losses from a disaster covered by the cat bond exceed a prespecified trigger. Then the interest on the bond or the principal, or both, is forgiven, depending on the specifications of the issued catastrophe bond. These funds are provided to SafeCompany to help cover its claims from the event. In addition to the interest rate on the cat bond, there are at least four other components for the investor to consider: the protection of the principal, the nature of the trigger, the size of the bond, and the maturity of the bond.

Protection of the Principal
The principal of a catastrophe bond often consists of different tranches, which might or might not be protected. A *protected tranche* guarantees that the investor will receive the principal from this tranche when the bond matures. For this tranche, if a covered event occurs, the SPV stops paying interest and can extend the maturity of the loan for several years. An *unprotected tranche* has both principal and interest at risk should a covered event occur.[8]

Trigger
The nature of the trigger varies from one bond to another. The trigger can be *indemnity based*, meaning that the transaction is based on the actual losses of the sponsor. This eliminates the basis risk for the sponsor, but also reduces the transparency of the transaction for the investors. The trigger can also be based on industry losses using a predetermined *industry index of losses* (e.g., the index is calculated by the property claim services in the United States). The trigger can also be determined by a *parametric index*, such as an earthquake of magnitude 7 or greater on the Richter scale occurring in the San Francisco Bay area or a Category 4 hurricane in Florida. A parametric index provides transparency for the investors, but sponsors may have significant basis risk (see the discussion above on basis risk for ILWs).

Size of the Bond
The size of the bonds issued has increased over time. For example, of the five bonds issued in 1997, only one had capitalization higher than $200 million; in 2000 there were two such

Table 8.2
Maturity of cat bonds issued between 1997 and 2007

Maturity	1 year	2 year	3 year	4 year	5 year	10 year
1997	2	1	1	0	0	1
1998	7	0	0	0	1	0
1999	5	0	3	0	2	0
2000	3	1	4	0	1	0
2001	2	1	3	1	0	0
2002	0	1	4	2	0	0
2003	0	1	3	1	2	0
2004	1	2	1	1	2	0
2005	1	2	7	0	1	0
2006	2	4	12	1	1	0
2007	4	5	12	3	5	0
Total (91)	27	18	50	9	15	1

Source: Authors' calculation, with data from Guy Carpenter.

bonds, and in 2005 there were four (out of a total of ten). Likewise, there were two bonds with capital lower than $50 million in 1997 (out of a total of five), but none of the seventy new bonds issued between 2003 and 2007 had capital lower than $50 million.[9] The transaction costs associated with the complex execution of these instruments (compared to traditional reinsurance) contributes to this trend toward larger bonds.

In 2007 State Farm issued a jumbo cat bond: a $1.2 billion risk capital bond, the largest cat bond ever issued. (The original attempt had been to issue a $4 billion bond, but it was scaled down to the $1.2 billion note and term loan.) The bond is innovative in that it is cumulative: the company covers its portfolio in the case of cumulative losses resulting from a series of predefined events (hurricanes in the United States, earthquakes in Japan, among others) over the three-year maturity of the bond.

Maturity of the Bond, or How to Stabilize Insurance and Reinsurance Prices

The maturity of a bond is the period during which the SPV will cover SafeCompany. One advantage of cat bonds over traditional one-year reinsurance contracts is that they can typically offer longer-term coverage—one to five years. Over time, the proportion of cat bonds with longer maturity has increased, an indication that these instruments are gaining trust within the reinsurance and finance community. Table 8.2 specifies the maturity of cat bonds issued between 1997 and 2007. The average maturity is about three years, with some cat bonds having only a one-year maturity and others having five years or more.

In the context of highly volatile reinsurance prices that often occur after large catastrophes, cat bonds offer an important element of stability for insurers by guaranteeing a predefined price over several years, assuming that the entire capital of the bond is not triggered (in which case a new bond has to be issued under price conditions that are likely to differ).

With many firms complaining about price increases for coverage against catastrophes in the aftermath of the 2005 hurricane season, and with pressure from rating agencies for more stringent catastrophe exposure management, the price stability offered by cat bonds with multiyear maturity might be important for insurance companies and other issuers as well. We believe that this stability has been largely undervalued so far.

Bonds do not have to cover only natural disasters. They are often issued to protect a commercial enterprise against other risks. For example, the first bond that insured against terrorism was issued in Europe in August 2003. The world governing organization of soccer, FIFA, which organized the 2006 World Cup in Germany, developed a $262 million bond to protect its investment. Under very specific conditions, the catastrophe bond covered losses resulting from both natural and terrorist extreme events that would have resulted in the cancellation of the World Cup final game without the possibility of re-scheduling to 2007.[10] Moreover, the government of Mexico, which through its FONDEN facility sponsored the $160 million CAT-Mex transaction in May 2006, was the first government to issue a cat bond.[11]

The sponsor of a cat bond also does not have to be an insurer. For instance, in 2002, Vivendi Universal (Universal Studios) issued a $175 million bond, Studio Re, to cover its production studios against an earthquake in southern California. The Walt Disney Company issued a bond to cover its large theme park in Japan. The first European corporate bond was issued in 2003 by EDF, the French electrical company; this $230 million bond, Pylon, covered the company against windstorms in France. In 2006, another corporate sponsor went with coverage by cat bond: Dominion Resources, an energy producer, obtained protection for oil-drilling assets located off the coasts of Louisiana and Texas by issuing a $50 million bond, Drewcat.

Increasingly, cat bonds cover against multiple events. In fact, in 2005, 2006, and 2007, over half of the capital at risk through cat bonds was for multi-event bonds rather than single-event bonds. In terms of capital outstanding, U.S. earthquakes and hurricanes represented the largest volume of cat bond at risk in both 2006 and 2007, followed by storm exposure in Europe, then typhoons and earthquakes in Japan. Whether more companies, trade associations, and state and federal governments, working in collaboration with experts in the field, will diversify their coverage through ILS will be a key factor in developing these instruments.

The maturity of cat bonds leads to an important distinction between issued bonds and outstanding bonds. Consider the following example. If a $200 million bond is issued on January 1, 2007, for one year, then the 2007 risk capital issuance is $200 million and the capital outstanding is also $200 million. Imagine now that this bond is issued for five years: the maturity of the bond is thus December 31, 2011. For 2007, the capital issued is $200 million, but for the next four years, the capital issued is $0. As the bond is

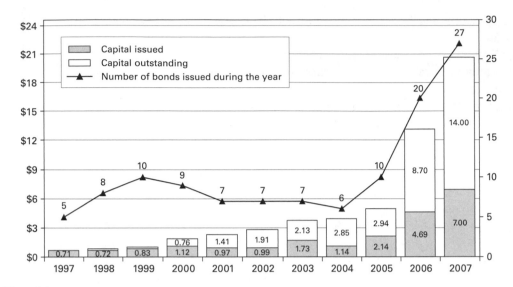

Figure 8.1
Natural catastrophe bonds: Capital risk issued and outstanding, 1997–2007 (billions of dollars).
Sources: Data from Swiss Re Capital Markets, Goldman Sachs, and Guy Carpenter.

outstanding for five years—each year between 2007 and 2011—the amount of capital outstanding is $200 million (if the bond has not been triggered in the meantime). In other words, issuance tells us about new deals, while outstanding capital tells us about present and past issuances.

Cat bonds have been on the market since 1997, which enables some comparisons as to the evolution of issuances and capital outstanding. At the end of 2004, there was nearly $4 billion in cat bond principal outstanding (including $1.14 billion of new issuances that year). At the end of 2005, outstanding risk capital grew to nearly $5 billion, with nearly $2.1 billion issued that year.

Figure 8.1 illustrates the evolution of risk capital issued and outstanding and the number of bonds issued between 1997 and December 2007.[12] The market recorded total issuance of over $4.7 billion in 2006 (twenty new issuances, twice as many as in 2005), a 125 percent increase over the $2.1 billion in 2005. This was a new record high, and a 75 percent increase over the $1.14 billion issued in 2004, and a 20 percent increase over the $1.73 billion issuance in 2003 (the previous record). The risk capital issued during 2005 and 2006 was equal to the total issued during the preceding five years. Bonds outstanding increased significantly as well, which reflects the issuance of multiyear bonds in previous years.

At the end of 2006, outstanding risk capital continued to grow significantly, to $8.7 billion, with nearly $4.7 billion of that being issued. In 2007, twenty-seven new catastrophe bonds were issued for a total of $7 billion in capital and $14 billion was outstanding. The

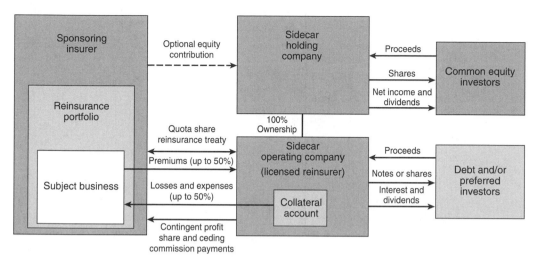

Figure 8.2
Operation of a sidecar. *Source:* Goldman Sachs.

2008 financial crisis had an impact on this market in the sense that no new cat bonds were issued between September and December 2008. Total cat bond volume for 2008 was $27 billion.

Sidecars

A phenomenon of the post–Hurricane Katrina market environment has been the development of so-called *sidecars*. A sidecar is a special-purpose company that provides reinsurance coverage exclusively to its sponsor (a reinsurer or a large insurer) by issuing securities to investors. The company that offers the sidecar has to be licensed as a reinsurer. Unlike ILWs or cat bonds, which generally provide excess-of-loss reinsurance, sidecars are often based on quota-share reinsurance. The sidecar company shares the risks of certain insurance or reinsurance policies with the underwriter in exchange for a portion of the premiums (generally up to 50 percent) and dividends in shares. Figure 8.2 shows a simplified diagram to illustrate the stakeholders involved in a sidecar.

Like cat bonds, sidecars are complex financial transactions. They typically require a larger investment than cat bonds (in the $200–$300 million range, although several sidecars have investments lower than $100 million). A sidecar company is designed to operate two years or less and then self-liquidate or renew, depending on market conditions, whereas cat bonds have been issued for five years for even longer. Another difference is that cat bonds are typically designed to hedge low-probability, high-impact events, whereas sidecars allow investors to take a slice of the whole business of a reinsurance program.

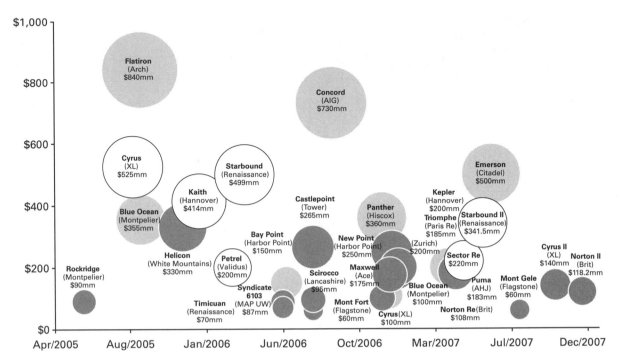

Figure 8.3
Reinsurer sidecars: Reaction to 2005 hurricane season, April 2005–December 2007. *Source:* Goldman Sachs.

Figure 8.3, compiled by Goldman Sachs, gives the name, capital, and sponsor of some of the sidecar companies that were created between April 2005 and December 2007. In 2005, the total volume was $2.2 billion, in 2006 it was $4.2 billion, and in 2007 it was $1.7 billion and in 2008 it was $700 million.[13]

While all the sidecars that were created in the aftermath of the 2005 hurricane season were sponsored by reinsurance companies, in August 2006, Lexington Insurance Company, a member of AIG, set up its own sidecar, Concord Re, to reinsure business on a quota-share basis. This was the first sidecar structured for a primary insurance company. Concord Re is capitalized with $730 million from equity securities issued by Concord Re's parent holding company, Concord Re Holdings.

To sum up, the 2005 hurricane season has led insurers and reinsurers, along with some other issuers, to use alternative risk transfer instruments at an unprecedented level, and the trend has continued. One important element to note here is that Hurricane Katrina swamped Kamp Re, a $190 million catastrophe bond arranged by Swiss Re for Zurich. It was the first cat bond to completely call in investor funds.[14] The 2005 hurricane season also wiped out a $650 million sidecar, Olympus Re.[15] These events might actually have had a favorable impact on the market. First, these losses did not stop investments in those new instruments in 2006. Investors that bet against the odds of devastating Atlantic hurricane seasons in 2006 and 2007 profited, as, contrary to expert predictions, both seasons turned out to be the mildest in years. Second, these were the first ILS to pay something back to their sponsors, which might make these instruments more "real" from a financial protection perspective.

We see the potential to increase this market more broadly. Over the past ten years, ILS market activities have been triggered primarily by the occurrence of major catastrophes, followed by significant increases in reinsurance prices, creating the need to gain access to less expensive financial protection. Although the data point to an increase in these extremely costly disasters in the coming years, it is unlikely that this will be sufficient to generate alone a large, liquid, and sustainable ILS market.

8.3   Benchmark: The Market for Credit and Weather Derivatives

Credit Derivatives

In order to think creatively as to how to enhance the ILS markets for extreme events, it is worth making a comparison with the development of other financial products over the past ten years. We now turn to two of them: credit derivatives and weather derivatives.

Credit derivatives are one of the most successful capital market developments despite being seriously compromised by the subprime crisis in 2007. With $20 trillion of outstanding credit derivatives in 2006 (figure 8.4), this market allows investors to trade the risk of

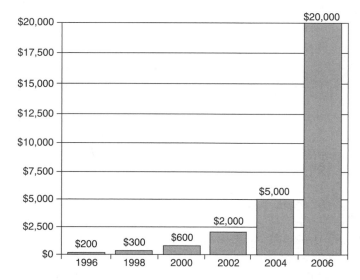

Figure 8.4
Global credit derivatives market, 1996–2006 (billions of dollars).

default on a certain security (in general, a debt or a loan) independent of the other risks they face. To put this figure into perspective, the credit derivatives market was "only" $40 billion of outstanding notional value in 1996, and $180 billion in 1997, according to the British Bankers Association.[16]

Credit derivatives can be structured in multiple ways, but the two dominant types of products are the credit default swap (CDS) and the collateralized debt obligation (CDO). The CDS is a contract that transfers, for a premium, the risk of default on a type of debt underlying and pays off if a registered case of default occurs. The cases of defaults have been progressively standardized, thanks to the work of the International Swaps and Derivatives Association. The CDO is a new type of security (or securities; there are many tranches for a single issue) that constitutes a pool of debt instruments securitized into one financial instrument. The pool typically consists of hundreds of individual debt instruments. CDOs are issued in several tranches that divide the pool of debt into bond with varying degrees of exposure to credit risk. One can buy different tranches so as to gain exposure to different levels of loss. While securitization has been criticized during the 2008 financial crisis, we believe it remains a useful risk transfer vehicle.

The comparison between credit derivatives and ILS is relevant, as both share common features, such as relative illiquidity of underlying risks and a high loss potential.

Weather Derivatives

The first weather derivative contract was developed in 1996, about the same time that the first cat bonds were created.[17] The weather derivatives market increased in 1997. As the market for these products grew, the Chicago Mercantile Exchange (CME) introduced the first exchange-traded weather futures contracts (and corresponding options) in 1999.

Recent years have seen a significant increase in this market. According to a survey released in June 2006 jointly by the Weather Risk Management Association (WRMA) and PricewaterhouseCoopers, the total weather derivatives market had grown more than tenfold over where it stood two years before (figure 8.5).

The WRMA's 2007 industry survey shows that the total number of contracts traded worldwide—both over-the-counter and on the CME—was 730,087 for the period April 2006 through March 2007. This reflects a decline from 2006's total of just over 1 million contracts, but is substantially higher than in earlier years. Likewise, the value of contracts traded between April 2006 and March 2007 was $19.2 billion, substantially higher than in other years (if one sees 2005–2006 as an exception due to very peculiar market conditions following the 2005 hurricane season in the United States that significantly increased the demand for these instruments): in 2004 and 2005, the total value of contracts was $4.6 billion and $8.4 billion, respectively.[18]

Temperature-related contracts on both CME futures and the over-the-counter (OTC) market accounted for the vast majority of deals, with a notional value of $18.9 billion. Notional values for rain- and wind-linked contracts were steady at $142 million and $36

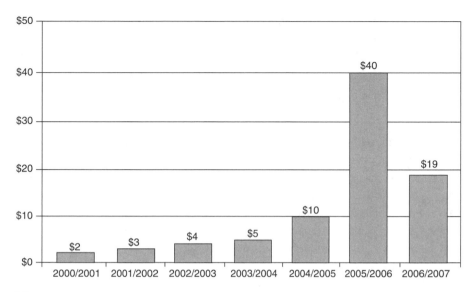

Figure 8.5
Global weather derivatives market, 2000–2006 (billions of dollars).

million only, respectively. To date, most of the activity in weather derivatives has occurred in U.S. markets. This might change, however, with the launching by Euronext of a joint venture with Meteo France in 2007 to develop a customized weather index to help corporations understand and design weather hedges.

8.4 Enhancing Capital Market Solutions: The Need to Address Stakeholders' Concerns

Capital market solutions, despite the recent movements, remain marginal in the global risk transfer market. But this picture can be misleading. Here we discuss some factors that have impeded more significant growth. If they are addressed, ILS is likely to play a more important role in covering the financial consequences of weather-related events and other extreme disasters.[19]

Issuers' Concerns

Issuers typically turn to ILWs because they are increasingly aware of their catastrophe exposure due to recent disasters, the resulting increased pressure from rating agencies to better manage their exposure, and regulatory changes.

Until recently, the regulatory pressure was mostly visible in the United States, but the situation is changing in Europe as well. With the new series of regulations under Solvency II, the landscape is evolving into more regulatory pressure. For example, under Solvency II, insurance companies will now be obligated to sustain a 1 in 200-year event. Interestingly, as the Committee of European Insurance and Occupational Pensions Supervisors's aim is to align solvency capital to risk-based economic capital, capital relief will be obtainable through risk transfer instruments, either reinsurance or securitization.[20] It is foreseeable that reinsurance programs and allocation of capital to Property and Casualty (P&C) lines of business will be affected by Solvency II, as it has been by changes in the capital adequacy models of rating agencies. These elements should have a positive effect on the insurance-linked security market.

One concern of potential issuers relates to the design of the ILS. The definition of the trigger is central, because it determines both the profile of risk transfer to capital markets and the impact on target return on investment for the issuer (e.g., how solvency margin, economic capital, or rating capital is affected, along with the distribution of expected profit and loss). Issuers typically favor indemnity triggers because they reduce the basis risk for the company (compared to parametric or index-based solutions). On the other hand, investors favor these latter solutions because they typically rely on a well-defined index provided by a third party (e.g., modeling firms) to measure the trigger.

Not surprisingly, the pricing of ILS remains a challenge. On one hand, ILS have often been noncompetitive with traditional providers of reinsurance from a single rate on line perspective, except for very specific risks like higher tranches of retrocession or peak exposures in risk-prone areas such as Florida.[21] They typically remain highly structured and customized products. On the other hand, ILS present important attractive features, even though they might be harder to quantify and price. As collateralized (largely or fully) and multiyear programs, ILS address the issue of credit risk and price volatility. They also allow issuers to draw from an alternative source of capital and leverage their bargaining power with traditional risk financing providers (insurance and reinsurance). These advantages have to be integrated into the price of these instruments.

Investors' Concerns

What is the demand for insurance-linked securities? Over the past few years, the investor base has not only surged in volume but has also changed its structure. Once viewed as an alternative source of financial protection for reinsurance and insurance companies familiar with the risks and eager to diversify their exposure, ILS have now become another family of investment products for alternative investors such as hedge funds, dedicated cat funds, and private equity funds. In 1999 these three categories of investors represented 40 percent of the new issue volume of cat bonds; in 2006 they represented over 90 percent.[22] These investors are highly specialized and sophisticated and are drawn by the features of the ILS (high Sharpe ratio and low correlation with traditional capital market assets).[23] Mutual funds and money managers are also becoming more active in the market, eager to benefit from the high-yielding instruments in the context of flat interest rates and historically low yield on government and corporate bonds.

In order to whet investors' appetite, several issues need to be addressed. First, it is important to make the risk/reward profile more explicit—a key element for investors who are faced with equity, bonds, credit, commodities, and other alternative investment opportunities. In this environment, insurance risks are appealing, but the further development of these products depends on the capacity to develop more standard quantitative models, the confidence of investors in these products, and the reliability of catastrophe models.

Second, the new investors in this market are yield sensitive (hedge funds and cat funds have minimum threshold for their investments, and leverage is often necessary to reach adequate rates of returns). As a result, investors until recently were interested only in high-yielding tranches, which translated into bonds attaching around 1 to 2 percent of annualized probability of first loss. These levels of attachment made the ILS unsuited for traditional investors, concerned about a loss in their principal. In parallel, the high level of due diligence that is required limited the penetration of these products among money managers. Recently, ILS were issued with a broader range of yielding tranches.

Moreover, while rating agencies did not usually rate investment-grade cat bond tranches for single-event triggers, Standard and Poor's decided in early 2007 to rate single-event cat bonds up to BBB+ if the first loss is sufficiently remote (below 20 basis points). For investors compelled to hold only investment-grade paper, this constitutes a critical move. As the products become more standardized and the range of issuers and programs increases, traditional investors will have more flexibility. For example, Pioneer, the asset manager, launched a fixed-income fund in July 2007 in which significant amounts of cat bonds were added to enhance yield.[24]

An additional point under scrutiny by investors was the liquidity of the investment. (Re)insurance risks can be underwritten under multiple wrappers, from retrocession contracts to ILWs, from cat bonds and cat swaps to shares of sidecars. Some hedge funds and private equity funds, given their expertise in illiquid and buy-and-hold strategies, would be keen on taking stakes in sidecars, high yielding but totally illiquid before dissolution of the sidecar. At the other end, mutual funds and cat funds focus on cat bonds that can be traded in the secondary market.

8.5   Looking Ahead: Solutions and Innovations for Reaching the Tipping Point in this Alternative Market

The ILS market is still developing and undoubtedly will be quite different five years from now. We conclude this chapter by providing four axes of development that will help structure the market in the near future.

Increasing Investors' Interest in Insurance-Linked Products through Tranching

To develop further, the ILS market must draw more investors beyond hedge funds and private equity firms. The increasing popularity of securitization among issuers will help increase the range of risks available in the market, but other solutions have to be found as well. Tranching is likely to help: several distinct risks are pooled together, and the resulting portfolio is divided into multiple layers with different expected returns. The tranching technology allows structuring firms to transform low-rated bonds into investment-grade securities by concentrating the risks in lower-quality tranches stemming from subordination and overcollateralization. These higher-risk tranches, called junior or equity, are usually bought by alternative investors attracted by the potential profit they would receive if no triggering event occurs. Some groundbreaking deals have reached the market, with notable transactions by ABN Amro and Guy Carpenter (Bay Haven Re in 2006 and Fremantle Re in June 2007).

So far, investors have been able to assume the risks they were offered when issuers went to the market. In the future, investors could approach insurers and define the risks they are seeking; structuring firms or risk transfer hubs would emerge to find these risks or create them through tranching.

Addressing the Basis Risk Challenge through Index-Based Derivatives

Because parametric insurance-linked securities will always retain basis risk, solutions to address this concern will be found in other corners. Standardized products such as Deutsche Bank–sponsored event loss swaps and index-based derivatives present attractive features for investors. The first attempt more than ten years ago to launch index-based products failed to attract attention and liquidity (cat index on the Chicago Board of Trade in 1995). Capital markets have dramatically evolved since then, and the investor base is deeper today. Recently the New York Mercantile Exchange and the Chicago Mercantile Exchange added natural catastrophe-related futures and options for trading.[25] Derivatives will be written on these indexes, and in years to come will further illustrate the attractiveness of insurance risks to capital market investors.

Innovating through the Development of New Products

Until 2005, the range of ILS was limited to a few products, among them cat bonds and ILWs. In 2005 and 2006, sidecars were developed. Other innovations will be developed to better tailor issuers' needs and investors' appetites, and also help lower the price of financial protection. A second generation of contingent capital products and "just-in-time capital" was developed recently and has been successfully marketed. For example, Goldman Sachs launched for XL the Stoneheath sidecar in November 2006, which also embeds contingent issues of capital in case of predefined events. Other solutions of convertible securities are being discussed but have not publicly emerged yet.

Derivative Solutions Based on Equity Volatility Dispersion

Alternative solutions will expand beyond the debt or equity forms, and even beyond the tradable securities form. Today the capital market offers a wide range of tools and products, especially in the derivative universe.

There is one innovation that we believe could lead to major value creation: developing investment strategies based on equity volatility dispersion will provide another promising solution. The idea is to reduce the volatility of a given portfolio by buying a product that pays off if the volatility of a given industry portfolio fluctuates more than the one of a given index (e.g., S&P 500) over a predefined period of time. By *equity volatility dispersion*, we mean the difference between the volatility of that portfolio (or basket) minus the volatility of the underlying index (e.g., S&P 500 or other predefined indices). Companies typically want to reduce their volatility, and there should be a market to cover excess volatility. While not specific to insurance, equity volatility dispersion would help in the face of catastrophic risks.

Insurance companies that conducted an in-depth analysis of their peak risk exposure (natural hazards, pandemics, megaterrorism risks) realized that the probability of these peak risks is often difficult to quantify with certainty.[26] Such large-scale events affect both underwriting results (huge claims) and equity investments (stock prices of insurance companies typically go down in the days following a major catastrophe and then go up again to reflect expected future gains from increased premiums). When structured adequately and based on a portfolio of stocks potentially highly affected by such extreme events (e.g., a portfolio representing the insurance and reinsurance companies operating in the United States), the derivative solutions have proven highly efficient by providing broad financial protection.

How does it work? The company buys a special product (e.g., a swap) that pays off if the volatility of the insurance industry portfolio is more than X points higher than the volatility of a given index. For instance, company A will receive $10 million for each point difference between the volatility of its portfolio and the volatility of the index; if at the maturity of the product (say, one year), the realized dispersion (difference between the two volatilities) is 5, then the company will receive $50 million. Having an industry portfolio (instead of the portfolio of a specific company) gives investors the advantage of higher transparency, but sponsors may have significant basis risk.

Figure 8.6a illustrates in a simplified way the payoff of such a strategy, designed to hedge a pandemic outbreak. In the case of a pandemic event or financial crash, the investment tested here would overperform, allowing the investors to recover their claim or asset losses with financial gains on the instrument. Indeed, we see in figure 8.6a that the volatility of the basket (highest curve) is much higher than the volatility of the index (middle curve). The dispersion curve (lowest curve) is the difference between the two. Figure 8.6b focuses on the volatility dispersion curve and depicts some major events between November 23, 1990, and April 28, 2007. We can see that dispersion would have remained relatively stable until the terrorist events of September 11, 2001, but would have increased significantly and steadily after 9/11, and continued to climb due to the uncertainty about the war in Iraq.

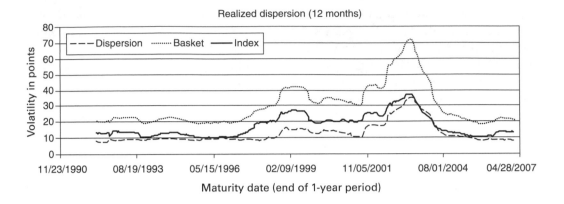

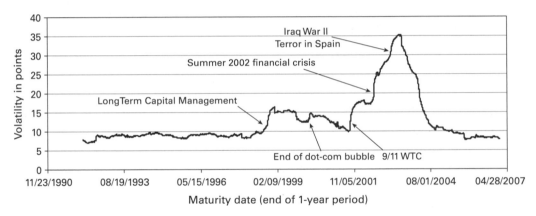

Figure 8.6
(*a*) Volatility of the basket and index, and dispersion between the two. (*b*) Dispersion solution graph based on impact of major events. *Note:* Simulated payoff ranging from less than 10 points to more than 30 points. Each point gets a payoff of several million dollars.

Fortunately, no pandemic event occurred during the studied period, but the payoff of the strategy illustrates that both insurance events and financial market events are covered thanks to the instrument. This last example of a capital market solution clearly illustrates the emergence of a new approach in the risk transfer industry that goes beyond the pure traditional underwriting management or pure asset management approach.[27] Innovative and simple ways are thus possible for leveraging new asset classes based on second-order risks, such as equity volatility dispersion. The potential of this new approach in hedging catastrophic risks remains mostly unexploited yet.

While securitization represents a small proportion of capital in the global insurance markets worldwide, the past three years have seen a significant increase in ILS use and the development of several new innovative products. Over $25 billion of outstanding capital was in place in 2007 for property and casualty coverage (including cat bonds, sidecars, and ILWs). Given the annual rate of growth we have witnessed in recent years despite the 2008 slow-down, we believe that in the next five years, outstanding capital could be as high as $50–$75 billion.

Summary

During the past ten years, new financial instruments in the form of insurance-linked securities have been developed to complement catastrophe risk coverage provided by traditional reinsurance. This chapter discusses the principal ILS products (industry loss warranties, catastrophe bonds, and sidecars) and tracks their development over time and the main drivers of the upward shift in the ILS market after the 2004 and 2005 hurricane seasons. We provide information on the evolution of this market for 2006, 2007, and 2008.

Notwithstanding this very encouraging development, it is still surprising that despite the tremendous capacity offered by financial markets today, the ILS market has not expanded to a larger extent. Securitization represents just a small proportion of capital in the global insurance markets worldwide.

We propose three complementary ways to increase interest in these instruments that could effectively trigger a much more significant volume of U.S. capital entering the ILS market: (1) increasing investors' interest through tranching, (2) addressing the basis risk challenge through index-based derivatives, and (3) developing new products such as investment strategies based on equity volatility dispersion.

9 A Framework for Linking Supply and Demand of Disaster Insurance

Key Findings

The supply of catastrophe insurance is determined primarily by the capacity of insurers and reinsurers, coupled with the availability of insurance-linked securities.

The price of catastrophe insurance is usually high relative to expected claims because of the large variance in losses that can be costly due to the insurer's need to allocate extra capital to provide protection against this risk.

The cycle in insurance prices is triggered by losses following major disasters due to the reduction in capacity. New inflow of capital normally expands capacity in a relatively short period of time.

One way to ration insurance capacity is to force policyholders to take higher deductibles so that the insurers can provide more coverage. Policyholders should then be more inclined to adopt protective measures because they have a higher stake in the potential loss.

In order to evaluate the effectiveness of current and alternative disaster insurance programs, one needs to understand not only the demand for protection by homeowners and the supply of coverage, but also how the two interact to create a specific market equilibrium. This chapter complements analyses provided in previous chapters and develops a framework at a conceptual level for understanding the interaction of supply and demand prior to a natural disaster as well as after a catastrophe occurs.

Our intention is to learn whether the insurance market is functioning effectively, given the play of market forces as shaped by existing regulations. To do this, we need some normative benchmarks to see whether the market provides an appropriate balance between the needs of consumers for adequate coverage and the needs of investors that provide this protection to secure an appropriate return on their investment. We separately look at the conditions governing the intersection of insurance demand and supply and ask whether the market clears at an acceptable price.

9.1 The Supply Side

Investors will supply capital to insurers if they believe they can realize an expected rate of return that more than compensates them for their risk. In turn, the insurer will allocate capital to underwrite catastrophic risk if the addition of that business improves (or at least maintains) the risk-return properties of its existing portfolio. Another way of expressing this is that the additional capital needed to underwrite catastrophe risk must bring a return that at least compensates the insurer or reinsurer for the additional costs of risk bearing that are imposed by the additional business.

Insurance supply is affected by the possibility of catastrophic losses due to the high correlation of risks within any confined region, thus imposing considerable tail risk. To deal with this problem in regions where there is the likelihood of catastrophic risk, insurers writing policies will need to be highly capitalized to deal with these potentially large losses. This implies that the cost of capital is a very important factor in determining insurance supply, as discussed previously. Alternatively, the insurer can economize on capital by reinsuring (or otherwise hedging) its catastrophe exposure through insurance-linked securities. In this case, the supply of insurance is largely conditioned by the price and availability of reinsurance and other alternative risk transfer instruments.

Insurance lore propounds that the insurance market is cyclical, with hard markets (capacity is scarce and prices are high) alternating with soft markets (capacity is abundant and prices are accordingly low). There is considerable research on the insurance cycle, and it is clear that markets are indeed sometimes hard and sometimes soft. However, the notion of a cycle implies there is some regularity and predictability in the turning of the market, and it is this regularity that is questionable.

The mainstream theory of the cycle is known as the Gron-Winter *capacity constraint model*.[1] The short-run insurance supply of each firm, and therefore of the market, is determined by the level of required capital. Short-run insurance supply is price elastic up to the point at which regulators, rating agencies, and customers consider existing capital to be inadequate given the additional liabilities. This is known as the *capital constraint model*. To induce investors to provide more capital requires higher premiums. Moreover, supplying additional capital takes time, as insurers, like most other firms, prefer to accumulate capital internally rather than going to the capital market for new equity.[2] This supply function is shown in figure 9.1, along with an insurance demand function. The short-run equilibrium is shown as price, P^*, and quantity, Q^*, which is met within the internal capital supplied by the industry. The capacity constraint is shown as Q^C.

The dynamics of the model are thrown into play when the industry suffers a capital shock, caused by either a sudden loss, such as Hurricane Katrina, Hurricane Ike, or the

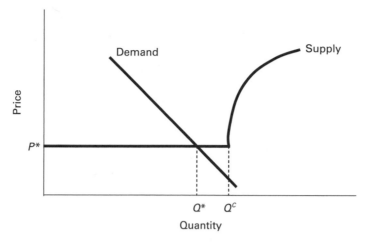

Figure 9.1
Demand with capital constrained supply function

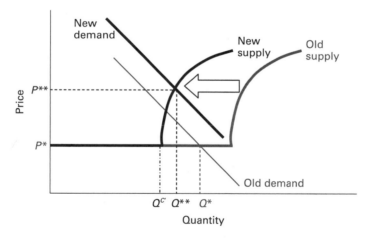

Figure 9.2
Gron-Winter capital constraint model

terrorist attacks of September 11, 2001, or by an asset loss, such as what happened at the end of the bull market in 2000. This loss of capital shifts the insurance supply function upward, as shown in figure 9.2. Depending on the circumstances of the loss, the demand function also might shift to the right. For example, after major disasters, more people purchase insurance to make sure they are protected should such an event happen again.

The new equilibrium price and quantity are shown as P^{**} and Q^{**} in this diagram. Notice several things. The equilibrium price has increased considerably, thus illustrating the post-loss hard markets that are typically experienced after such capital shocks. Figure 9.2

also shows that the new output, Q^{**}, exceeds the new capital constraint $Q^{C'}$, so supply can be generated only with a very large price increase to compensate the insurer for its deterioration in credit quality. Such pressure on credit quality was felt, for example, by all reinsurers in the early 2000s following the combination of the burst of the asset bubble (which affected mostly European insurers, who tended to be more heavily invested in stocks) and the cost of insured losses due to the September 11, 2001, terrorist attacks. Thus, the post-loss hard market interestingly combines higher prices and pressure on credit quality.

The hard market typically does not last. Since internal capital is cheaper than external capital, insurers prefer to replenish gradually through retained earnings because of the hard market. However, if the price increase is sufficient to overcome the additional costs of external capital, then new capital may indeed flow in. For example, as discussed in chapter 7, while Hurricane Katrina alone accounted for over $46 billion in insured losses, the new capital flow to the industry in the ten months that followed the catastrophe was estimated to be between $26 and $27 billion.[3]

The combination of retained earnings and new capital will begin to push the supply function outward again, as shown in figure 9.3. Eventually a new equilibrium is established with the market clearing at an output level within the limits of the replenished capital.

The capacity constraint model shows that the cycle of hard and soft markets (triggered by capital shocks) is a normal market mechanism for allocating scarce and varying capital. It does lead to the uncomfortable result that price and availability of insurance are adversely affected by catastrophic losses: the markets will clear, though at a higher price. The market will self-correct in time with the inflow of new capital. Under this model, insurance is not rationed.

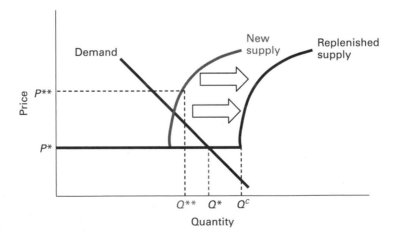

Figure 9.3
Long-run equilibrium with capital replenishment

Further empirical evidence suggests that the disruption can be more severe. Prices usually rise after major losses, and this alone (absent other effects such as an increase in the demand function) would tend to depress insurance purchases. However, insurers sometimes wish to ration coverage even at the higher prices. There may be several reasons for this. One is that insurers need to keep the geographic diversity of their portfolios in balance. If a disaster in one region leads to a reestimate of risk, which shows an increase in local probability or severity, then insurers may need to reduce local capacity. This will be necessary to rebalance their spread of risk and thereby preserve their credit status. However, there is a compounding reason that coverage might be rationed after a loss. Insurers will be more willing to allocate capacity to states if they retain the flexibility to withdraw that capacity after a loss when their capital is highly depleted.[4] This model, for which there is empirical support, suggests that any attempt by regulators to retain capacity in a post-loss situation is likely to impede the future flow of capital into that state.

9.2   The Demand Side and Role of Deductibles

The demand for insurance stems from many factors, including financial concerns and a latent aversion to risk, hence the desire to transfer risk to another party that can absorb that risk more effectively. The demand is also influenced by the consumer's knowledge and perception of the risk. In an ideal rational world where consumers were fully informed of the risk they face and maximized their expected utility, the risk was perfectly known, and there were insurers that could bear that risk with no transaction costs, consumers would buy full insurance.

Consumers would avoid all the costly risk they would otherwise face, without imposing any real cost on insurers, which could easily diversify that risk. In reality, consumers may be ill informed of their risk exposure—even insurers cannot model this risk with great accuracy—and the risk itself is not easily diversifiable, thereby requiring insurers to hold considerable costly capital to support the underwriting of catastrophe risk.

Just as it would be nice to offer all people unlimited and free medical care and education, it would be nice to make available unlimited free risk transfer, that is, where the premium simply equals expected claim cost and no reward is given to the insurer for transferring risk. But of course, there is an opportunity cost, and the best we can do is to allocate coverage (and health care and education) in a manner that balances the costs and benefits. In effect, this means that full coverage is not ideal. Rather, it is reasonable for policyholders to carry a deductible on their policy.

Paying for small losses does not usually stress people's budgets or increase their risk very much (since small losses are affordable and fairly frequent). Furthermore, deductibles can result in significant premium savings, by preventing the transaction costs of handling small claims (which would have to be built into the premium). Deductibles also put some of the

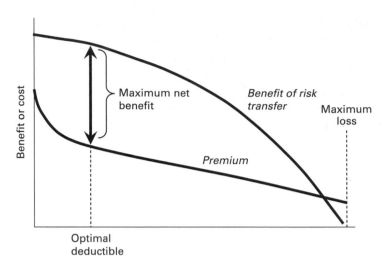

Figure 9.4
Optimal deductible when insurance has transaction costs

policyholder's "skin in the game," thus providing an incentive for loss mitigation and alleviating potential moral hazard problems. This reinforces the social objective of reducing overall exposure to catastrophes.

The benefit of insurance to the policyholder is more than the value of the expected losses transferred to the insurer; the benefit includes the removal of the uncertainty or risk surrounding the expected loss. In figure 9.4, we show the benefit declines as the level of the deductible increases. With small deductibles, there is little decline, because the small losses are frequent and predictable and bearing such losses imposes little uncertainty on the policyholder. Increasing the deductible significantly reduces the benefit, because the policyholder now has a large stake in the low-frequency, high-consequence losses. In contrast, the premium may fall quite dramatically because the insurer avoids the transactional expenses of handling frequent small claims. A further reduction in premiums can arise because the policyholder now has a stake in the loss and will be more inclined to invest in protective measures such as installing storm shutters to reduce hurricane losses. The optimal deductible maximizes the difference between expected benefits and costs, as illustrated in figure 9.4.

9.3 Market Clearing Prices and Quantities at the Equilibrium

As with other markets, the interaction of supply and demand should result in a price that will clear the market. The considerations already explored suggest that the clearing price for catastrophe insurance might be high relative to the expected losses. This does not re-

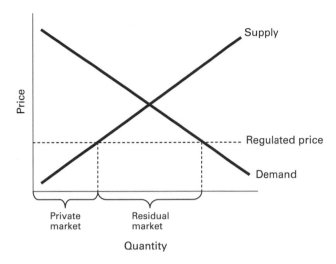

Figure 9.5
Suppressing the market clearing price with a residual market

flect excess profits by insurers, but simply the high cost of capital associated with providing protection against possible catastrophic losses.

Impact of Regulation

One way in which regulators can affect insurance supply is through pricing restrictions. Insofar as regulators are able to hold prices below their normal market clearing level, there will be excess demand (supply shortage) for insurance. The normal mechanism that regulators adopt to address this excess demand is to establish a residual market mechanism (see the discussion of Florida's Citizens in chapter 2). This can lead to a higher volume of insurance transacted at a lower price than for an unregulated market, as depicted in figure 9.5.

Undiversifiable Catastrophe Risk and Policy Design

As we have shown, basic economic theory holds that when insurance encounters transaction costs (so that the competitive premium exceeds the expected loss), it is desirable for a policyholder to retain some risk in the form of a deductible. In other words, individuals should share in their own risk, absorbing the smaller losses, which they can usually afford to pay, and thereby saving on expensive insurance premiums. We now make additional supply-side arguments as to why it is desirable for policyholders to share in their own losses.

It is the nature of catastrophes that risk is highly correlated among sections of the population. The same hurricane hits many property owners in the same coastal region, and the same earthquake damages houses of many thousands of people in that locale.

The implication is that the insurer cannot diversify the risk by simply holding more policies in its portfolio. Certainly insurers can and do reinsure, and reinsurance companies will hold geographically diversified portfolios. This helps spread the catastrophe risk widely through the market, but the diversification is not complete. Thus, insurers can, and do, have sudden spikes in their profitability and sudden hits to their capital when large catastrophes occur.

For this reason, catastrophe insurance is not like automobile or life insurance, where pooling in the insurance market, in effect, makes the risk disappear.[5] No matter how far catastrophe insurance risk is spread, there is some unavoidable residual risk cost that must be absorbed somewhere. If this were to be borne by investors, then insurers would charge a risk premium and policyholders would be better off economizing on their premiums by accepting a co-share in the risk, such as a deductible.

Alternatively, the remaining risk could be borne by the government. The government could be the last-resort reinsurer or could provide ex post compensation to victims, as happened after Hurricane Katrina. But of course, government aid ultimately comes from the taxpayers and firms that would end up bearing their own risk (or those of others) through either additional taxes or cuts in other federally supported programs.

This reasoning takes us to the basis of modern insurance theory, the Borch theorem.[6] Insofar as risk is undiversifiable, the optimal social arrangement is that individual risk is insured, but the undiversifiable component is shared among the population. Thus, each policyholder should retain a stake in the social risk. In practical terms, this can be achieved in several ways:

• Deductibles could vary according to the size of the aggregate loss. With large losses such as those caused by Hurricane Katrina, the deductible would be very large, and conversely would be small when smaller catastrophes occurred.

• Policyholders could be reimbursed for their total losses, but pay an ex post assessment so that the industry could recover part of its capital. The practical problem with such assessments is that they may not be collectible, especially from victims with low income or those who suffer severe damage.

• Policyholders could pay higher initial premiums to contribute to the insurance pool's capital and be given an ownership stake in the insurance pool. In other words, insurance could be mutualized. Policyholders would then receive a dividend, which would vary according to the overall results of the pool, so that when a large catastrophe occurred, the dividend would fall to zero (or perhaps be negative—an assessment).

The policy task is to recognize that insurance does not provide full protection when applied to catastrophic risk and that we all have to bear the undiversified risk. What, then, is the most efficient way of distributing this lumpy risk over policyholders or over society more widely? There is no easy answer to this question, but it provides a basis for understanding the importance of mitigation and the need for public-private partnerships for dealing with the risk. In the next chapter we examine the status of demand and supply of insurance by analyzing empirically the market equilibria for homeowners' insurance in four states, Florida, New York, South Carolina, and Texas.

Summary

The supply of catastrophe insurance is determined primarily by the capital that insurers can and wish to allocate to protect themselves against large losses and by the availability of reinsurance and insurance-linked securities. In turn, reinsurance capacity is determined by the reinsurers' capital base. However, the underlying capital varies according to both the claims experience and the investment experience of insurers and reinsurers, thus causing the cycle in prices and insurance capacity. Hard markets (capacity is scarce and price is high) following major losses do arouse policy concerns, though these conditions are usually self-correcting over time with the inflow of new capital. The price of catastrophe insurance is usually high relative to expected claims primarily because of the high cost of capital needed to back this type of coverage. Requiring policyholders to take deductibles is an efficient way to ration expensive insurance capacity.

While we expect an unregulated market to clear with some risk sharing in the form of deductibles and at prices that reflect claims and transaction costs, this equilibrium will be disturbed by regulation. Price suppression and the inability of insurers to base premiums on risk affect insurance capacity, the incentive to mitigate risk, and the participation of different risk groups in the insurance market.

10 A Multistate Empirical Analysis of Homeowners' Insurance

Key Findings

Demand for insurance is approximately unit elastic at the county level. *Unit elastic* means that a given percentage increase in price will result in a similar percentage decrease in demand. For example, our results indicate that a 10 percent increase in the average premium will result in an 8.9 percent decrease in the amount of insurance purchased. This level of sensitivity to price is not surprising as the home is a typical household's biggest asset and there is no other way to hedge fire or wind risks except through insurance. In Florida, the cross-elasticity between private insurance and insurance supplied by Citizens, the state's insurer of last resort, is 0.159. This cross-elasticity implies that a 10 percent increase in Citizens' premium is associated with only a 1.59 percent increase in the amount of insurance demanded by homeowners from private insurers.

The elasticity of supply at the county level is very high using the number of policies as a proxy for quantity of insurance demanded. The elasticity suggests that a 10 percent increase (decrease) in price that homeowners are willing to pay for coverage will yield a 27 percent increase (decrease) in the quantity of policies supplied by the insurers. This high supply elasticity has important implications for rate regulation. If rates are suppressed too much, then there is likely to be a severe availability problem because of a large decrease in the quantity of policies offered by private insurers.

Insurance premiums are high in Florida, Texas, and South Carolina relative to New York. The price of insurance in Florida and South Carolina is high relative to other states. The mean policy premium for our sample companies is $6,164 in Florida and approximately $5,000 in South Carolina. In contrast, the mean premium is $2,375 in Texas, and $761 in New York. In terms of mean premiums per thousand dollars of coverage, we found that Florida had the highest, at $8.13, followed by Texas ($7.89), South Carolina ($5.14), and New York ($3.94). Florida faces the highest risk of hurricane losses, so it is not surprising that it has the highest mean premium. South Carolina faces a lower but still significant level of hurricane risk. New York faces the lowest hurricane risk among the four states.

Hence, the pattern we see in mean premiums among these three states is consistent with what we would expect. We should note that our data for this analysis are for the period 2001–2005. Based on updated risk analysis following the 2004 and 2005 storm seasons, insurers increased their rates.

Demand is unstable in Florida. In Florida, estimates of price and income elasticity of demand are unstable over the period 2001–2005. The price elasticity ranged between 0.06 and 0.50. This could be due to shifting consumer perceptions of risk and the importance they placed on having adequate insurance coverage, among other factors. For the same four-year period, the results in South Carolina and New York are more stable. In South Carolina the price elasticity was between 1 and 1.5, implying a 10 percent increase in price yields a 10 to 15 percent decrease in quantity demanded. In New York, the price elasticity was approximately 0.60, suggesting that a 10 percent increase in price causes a 6.0 percent decrease in quantity demanded.

Many people choose low deductibles for their homeowners' policy. A large percentage of the policies from our sample have relatively low deductibles. In Florida, over 50 percent of the homeowners have wind deductibles of $500, while the average wind deductible was $1,565. The difference between the median and mean wind deductible suggests some homeowners chose much higher deductibles. We would expect this to be especially true in the highest-risk coastal areas, where the premium savings from choosing higher deductibles will be the greatest. Furthermore, we expect that median and average deductible levels have risen since 2005. In South Carolina, with an average wind deductible of $531, over 50 percent of the policyholders have $500 or less in wind deductibles. For New York, the average wind deductible is $508, but 75 percent of homeowners have a wind deductible of $500 or less.

10.1   Developing a Model of the Demand and Supply of Insurance

The basic demand problem for the homeowner is to select the best insurance policy from among the menu of policies offered in the market.[1] Demand arises from the optimal consumer choice of a bundle of product and company attributes, given the personal characteristics of each homeowner and the economic and demographic characteristics of the neighborhood (postal zone) where he or she resides. The theoretical foundation for this demand analysis and the interacting market equilibrium are based on a model of price-quality competition.[2] In a perfectly competitive market, the differences in what homeowners are willing to pay for various features will be reflected in the price at which various bundled products with these features sell.

Thus, in our analysis of the demand for and supply of property insurance in hurricane-prone areas, we model a regression of observed price in the market against various features of the products sold and the companies that sell them. We are interested in the factors that seem to influence demand. We determine whether these factors appear reasonable on the basis of theory, and if so, we quantify the effect of each of these factors. Since there is considerable evidence that many homeowners do not search thoroughly for best offers, we are also interested in aspects of the market that appear to arise from behavioral considerations, including the price dispersion of similar policies offered in the same geographic area or "rating territory."[3] We should note that one source of price dispersion is the fact that insurance companies differentiate themselves in term of underwriting stringency. Insurers with more stringent underwriting standards, labeled "preferred insurers," tend to have the lowest prices. "Standard" and "nonstandard" companies tend to have higher prices. Some insureds may pay higher than necessary prices if they would qualify for coverage from a preferred insurer, but intentionally or inadvertently purchase coverage from a standard or nonstandard insurer.

We rely on the following features of the homeowners' insurance market in modeling the supply and demand for insurance. Although the structure of this market may be workably competitive, it is nonetheless a regulated market.[4] On the demand side, this does not cause any theoretical difficulties as the model we develop only attempts to explain, for policies actually offered in the market, how various features are valued. We examine within-feature changes (e.g., various deductible levels) and across-features trade-offs (e.g., deductible levels versus type of coverage). It is important to bear in mind that because of regulation, the policies offered in the market, and their prices in particular, are not the result of a perfectly competitive market. In other words, the prices, products, and other aspects of insurance transactions are subject to certain regulatory constraints and mandates.

The insurer's basic supply decision is guided by its expectation that a commitment of capital will yield an adequate rate of return. In turn, this requires that the insurer be able to underwrite a portfolio with an adequate spread of risk (or that it have access to adequate reinsurance) and that the insurer can price its policies to cover the expected costs of claims with some margin for risk and its cost of capital. In most states, the insurer is not operating in an entirely free market, though the effect and form of regulation vary among states (see chapter 2 on insurance regulation). In designing its policies and coverage decisions, we assume that an insurer seeks to maximize expected profits, subject to regulatory constraints. This implies that insurance companies find the imposed regulatory constraints are not so onerous as to cause them to leave the state. Nonetheless, because of such constraints, catastrophe coverage in some areas might require cross-subsidies from other lines of business such as noncatastrophe coverage and catastrophe coverage in low-risk areas.

These cross-subsidies may be sustainable if they allow insurance companies to earn an acceptable rate of return on all lines of business. At the same time, we must recognize that there are limits to the magnitude of the cross-subsidies that can be sustained in a private, competitive market when consumers can choose among multiple insurers. The continuation of these cross-subsidies over time implies further inertia by insurers (and insureds) that may at least in part be due to regulatory restrictions on terminating policies and other insurer and consumer considerations.[5] Beyond the obvious implications for understanding rate adequacy and precision, this suggests the importance of detecting cross-marketing synergies in the demand and supply analysis, as well as detecting trends in the aggregate supply of particular insurers in terms of increasing the diversification of their portfolios of insurance policies.

10.2   Study 1: County-Level Supply and Demand Analysis

We have obtained a data set at a county level from the Florida Office of Insurance Regulation (FLOIR), which represents the entire homeowners' insurance market for the state of Florida in 2006 (both private insurers and the state-run company, Citizens). From this data set, we have information concerning the policies in force and the average premium on a company basis for each county. This allows us to estimate both a supply and demand function for Florida. An important caveat is that the aggregation level of the data is at the county level, which may not provide enough variation to test all hypotheses. However, it does provide a glimpse at the Florida homeowners' market that previously has not been seen. The advantage of this analysis, compared with our postal zone–level analysis discussed later in this chapter, is that it reflects all insurers writing homeowners' insurance in Florida. Our postal zone–level data analysis uses more detailed information but it is confined to a select number of major writers of homeowners' insurance in Florida. Hence, we conducted analyses using both data sets to obtain the best insights possible with respect to demand and supply conditions.

In addition to the data provided by the FLOIR, we used three other sources of data. From the 2000 U.S. Census Bureau, we obtained information about the Florida counties' demographics as well as housing characteristics. From the National Association of Insurance Commissioners (NAIC) financial database (based on insurers' regulatory annual financial statements), we obtained information for each company writing in Florida. And from A.M. Best, a nationally known insurance rating agency, we were able to obtain some information about most insurers operating in Florida.

We employ the two-stage least-squares methodology to estimate a demand and a supply function for Florida at the county level. Table 10.1 provides a description of the variables that we use in the analysis. We break our data into six categories for the demand analysis: prices, income, housing characteristics, location characteristics, insurance company characteristics, and other factors.

For the supply analysis, we break the variables into four groups: price of insurance, reinsurance, insurer characteristics, and government. These categories correspond roughly to elements of the demand equations we estimate.

Table 10.1
Descriptive statistics of variables employed in supply and demand analysis

Variable	Mean	SD	Maximum
Insurer Characteristics			
A.M. Best Rating of A	0.168	0.374	1.000
A.M. Best Rating of A–	0.155	0.362	1.000
A.M. Best Rating of B+,B,B–	0.161	0.367	1.000
A.M. Best Rating of C+,C,C– and NR	0.258	0.438	1.000
Age of company in years	37	42	196
Independent agency marketing system	0.552	0.497	1.000
Reinsurance assumed (premiums assumed to DPW)	0.645	2.324	18.730
Reinsurance ceded (premiums ceded to DPW)	0.911	1.449	12.311
A.M. Best rating downgrade 2005	0.869	0.338	1.000
Florida-domiciled company	0.409	0.492	1.000
Florida-domiciled company part of a group	0.252	0.434	1.000
Member of a group	0.808	0.394	1.000
HHI Index of concentration at county level	1.447	41.533	2578.00
Publicly traded company	0.057	0.231	1.000
Stock company	0.904	0.295	1.000
South Florida indicator for wind risk	0.099	0.299	1.000
Housing characteristics and location characteristics: Number of homes (1–4) units	86,221	111,065	503,864
Median age of home in county	1982	3.614	1989
Median value of occupied home	97,141	29,274	241,200
Population density	346	524	3,291
Indicator for coastal county	0.572	0.495	1.000
Overall liquidity ratio (%)	234	226	999.900
Percent HH in urban areas	0.649	0.317	0.999
Percentage of housing units with mortgage	0.641	0.101	0.829
Percent of county covered by water	0.153	0.125	0.733
Price and income			
Average premium for company in county	1,667	1,806	37,877
Policies in force	615	2,623	61,688
Median income 2004	38,351	6,728	55,712
$N = 5,277$ (except for liquidity ratio where $N = 5,089$)			

Note: Age of home is the construction date here

One of the major problems with undertaking an analysis of demand or supply in the insurance sector is that defining the quantity demanded (or supplied) is difficult.[6] Similarly, constructing a theoretically justified proper definition of price of insurance is also difficult. Here we use policies in force as our measure of quantity (Q). This is obtained from the Florida Office of Insurance Regulation's county level Quarterly Supplementary Report (QUASR) 2006 data. Each company reports the number of policies in force in each county, as well as the total premiums written. For price, we use the average premium (which is the total company premiums in a county/company policies in force in the county).

Demand Equation Estimation

The demand model is a two-stage model. The first stage is a price regression to determine which variables affect price.[7] The second stage estimates a quantity demanded for company i in county $c(Q_{i,c}^d)$ using the estimate of price from the first stage regression along with other explanatory variables, as shown in equation 10.1:

$$Q_{i,c}^{d^*} = f(prices,\ income,\ housing\ characteristics,\ company\ characteristics,\ other) + e \quad (10.1)$$

where the * represents the equilibrium value of quantity demanded.

For prices, we include the firm's own premium, the average premium of a Citizens' policy in the county, and the average premium of all policies (excluding Citizens) in the county. These are the three prices that influence the demand for homeowners' insurance. It should be pointed out here that these are the actual premiums charged by the insurer and therefore do not provide the best measure of the cost of transferring risk because we do not have explicit levels of loss costs. In addition to expected losses, premiums also account for loss control services, expected claims payment costs, and marketing and other expenses. In contrast, in the contract-level demand analysis undertaken later in this chapter, we measure price as the premium loading, which measures the markup above the expected loss. We discuss this further below, pointing out why the price markup is a more accurate representation of price. However, for this first analysis, the best available data are based on the actual premiums in the market.

As shown in table 10.1 we obtained information from the U.S. Census Bureau on county-wide median income and information on housing characteristics, such as the number of units eligible for homeowners' coverage in the county (one or more single or attached homes with four or fewer units), the percentage of households in urban areas, the median value of an occupied home, the percentage of household units with a mortgage, the number of building permits in the county, and the median age of an owner-occupied home in the county.

We also obtained firm-specific information about the insurer. For example, as shown in table 10.1, we use an indicator for whether the insurer uses an independent agency marketing system. Agents provide consumers with information as well as loss adjustment services.

Finally, we also have indicators for whether the insurer is a stock or mutual company or is a member of a group. A stock company is owned by shareholders who are not necessarily policyholders, while a mutual company is owned exclusively by the policyholders. It is likely that a mutual company may have different ties to the consumer, and thus we use the stock or mutual variable to control for this relationship. In addition, many of the insurers in Florida sell only homeowners' coverage. If the insurer is a member of a group of affiliated insurance companies, it is more likely that the insurer can cross-market life and other nonlife types of policies, such as auto or boat owner. There could be other relevant differences between stand-alone companies versus companies belonging to groups, such as potential access to group capital infusions in the event of heavy losses (a broader pooling of risk and geographic and product diversification).[8]

Because prices are endogenous, we estimate the demand equation using the two-stage approach described. Our first-stage regressions (not shown) provide evidence of reasonable explanatory power so that we can use these predicted prices in the second stage with some degree of confidence that we are estimating a demand equation.

Demand: Discussion of Results

Table 10.2 provides the results of our estimation. The second column of the table, titled "Coefficient," is the main focus of our analysis. This coefficient is an estimate of the

Table 10.2
Two-stage least-squares demand equation at the county level—Dependent variable: Log of policies in force by company in county

Variable	Coefficient	SE	T-statistic	Probability > 0
Intercept	−1.522	3.078	−0.490	0.623
Prices				
* Log of average premiums	−0.893	0.145	−6.150	0.000
* Log of average premium in county	0.226	0.137	1.650	0.104
* Log of citizens average premium	0.159	0.085	1.860	0.067
Income				
Log of median income	0.025	0.461	0.050	0.958
Housing characteristics				
Log of the number of housing units (1–4)	0.850	0.065	13.160	0.000
Percentage HH in urban areas	−0.139	0.204	−0.680	0.499
Percentage of housing units with mortgage	0.188	0.258	0.730	0.467
Log of the number of building permits	0.028	0.044	0.640	0.526
Log of median home value in county	0.272	0.300	0.910	0.368
Log of the age of median home	−0.895	0.310	−2.890	0.005
Company characteristics				
Independent agency marketing system	−0.434	0.047	−9.280	0.000
Stock company	0.151	0.055	2.740	0.008
Member of a group	−0.145	0.064	−2.260	0.027

Note: Robust standard errors reported. $N = 5{,}121$; $R^2 = .245$.
* Endogenous variable.

elasticity between the quantity demanded and the variable of interest.[9] The elasticity is defined as how a percentage change in the variable under discussion is related to a percentage change in the quantity demand for insurance. For example, the elasticity with respect to the average premium for the insurer in the county is −0.893. This means that a 10 percent increase in the average company premium will yield a reduction in the number of policies sold for that company of 8.93 percent $(10^* \cdot 0.893)$, implying that demand is inelastic. A relatively high number implies sensitivity to price changes, and demand would then be classified as elastic. In addition to examining the effect of the individual company's price (the so-called own price elasticity), we can also look at how other prices influence the demand for the insurers' products. We can examine the cross-price elasticity, that is, the sensitivity between a competitor's price and the firm's quantity demanded. In particular, it would be interesting to know how the price of a Citizens' contract, measured by the average premium for a Citizens' contract in the county, affects private insurers' quantity demanded. The cross-price elasticity here is 0.159. This implies that a 10 percent increase in Citizens' premium is associated with a 1.59 percent increase in the quantity demanded by homeowners from private insurers. The reverse is also true: a Citizens' price reduction will reduce the quantity demanded in the private market. This is especially important today, as Citizens is allowed to compete with private market companies. Prior to 2007, Citizens was required to set prices in a manner that would not undercut the private market. As discussed in chapter 2 and elsewhere, the more risk underwritten by Citizens (i.e., the state) the greater is the risk that may ultimately be transferred to other insurance buyers (and even taxpayers) across the state.

Finally, we see that the average premium in the county for private market insurers is also positively (but not significantly) related to the quantity demanded. This is consistent with the fact that competitors' policies are substitutes to the insurer's own products. Although the elasticity is not significant, it is close to standard levels of statistical significance (10 percent) and is consistent with economic theory.

More generally, table 10.2 reveals that the demand for insurance (based on policies in force) is relatively insensitive to the price of insurance. The income elasticity is not significant, indicating that the quantity of insurance purchased is insensitive to homeowners' earnings. This compares with the findings of Grace, Klein, and Kleindorfer (2004) where there was a slightly positive income elasticity for Florida homeowners' insurance, though they employed a different definition of price and quantity from the ones used here.[10] Furthermore, there may not be enough variation in income across the counties to provide a strong enough statistical test of differences.

In terms of housing characteristics, two variables are significant. First, the number of eligible residences (single and attached houses up to four units) is significantly related to the policies in force, as is the median age of a home within the county.[11] A 10 percent increase in the number of eligible homes in a county leads to an 8.5 percent increase in the demand for policies. Similarly, a 10 percent increase in the age of the housing stock in a county yields a decrease in the demand for insurance by approximately 8.95 percent. While one might expect a relationship between quantity demanded and housing value, we do not find significant relationships for the median value of the home.

Two reasons exist that one might not see a relationship with these data. First, there may be multicollinearity between housing value and income. This implies that multiple variables are essentially explaining the same thing (people with higher incomes tend to live in more valuable houses). We checked using a number of techniques and found that the resulting estimates were similar to those presented in table 10.2. In addition, our definition of quantity is a policy. The purchase of a policy by itself is less likely to be influenced by the value of a home. Our data at the county level do not allow us to examine the type of policy purchased. For example, certain policies contain more options, which may be valuable to people with higher-valued homes but too expensive for people with lower-valued homes.

Company characteristics are also related to the demand for insurance. Insurers using agents, companies that are members of a group, or companies that have a specific organization form (stock or mutual), may also influence consumers' preferences as to whom they choose to purchase homeowners' insurance from. Agents, traditionally thought of as information providers, have a negative influence on demand, all other things equal. Since we are examining the decision as to whether to purchase a policy (and not the details of all the optional contract terms), the agent does not appear to create additional demand for coverage. In fact, the presence of a company's independent agency marketing system is associated with lower demand for the company's products, all other things held constant. This result is a bit puzzling, but there are some possible explanations. One is that insurers identified as exclusive agency insurers or direct writers may have a stronger brand reputation because of their extensive advertising efforts, and this may cause consumers to have a higher demand for their products.

The firm's organizational form also appears to influence demand. One might hypothesize that policyholders who are also owners of a company (as in the case of a mutual) may have a different relationship with a company than policyholders who are merely customers. We see that stock companies have higher demand for their products, all other things held constant. Finally, one might buy from a company that is a member of a group. Groups are often able to offer more types of coverage because of the broader reach of the expertise within the overall company. Thus, a company may be able to offer life as well as nonlife coverage. In Florida, many of the companies writing homeowners' policies specialize in one line of business. Thus, there might be a benefit in terms of greater opportunities for selling across lines of business if a firm is a member of a group. In fact, we see that group membership is negatively associated with demand, suggesting that the consumers do not value these potential cross-opportunities when purchasing homeowners' insurance.[12]

Supply Estimation

We now turn to the estimation of a supply function in a manner similar to the demand function. Again, we employ a two-stage approach where the first stage is the same as in the demand analysis. Our quantity supplied $(Q_{i,c}^s)$ is the number of policies in force, and the price is the average premium for policies written by company i in a county c. Again, our underlying first-stage results, while not as powerful as those in the first-stage demand equations, provide the proper signs for our supply function.

$$Q_{i,c}^{s^*} = f(Prices, Reinsurance, Risk, Company\ Cost\ Characteristics, Government) + v \tag{10.2}$$

where * represents the equilibrium value of quantity supplied.

Discussion of Results

Table 10.3 details the results of the two-stage least-squares regression. The first variable of interest is the price variable. The average premium's coefficient, which reflects the price

Table 10.3
Two-stage least-squares estimation of supply function—Dependent variable: Policies in force by company in county

	Coefficient	SE	T-statistic	Probability > 0
Intercept	−14.645	5.881	−2.490	0.015
Price				
Log of average premiums	2.754	0.903	3.050	0.003
Reinsurance				
Log of ratio of premiums ceded to total premiums	0.097	0.032	3.000	0.004
Log of ratio of assumed premiums to total premiums	−0.185	0.061	−3.030	0.003
Risk				
Indicator for coastal county	0.081	0.448	0.180	0.858
South Florida indicator for wind risk	−0.641	0.589	−1.090	0.280
Company characteristics				
Stock company	−1.837	0.218	−8.410	0.000
Publicly traded company	−0.662	0.176	−3.770	0.000
Member of a group	1.161	0.319	3.640	0.001
Florida-domiciled company	1.561	0.427	3.650	0.001
Florida-domiciled company part of a group	−0.379	0.435	−0.870	0.387
Independent agency marketing system	−0.906	0.093	−9.760	0.000
A.M. Best rating of A	0.183	0.149	1.230	0.223
A.M. Best rating of A−	0.642	0.216	2.970	0.004
A.M. Best rating of B+,B,B−	0.977	0.079	12.370	0.000
A.M. Best rating of C+,C,C−, and NR	−0.489	0.127	−3.850	0.000
A.M. Best rating downgrade 2005	−0.018	0.072	−0.250	0.800
Overall liquidity ratio (%)	−0.0005	0.000	−3.090	0.003
Government				
Log of Citizens market share	−0.068	0.130	−0.520	0.605

Note: $N = 5{,}089$; $R^2 = .26$.

elasticity, is positive and is 2.754. The elasticity suggests that a 10 percent increase (decrease) in price will yield a 27 percent increase (decrease) in the number of policies supplied. This price elasticity has an important implication for rate regulation. If rates are suppressed, then the high price elasticity implies that there would be a severe availability issue resulting from the large decrease of policies supplied by private insurers. If rates were most suppressed in high-risk areas, then availability would be especially severe in these regions of the state. We do see significantly higher proportions of policies written by Citizens in high-risk areas, but we cannot measure how much of this is due to rate suppression or compression versus other factors. The supply elasticity result also suggests that if Florida reversed its policies that cause insurers to exit the state completely or to refrain from selling in high-risk areas of the state, it would likely spur entry and marketing of coverage in these regions.

We also control for the reinsurance profile of the insurer. We calculated the ratio of ceded premiums to direct premiums written, as well as a ratio of assumed to direct premiums. If an insurer reinsures a greater proportion of its risks, then it will have a high ratio of ceded premiums to direct premiums. If an insurer assumes reinsurance, then it is taking on risks. We find that firms that cede premiums to a reinsurer are more likely to increase their supply of policies in Florida and that firms that assume risks from others are less likely to supply insurance. This is consistent with our expectations, as insurers can increase their capacity by ceding certain risk to others. In fact, our results suggest a 10 percent increase in the ratio of ceded premiums to direct premiums written yields just under a 1 percent increase in the quantity of policies sold. In contrast, a 10 percent increase in the ratio of assumed to total premiums reduces supply by 1.85 percent ("assumed premiums" refer to reinsurance premiums received by an insurer for assuming a portion of the risk and premiums ceded to it by another insurer).

We also make a crude attempt to control for location as it relates to the wind risk associated with hurricanes by employing the coastal county indicator and a south Florida indicator, but neither is significant. This lack of significance is likely due to the high level of aggregation of the data so that one cannot easily distinguish high-hazard areas from other parts of the county.

Our regression estimation also included a number of company indicators that may affect the costs of doing business for the firm. The first significant variable is an indicator for whether the firm is publicly traded. It is statistically significant and negative. There is an argument that shareholders of publicly traded companies are not willing to risk their capital in a market like Florida if they can earn a higher, and perhaps more secure, return in other parts of the insurance industry or in other business. This hypothesis suggests a negative sign on this coefficient, and that is what we observe.

A company that is a member of a group is statistically more likely to have a higher level of supply than a company outside a group. As a member of a group, a company may access lower-cost internal capital to increase supply. A company that is not a member of a group may have a harder time raising capital, as it must either raise prices or seek additional capital from the market. This is also consistent with what we observe in table 10.3.

According to our regression results, companies domiciled in Florida (members of a group and single companies) are also more likely to supply insurance. This is likely due to the recent growth in the number of Florida domestic start-ups, as well as increased wind risk, which caused national companies to readjust their homeowners' insurance portfolios downward. Furthermore, the state encouraged Florida companies to enter the market and take policies from the Florida Hurricane Catastrophe Fund (FHCF), the state-backed entity of last resort. Many national companies have established Florida subsidiaries as a risk management strategy. In the event of the "big one," a company with a Florida subsidiary could have the option of recapitalizing the Florida subsidiary, thus avoiding a mandatory and immediate charge to its equity.[13] We find that this does not seem to have a significant effect on supply, but it does provide value to the holding company by protecting it from a forced recapitalization. Independent agency distribution systems are more costly than exclusive agent or direct operations. The agents selling insurance for an "exclusive agent" insurer sell insurance for only that insurer. Independent agents typically represent or sell insurance for multiple insurers. Direct writers use company personnel to distribute insurance and make greater use of mail, telephone, and Internet devices for interacting with consumers and policyholders. The regression analysis indicates that companies with independent agency systems have a lower quantity supplied, all other things equal.

In terms of A.M. Best ratings, we see that relative to A++ and A+ rated companies (which is the omitted variable), firms in the A− and B range have a higher supply of policies than all other rating categories. This is consistent with the principal-agent theory, which posits that shareholders (the agents, in this case) of a higher-risk firm are more willing to increase supply because more of the downside risk of default is borne by existing policyholders (the principals, in this case).[14] For this strategy to succeed, the price of new policies should be insensitive to default risk. Thus, one might conclude that new policyholders are relatively unconcerned, or unaware, of the difference between A and B ratings. However, when the rating is in the C categories, supply is reduced relative to the A+ and A++ rated companies. This suggests that insurers anticipate that policyholders would not tolerate such a low rating and simply reduce their market participation. Finally, we see that recent ratings downgrades do not have an effect on the supply of insurance.

We also examine the impact of the A.M. Best liquidity ratio on supply. This is the ratio of total assets to total liabilities. Essentially it is the inverse of a leverage ratio. Supply capacity is related to the total assets brought to financially backed risks in the market. One could believe that highly liquid firms have sufficient cash to support increased supply.

Alternatively, one could envision that the managers (acting on behalf of the shareholders) and the policyholders may have different interests. As the managers have little downside risk resulting from the possibility of bankruptcy, they can reduce liquidity (become more leveraged) to take bigger risks. Essentially the managers acting on behalf of the shareholders increase the probability of default at the expense of the policyholders.

One can view our results in two ways. First, higher levels of firm liquidity are associated with lower insurance supply in Florida. Alternatively, a higher level of leverage is associated with a higher level of supply. Thus, firms with "excess" liquidity will not invest in Florida. This result is consistent with the principal-agent theory whereby higher-risk insurers are willing to exploit their default potential at the expense of the policyholders by increasing supply. Again, the success of this strategy relies on the insensitivity of premium rates to the enhanced leverage risk. Normally firms try to raise prices if risk increases. However, if prices are fixed, increased leverage increases the risk of the insurer.

The results on credit rating and leverage are largely consistent with a principal-agent story. Alternatively, these results can be explained, or enhanced, by regulatory factors. First, the failure of prices to change for high-risk insurers might be due to regulatory price controls in which suppressed rates offer no flexibility for premiums to vary with credit quality. Second, the regulatory environment may have encouraged or otherwise facilitated the presence of lower-risk insurers.[15] Whatever the reason, these low ratings imply significant pressure on the companies' ability to pay claims in the event of a severe hurricane. If a company defaults, any shortfall in its ability to pay claims is made up for by assessments on the companies remaining in the market. The assessment is made based on the remaining companies' market shares.

The final variable in the supply equation is the presence of Citizens Property Insurance Company in the marketplace. The coefficient on Citizens' market share is insignificant, suggesting that Citizens is not having a significant effect on the market. In 2006, Citizens was not allowed to compete directly with private market companies. It was not until 2007 that Florida allowed Citizens to price its premiums at levels competitive with (or lower than) the private market participants.

Conclusions for County-Level Supply and Demand

As a result of our analysis at the county level we can draw some conclusions about behavior in Florida markets.

1. The price elasticity of demand is unit elastic, indicating that consumers have some loyalty to their current insurer.

2. However, the cross-elasticity for Citizens' policies is significantly higher, suggesting that customers are willing to switch to those policies on the basis of price comparisons if, and when, they are able to do so. This implies that if Citizens can underprice the private

market, it will attract significant new business. This is consistent with what we have observed recently in Florida, as Citizens is the largest insurer in the state.

3. Supply is highly price elastic: firms would supply more insurance if they could raise prices. This implies that even moderate price suppression will have a severe affect on availability in the private market. Further, insofar as price suppression is greatest in high-risk locations, the availability crunch in these locations will be especially severe.

4. The availability of reinsurance increases capacity.

Higher-risk firms (as indicated by leverage or credit quality) are more willing to supply policies. This may be because they are able to pass on the increased default risk to other policyholders without being penalized in prices. Additionally, the higher supply of high-risk insurers may have been directly facilitated by regulatory strategies that have encouraged their growth. This is consistent with actual experience (discussed in chapter 3) in which five highly leveraged Florida insurers wrote excessive concentrations of high-risk exposures and subsequently failed as a result of losses from the 2004 and 2005 storm seasons.

The county-level study looked at the supply and demand for insurance in one state, Florida. In this study, the price was measured as the average premium paid for homeowners' insurance in the county, and the quantity was the number of policies sold in that county. Thus, when we are talking about the demand elasticity, we are referring to the sensitivity of the number of policies demanded to the premium charged. Thus, in saying that demand is inelastic, we mean that differences in premiums between companies in a county and across counties do not seem to be associated with big differences in demand for insurance. Similarly, our conclusion that supply is elastic means that insurers seem to be quite willing to increase (decrease) the number of policies they sell as premiums change. The analysis does not investigate the impact that premiums have on the amount of coverage that a homeowner purchases, as we focus in this section on the decision to sell an insurance policy, not the level of coverage provided.

There are two major issues with this analysis. First, while it is useful to examine how the number of policies supplied and demanded changes with price, this does not take into account how much insurance is purchased (which is best proxied by a measure of expected loss). Second, the measure of price—the actual premium—is not the best measure of the economic price to the insured of transferring risk. Much of the premium will, when averaged across the portfolio, be returned to the policyholder in the form of a claims payment. A more usual measure of the economic price to the consumer is the spread between the premium and expected losses. This corresponds more closely with what economic theory says about insurance supply and demand.[16] To address these issues, we undertook a second analysis of insurance demand across Florida, South Carolina, New York, and Texas, using insurance company contract data.

10.3   Study 2: Cross-State Analysis of Insurance Demand Using Insurance Company Contract Data

Defining Price and Modeling Demand for Homeowner Policies

Assume that a particular homeowner, with characteristics Z (income, family status, type of structure of the house or apartment building, and so forth), faces a choice among different policy options for insuring his home, where the set H gives the available policy options in the homeowners' market. A typical such option h in the set H would be one offered by insurer i, with characteristics X_i (such as implied quality levels based on surplus level, size and visibility in the market, distribution system type—direct marketing or independent agent). Or a typical such option h in the set H would be one offered by insurer i (with characteristics X_i that include characteristics such as claims-paying ability, organizational form, marketing methods, and the ability to offer complementary products such as auto insurance) with certain policy features (such as deductible levels, loss settlement provisions, actual cash value, or replacement cost) and with premium $P(h)$. The homeowner must choose one of the options in H and is assumed to do so by maximizing his expected utility over the risks or gambles implied by each choice h. Let us represent this expected utility $U(h, P(h))$ in quasi-linear form[17] as:

$$U(h, P(h), Z) = V(F(h), Z) - P(F(h), Z) \tag{10.3}$$

where V represents the consumer's willingness to pay for various types of coverage or features of an insurance policy and $F(h)$ represents the vector of such features, including the characteristics of the company offering the policy that may make a difference to consumers.

Note that both V and P depend only on the vector of features F and the characteristics of the homeowner (possibly only the type of structure, but perhaps also on locational characteristics such as community rating or location of nearest fire department). One of these features could itself be the premium level $P(h)$. The homeowner then maximizes the function $U(h, P(h), Z)$ over the set H.

Assuming that there is a rich menu of policies available in the market, we can represent the choice problem as selecting an insurance policy by choosing optimal features of the policy. The solution is found where the marginal benefit of policy features is equal to the marginal cost. This leads to estimation problems of the following general type, neglecting for the moment the details here of functional form:

$$P(F, X, Z) = aF + bX + cZ + \varepsilon \tag{10.4}$$

We have separated the policy features into categories: those pertaining to the policy itself (the vector F), those that pertain to the company (the vector X), and those pertaining to neighborhood characteristics (the vector Z). In this model, $P(F, X, Z)$ could be either the total premium for a given policy or, more likely, normalizing by units of coverage (e.g., the expected or indicated loss costs), premium per unit of coverage.

The price for insurance products, as for other products and services, is defined as the value added per dollar of output. At the policy level, this value-added measure of price can be captured by subtracting the discounted value of expected losses covered by the policy from the premium.[18] Denoted by $L(F,Z)$, the expected losses for a policy h with features F and by $P(F,X,Z)$ its premium, we obtain the following definition of price $p(F,X,Z)$ for a homeowners' policy $h = (F,X,Z)$ characterized by the parameters (F,X) and indexed by consumer and loss characteristics Z:

$$p(F,X,Z) = \frac{P(F,X,Z) - PV(L(F,Z))}{PV(L(F,Z))} = \frac{(1+r)P(F,X,Z) - L(F,Z)}{L(F,Z)} \tag{10.5}$$

where $PV(L(F,Z)) = L(F,Z)/(1+r)$ is the present value of expected losses on the policy for the policy period and (r) is the insurer's return on equity for the period, which is the discount factor used to calculated present value. $L(F,Z)$ is the indicated loss costs per unit of coverage for the policy features (F) and structure (Z) in question. This was the underlying methodology used in Grace et al. (2004).

The value of the $L(F,Z)$ is calculated using ISO procedures for our sample data. Examining the data across the sample firms (see description below), we have a number of variables unique to a particular firm. This is because each company has different needs for the data it collects. However, we are able to take a set of common variables to calculate an indicated loss cost for each contract. We used the ISO procedures to develop relativities for the coverage A (or the dwelling) limit, the policy deductible, the wind deductible, and the location (by ISO territory). The coverage A limit in a homeowners' insurance policy is the amount of insurance on the principal dwelling and attached structures. This is usually set at the estimated replacement cost of the dwelling. Other coverages (e.g., for contents, unattached structures, loss of use) are typically set as a percentage of the coverage A limit. Normally consumers opt for standard percentages for these other coverages but can choose higher or lower percentages if they wish.

Quantity Demanded

In previous work, the indicated loss cost (ILC) is employed as a measure of the risk shifted to the insurer through the insurance contract.[19] We hypothesize that the ILCs offer a good proxy for the expected losses of the policy contract. In our current data set, we do not have an indicator for losses. Thus, we employ the coverage A (dwelling) limit as an alternative measure of demand. While this is a maximum probable loss rather than an expected loss, it is used to proxy for quantity of insurance coverage demanded.

We received data from five sponsoring companies (State Farm, Allstate, Liberty Mutual, Travelers, and Nationwide) and from Fireman's Fund and Citizens Property Insurance Corporation. These insurers accounted for approximately 50 percent of the Florida homeowners' insurance market in 2005. For New York, the market share coverage was approximately 20 percent, for South Carolina it was approximately 30 percent, and for Texas it was approximately 40 percent. Data were provided for a number of years over the period 2000–2005. Not every company was able to provide data for all years for every state. It is important to note that although this is not a random sample of policies across all states, it is a relatively large sample of the market.

Our data consist of individual contract information from the various insurers in Florida, South Carolina, New York, and Texas. Table 10.4 shows summary statistics for the state databases. Florida's average written premium is the highest among the four states, followed by South Carolina, Texas, and New York. However, the average premium is not necessarily a good indicator of price. We also calculate the average premium per $1,000 of coverage using the coverage A (or dwelling limit). We see that Florida still has the highest price per dollar of coverage at $8.13. However, Texas is a close second with $7.89. The other two states are lower, with New York having a "price" of $3.94 and South Carolina a price of $5.14. While these prices are illustrative of differences in state markets, they do not account for the expected loss, or indicated losses, from the policy.

Table 10.4
Descriptive statistics for contributing companies' data measured at the postal zone level, 2005

	Number	Mean	Median	SD	Minimum	Maximum
Florida						
Written premium	2,009,576	$6,164	$1,696	8,642	$101	$482,014
Wind deductible	2,009,576	1,850	500	6,884	—	894,852
Policy deductible	2,009,576	1,998	500	6,858	—	894,852
Premiums per $1,000 of coverage A limit	2,009,573	8.13	7.10	4.634	0.407	788.00
South Carolina						
Written premium	423,818	4,977	4,185	5,616	100	187,684
Wind deductible	423,818	2,517	500	8,737	—	490,688
Policy deductible	423,818	2,754	500	8,678	—	490,688
Premiums per $1,000 of coverage A limit	423,818	5.14	4.64	2.10	—	74.33
New York						
Written premium	1,033,066	761	656	756	101	85,588
Wind deductible	1,033,066	508	500	433	—	25,000
Policy deductible	1,033,066	508	500	433	—	25,000
Premiums per $1,000 of coverage A limit	1,033,066	3.94	3.42	3.72	0.32	791.40
Texas						
Written premium	834,520.00	2,376	974	4,172	101	170,364
Wind deductible	834,520.00	3,136	1,082	7,363	—	1,201,392
Policy deductible	834,520.00	1,165	1,000	1,255	—	391,250
Premiums per $1,000 of coverage A limit	834,520.00	7.89	7.24	3.31	0.72	71.75

Other differences exist among the states. These arise in part because we do not have the universe of policies in each state. Instead we have the policies actually written by the sample companies. Furthermore, in each state, there are significant differences in property values written by the companies. For example, the sample companies have a higher coverage A limit for South Carolina than they do for New York. The coverage A limit average may be influenced by spectacular outliers; thus, we include the median coverage A limit too. However, we still see that South Carolina has a higher median coverage A limitation than New York. In addition to the different mix in companies in each state, we also have the possibility that each of the sample companies may have a different business model in each state and write in different areas of relative risk.

Methodology

We estimate a demand model for each state using a two-stage least squares. The process is similar to that described for the county-level analysis in section 10.2. We estimate a price equation at the postal zone level to control for the endogeneity of price and estimate the deductibles as endogenous variables.

The instruments for the first-stage regressions are the percentage of the postal zone covered by water, the percentage of the postal zone categorized by the Census Bureau as urban, the median value of homes in the postal zone, the number of housing units in the postal zone, the median year housing was built in the postal zone, the percentage of homes in the postal zone covered by a mortgage, the number of homes without heat, the number without plumbing or full kitchens, elevation above sea level, and ISO territory. Depending on the state, the first-stage regression R^2 range from 0.2 to 0.6.[20] The initial results for each state are summarized in tables 10.6 to 10.8.

Discussion of Results

Our main task is to show the sensitivities of insurance demand to changes in price, income, and levels of deductibles and to compare these results across states that have very different regulations. To set the stage, we present comparisons of prices across the states and across risk groups within each state in table 10.5.

We first break the data into four quartiles based on the ratio of modeled wind losses to total indicated losses. We rank all of the contracts based on this ratio and then break the sample into four equal-sized groups. The first quartile contains the first one-fourth of the data with the lowest levels of wind risk as a percentage of total risk. The second quartile contains the next one-fourth of the contracts, which represents the next 25 percent of the contracts based on wind risk. The third and fourth quartiles are defined similarly. By breaking the contracts up into these wind risk quartiles, we can examine the influence of risk on prices.

This table shows the prices of insurance for the different risk quartiles in Florida, South Carolina, and New York. We are not able to calculate similar prices for Texas because the

Table 10.5
Examination of prices across risk categories measured by percentage of wind loss costs to total loss costs, 2005

	Price	Number	Mean	SD	1 percentile minimum	99 percentile maximum
Florida	Quartile 1	157,207	1.871	3.570	−0.726	13.522
	Quartile 2	157,192	1.233	0.877	−0.486	3.653
	Quartile 3	157,311	1.037	0.817	−0.329	3.712
	Quartile 4	157,118	0.672	0.701	−0.477	2.871
	Overall	628,828	1.203	1.964	−0.595	5.730
South Carolina[a]	Quartile 1	78,267	1.956	0.994	0.319	4.962
	Quartile 2–3	104,655	1.835	1.122	0.168	5.496
	Quartile 4	61,144	1.902	1.509	−0.368	5.977
	Overall	244,066	1.891	1.135	−0.029	5.518
New York	Quartile 1	81,904	2.148	1.098	−0.127	5.103
	Quartile 2	81,520	1.850	1.002	−0.141	4.584
	Quartile 3	84,480	1.739	1.239	−0.315	5.398
	Quartile 4	76,119	1.9109	1.054	−0.251	4.417
	Overall	324,023	1.9106	1.104	−0.232	4.885

[a] South Carolina quartiles 2 and 3 had the same level of wind risk.

ISO did not create the loss cost rating program for this state.[21] In each state, the first quartile refers to the policies with the lowest level of catastrophe risk (measured as the ratio of wind loss costs to total loss costs), with succeeding quartiles having higher relative catastrophe risk. The price is an index of the percentage price-cost spread in the premium. The results show a very clear pattern in Florida. The price is much higher in lower-risk quartiles and much lower in later-risk quartiles. This reflects a pattern observed earlier by Grace et al. (2004) whereby premiums in high-risk areas are subsidized by premiums in low-risk areas. This cross-subsidization flattens out the risk sensitivity of premiums. In contrast, in South Carolina and New York, the premium index shows little variation across quartiles. This finding would be consistent with risk based premiums.[22]

Tables 10.6 to 10.8 contain the results for each state's demand estimation. Two panels are presented in each table. The top panel is a demand equation elasticity results over the time period (2001–2005) for each state. The second panel shows the elasticities estimated at various level of wind risk as a percentage of total risk in the year 2005. As in table 10.5, the state samples are broken up into quartiles based on the percentage of wind loss costs to total loss costs. This is used as a proxy for the importance of wind risk to the homeowners' demand for insurance.

Florida

Panel A in table 10.6 shows elasticity estimates for important variables in the demand equation. Each elasticity estimate is in relation to the quantity of insurance demanded. So we examine how price, income, deductibles, the percentage of homeowners with mortgages, and the coverage limits influence the quantity of insurance demanded. The first finding from the results in panel A in table 10.6 is that demand is price inelastic, since all the coefficients are less than 0.5 in absolute value. This is consistent with the result from the county-level analysis, though the coefficients are not directly comparable because of the different measures of price and quantity used in the two studies. It is of interest, however, that the degree of price inelasticity appears unstable over time. This may not be surprising given the rapidly changing regulatory environment and the corresponding changes in Citizens' market share. The instability might also be associated with the market disruptions caused by actual storm losses. In other words, it is reasonable to surmise that as hurricanes began hitting Florida and other states in 2004, this caused consumers to place greater importance on having adequate insurance, which would effectively increase their demand for insurance. One way this greater demand might be manifested is that homeowners might increased the coverage A limit on their policy to make sure that it would fully cover the replacement cost of their home. It also appears that the price becomes less inelastic as perceived risk increases (in 2004 and 2005, based on the hurricanes), indicating that customers are more likely to engage in price shopping in high-risk locations. This makes sense when one considers that despite the cross-subsidization between risk classes, insurance will form a larger portion of the consumers' budget in high-risk areas.

In general, demand is fairly inelastic with respect to income, which is consistent with the county analysis (table 10.6, panel A) ranging from -0.372 to -0.461. The county-level results showed that variations in income were associated with very small variations in the number of policies purchased. In contrast, the contract data result shown here reveal that insofar as people do buy insurance, the amount of insurance they buy is more closely related to price and income and, in the more recent data, less closely associated with the presence of a mortgage. For example, in 2005, the price elasticity and income elasticity are higher than the elasticity with respect to the percentage of mortgages in the postal zone.

Finally, the elasticity with respect to the percentage of homes with mortgages is positive, suggesting that an increase in the percentage of homes with mortgages increases the quantity of insurance demanded. Over the five years of our study (2001–2005), this elasticity ranges from 0.113 to 0.509. Thus, a 10 percent increase in the percentage of homes with a mortgage yields an increase in the range of 1.1 percent to 5.1 percent for the quantity of insurance demanded.

In table 10.6, panel B, we focus on the wind risk quartiles for 2005. Recall that the quartiles are defined based on the ratio of modeled wind loss costs to total indicated losses. Again, quartile 1 has the lowest wind exposure and quartile 4 the highest. We see that as wind exposure increases, the price elasticity becomes highly inelastic. In quartile 1, it is -0.773, and in quartile 4, it is -0.003. We also see that the income elasticity becomes more inelastic and negative at the higher levels of wind exposure. In terms of the other

Table 10.6
Florida: Important elasticity estimates by year and by wind risk percentage quartile, 2005

		Elasticities with respect to			
		Price	Income	Percentage of homes with mortgage	R^2
A. Two-stage least-squares regression elasticity estimates by year	2001	−0.067***	−0.372***	0.113***	0.848
	2002	−0.208***	−0.386***	0.182***	0.847
	2003	−0.094***	−0.414***	0.178***	0.800
	2004	−0.475***	−0.384***	0.509***	0.836
	2005	−0.382***	−0.461***	0.267***	0.891
B. Two-stage least-squares regression elasticity estimates by quartile (% wind risk)	Quartile 1	−0.773***	0.244***	0.005	0.975
	Quartile 2	−0.629***	0.063***	0.313***	0.758
	Quartile 3	−0.032***	−0.027***	0.085***	0.986
	Quartile 4	−0.003	−0.018***	0.018***	0.996
	Overall	−0.382***	−0.461***	0.267***	0.891

Note: Quartile is based on the ratio of indicated loss costs for wind to total indicated loss costs. Higher quartiles have higher wind components.
***Significance at the 0.01 level.

elasticities, we see no pattern as wind risk increases, suggesting no pattern in how the elasticities are related to the wind risk. This implies that as wind risk increases, people become less sensitive to changes in price when determining their demand for insurance.

South Carolina
In contrast with the Florida results, the insurance demand is elastic with response to price, and this elasticity is more stable over time. Demand is income inelastic, though showing a lower elasticity than in Florida. These results reflect a more stable regulatory environment than in Florida, and the absence of market shocks caused by major storm losses such as Florida experienced. The percentage of homes with a mortgage is not stable. This elasticity switches signs over time, going from approximately 0.09 to −0.245 (income column in panel A of table 10.7). However, the elasticity is always inelastic, so it does not have much effect on the quantity of insurance demanded.

Panel B of table 10.7 shows the demand elasticities at various levels of wind risk. Again, in contrast to the Florida results, we see that as wind exposure increases, the price elasticity becomes more elastic in South Carolina. Furthermore, there is no consistent pattern to the income elasticity over the risk quartiles. This also suggests, at least on the surface, that the market dynamics and regulation are different between the two states. From table 10.6, panel A we saw evidence of regulatory price suppression in Florida but not in South Carolina (table 10.7, panel B).

Table 10.7
South Carolina: Important elasticity estimates by year and by wind risk percentage quartile, 2005

		Elasticities with respect to			
		Price	Income	Percentage of homes with mortgage	R^2
A. Two-stage least-squares regression elasticity estimates, by year	2001	−0.949***	−0.248***	0.089***	0.726
	2002	−0.968***	−0.221***	0.025**	0.812
	2003	−1.637***	−0.139***	−0.293***	0.738
	2004	−1.550***	−0.098***	−0.286***	0.747
	2005	−1.103***	−0.149***	−0.245***	0.860
B. Two-stage least-squares regression elasticity estimates, by % wind risk	Quartile 1	−0.043	−0.408	0.130	0.294
	Quartile 2–3	−0.225**	0.354***	0.007	0.466
	Quartile 4	−1.730***	0.117	0.185*	0.653
	Overall	−1.158***	−0.099***	−0.323***	0.850

Note: Quartiles 2 and 3 had the same level of wind risk and are thus included together.
*** Significance at the 0.01 level.

New York

New York's results are shown in table 10.8. As in South Carolina, the price and income elasticities are fairly stable over time, though the demand is less responsive to price, hovering in the −0.6 range (compared with South Carolina, where it ranges from about −1.0 to −1.6). The income elasticity measure is comparable to South Carolina in the −0.1 through −0.3 range (table 10.8). While relatively stable, the price and income elasticities do seem to follow a time trend. Demand has become progressively less sensitive to price and progressively more sensitive to income between 2002 and 2005. Thus, in the markets where regulation is more predictable and major storm losses less frequent, demand elasticities with respect to price and income seem to be better behaved than in the more volatile market environment of Florida. In regard to the different risk quartiles, New York shows no substantial variation in price elasticities between risk groups, though the demand becomes more sensitive to income variation in the high-risk quartiles.

Another interesting pattern that emerges in both New York and South Carolina is that the temporal trends in price elasticity and in income elasticity move in opposite directions. Thus, as demand becomes more price sensitive, it also becomes less income sensitive. Given that the demand elasticity measures the sensitivity of the amount of insurance purchased from company x to the price charged by that same company, an increased elasticity can mean either that people buy less insurance when the incumbent increases its price or that they switch to another insurer. Given other results on cross-elasticities, the likely interpretation is that increased price elasticity reflects more shopping around. Thus, it seems

Table 10.8
New York: Important elasticity estimates by year and by wind risk percentage quartile, 2005

		Elasticities with respect to			
		Price	Income	Percentage of homes with mortgage	R^2
A. Two-stage least-squares regression elasticity estimates, by year	2001	−1.275***	0.009	0.076***	0.116
	2002	−0.633***	−0.105***	0.116***	0.319
	2003	−0.659***	−0.135***	0.145***	0.318
	2004	−0.645***	−0.142***	0.114***	0.320
	2005	−0.599***	−0.153***	0.096***	0.294
B. Two-stage least-squares regression elasticity estimates, by % wind risk	Quartile 1	−0.646***	−0.071***	0.061**	0.253
	Quartile 2	−0.673***	−0.091***	−0.022	0.204
	Quartile 3	0.113	−0.212***	−0.031	0.042
	Quartile 4	−0.676***	−0.225***	0.221***	0.536
	Overall	−0.599***	−0.153***	0.096***	0.294

Note: Quartile is based on the ratio of indicated loss costs for wind to total indicated loss costs. Higher quartiles have higher wind components.
*** Significance at the 0.01 level.
** Significance at the 0.05 level.

that insurance is becoming more of a necessity even as incomes rise, but these state markets at least are showing a degree of competition in the form of more shopping around.

If we look at the three states as a group, it is clear that Florida is different from New York and South Carolina. Florida's price elasticity is volatile over time, but as the amount of wind risk increases across risk quartiles, the demand for insurance becomes more inelastic. New York and South Carolina do not show similar results, and we suggest that this is due to the fact that regulation is stricter in Florida and that the underlying wind risk is also greater in Florida than in the other states. It is also important to note that high-risk exposures in coastal areas represent a much higher percentage of the total number of exposures in Florida than they do in South Carolina and New York. This may also partly account for the greater stability in the latter two states.

Deductibles

We also examined the effect of prices, expected losses (indicated losses), and income on the two types of deductibles common to our data: the hurricane wind deductible and the policy deductible. The hurricane wind deductible is specified separately from the policy deductible in the insurance contracts covering hurricane-related wind losses. As shown in table 10.9, the wind deductibles are much different from the general (nonwind) policy deductible for Florida and South Carolina. For Florida, the average policy deductible

Table 10.9
Wind and policy deductibles by state, 2005

	Wind			Policy		
	Florida	South Carolina	New York	Florida	South Carolina	New York
99%	$27,900	$1,000	$1,000	$26,400	$1,000	$1,000
95%	5,000	1,000	1,000	3,900	1,000	1,000
90%	2,000	1,000	1,000	1,700	1,000	1,000
75% Q3	1,000	1,000	500	1,000	1,000	500
50% median	500	500	500	500	500	500
25% Q1	0	500	250	500	500	250
10%	0	0	250	500	500	250
5%	0	0	250	500	500	250
1%	0	0	100	0	500	100
0% Minimum	0	0	0	0	50	0
Average	$1,565	$531	$508	$1,658	$700	$508

($1,658) is slightly higher than the wind deductible ($1,565). For South Carolina, the average wind deductible is about $531, while the average policy deductible is $700.[23] These differences may be due to the fact that while both Florida and South Carolina have relatively high insurance prices, the Florida prices are higher, and consumers in Florida are more likely to employ higher deductibles as a way of reducing premiums. In addition, since our policy samples are not random but are based on the data supplied by the various companies, it may be that the mix of high- and low-risk policies differs between the states.

Looking at the distribution of deductibles across the sample companies and states, we see that a relatively large percentage of policyholders has low deductibles. For example, if we look at the percentiles at the lower end of the distribution, both Florida and South Carolina have significant numbers of policyholders with either zero or $500 deductibles. The same is true in New York, where at least 75 percent of the sample has a deductible of $500 or less. This is consistent with the evidence detailed in chapter 4 with respect to the National Flood Insurance Program for Florida, which shows that approximately 80 percent of the insureds have the minimum deductible and is consistent with other empirical data indicating that many individuals prefer low deductibles.[24] We must also note that homeowners in noncoastal areas represent a much larger proportion of all homeowners in New York and South Carolina than they do in Florida. Presumably there would be little incentive for noncoastal homeowners to opt for a high wind deductible.

As part of our demand estimation, we also estimated relationships between deductibles and other explanatory variables. These results in elasticity form are presented in table 10.10. For each state we estimated two equations of the form:

Table 10.10
Deductible elasticities for Florida, New York, and South Carolina, 2001–2005

		Elasticities with respect to					
		Indicated loss costs		Price		Income	
		Wind	Policy	Wind	Policy	Wind	Policy
Florida	2001	0.751	0.000	−0.533	0.087	0.489	−0.005
	2002	0.845	0.039	−1.132	0.144	0.000	0.023
	2003	0.812	0.049	−0.997	0.176	0.024	0.012
	2004	0.822	0.065	−0.905	0.238	0.030	0.000
	2005	0.851	0.123	0.067	0.123	0.067	0.054
New York	2001	5.986	0.060	1.858	0.203	−0.663	0.111
	2002	9.533	0.587	5.947	0.405	1.019	0.194
	2003	7.644	0.608	5.252	0.415	0.847	0.214
	2004	8.989	0.712	6.344	0.465	1.534	0.270
	2005	5.837	0.713	4.796	0.456	0.932	0.286
South Carolina	2001	−0.622	0.065	0.144	0.000	−2.299	0.239
	2002	−0.528	0.061	0.557	−0.053	−2.021	0.237
	2003	−4.725	0.173	14.364	−0.437	−2.808	0.106
	2004	−4.283	0.171	11.535	−0.352	−1.913	0.051
	2005	−3.621	0.145	11.342	−0.350	0.190	−0.005

Note: Elasticities calculated from a 2sls regression estimated with the demand equation of the form log deductible $= f$(log price, log of ILC, log of other deductible, log of median income, percent area covered in water, percent urban, median year home was built, elevation).

$$\log(Deductible_i^D) = f\left(\log(price_i), \log(median\ income_z), \log(ILC_i),\ others\right) + v \qquad (10.6)$$

where i is the contract, z is the postal zone, D is the deductible type (wind or policy), and ILC is the indicated loss costs. Price is endogenously determined, and the other variables include the complementary deductible, which is also endogenously determined; the percentage of the postal zone area that is water; the percentage of homes in urban areas in the postal zone; the median year the home was built; and the mean elevation above sealevel of the postal zone.

Florida

For the elasticity with respect to the indicated loss cost (our measure of quantity) we see a relatively stable relationship over time (see table 10.10). A 10 percent increase in indicated losses yields a 7.5 to 8.5 percent increase in the wind deductible. In addition, the policy deductible is also stable and relatively inelastic over time. This suggests that consumers increase their policy deductible with an increase in expected losses. This would also be consistent with consumers' attempting to maintain the same coverage limit for protecting

themselves against a hurricane that causes severe damage to their property without having
to increase their total insurance premium significantly. The price elasticity is unstable over
time with respect to the wind deductible. However, if we look at the beginning and end
periods, we see that the elasticity increased from −0.5 in 2001 to 0.067 in 2005. This suggests that consumers' behavior with regard to the wind deductible has changed significantly over time. A number of things have happened during this period in Florida. First,
there was an increase in the frequency of hurricanes in 2004–2005, and second, there was
an increase in home values. While the elasticity was negative in 2001, a 10 percent increase
in the deductible in 2005 yielded a 0.67 percent increase in the price. This positive elasticity
reflects the increase in insurance premiums following the 2004 hurricane. In other words, it
appears that homeowners maintained their demand for insurance at higher premiums but
decided to reduce their total costs by taking a higher deductible. The policy-deductible
price elasticity, in contrast, has been relatively stable at about 0.1 to 0.2, suggesting
increases in prices were associated with increases in the policy deductible.

For income, we see a relatively stable relationship between income and the deductibles.
With the exception of 2001, the wind and policy deductible income elasticities are quite
low, in the near zero range, suggesting almost no relationship between income and
deductibles.

The results shown in table 10.11 are derived from a two-stage least-squares model akin
to the one used to estimate the results in table 10.10. The first row shows the elasticities
with respect to our measure of quantity demanded. Thus, the price elasticity is −0.32, consistent with our results in table 10.6. The second row is a regression estimation reflecting
the determinants of the wind deductible, and the third line shows a similar regression for
the policy deductible. The main difference between these results and the results described
above is that we include another variable that accounts for the wind risk in the postal
zone. This risk variable comes from RMS, which calculated the modeled average annual
loss (AAL) for the postal zone for Florida in 2005. In addition to the AAL, RMS provided
the standard deviation of the AAL. So we have a measure of the pure modeled expected
hurricane loss as well as the standard deviation of the measure. A good proxy risk measure

Table 10.11
Demand, deductibles, and risk elasticity results for Florida, 2005

	Price	Hurricane deductible	Policy deductible	Income	Risk	R^2
Demand	−0.320***	−0.077***	−0.334***	−0.433***	−0.081***	0.93
Hurricane deductible	−0.096***		−3.018***	0.110**	−0.116***	0.38
Policy deductible	0.237***	−0.069***		0.033***	0.013***	0.14

Note: Risk is defined as the log of the ratio of the standard deviation within the postal zone of RMS-modeled
average annual loss (AAL) divided by the mean of the AAL for the postal zone.
*** Significance at the 1 percent level. ** Significance at the 5 percent level.

is the coefficient of variation, which is defined as the ratio of the standard deviation to the mean of a variable. Essentially the coefficient of variation allows us to compare different levels of uncertainty about the wind risk relative to its mean (or what one expects).

In table 10.11, the results are reported in elasticity form. Thus, a 10 percent increase in price will yield a reduction in quantity demanded of 3.2 percent. We see that for both the hurricane and policy deductibles, the relationship to demand is relatively inelastic, with the quantity demanded being particularly insensitive to the hurricane deductible. This implies that consumers' choices about the total limit on their policy are not closely related to their choices of deductible. In other words, insureds may want to be sure that they have adequate coverage in terms of having the full replacement cost of their home covered (which would be important in the event of a total or severe loss) but may be willing to accept a higher deductible regardless, as the deductible is something they may be prepared to pay out of their assets in exchange for a lower premium, all other things being equal. This would be consistent with insurance principles that place greater emphasis on transferring the risk of "unaffordable" losses and retaining smaller, affordable losses. Looking at the risk as measured by the log of the coefficient of variation of the AAL, we see that a 10 percent increase in risk lowers the quantity demanded by 0.8 percent. This is consistent with the fact that there are no real substitutes for insurance and that consumers will still purchase insurance even if risk increases.

We also see that increases in risk influence the deductibles. For the hurricane deductible, an increase in risk of 10 percent yields a 1.116 percent decrease in the deductible. However, for the policy deductible, there is a positive but almost negligible effect of 0.13 percent increase in the level of deductible for a 10 percent increase in risk. These results seem to suggest that consumers' demands for protection (at the low end where the deductible might come into use) are different for wind losses than for nonwind losses. Consumers will increase deductibles in conjunction with higher prices for nonwind risk but not for wind risk.

New York

New York is very different from Florida in terms of the consumers' behavior toward changes in the indicated loss costs (see table 10.10). New York shows high elasticities between wind deductibles and indicated losses, suggesting that small increases in expected losses cause a large increase in the deductible level. It should be noted that New York's levels of deductibles are quite low compared to the other states, so this is not too surprising. Similarly for the policy deductible, the elasticity is more sensitive than Florida's, but it is much lower than the New York wind deductible in terms of sensitivity.

The price elasticity for both deductibles is positive, which suggests that an increase in the price causes an increase in the level of the deductible. Again, like the elasticity for the indicated loss costs (ILC), our measure of output, the wind deductible price is quite elastic relative to the policy-deductible price elasticity.

The New York deductible income elasticities are mostly positive. The wind elasticity is negative in one year (2001) and somewhat unstable in the other years, ranging from 0.85 to 1.5. The policy deductible is relatively stable, ranging from 0.11 to 0.29. Thus, as the median income increases by 10 percent, the deductible increases between 11 and 29 percent depending on the year.

South Carolina

South Carolina has a negative elasticity for wind deductible with respect to indicated losses, as shown in table 10.10. It is also quite high in terms of absolute value in 2003–2005. One would expect that the elasticity would be positive. A negative elasticity suggests that as indicated losses go up, deductibles decrease. In contrast, we find a positive relationship for the indicated loss costs with respect to the policy deductible in approximately the same range as for Florida. For price elasticities, we see that the wind deductible has a high price elasticity for the period 2003 to 2005. Thus, a 10 percent increase in the price is associated with a 140 percent increase in deductibles. This would be consistent with consumers going from $500 deductibles to deductibles based on a percentage of the limits for the dwelling. For the policy deductible, the price elasticity is negative; thus, a 10 percent increase in price is associated with a decrease in the deductible. We found opposite results in New York and Florida. While this result is somewhat perplexing, there are possible explanations. One might be that in South Carolina, consumers respond to higher risk (reflected in higher prices) by lowering their deductible because they believe that they are much more likely to have a loss. In Florida, however, the price of insurance in coastal areas is much higher (as is the price of lower deductibles), and this crosses a tipping point for consumers, causing them to opt for higher deductibles to make their insurance more affordable.

Finally, we see that with respect to income elasticity, both the wind and policy deductible are moving toward zero over time. The wind deductible started at −2.3 in 2001 and in 2005 was 0.19. The policy deductible started in 2001 at approximately .24 and by 2005 was −0.005. This is consistent with the results in Florida, where the income elasticity for the deductibles was close to zero.

We have examined the demand for insurance in three states. Each state has a different political and regulatory environment as well as experience with hurricanes. Because it is not possible to control for these types of variations among the states, it is not possible to make generalizations. Each state is a separate case study. Florida, the state with the most severe regulatory environment, has had the worst experience with hurricanes. This experience has led, in part, to the development of regulatory policy unique to this state. South Carolina, while it has had experience with large hurricanes, has not had the frequency experienced by Florida. Its wind insurance availability problem is also focused on the coastal areas. Florida, in contrast, has potential availability problems in most of the state. New York has not had the same type of experience with major wind storms. While it is not completely free from risk of hurricanes, a large portion of the state's valuable property and the source of its major economic activities is within the reach of a severe hurricane. Each state has different issues with regard to wind risk, and thus the demand for insurance is likely to be quite different.

10.4 Conclusion

In this chapter we provide an initial examination of the supply and demand conditions for Florida. We note first that the demand elasticity for the purchase of any insurance is unit elastic in Florida and that the state's intervention through Citizens provides a substitute for private market insurance.

In terms of supply, we note that it is highly elastic. This implies that insurers are willing to provide coverage, assuming that they can obtain risk-based prices. We note from table 10.6 that the highest-risk areas have the lowest price markups in Florida, suggesting a degree of price suppression that reduces the availability of insurance to high-risk areas. Also, the availability of reinsurance increases the supply of insurance. Furthermore, higher-risk firms (indicated by leverage or credit quality) are more willing to supply coverage in Florida. This may be because these firms are able to pass on the increased default risk to existing consumers without being penalized in prices. Indeed, the presence of guarantees means that consumers do not have to worry too much about credit risk. It is also the case that the state has encouraged single state entities, often with low credit ratings, to address capacity shortages. Alternatively, the larger supply of high-risk insurers may have been directly facilitated by regulatory strategies that have encouraged their growth.

This study examined Citizens' participation in the market when it was mandated to have the highest price in relation to what was offered in the private market. Thus, it really was not competing with insurance companies but was acting as an insurer of last resort. Even so, there was a positive cross-price elasticity, suggesting that the public market was a substitute for private insurance products. Indeed, with cross-elasticity of demand, the size of Citizens would have been constrained by its imputed high prices. In 2007 the Florida legislature allowed Citizens to compete for customers (by pricing at what some would designate as below risk-based rates). Given cross-elasticity, this would imply that Citizens could capture considerable market share from private insurers as it competes directly. This new competition might have a further effect on the long-run desirability of private insurers marketing homeowners' coverage in Florida.

For our demand analysis for three states, we have a number of interesting results. In the highly regulated and loss-prone state of Florida, estimates of price and income elasticity of demand are highly unstable. While this may be indicative of some market disorder, we need to study further whether the fluctuations are systematically related to regulatory and other factors. In South Carolina and New York with lower regulation and no major losses during the study period, we find that our results on price and income elasticity are more robust. The amount of insurance purchased (conditional on one buying insurance at all) is quite sensitive to price spread and even ventures into the price elastic range in South Carolina. Demand is also income inelastic, although not as extreme as in the Florida county-level study reported earlier.

Also, the deductibles are generally sensitive to the indicated loss costs (Florida and New York are positive and South Carolina is negative). However, the state markets differ in terms of price elasticities with respect to the deductibles. What is interesting is that New York, with arguably the lowest wind risk, has the typically expected relationships (as price increases, deductibles increase). Florida has negative elasticities for the wind deductible, and South Carolina has negative elasticities for the policy deductible. Finally, while the income elasticities with respect to the deductibles are different across states, by 2005 both Florida and South Carolina reported a near-zero income elasticity for both hurricane and policy deductibles, suggesting that changes in income have no effect on the deductible.

Summary

In this chapter, we undertake a number of analyses. First, we present an analysis of the supply and demand for homeowners' insurance for Florida. Second, we examine various measures of premiums in four states (Florida, New York, Texas, and South Carolina). Third, we estimate at a more refined level the demand for homeowners' insurance in Florida, South Carolina, and New York. The purpose is to examine how effectively the private market functions and what prices and availability result. We also address the impact on the market of various interventions, ranging from price controls to residual market mechanisms.

III PROTECTING HOMEOWNERS AGAINST NATURAL DISASTERS

Impact of Insurance Status on Economic Welfare of Homeowners in Hazard-Prone Areas: The Affordability Challenge

Key Findings

Defining the affordability of homeowners' insurance requires making value judgments about how much income a homeowner should have left over to spend on other things after paying for insurance coverage. This value judgment is typically specified relative to some poverty line (which adjusts for family size and composition). The affordability threshold thus represents a community's values and standards.

Data from the American Housing Survey on eight cities in our target states show that in all cities, for several different definitions of the affordability threshold, a significant number of owner-occupied homes are owned by households with incomes below those thresholds. If the affordability threshold is set at 200 percent of the federal poverty line, between 16 percent (Dallas) and 31 percent (Tampa) of owner-occupied homes are owned by households that cannot afford insurance. At 125 percent of the federal poverty line, the percentage varies from nearly 7 percent in Dallas to 17 percent in Tampa.

Among low-income households judged unable to afford insurance, a large fraction of homes are nevertheless insured, even when there is no mortgage requiring coverage. Fewer than 27 percent of low-income homeowners (San Antonio; 125 percent of the federal poverty line) fail to purchase insurance coverage in any of the cities studied. Any program that directs subsidies to all low-income homeowners will allocate much of the funds to those who are already insured.

While measures based on purchasing power and on household choices capture static notions of affordability, people may have in mind a notion of equity that relates to the fairness in changes in homeowners' premiums. In particular, if changes in premiums are distributed unevenly across households, one might take the view that those subject to large increases are not being treated fairly and justly. If some homeowners see their premiums jump by thousands of dollars in a single year while others have modest changes, a case could be made that one subgroup is being singled out for unfair premium increases. This perceived inequity could be addressed through innovative public or private sector programs.

In determining the future of insurance as a policy instrument for financing recovery from natural disasters and enhancing the adoption of adequate mitigation measures, we need to have a clearer understanding of what proportion of homeowners in hazard-prone areas currently have homeowners' insurance. Furthermore, we need to understand why some have (or should have) homeowners' insurance while others do not. (Homeowners' insurance usually does not cover losses from flood damage, but covers damage from other perils.) The first portion of this chapter tackles these issues by looking at American Housing Survey data, the primary source of data on housing expenditures for metropolitan areas in the states of interest. The final section discusses the policy implications of these findings.

11.1 Who Should Have Insurance, and Why?

The most serious public policy problems occur when a substantial fraction of homeowners suffering losses do not have homeowners' insurance. If this fraction is large, there will be considerable pressure, partly political but partly altruistic, for special legislation to provide them with disaster assistance, as discussed in chapter 5. In the United States, most homes are covered by some type of homeowners' insurance, but some are not. It is these victims' financial plight that raises the loudest calls for public assistance following natural and man-made catastrophes. When a disaster strikes, uninsured homeowners become more impoverished unless local, state, and federal governments step in, commonly in delayed, incomplete, inefficient, and arbitrary ways. Encouraging or requiring uninsured homeowners to obtain insurance prior to a disaster will lead to better outcomes than relying on disaster assistance after losses occur. Gaining a clearer understanding as to the socioeconomic characteristics of homeowners who lack insurance coverage is a key to designing or evaluating public policy.

To help fill this gap, we reviewed data on the proportion of homeowners without insurance and the characteristics of purchasers and nonpurchasers. We were particularly interested in the insurance status of relatively low-income households, which, as the data demonstrate, are much more likely to be uninsured. We used the American Housing Survey (AHS) data for 1998, 2000, and 2002. Our analysis is limited to owner-occupied homes. The AHS data were collected in eight large metropolitan areas in three of our focus states, Florida, New York, and Texas; different cities were surveyed in different years. The data provide detailed information on insurance, housing, and homeowner characteristics.

11.2 Defining "Affordability"

There is no unique technical definition of *affordability* or *afford* in economics or insurance-related policy analysis. We propose and use an interpretation that represents what policy-makers and decision makers have had in mind, based on other uses of the term in policy discussions in the literature. In section 11.4 we also discuss alternative definitions of both *affordability* and *equity* that might be considered. The most common interpretation of *affordability* is a normative concept: a consumer expenditure on a particular good is said to be affordable by a household if the expenditure buys an adequate amount of the good in question and the household has enough income to pay for the expenditure on the particular good and enough money left over to buy adequate amounts ("an adequate basket") of other goods. For example, Bramley (1991) defines the affordability of a given good as entailing a household's having enough income to buy the quantity of the good "that meets well established (social sector) norms of adequacy" at a total cost "that leaves them with enough income to live on without falling below some poverty standard."

While some variant of this definition (normative, in the sense that it depends on norms) is the basis of the most common uses of the term *affordability* or *affordable*, there are other definitions as well. For example, one could define the income at which some amount of a good is affordable as that level at which more than half (or some other fraction) of otherwise similar households choose to obtain the item. This behavioral definition cannot be explored fully with the data at hand, since we do not know how purchase decisions are affected by changes in prices, but it could be implemented when information on price responsiveness of the purchase or nonpurchase decision becomes available.

11.3 Why No Insurance? Concepts and Results

We explored the association between having or not having homeowners' insurance and (1) whether the home carried a mortgage and (2) the income of the homeowner relative to the poverty line. We anticipate that homeowners without mortgages are more likely to be uninsured than homeowners with mortgages, because mortgage lenders typically require the purchase of at least enough insurance to protect their assets at risk.

Homeowners with mortgages agree to pay for insurance because they are required to do so if they want to take out and maintain the loan that makes ownership of their home possible. These requirements are generally decided by the lender, but if the mortgage balance falls to a low level relative to the value of the property, rational lenders may be less concerned about continuing insurance protection, expecting that any remaining exposure might be covered by the salvage or land value of the property. Homeowners without mortgages generally ought to seek insurance as well, since damage can wipe out this important asset that they own. However, they are not required to have insurance as a condition of retaining ownership of the home.

Household income or wealth has a less obvious relationship to insurance coverage. For a given asset value at risk, the normative theory of insurance suggests that lower-income households are more likely to be insured, since a total loss would often be a larger proportion of their wealth and therefore more devastating to them. (Lower-income people might have lower-valued houses as well, but the value of the house would not generally decline enough to be a lower proportion of their wealth.) They might also be expected to display higher risk aversion. However, it is often said that lower-income homeowners are less able to afford insurance as part of housing costs. It is surely true that a given lower-income household paying an insurance premium would generally have lower levels of other consumption than if it had not purchased coverage (except when it actually experienced a loss).

For lower-income households without mortgages that find the insurance premium on their current home to be too burdensome, there is, in theory, an economically more attractive option to risking an uninsured loss of the asset from a disaster: sell the house, use the proceeds to buy a less expensive home, and use the savings to cover the insurance premium on the new residence. This strategy works well on paper. (Or they might have been better advised not to tie up so much of their assets in this house in the first place.) In reality, however, sentimental attachment to a particular home, the desire to stay in a bigger house or in a nicer area, inertia, location of one's employment, the high transaction costs associated with selling and buying a new home (including the time and expenses associated with moving), lagged responses to insurance premium increases resulting from the appreciation in house value and higher replacement cost, or poor planning may make this strategy unattractive.

The AHS data indicate how these conflicting motives for purchasing insurance play out. The specific wording of the question in the AHS questionnaire was, "Does this household have homeowners' insurance (HO) (household property insurance)?" Some people may have interpreted "homeowners' insurance" to mean more comprehensive fire and hazard protection than what they currently have. So the fraction of people who said no may be an upward-biased measure of those without any financial protection for their house whatsoever.

We explore the implications of using different specifications of affordability in terms of household income. We assume that society chooses a lower boundary for adequate spending on the household's consumption of other goods and services, and therefore defines a household as unable to afford insurance if its income is below the amount needed to buy those other items as well as homeowners' insurance. We explore two levels of this minimum adequate consumption standard: 125 percent of the federal poverty line and 200 percent of the poverty line.[1]

Table 11.1 shows the proportion of uninsured homeowners in the metropolitan areas in the AHS survey in Florida, New York, and Texas for the two different measures based on the federal poverty line. The proportion of homes owned by low-income households is sub-

Table 11.1
Percentage of owner-occupied houses in households with income below various affordability thresholds, 1998–2002

Threshold	City and year							
	Houston 1998	Tampa 1998	Rochester 1998	Dallas 2000	Miami 2000	Fort Worth 2000	Buffalo 2000	San Antonio 2002
200% of FPL	25.7	30.8	18.0	16.3	27.6	19.0	21.1	29.4
200% of FPL plus triple premiums	26.8	32.8	18.8	18.1	29.9	20.9	23.0	30.7
125% of FPL	15.8	17.2	9.0	6.8	12.6	8.7	7.8	14.5
125% of FPL plus triple premiums	17.3	18.7	9.7	8.4	14.7	10.8	9.0	16.8

Note: FPL = federal poverty line.

stantial in all of the areas. It is highest in Miami and Tampa and lowest in the two New York cities, Rochester and Buffalo, where lower-income families are more likely to rent rather than own.

Suppose that we use 200 percent of the federal poverty line (FPL) as a measure of the affordability threshold. The data in the first row of table 11.1 show that a significant portion of owner-occupied houses had owners with incomes below this line. Consider Houston, Texas. Based on the normative poverty-line definition, 25.7 percent of the homeowners in this city could not afford homeowners' premiums even at their then-current level of income. What if we use 125 percent of the poverty line, a lower income level, as a threshold? Fewer homes were owned by people with such low incomes, so the proportion of Houston homes owned by families labeled unable to afford by this measure falls to 15.8 percent.

How would an increase in premiums, (e.g., from adherence to risk-based pricing) affect the proportion of those who could not afford coverage? We simulate such an increase using data results from table 11.1 by asking what the percentage of individuals in this category would be if the premiums were raised by a substantial amount. Specifically, we assume that the premium to be paid would more than triple; we estimate this increase by adding twice the median premium to the threshold premium. Continuing with the Houston example, the median annual insurance premium in 1998 for those who bought homeowners' insurance was approximately $852. Homes owned by low-income homeowners generally had smaller premiums than this, but we use this measure in our illustration. If premiums had risen by triple the average premium, or $1,704, the percentage of homeowners unable to afford insurance would increase, but only moderately, from 25.7 percent to 26.8 percent. That is, while the proportion of homes owned by people who cannot afford premiums is fairly high, it does not increase much if premiums increase substantially. Similar findings hold for the other seven cities, as shown in table 11.1. The findings are not changed for

Table 11.2
Mortgage and insurance status, low-income households, 1998–2002

	City and year							
	Houston 1998	Tampa 1998	Roch- ester 1998	Dallas 2000	Miami 2000	Fort Worth 2000	Buffalo 2000	San Antonio 2002
Affordability: 200% of FPL								
% without mortgage	62.6	58.6	64.1	49.0	48.9	65.6	65.8	63.0
% without mortgage and without insurance	31.6	11.6	7.7	20.1	26.8	26.9	6.5	31.8
Overall % without insurance	23.2	8.3	6.3	15.5	21.0	22.8	5.1	23.1
Affordability: 125% of FPL								
% without mortgage	66.8	59.1	67.1	49.4	55.0	71.0	62.6	70.6
% without mortgage and without insurance	32.0	11.7	10.0	26.1	31.1	27.9	7.7	34.0
Overall % without insurance	25.0	9.0	8.3	22.2	26.1	24.8	6.9	27.2

Note: FPL = federal poverty line.

any of the eight cities when a lower standard of affordability such as 125 percent of the poverty line is used. The reason these households are not able to afford insurance is that their incomes are low, not that their premiums are high.

This common normative definition of *affordability* does, however, lead to a puzzle in this regard. While many lower-income homeowners might be said to be unable to afford insurance, a very large fraction of them did pay for this insurance. In fact, 96.6 percent of nonafforder homeowners with mortgages had insurance (data not shown). This high proportion presumably reflects lender requirements.[2] Table 11.2 shows that even among homeowners below the FPL who had no mortgage, a surprisingly small proportion had no insurance. The percentages without insurance ranged from a low of 6.5 percent (Buffalo, New York) to a high of 31.8 percent (San Antonio, Texas). Mortgages for poor households are most common in Miami, Florida; Dallas, Texas; and Tampa, Florida, which explains the relatively low overall uninsured percentage among low-income homeowners in these three areas. We conjecture that the very low uninsured percentages in Rochester and Buffalo are due to the fact that a much larger proportion of low-income individuals rent in these two cities than in the other six, so that almost all of those who choose to own a home can afford to pay for the insurance.

Aside from having a mortgage, what other variables are related to the purchase of homeowners insurance for low-income homeowners? Table 11.3 shows that homeowners below 200 percent of the FPL without mortgages are more likely to have insurance coverage if the home has a higher value and the owner is older. Since the insurance premium is

Table 11.3
Sample data on owner-occupied housing among households without mortgages, under 200% of FPL, by home-owners' insurance status

	1998 AHS			2002 AHS				2004 AHS
	Houston	Tampa	Roch-ester	Dallas	Miami	Fort Worth	Buffalo	San Antonio
Among uninsured (N)	104	44	21	39	79	62	16	136
Mean value of house ($)	37,402	45,181	37,528	55,024	71,852	48,458	37,144	55,571
Mean age of homeowner	57	58	63	57	65	57	57	61
Among insured (N)	249	366	273	146	232	184	252	300
Mean value of house ($)	77,174	65,440	77,361	102,049	136,958	83,908	83,168	83,570
Mean age of homeowner	63	71	69	63	69	64	72	63

Source: Authors' calculation; data from American Housing Survey.

almost always higher for higher house values, this finding shows that households do not necessarily drop coverage when they have to pay more for insurance. If the higher premiums reflect protection of more assets at risk, households somehow find a feasible way to protect their property.

11.4 Alternative Definitions of Affordability

While the definition of affordability based on income (minus premiums) relative to the poverty line is a reasonable one and common in the literature that deals with affordability, other definitions are possible. One alternative is a definition that makes affordability dependent not on value judgment about what people can pay for but rather on what they typically choose to pay for. This behavioral definition says that a household with a given set of characteristics can afford some particular item of consumption if most households with the same set of characteristics do in fact choose to buy that item.[3] Here, this definition might suggest that if most households at a given income level without mortgages owning a house of a given value do obtain homeowners' insurance, households with those characteristics that do not obtain insurance could have afforded it but chose not to purchase it. One could then investigate what proportion of uninsured homeowners could have afforded insurance. If in almost every set of characteristics that one might construct, including income, a majority of homeowners do buy insurance, we would conclude that almost everyone could afford insurance.

There are still some important value judgments here. For example, rather than judging something as affordable if a certain percentage of people already buy it, one could increase the criterion from 50 percent to a larger fraction, such as 75 or 90 percent. The set of characteristics also represents a value judgment. What about respondents who say they "live from paycheck to paycheck"? Probably a larger fraction who indicate that this behavior matches their own will be uninsured, but that kind of budgeting strategy is not imposed on people; they choose to budget in a particularly risky way (in contrast to other households similar to them on objective measures), and we would not want to let them be labeled "unafforders" just because they chose a dysfunctional pattern of family budgeting. Even measures like the value of the house or the presence or absence of a mortgage are endogenous to households; they choose to be or not to be in one of these sets.

To estimate the proportion of uninsured homeowners who cannot afford insurance by this criterion, we would need to specify and estimate an empirical behavioral model of the decision to obtain some insurance, which we have not done. The AHS contains only some measures of household characteristics, perhaps not all that one might want. Based on the data presented, it is very likely that most low-income people who own relatively high-value homes will have insurance, so that the minority who are uninsured would be labeled "afforders." If uninsured households are a minority in most income and demographic categories, one would be able to conclude that most uninsured could have afforded insurance.

Another possible definition of affordability of homeowners' insurance is based on definitions of affordable housing used by the U.S. Department of Housing and Urban Development (HUD). HUD usually classifies people as unable to afford housing in a given market area if the total cost of housing (including insurance) is more than 30 percent of their income *and* their income is less than half the median income in their market area. The basis for this definition is again a value judgment: such families "are considered cost burdened and may have difficulty affording necessities such as food, clothing, transportation, and medical care."[4] This definition differs from our earlier normative version in being based on total housing costs and on requiring necessarily subjective judgments about what levels of spending on other necessities are affordable. Although we do not apply this definition to the AHS data since it seems to go to factors other than premiums and their regulation to define social objectives, we do note that it makes the interesting point that society might be more concerned about the total cost of housing rather than any component of it. For example, if property taxes are very high in an area, a relatively low-income household might be said to be unable to afford housing even if homeowners' insurance premiums were quite low.

Another alternative definition of affordability is one that was established by the U.S. Environmental Protection Agency (EPA) to meet guidelines established by the 1996 amendments to the Safe Drinking Water Act. The amendments specified that small public water systems would be allowed to use less effective pollutant control technologies when the designated technologies for satisfying treatment technique requirements were not "affordable." EPA judged that a technology was not affordable for a small system if the associated average expense per household served exceeded 2 percent of the median household income in the service area.[5] Using this definition for judging whether a household could pay for homeowners' insurance, one could determine what proportion of those residing in any given region woul be considered unable to afford to pay the premium. The federal poverty line for a family of four is nearly $20,000 per year, which means that if the insurance premium were above $400, it would be considered unaffordable. By this definition, a much larger percentage of homeowners in the hazard-prone areas under study would be classified as being unable to afford insurance. The qualitative conclusions of the previous section would still hold: most of the homeowners in the "unaffordability" class would still have purchased insurance.

11.5   Equitable Changes in Premiums

While measures based on purchasing power and on household choices capture static notions of affordability, there may also be a notion of equity that people have in mind that relates to the fairness in changes in homeowners' premiums. In particular, if increases in premiums are distributed very unevenly across households, one might take the view that homeowners subject to very large increases are not being treated fairly and justly. To be specific, suppose a population of owners of similar homes (but in different locations) with initially similar premiums unexpectedly face increases in premiums that are much larger for homes in some locations than in others. Some homeowners see their premiums jump by thousands of dollars per year, while others, perhaps most homeowners, have modest changes. While the increase in premiums might not be large enough to push the unlucky families' consumption levels down below the poverty line and while all households might continue to buy coverage, there might be a public policy argument that one subgroup is being inequitably singled out for substantially higher premium increases (disregarding the reasons why this huge increase happened).

Whether this pattern is inequitable is obviously a value judgment, and such judgments may differ across voters, policymakers, insurers, or regulators. It seems plausible that views might differ depending on the reason for the premium change. If it reflects a dramatic change in relative risk estimation, views might be different than if it reflected a movement to risk-based premiums after a time period of regulation-required community rating. If in the former case, insurers and homeowners alike had previously believed risk levels to be both lower and more uniform than the risk levels indicated by new risk models with new data, then it might be possible to make the case for some regulatory cushioning of large changes in market-based premiums. If such protection can be provided to existing homeowners in ways that do more good than harm, it should be sanctioned. But inhibiting the ability of insurers to obtain premiums reflecting risks from new or prospective homeowners can have substantial inefficiency costs in the form of distorted incentives toward housing purchases in higher-risk locations, and inhibit investment in mitigation, so in this sense it is less desirable.

As suggested, an equity-based argument would seem at most to be one that applies to people who owned the homes before the risk estimate changed. Whether they remain in those homes and pay high premiums or decide to sell their homes at a lower price, they do bear an unexpected cost, and they, as well as society, might wish some protection on the basis of efficiency in risk spreading as well as equity. The only sensible standard here would seem to be what the full subset of homeowner-taxpayers might prefer as public policy, with options presented clearly and tax or premium cost differences made transparent. The tendency to imagine that insurers have the power to absorb higher expected costs should be resisted.

11.6   Implications for Policy

The results of our analysis indicate a policy puzzle. If the government wanted to make insurance more affordable to homeowners that it thought were unable to afford the premiums and based eligibility for a specific subsidy program only on a homeowner's having a low income relative to the poverty line, it would subsidize a large fraction of homeowners in many areas who are already paying for insurance. For example, at 200 percent of poverty line standard, more than a quarter of homeowners would be eligible for subsidy in a number of areas we studied. In all the cities we reviewed, at least 16 percent of all homeowners would be eligible for subsidy.

However, no more than 27 percent of needy households now fail to buy their own insurance even when not required to do so by a mortgage lender (San Antonio; 125 percent of poverty). The type of subsidy program that would have the highest likelihood of homeowners buying or retaining coverage (and might also be regarded as fair) would be one that subsidized all low-income homeowners. To direct these subsidies only to those uninsured at a given low income level at a given point in time would offer strong incentives for the majority with coverage to cancel their insurance and would deny subsidies to owners who behaved responsibly by maintaining their coverage. However, such a globally efficient and equitable subsidy program to reduce the number of uninsured homes would direct the bulk of subsidies to homes that were already insured. If the goal was primarily to subsidize currently uninsured homes or to reduce the number of uninsured homes, such a uniform program would probably have low target efficiency, in the sense that the government would be paying a lot per uninsured homeowner subsidized, and therefore potentially now able to purchase insurance.

Consider Houston, where about 23 percent of low-income homeowners lack insurance (but 77 percent of low-income homeowners already have it). An across-the-board subsidy of, say, $1,000 per house per year in Houston that caused all formerly uninsured households to buy insurance would have a subsidy cost per newly insured home of $4,348. That is, for every uninsured household that bought insurance because it received a subsidy, there would be about three other households receiving the subsidy that had already bought homeowners' insurance.

It seems that unaffordability by the usual normative definition and standard does not do a very good job of identifying households without insurance. Instead, it identifies many households that may have problems or may be strained by homeowners' insurance premiums, but not to the extent that they forgo coverage. This definition of affordability says that many homes are owned by families that cannot fully afford anything. Their incomes are so low that they cannot afford the other components of housing expense (e.g., taxes and utility bills) for those with no mortgage. Rather than subsidize insurance by maintaining artificially low insurance prices through regulation, it might be better to provide these families with more income though such provisions as the earned income tax credit, which simply transfers income to low-income households, regardless of their current consumption patterns.

More generally, these results offer little support for the view that insurance premiums (or higher insurance premiums) are a major cause of fiscal distress among homeowners. There are some families that should have chosen a less expensive house or a rental option. But when low-income households own higher-value property, and so have a stronger incentive to have coverage, they are in fact more likely to buy insurance. This indicates that insurance purchase is not so much related to a normative definition of affordability based on low income as it is related to low demand because of less wealth at risk.

Even so, an increase in insurance premiums unaccompanied by an increase in house value will add to the financial problems these families already face. For a large portion of these homeowners, a premium increase will not be the proximate cause of the problem of insurance unaffordability. Rather, the cause is low income or high levels of other expenses, including other housing costs. By a similar argument, lowering premiums through moderate subsidies will not lead to major increases in either the probability that an uninsured household will buy insurance or that the household's overall financial picture will brighten appreciably.

These data indicate that low-income homeowners (even very low-income homeowners) largely seek to buy and retain insurance even when they do not have to do so because of mortgage requirements. Ideal public policy should still deal with cases where homeowners do not have insurance that they ought to have, or with cases where low-income families have a lower than desirable ability to obtain adequate amounts of all goods, but altering insurance prices across the board is much too blunt an instrument to deal with this relatively small fraction of low-income homeowners. If, nevertheless, there were a substantial alteration of relative premiums, what impact would this have? We have shown that it would not push many additional families below the threshold of affordability.

These data cannot tell us, however, how many low-income homeowners might significantly decrease their coverage (selecting higher deductibles and lower limits), or even drop coverage, if their premiums increased and the value of their property remained constant. Our preliminary analyses in this chapter show that it is possible to find variables that strongly predict a higher chance of not having coverage, so using some of those characterizing variables to target a subsidy program might make more sense than using an indiscriminate approach.

Summary

This chapter characterizes the socioeconomic features of the insured and uninsured population of homeowners. After defining the meaning of *affordability*, we use data from the American Housing Survey to determine the proportion of low-income households that do not have homeowners' coverage in eight metropolitan areas of Texas, Florida and New York. At least 73 percent of low-income homeowners in these regions had purchased homeowners' insurance. Almost all homes with mortgages have insurance, and coverage is more likely if the home has a higher value and the owner is older.

The chapter concludes with implications for public policy. The results offer little support for the view that higher insurance premiums are a source of financial distress among homeowners, suggesting that there may not be a large increase in uninsured homeowners if premiums are increased to reflect risk. To decrease the number of uninsured homeowners, one should find variables that strongly predict a chance of not having coverage and provide special treatment to those individuals. The poverty line is not necessarily one of these variables.

12 Enhancing the Implementation of Risk Reduction Measures

Key Findings

The adoption of building codes significantly reduces damage from hurricanes. Based on a sample of over 5,600 homeowners affected by Hurricane Charley in 2004, residences built under the wind-resistant standards that were enforced beginning in 1996 had a claim frequency that was 60 percent lower than those that were built pre-1996. Moreover, claims for pre-1996 damaged homes resulted in an average of $24 per square foot compared to $14 per square foot for those constructed between 1996 and 2004.

Many homeowners do not voluntarily invest in cost-effective risk reduction mitigation measures. The principal reasons that homeowners do not invest in these mitigation measures are that they overweight short-term cash expenditures, underestimate the risk because of excessive optimism, and do not learn enough from experience. Social norms can lead individuals to take steps to reduce future disaster losses. If all homeowners in your hurricane-prone neighborhood installed strong storm shutters, then you would likely want to follow suit.

It is possible to significantly increase adoption of mitigation measures by enforcing building codes, developing economic incentive programs such as tax rebates, and adopting zoning ordinances. Collaboration between the public and private sectors is critical in this regard. For instance, tax credits can be given to property owners who purchase building supplies used to make their homes more storm resistant. Mitigation grants are available to low-income families for retrofitting their homes, and matching grants (on a dollar-for-dollar basis) can be made available to all homeowners.

This chapter discusses the role that risk reduction measures (mitigation) can play in reducing losses from natural disasters and the positive role that insurance could play in encouraging more homeowners to adopt cost-effective protective measures. It also raises a set of challenges for encouraging the adoption of mitigation measures.

12.1   The Role of Insurance as a Bridge between Mitigation and Risk Financing

The challenge society faces today is how to promote investments in cost-effective loss reduction mechanisms while at the same time placing the burden of recovery on those who suffer losses from natural disasters.[1] In theory, insurance is one of the most effective policy tools for achieving both objectives, because it rewards investments in cost-effective mitigation with lower premiums, and provides claims payments to policyholders should a disaster occur.

In recent years, insurance has not played this role as much as it could. Insurers generally have not fully implemented pricing adjustments that encourage the adoption of cost-effective loss prevention measures for several reasons. First, they feel that few people would voluntarily adopt these measures based on the small annual premium reductions for taking these actions compared to the up-front cost. If individuals have short time horizons, they would have little interest in investing $1,500 in return for a reduction in annual premiums of, say, $200.

As discussed in Part I of this book, insurance is a highly regulated industry. Rate changes and new policies generally require the approval of state insurance commissioners. If premiums are artificially low in hazard-prone areas, insurers have no economic incentive to offer premium discounts for those who adopt mitigation measures. In fact, they prefer not to offer coverage to these property owners because it is a losing proposition in the long run.

For insurance to play a positive role in encouraging homeowners to adopt mitigation measures, it is necessary that premiums reflect risk so that insurers will want to provide price reductions for those who adopt these risk reduction measures. Furthermore, there is a need to study the decision-making processes of homeowners to understand more fully why some invest in mitigation measures and others do not.

There is also a need to involve other key interested parties from the private sector, such as the construction and banking industries, so that property owners can see mitigation as an attractive investment. Well-enforced building codes may play an important role in encouraging the private sector to become proactive with respect to fostering cost-effective mitigation measures.

12.2   Mitigation Measures for Hurricane-Related Damage

Table 12.1 summarizes the level of damage associated with different categories of hurricanes along with sustained wind speed and anticipated storm surge. The actual damage depends on the level of mitigation measures in place at the time of the disaster.

The damage to property from natural disasters falls into two categories: structural damage and contents damage (damage to the land itself can also occur, but it is generally not a

Table 12.1
Anticipated damage to structure on the Saffir-Simpson Hurricane Scale

Scale number (category)	Sustained winds (mph)	Damage	Storm surge
1	74–95	Minimal: Damage is done primarily to shrubbery and trees; unanchored mobile homes are damaged; some signs are damaged; no real damage is done to structures.	4–5 feet
2	96–110	Moderate: Some trees are toppled; some roof coverings are damaged; major damage is done to mobile homes.	6–8 feet
3	111–130	Extensive: Some structural damage is done to roofs; mobile homes are destroyed; structural damage is done to homes and utility buildings.	9–12 feet
4	131–155	Extreme: Extensive damage is done to roofs, windows, and doors; roof systems on buildings completely fail; some curtain walls fall.	13–18 feet
5	More than 155	Catastrophic: Roof damage is considerable and widespread; damage to windows and doors is severe; there are extensive glass failures; some buildings fall.	Greater than 18 feet

Source: Federal Emergency Management Agency (2002).

major consideration). *Structural damage* refers to the damage to the foundation, frame, roof, and other features—exterior and interior—of the property at risk. *Contents damage* refers to the damage to valuable items located at the property: automobiles, furniture, fixtures, appliances, electronics, and other contents with a monetary or nonmonetary value (the latter can include irreplaceable documents and items with sentimental value). Structural damage can cause contents damage (e.g., when a broken window allows in water from a flood or hurricane), and contents damage can cause structural damage (as when an unsecured water heater topples during an earthquake, causing fire damage to the property). Either kind of damage can cause injury or loss of life, whether from broken glass windows or the collapse of a structure destroyed by fire.

Wind Damage

Wind from hurricanes poses a major danger to the structure of the property, particularly to the roof, windows, and doors. Mitigation measures to roofs include replacing old or damaged sheathing, sealing sheathing joints, and installing a roof covering that can withstand high winds. Connections, where the roof meets the walls and the walls meet the foundation, should be well anchored. Mitigation measures to windows include impact-resistant window systems or storm shutters. Patio doors should be nonsliding, and high-wind-resistant garage door and track systems are recommended. Another measure homeowners can take is to ensure that objects on the property that could become debris in a windstorm, especially overhanging tree branches, are cleared.

Water Damage

To reduce water damage from floods and hurricanes, property owners can undertake a variety of flood-proofing measures that include the use of flood-resistant building materials, bracing roof trusses and gable end walls, applying wood adhesive where the roof decking and roof supports meet, installing hurricane straps or clips where the roof framing meets the top of the studs, and elevating the structure.[2]

12.3   Cost-Effectiveness of Risk Reduction Measures

The challenges associated with encouraging homeowners to mitigate against catastrophic risks lie in demonstrating the effectiveness of risk reduction measures and a sufficient expected return on the investment over the relevant time horizon. As the government has been allocating money to support mitigation efforts, an important question relates to the effectiveness of these governmental grants.

This was the purpose of a multiyear study undertaken by the U.S. National Institute of Building Science and released in 2005. This initiative systematically assessed the future savings from hazard mitigation activities supported by the U.S. Federal Emergency Management Agency's grants for the period 1993 to 2003. The study quantified these savings for three types of hazards: wind, flood, and earthquake. Benefits were defined as losses avoided and included reduced direct property damage, reduced direct business interruption, reduced indirect business interruption (ripple effects), reduced environmental damage (to wetlands, parks, or historical structures), and reduced human losses (deaths, injuries, homelessness). Benefits also included the reduced cost of emergency responses, as well as reduced amount of federal funds being used for disaster assistance and recovery (including post-disaster tax revenue decreases because of tax breaks or interruption of activities).

These findings are interesting because they demonstrate a high benefit-to-cost ratio of mitigation grants. The study estimates that the benefits from FEMA mitigation grants represent $14 billion (in 2005 dollars) compared to $3.5 billion for grants made by FEMA on the studied programs. In other words, a statistically representative sample of FEMA grants awarded between 1993 and 2003 can be used to show that $1 spent on mitigating the risk of wind, flood, and earthquake in the United States saves an average of $4.[3]

On the human side, it is estimated that these mitigation measures are likely to save over 200 lives and prevent almost 4,700 injuries over fifty years. The U.S. National Institute of Building Science's Multihazard Mitigation Council (MMC) indicates that federal grants are not only cost-effective, but that they often lead to the implementation of additional mitigation measures that are supported by other sources, especially in communities that have implemented specific mitigation programs in a systematic way. Appendix 12 highlights two examples of mitigation projects undertaken recently by Florida with funding support from FEMA: the Miami-Dade Flood Control Project and the Miami Children's Hospital, which recently underwent a state-of-the-art retrofit to enable it to withstand a Category 4 hurricane. The MMC recommended that "the federal government should support ongoing evaluation of mitigation by developing a structured process for assessing the performance of buildings and infrastructure after all types of natural disasters and by measuring the benefits that accrue from process mitigation activities."[4]

12.4 The Importance of Building Codes

Building codes require property owners to meet standards on new structures but normally do not require them to retrofit existing structures. Often such codes are necessary, particularly when property owners are not inclined to adopt mitigation measures on their own because of their misperception of the expected benefits resulting from adopting the measure or their inclination to underestimate the probability of a disaster occurring.

Cohen and Noll (1981) provide an additional rationale for building codes. A collapsed structure may create negative externalities in the form of economic dislocations and other social costs that are beyond the owners' financial loss. For example, a poorly designed structure that collapses in a hurricane may cause damage to other buildings that are well designed and still standing in the storm. Knowing this, an insurer may offer a smaller premium discount than it would otherwise have given to a homeowner investing in loss reduction measures.

Two agencies that rate building codes in the United States are the International Code Council (ICC) and Insurance Services Office (ISO). ICC is a membership association that produces model building codes that individual states can implement or modify. The fifty states plus Washington, D.C., use the International Building Code (which focuses on nonresidential property). Forty-eight states plus Washington, D.C., use the International Residential Code (which deals with the construction of one- and two-family dwellings and townhouses up to three stories high). Forty-two states plus Washington, D.C., use the International Fire Code (which addresses fire safety in new and existing buildings).[5]

Building Code Effectiveness Grading Schedule

The Building Code Effectiveness Grading Schedule (BCEGS) is a community-level mitigation rating system administered by the ISO. It assesses the building codes in effect in a particular community and how the community enforces those codes, with special emphasis on mitigation of losses from natural hazards. The BCEGS program places particular emphasis on reducing losses caused by hurricanes, tornadoes, and earthquakes. It judges adherence to building codes, since the score is based not only on the building code in place but also on field inspector staffing and qualifications.

Figure 12.1
Effectiveness of mitigation measures in place in Florida. *Source:* National Oceanic and Atmospheric Administration/Department of Commerce.

The BCEGS ratings that communities receive are provided to insurers to use as an underwriting tool. According to the U.S. Government Accountability Office, few insurance companies are using the BCEGS report to provide premium discounts.[6] The one exception is Florida, where insurers are required by law to offer discounts on wind protection premiums based on a community's BCEGS rating. Communities that do not participate in the program are assessed a 1 percent surcharge on wind protection premiums.

Figure 12.1 shows in stark detail how the stringency of building codes can translate into vastly different levels of damage (compare the upper left-hand corner of the photo with the lower right-hand corner of the photo). This photo, taken in south Florida after Hurricane Andrew, shows that homes on one side of a street were completely destroyed, while homes on the other side were still standing. Later inspection determined that in many cases, construction of the destroyed buildings was well below the standard required by the building code in effect.[7]

The ISO uses the BCEGS as part of the Community Rating System (CRS), a component of the National Flood Insurance Program (NFIP), which allows communities to achieve lower flood insurance rates through mitigation (see chapter 4).[8] Depending on the level of activities that communities undertake in four areas (public information, mapping and regulatory activities, flood damage reduction, and flood preparedness), communities are rated on a scale from 1 to 10. A class 1 rating provides the largest flood insurance premium reduction (45 percent), and a community with a class 10 rating receives no premium reduction.[9] Only a small number of communities (around a thousand at risk from flooding nationwide) participate in the CRS, so it is an incomplete national indicator of code adherence. More detailed assessment of building code enforcement at the local level often takes place on an ex post basis, with disasters such as Hurricane Katrina serving as the impetus for such a review.

Application to Florida

Florida has several insurance mandates regarding mitigation measures and rating that make it an interesting test case. First, rating on mitigation measures, such as adherence to latest building codes, is mandatory in Florida. Florida also has a permit and inspection system that allows insurers to verify that mitigation measures are in place without the expense of independent verification. A qualified inspector is defined as a Florida licensed building inspector, building contractor, general contractor, residential contractor, structural engineer, or architect.

"My Safe Florida Home" Program

The Florida Department of Financial Services operates this program to help Florida residents identify ways to strengthen their homes to reduce damage from hurricanes. The program offers a free home inspection to homeowners that meet income and other eligibility requirements to help them identify appropriate mitigation measures. The state provides matching grants of up to $5,000 to make recommended mitigation improvements.[10]

Florida Building Codes

Following Hurricane Andrew in 1992, Florida reevaluated its building code standards and their enforcement. In 1995, coastal areas of Florida began to use and enforce high-wind design provisions for residential housing. Toward the end of the 1990s, the state began the process of developing and enforcing a statewide building code. The Florida Building Code (FBC) 2001 edition, adopted in mid-2002, was accompanied by an extensive education and training program that included a requirement that all licensed engineers, architects, and contractors take a course on the new building code.[11]

Hurricane Charley in 2004 demonstrated the impact of the new building code. One insurance company provided the Institute for Business and Home Safety data on 5,636 policies in Charlotte County at the time that this hurricane made landfall on August 13, 2004. There were 2,102 reported claims from the hurricane (37 percent of all the homeowners insurance policies in Charlotte County for this insurer). Figure 12.2 reveals that homes built under the new wind-resistant standards that were enforced in 1996 had a claim frequency that was 60 percent less than those that were built prior to 1996.

Moreover, this insurer's claims for pre-1996 homes resulted in an average claim amount of $24 per square foot, compared to $14 per square foot for those constructed between 1996 and 2004, as shown in figure 12.3. For an average home of 2,000 square feet, the average damage to each of these homes would be $48,000 and $28,000, respectively. In other words, the average reduction in claims from Hurricane Charley to each damaged home in Charlotte County built according to the newer code was approximately $20,000.[12]

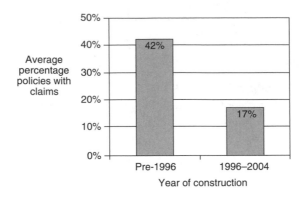

Figure 12.2
Average claim frequency by building code category from Hurricane Charley. *Source:* Institute for Business and Home Safety.

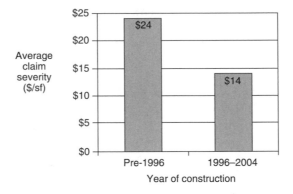

Figure 12.3
Average claim severity by building code category from Hurricane Charley. *Source:* Institute for Business and Home Safety.

Rewarding Mitigation with Premium Discounts

In order to quantify the mitigation discounts that insurers give to their policyholders, we examined the rate manuals for four major homeowners' insurance companies in Florida: Allstate, State Farm, Travelers, and Citizens Property Insurance Corporation. What we present here is a sample of mitigation discounts.

Properties constructed prior to new building code requirements are permitted exemption until the next improvement to the home. Therefore, there are three levels of building code compliance in Florida: non-FBC (grandfathered structures), existing homes FBC compliant (pre-2001 constructions that are retrofitted to the latest building standard), and FBC new construction (homes built after adoption of the new building code).

All four companies have two types of mitigation discount plans: one for FBC-compliant homes (whether existing or new construction) and one for non-FBC-compliant homes with verified mitigation measures. Measures that garner discounts include roof covering, roof deck attachment, roof-wall connection, roof opening protection, and secondary water resistance measures. This discount generally applies to the hurricane portion of the premium (premium structures are generally split between nonhurricane and hurricane premiums).

One other measure of interest is rewarding superior construction—structures that are built with mitigation features above and beyond those required by building codes. An example of this is the Fortified Home seal of approval offered by the Institute for Business and Home Safety. Of four insurers' programs we examined in detail,[13] only one explicitly makes use of this mitigation measure, awarding policyholders a 10 percent discount on total premiums (hurricane and nonhurricane premiums). Another insurer defines a superior construction measure (one that can encompass other types of well-designed structures) and awards policyholders a 15 percent discount on total premiums.

12.5   Factors Influencing the Adoption of Mitigation Measures

A Normative Model of Choice: Cost-Benefit Analysis

Consider the Lowlands, a hypothetical family whose home was destroyed by one of the four hurricanes that hit Florida in 2004.[14] They have decided to rebuild their property in the same location but are undecided as to whether they want to invest in a wind-reduction measure (e.g., storm shutters).[15] Suppose that scientific experts have estimated that the annual chance of a severe hurricane in the area where the Lowlands live is 1 in 100. If they invested in a wind mitigation measure, they would reduce damage from this hurricane by $40,000. In other words, the expected annual benefit from investing in such a measure would be $400 (1 in 100 × $40,000). The longer the time period (T) that the Lowlands expect to live in their house, the greater the expected benefit from hurricane-proofing their house. More specifically, let B represent the expected net present value of the benefit of mitigation over T.

Suppose the extra cost to the Lowlands of undertaking windproofing measures is $C = \$1,200$. Let T^* represent the minimum number of years for the loss-reduction investment to be cost-effective. In other words, T^* is the smallest time period where $B/C > 1$. The second column in table 12.2 depicts the expected benefit-cost ratio as a function of T associated with such an investment if the Lowlands' annual discount rate was 10 percent.

If the family planned to live in their home for more than four years they would want to windproof their house if they were risk neutral and utilized cost-benefit analysis. To the extent that the windproofing expenditure was capitalized in the value of the house, T^* would be less than 4. Furthermore, if the Lowlands were risk averse, then $T^* < 4$, because

Table 12.2
Expected benefit-cost ratio of investing in mitigation measure as a function of time horizon, perceived loss reduction, and perceived probability (p)

Time horizon (years)	Loss reduction ($40,000)	
	$p = 1/100$	$p = 1/300$
1	.30	.10
2	.58	.19
3	.83	.28
4	1.06	.35
5	1.26	.42
10	2.05	.68
15	2.54	.84
20	2.83	.94
25	3.03	1.01

they would be even more concerned with the financial consequences of suffering a large loss from the next disaster and would thus find the expected benefits of mitigation more attractive than if they were risk neutral.

Behavioral Considerations

In the absence of analytical guidance such as the information provided in table 12.2, the Lowlands will make their decision on whether to invest in mitigation measures by using informal heuristics that have proven useful for guiding day-to-day decisions in more familiar contexts, but they are likely to be unsuccessful when applied to the kind of low-probability, high-consequence event the family is now considering. Below we review the range of informal mechanisms that might be used to make mitigation decisions and discuss how they might explain the widespread lack of investment.

Budgeting Heuristics

The simplest explanation as to why individuals fail to mitigate in the face of transparent risks is affordability. If the Lowland family focuses on the up-front cost of windproofing their house and they have limited disposable income after purchasing necessities, there would be little point in undertaking a cost-benefit analysis regardless of its recommendations. Residents in hazard-prone areas have used this argument explicitly as to why they have limited interest in buying insurance voluntarily.

In focus group interviews to determine factors influencing decisions on whether to buy flood or earthquake coverage, one uninsured homeowner responded to the question, "How does one decide how much to pay for insurance?" in this way: "A blue-collar worker doesn't just run up there with $200 [the annual insurance premium] and buy a policy. The world knows that 90 percent of us live from payday to payday.... He can't come up with that much cash all of a sudden and turn around and meet all his other obligations."[16]

The budget constraint for investing in protective measures may extend to higher-income individuals if they set up separate "mental" accounts for different expenditures.[17] Under such a heuristic, a homeowner who is uncertain about the cost-effectiveness of mitigation might simply compare the price to that which is typically paid for comparable home improvements. Hence, the $20,000 investment may be seen as affordable by those who frame it as a large improvement similar to installing a new roof, but unaffordable to those who frame it as a repair similar to fixing a leaky faucet.

Making mitigation decisions in this manner does not conform to guidelines implied by cost-benefit analysis, but there is evidence from controlled laboratory experiments that it may not be uncommon. For example, in a study that asked individuals why they were willing to pay only a fixed amount for a deadbolt lock when the lease for their apartment was extended from one to five years, one respondent said, "Twenty dollars is all the dollars I have in the short run to spend on a lock. If I had more, I would spend more—maybe up to $50."[18] Similarly, we suspect that some residents in coastal zones are discouraged from buying and installing storm shutters because the cost exceeds that of the window itself, a logical benchmark expenditure.

Biases in Temporal Planning
While individuals' decisions about mitigation are undoubtedly constrained by considerations of affordability, trade-offs between costs and benefits invariably arise at some level. How skilled are people at performing intuitive cost-benefit analysis? The empirical evidence on how individuals make intertemporal judgments is not encouraging. Although decisions often follow the directional advice of normative theory (such as by giving less value to temporally distant events than immediate ones), they frequently depart from those prescribed by rational theories of intertemporal choice. Moreover, they depart in a way that collectively discourages farsighted investments in mitigation. In particular, homeowners are likely to overweight short-term cash expenditures, have distorted beliefs about probabilities, and value common outcomes differently over time. The implications of these biases for mitigation decisions will be reviewed in turn.

Underweighting the Future
A fundamental feature of human cognition is that we are influenced more by cues that are concrete and immediate than by those that are abstract and delayed. To some extent, of course, rational intertemporal choice theory prescribes that we should give less weight to distant future outcomes. There is extensive experimental evidence, however, showing that human temporal discounting tends to be hyperbolic, where temporally distant events are disproportionately discounted relative to immediate ones. As an example, people are willing to pay more to have the timing of the receipt of a cash prize accelerated from tomor-

row to today than from two days from now to tomorrow.[19] The implication of hyperbolic discounting for mitigation decisions is that we are asking residents to invest a tangible fixed sum now to achieve a benefit later that we instinctively undervalue—and one that we, paradoxically, hope never to see at all.

The effect of placing too much weight on immediate considerations is that the up-front costs of mitigation will loom disproportionately large relative to the delayed expected benefits in losses over time. A homeowner might recognize the need for mitigation and see it as a worthwhile investment when it is framed as something to be undertaken a few years from now when both up-front costs and delayed benefits are equally discounted. However, when the time arrives to make the investment, a homeowner subject to hyperbolic discounting might well get cold feet.

We should add that less formal, psychological mechanisms could also produce perpetual postponements of investments in mitigation. The most salient is the observed tendency for individuals to defer ambiguous choices. The less certain one is about a correct course of positive action, the more likely one is to choose inaction.[20] This ambiguity would seem particularly acute in the context of mitigation decisions where the question of whether it is optimal to mitigate is often unknowable for a single household, and there is infinite flexibility as to when one can undertake the investment.

Underestimation of Risk Due to Excessive Optimism
In addition to overweighting immediate costs, underweighting future benefits of mitigation, and procrastination, another factor that could suppress investments in mitigation is excessive optimism by underestimating the likelihood of the hurricane occurring. Although underestimation of risk is perhaps the simplest explanation as to why people fail to mitigate, the empirical evidence in the domain of natural hazards is far from complete.

On the one hand, we do know that decisions about mitigation are rarely based on formal beliefs about probabilities. There is considerable empirical evidence that individuals do not seek information on probabilities in making their decisions.[21] Huber, Wider and Huber (1997) showed that only 22 percent of subjects sought out probability information when evaluating risk managerial decisions. When consumers are asked to justify their decisions on purchasing warranties for products that may need repair, they rarely use probability as a rationale for purchasing this protection.[22]

This evidence that individuals do not find statistical probability to be a useful construct in making risky decisions does not, of course, imply that decisions are not based on subjective beliefs about relative risk. To the contrary, Lerner, Gonzalez, Small, and Fischhoff (2003) find that when asked, individuals have no problem expressing beliefs about the relative riskiness of hazards. But these beliefs are not well calibrated. When directly asked to express an opinion about the odds of being personally affected by different hazards, people consistently respond with numbers that, perhaps surprisingly, are far too high relative to actuarial base rates. For example, Lerner et al. found that when people were asked to provide an estimate of the probability that they will be the victim of a violent crime over the coming year, the mean estimate was 43 percent—an estimate that was far too high compared to actuarial base rates and comparable to that which they expressed when asked to estimate the odds of getting the flu (47 percent). If these estimates actually reflected heightened fears about being exposed to hazards, it would strongly argue against the idea that people fail to mitigate simply because they assume that they will be immune. But these results may be speaking more to individuals' lack of familiarity with statistical constructs than real evidence that people are pessimistic.

There is also evidence that people tend to ignore risks whose subjective odds are seen as falling below some threshold. Many homeowners residing in communities that are potential sites for nuclear waste facilities have a tendency to dismiss the risk as negligible.[23] Prior to the Bhopal chemical accident in 1984, firms in the industry estimated the chances of such an accident as sufficiently low that it was not something they planned for. Similarly, even experts in risk disregard some hazards. For instance, after the first terrorist attack against the World Trade Center in 1993, terrorism risk continued to be included as an unnamed peril in commercial insurance policies, so insurers were liable for losses from a terrorist attack without their ever receiving a penny for this coverage. Because U.S. insurers had not integrated the threat into their portfolio management, the September 11, 2001, attacks obligated them to pay over $35 billion in claims.[24] If the Lowland family exhibits similar threshold-based behavior, they would not have any interest in investing in a loss mitigation measure no matter how large the savings would be.

Furthermore, levees or other flood control projects are likely to have given residents a false sense of security with respect to suffering damage from floods or hurricanes. In fact, Gilbert White pointed out many years ago that when these projects are constructed, individuals believe that they are fully protected against future disasters and, hence, there is increased development in these "protected" areas. Should a catastrophic disaster occur so that residents of the area are flooded, the damage is likely to be considerably greater than before the flood control project was initiated. This behavior and its resulting consequences have been termed the *levee effect*.

Learning Failures

The discussion offers a clear argument that if individuals make mitigation decisions by performing intuitive cost-benefit analysis, they will likely underinvest by focusing too much on up-front costs, undervaluing long-term benefits, or underestimating the likelihood that the disaster will strike them. While an individual (or institution) making a one-time mitigation decision might err by underinvesting, such errors would appear to be transient. Once the consequences of undermitigation are observed, intuition suggests that there would be a natural tendency to correct the biases that led to the initial error. Indeed, there is some evidence that mitigation errors are naturally correcting; early Mayans learned (no doubt by experience) that it was safer to build cities inland than on the hurricane-prone coasts of the Yucatan, the loss of 8,000 lives in Galveston in 1900 taught the city that it needed a seawall to protect against future storms, and the disaster of Hurricane Katrina spurred federal and state government to discuss the allocation of funding for repairing and expanding the levees surrounding New Orleans.[25]

The problem, however, is not that we do not learn, but rather that we do not seem to learn enough from the experiences of disaster. While the 1900 Galveston hurricane precipitated the construction of a protective seawall around the city, little attempt was made to expand this protection to the north and south as the region's population expanded—areas that are no less prone to hurricanes than Galveston. The costs of this oversight were dramatically apparent in the summer of 2008 when Hurricane Ike hit the area; whereas the city of Galveston itself experienced limited damage from flooding, Ike's storm surge destroyed most of the existing homes on the unprotected Bolivar Peninsula just to the north. Other familiar examples exist as well, such as the tendency to resettle in floodplains after major floods and to become increasingly lax in earthquake preparedness as the time since the last quake lengthens.

What explains the seeming lack of learning by residents? The reason, we suggest, is that we instinctively learn to protect ourselves against hazards by relying on the same trial-and-error heuristics that have proven successful in other walks of life—heuristics that encourage us to repeat behaviors that yield positive rewards and avoid those that yield negative outcomes. But while reinforcement learning is a highly efficient way to learn multiplication tables and how to play tennis, it is particularly ill suited for learning how best to respond to low-probability, high-consequence hazards. The reason is simple: most protective behaviors will be negatively reinforced far more often than they will be positively reinforced.

As an example, when Hurricane Wilma approached south Florida in 2005, the vivid news depictions of suffering Katrina survivors were counterbalanced by a different and more salient source of information: residents' recollections of the seven false alarms that the area had received during the previous two years. For many, the hurricane warnings posted for Wilma triggered memories of rushing to secure supplies of water and gas before a storm, only later to find out that their efforts were unnecessary. For everyone else, it was memories of how gambling paid off; their decisions not to prepare for all the previous storms had turned out to be the right ones (in hindsight).

A second major impediment to learning is the inherent ambiguity of feedback about what constitutes optimal mitigation. In the course of disasters, one can rarely observe the counterfactuals critical to learning: what damage would have occurred had certain mitigation steps been taken (or not taken). One consequence of this feedback property is that it supports the persistence of superstitious beliefs about mitigation strategies. A good example is the old adage that one should open windows in advance of a tornado so as to equalize pressure. It took structural engineers years to discover that open windows were more likely to be the *cause* of building failures than the cure (entering wind exerts upward pressure on roofs), yet the myth is still widely held. The reason, of course, is that it is impossible to infer from observing a destroyed house whether it would still be standing had the windows been closed—or indeed whether they were open or closed to begin with.[26]

We should emphasize that it is not the rarity of hazardous events that limits learning. While individuals may encounter a major earthquake or hurricane only once in their lives (or, more likely, never), there are ample opportunities to learn by observing the experiences of others. Indeed, the plethora of books describing great disasters of the past and the intense new attention that is given to disasters suggest that we have deeply ingrained instincts (however morbid) for trying to learn from others' misfortunes. There is suggestive evidence, however, that people often learn much less from vicarious feedback than one might hope. As an example, in a laboratory study designed to measure people's abilities to learn optimal levels of investment to protect against hurricanes, Meyer (2006) found that decisions to increase investment were driven almost exclusively by whether the decision maker personally suffered losses in the previous period; in contrast, losses suffered by others did not have such a triggering effect.[27]

Social Norms and Interdependencies

Suppose the Lowland family was considering elevating their house on piles so as to reduce flood losses from a future hurricane. If no neighbors have taken this action, their house would look like an oddity in a sea of homes at ground level. Should the Lowlands choose to move, they would be concerned that the resale value of their home would be lower because the house was different from all the others. Given that there is a tendency not to think about a disaster until after it happens, the Lowlands may reason that it would be difficult to convince potential buyers that elevating their house should increase its property value.

The question as to how actions of others influence one's own decisions relates to the broader question of social norms and interdependencies. With respect to social norms, if all homeowners in the neighborhood had elevated their houses, then the Lowlands would very likely want to follow suit; if none of them had taken this step, they would not have an interest in doing so. The problem of interdependencies arises if there is the possibility that unprotected homes can cause damage to a home that has adopted mitigation measures. If the Lowlands decide to elevate their house but their neighbors have not taken this action, then during the next hurricane, flying debris from one of these nonprotected houses could cause damage to the Lowlands' home, which would otherwise have been spared.

It is conceivable that if a few leaders in the community protect their houses, then others will do the same. This type of tipping behavior is common in many situations and has been studied extensively by Schelling (1978) and popularized by Gladwell (2000). Heal and Kunreuther (2005) provide a game-theoretic treatment of the topic and indicate that a wide range of problems comes under this rubric. They suggest ways to coordinate actions of those at risk ranging from subsidization or taxation to induce tipping or cascading to rules and regulations such as well-enforced building codes.

12.6 Collaboration between the Public and Private Sectors

The Natural Disaster Syndrome

Recent extreme events have highlighted the challenges associated with reducing losses from hurricanes and other natural hazards due to the *natural disaster syndrome*.[28] Before a disaster, many homeowners, private businesses, and public sector organizations do not voluntarily adopt cost-effective loss-reduction measures. Hence, the area is highly vulnerable and unprepared in the event of a severe hurricane or other natural disaster. The magnitude of the destruction following a catastrophe often leads public sector agencies to provide disaster relief to victims even if the government claimed it had no intention of doing so prior to the event. This combination of underinvestment in protection prior to the event leading to large disaster losses, together with the general taxpayer financing some of the recovery, can be critiqued on both efficiency and equity grounds.

One of the reasons for the natural disaster syndrome relates to the decision processes of individuals with respect to events such as a category 3 or 4 hurricane or a major earthquake. Prior to a disaster, many individuals perceive its likelihood as sufficiently low that they argue, "It will not happen to me." As a result, they do not feel the need to invest voluntarily in protective measures, such as strengthening their house or buying insurance. It is only after the disaster occurs that these same individuals claim they were sorry they did not undertake protective measures.

Kydland and Prescott (1977) in their Nobel Prize–winning contribution, show that a discretionary policy, which may be optimal given the current situation, may not necessarily result in a socially optimal policy in the longer run. As a specific example of this general proposition, the authors note that unless individuals are initially prohibited from locating in a floodplain, it will be very difficult politically to force these people to leave their homes. In making their decisions to locate there, Kydland and Prescott indicate that these individuals believe that the Army Corps of Engineers will subsequently build dams and levees if enough people choose to build homes there. A large number of homeowners then decide to locate in these high-hazard areas for that reason, and the Corps of Engineers is forced to invest in flood control projects.

Kunreuther and Pauly (2006b) extend the Kydland-Prescott argument by introducing behavioral considerations into the picture. They contend that because individuals underestimate the likelihood of a future disaster, it may be important to require homeowners to purchase insurance and have well-enforced rules such as land use regulations and building codes to avoid the large public sector expenditures following these events. To support this point, they provide empirical evidence that many individuals do not even think about the consequences of a disaster until after a catastrophe occurs, and hence do not invest in protective measures in advance of a disaster. After a large-scale flood, earthquake, or hurricane, the government provides some financial assistance to aid the recovery of the unprotected victims.

There is extensive evidence that residents in hazard-prone areas do not undertake loss prevention measures voluntarily. A 1974 survey of more than a thousand California home-owners in earthquake-prone areas revealed that only 12 percent of the respondents had adopted any protective measures.[29] Fifteen years later, there was little change despite increased public awareness of the earthquake hazard. In a 1989 survey of 3,500 home-owners in four California counties at risk from earthquakes, only 5 to 9 percent of the respondents in these areas reported adopting any loss reduction measures. Other studies have found a similar reluctance by residents in flood-prone areas to invest in mitigation measures.[30]

In the case of flood damage, Burby (2006) provides compelling evidence that actions taken by the federal government, such as building levees, make residents feel safe when in fact they are still vulnerable to catastrophes should the levee be breached or overtopped. This problem is reinforced by local public officials who do not enforce building codes or impose land use regulations to restrict development in high-hazard areas. If developers do not design homes resistant to disasters and individuals do not voluntarily adopt mitigation measures, one can expect large-scale losses following a disaster, as evidenced by the prop-erty damage to New Orleans caused by Hurricane Katrina.

Even after the devastating 2004 and 2005 hurricane seasons, a large number of residents had still not invested in relatively inexpensive loss reduction measures with respect to their property, nor had they undertaken emergency preparedness measures. A survey of 1,100 adults living along the Atlantic and Gulf coasts undertaken in May 2006 revealed that 83 percent of the respondents had taken no steps to fortify their home, 68 percent had no hur-ricane survival kit, and 60 percent had, still, no family disaster plan.[31]

The Politician's Dilemma

The fact that politicians can benefit from their generous actions following a disaster raises basic questions as to the capacity of elected representatives at the local, state, and federal levels to induce people to adopt protection measures before the next disaster. The difficulty in enforcing these mitigation measures has been characterized as the *politician's dilemma*.[32]

Consider an elected representative at the city or state level. Should he or she push for people and firms in this city or state to invest in cost-effective mitigation measures to pre-vent or limit the occurrence of a disaster? From a long-term perspective, the answer should be yes. But given short-term reelection considerations, the representative is likely to vote for measures that allocate taxpayers' money elsewhere that yield more political capital. It is another example where little consideration is given to supporting mitigation measures prior to a disaster because they believe that their constituents are not worried about these events occurring, but where there is likely to be a groundswell of support for generous assistance to victims from the public sector after a disaster to aid their recovery. The one silver lining to this behavior is that following a natural disaster when residents and the media focus on the magnitude of the losses, politicians will respond by favoring stronger building codes and other loss reduction measures, but only when there is a consensus among constituents that this is a good thing to do.

Tax Incentives

One way for communities to encourage residents to pursue mitigation measures is to provide tax incentives. For example, if a homeowner reduces the chances of damage from a hurricane by installing a mitigation measure, then this taxpayer would get a rebate on state taxes to reflect the lower costs for disaster relief. As part of South Carolina's Omnibus Coastal Property Insurance Reform Act of 2007, tax credits are given to property owners who purchase building supplies used to make their homes more storm resistant. Mitigation grants of up to $5,000 are available for low-income families, and matching grants (on a dollar-for-dollar basis) of up to $5,000 are available for all homeowners in the state.

The city of Berkeley, California, has instituted a transfer tax rebate to encourage homebuyers to retrofit newly purchased homes to reduce the damage should an earthquake occur in the area. The city has a 1.5 percent tax levied on property transfer transactions; up to one-third of this amount can be applied to seismic upgrades during the sale of property. Qualifying upgrades include foundation repairs or replacement, wall bracing in basements, shear wall installation, water heater anchoring, and securing of chimneys. The Berkeley program has been a great success. According to Arrietta Chakos, the assistant city manager, about 40 percent of Berkeley's homes have been improved using this tax incentive.[33]

Better Zoning Ordinances

One of the more vexing problems facing policymakers after major catastrophes is whether to permit rebuilding in areas that have been damaged. As demonstrated by the response after Hurricane Katrina, there is usually strong political support for wanting to rebuild. Indeed, not to do so seems somehow unpatriotic. But in some cases, common sense should take precedence. In areas that have suffered multiple catastrophes—say, three or more—nature may be telling us something: that these locations are naturally much more likely to be damaged than others. In effect, this is recognized in FEMA's flood maps, which the agency is in the process of updating.

Ideally, local authorities would adopt zoning policies that prohibit rebuilding in hazard-prone locations. But this is unlikely, since much of the pressure to permit, if not encourage, such rebuilding exists at the local level. This pressure is unlikely to be as intense at the state level, and thus one way of addressing the problem is for states to adopt policies that prevent or discourage localities from allowing rebuilding in areas that are subject to natural catastrophes by undertaking some type of benefit-cost analysis. States might consider announcing rules before a catastrophe, prohibiting reconstruction should a severe disaster occur. The political challenge will be their ability to enforce this rule.

An even bolder suggestion is to have the federal government encourage state governments to take this step. This could be done through positive incentives. Alternatively, the federal government could use penalties to accomplish the same objective—withholding federal highway monies, as one example, unless the state adopted this zoning policy.

Future Challenges for Encouraging Mitigation Measures

A U.S. Government Accountability Office (GAO) report noted a number of opportunities for private-public collaboration with respect to encouraging adoption of cost-effective mitigation measures.[34] It pointed out that in Florida where the population continues to grow rapidly, most of the new residents were unfamiliar with the state's hazard risks and mitigation options. The report calls for public education and outreach programs that can take many forms, including distributing literature to individuals, organizing community events that discuss mitigation options, and incorporating hazard information into school curriculums.

Local governments may be reluctant to take actions to mitigate natural hazards because community goals such as building housing and promoting economic development may be higher priorities than formulating mitigation regulations that may include more restrictive development regulations and more stringent building codes. Local communities may also encounter difficulties in implementing and maintaining mitigation-related policies due to cost concerns such as the expenses in hazard mapping, land use planning, and local ordinances to address natural hazard risks.

Officials from the National Homebuilders Association told the GAO that the economic cost of mitigation should be considered because every $1,000 increase in median home prices can force about 240,000 homebuyers out of the market. Similarly, private property owners may be reluctant to pay for the additional cost of features that exceed local building codes, such as reinforced concrete walls and flood-proofing materials.

In chapter 14, we discuss innovations for dealing with catastrophic risks, such as long-term homeowners' insurance. Unless there are economic incentives provided to property owners to adopt cost-effective mitigation measures, coupled with well-enforced regulations and standards, it will be extremely difficult to make headway in having these measures adopted for reasons outlined here.

12.7 Conclusion

The 2005 hurricane season provided empirical evidence that many victims suffered severe losses from flooding because they had not mitigated their home and did not have flood insurance to cover the resulting damage. As a result, an unprecedented level of federal disaster assistance was promised to aid these victims. Nevertheless, the amount of disaster relief will never cover all the losses that could have been avoided by the implementation of effective protection measures.

There are many reasons that those in harm's way have not protected themselves against natural disasters. The principal ones are budgeting or affordability constraints, underestimating the likelihood of the event occurring, underweighting the future, myopia, and failure to learn from the past. These beliefs, coupled with artificially low insurance rates in high-risk areas, have led to increased development in areas subject to natural disasters. At the local level, government representatives might also prefer to allocate taxpayers' money where they can gain more political capital in the short term; investing in mitigation might not be their first priority until a disaster occurs.

If we as a society are to commit ourselves to reducing future losses from natural disasters and limit government assistance after this event, then we have to engage the private and public sectors in a creative partnership that would include well-enforced building codes and land use regulations, coupled with insurance protection.[35] In order to develop these measures, we need to examine the economic welfare of homeowners and their ability to afford protective measures as discussed in chapter 11.

Summary

This chapter analyzes mitigation measures for reducing the physical consequences of specific types of catastrophes (wind, flood, and earthquake). Many of these measures have proven to be cost-effective. Data collected by the Institute for Business and Home Safety following Hurricane Charley in 2004 illustrate that poorly designed homes sustained greater damage relative to homes constructed to meet building codes.

Homeowners do not seem to use cost-benefit analyses when deciding about whether to invest in mitigation measures. Instead, individuals may decide not to adopt cost-effective measures because they use budgeting heuristics, are somewhat myopic in their planning, underestimate the risk due to an optimism bias, or fail to learn from experience. Social norms and interdependencies also affect homeowners' decision processes. Given the reluctance of individuals to invest in cost-effective mitigation measures voluntarily and politicians' reluctance to push for cost-effective mitigation measures unless a disaster has recently occurred, there is a need to develop innovative strategies that involve creative collaboration between the public and private sectors. The chapter concludes by providing examples of tax incentives coupled with zoning ordinances that would better protect residents in hazard-prone areas against future disasters.

APPENDIX 12:   BEST PRACTICES IN FLORIDA

The C-4 Basin Project: Moving Water to Prevent Flooding

The Miami-Dade Flood Control Project, or C-4 Basin Project, built on the existing canal system, was created to address the county's extensive flooding problem and to relocate excess water from one area to another so it could be absorbed into the groundwater or held in reserve.[36] At the heart of the C-4 basin is the Tamiami Canal, which begins in the Everglades National Park and traverses the Miccosukee Indian reservation, the critical Pensuco Wetlands, and several municipalities before flowing into the environmentally sensitive Biscayne Bay. The driving force of the C-4 Project is the forward pump station at the mouth of the canal, which is designed to push water flow downstream against the tide. A second station, at the mouth of the Miami River Canal in the C-6 basin, was built to offset the flow from the C-4 canal and prevent flooding upriver. There are three pumps in each station that can process approximately 4,500 gallons of water per second.

When the canals cannot handle the water volume necessary to prevent flooding, an emergency detention basin, comprising two reservoirs, was created to receive and store the excess water. In addition, a separate supply canal was built to divert excess water from the C-4 canal to and from the detention basin, which allows water to be shifted from area to area not only in times of heavy rainfall or potential flooding, but also when a need for water in other areas arises, such as when droughts occur.

The cost of the project totaled $70 million. Florida was awarded $52.5 million from FEMA's Hazard Mitigation Grant Program. The Quality Neighborhood Improvement Program, along with the South Florida Water Management District and Miami-Dade County, contributed remaining funds.

Miami Children's Hospital

Beginning in 2001, the Miami Children's Hospital (MCH) underwent a state-of-the-art retrofit to enable it to withstand a Category 4 hurricane. The hospital serves seven counties in southern Florida, including populous Miami-Dade County, and is the region's only specialty hospital for children. The 268-bed medical facility has expertise in all aspects of pediatric medicine and is an important community resource. An assessment of the facility's exterior construction, built in the mid-1980s, found that it was unsafe at wind speeds associated with a Category 2 hurricane, a familiar occurrence in southern Florida. Hospital administrators had to solve a twofold problem: how to fund the renovation project and how to conduct the retrofit and renovations without disrupting medical services.

MCH received $5 million through FEMA's Hazard Mitigation Grant Program, administered by the Florida Department of Community Affairs, to help pay for the $11.3 million project. The retrofit involved strengthening the building by encapsulating the three-story structure in premolded panels of concrete reinforced with glass fibers. The panel system, anchored into the building's existing support structure, forms a protective cocoon around the hospital and, with impact-resistant windows and a strengthened roof, enables the building to withstand winds of up to 200 miles per hour.

The project was completed in spring 2004 and proved to be effective in the following months: young patients and their families did not need to evacuate from the hospital when Hurricanes Frances and Jeanne struck. In addition, MCH welcomed over sixty children who live at home but depend on ventilators or other powered medical equipment.

During Hurricane Frances, MCH was the refuge for nearly a thousand staff members and their families. The hospital hosted medical evacuees and families during Hurricanes Katrina and Wilma in 2005.

13 Policy Analysis of Alternative Programs: Comparing the Status Quo with a True Competitive Insurance Market

Key Findings

The proportion of hurricane losses covered by private insurers for the 100-year return period under current insurance programs in place differs widely among the four states studied. Should this event occur in South Carolina, private insurers would cover 80 percent of the loss, compared to about 70 percent in New York and 50 percent in Texas. In Florida, private insurers would cover 25 percent of the loss and the state-operated insurer, Citizens, 10 percent. The actual dollar amounts of loss to residential properties are much lower in South Carolina and New York than in Texas and Florida.

If a hurricane with a return period of 500 years were to occur in 2009, the deficits from residential losses to the Florida Hurricane Catastrophe Fund (FHCF) would be $19.5 billion. The FHCF would assess private insurers operating in Florida to recoup the necessary funds for the claims it could not meet from its reserves. In turn, insurers would levy charges against their own policyholders. An open question is whether these policyholders realize the extent of this postdisaster payment. If they do, this might create a disincentive for them to purchase insurance voluntarily.

Metropolitan areas in these four states are subject to a hurricane risk disproportionate to other parts of their states. Should a 100-year hurricane hit tomorrow in each of the four states, Miami-Dade metropolitan area will suffer 21 percent of the total direct loss of Florida, New York City area 24 percent of the loss in the state of New York, Charleston area 56 percent of the loss in South Carolina, and Houston area 89 percent of the loss in Texas.

Mitigation has the potential to provide significant cost savings in all four states. In our analysis of the impact of mitigation, we consider two extreme cases: one in which no one has invested in mitigation, the other in which everyone has invested in predefined mitigation measures. For a hurricane with a 1-in-100-year return period, mitigation would reduce the potential losses by 61 percent in Florida, 44 percent in South Carolina, 39 percent in

New York, and 34 percent for Texas. In Florida alone, the use of mitigation leads to a $51 billion savings for a 100-year event and $83 billion for a 500-year event. These findings are important given the costly capital needed to cover the tail of the distribution of extreme events. Enforcing mitigation significantly reduces, if not eliminates, this tail.

Under a scenario where insurers are permitted to charge premiums reflecting risk, the private sector will be able to cover most (if not all) losses from severe hurricanes if homeowners mitigate their property and private reinsurance is in place. In this case, if insurers were to devote 10 percent of their surplus to provide coverage against a 100-year hurricane in a given state, they would be able to cover 100 percent of the market in all four states. For a 500-year event, they would continue to cover 100 percent of the market in New York and South Carolina, 94 percent of the market in Texas, and 66 percent in Florida.

Except for Florida, which constitutes a peak zone for catastrophe exposure, insurers would need to allocate only a small portion of their surplus to provide the market with full coverage under a competitive market if adequate mitigation and private reinsurance were in place. If all single-family dwellings in the state were mitigated and if private reinsurance and alternative risk transfer mechanisms were in place, based on the status quo, the percentage of insurers' surplus necessary to insure all homes against a 100-year hurricane is 1.1 percent in South Carolina, 1.4 percent in New York, 6.7 percent in Texas, and 15.4 percent in Florida.

If one determines premiums based on loss costs and adds a 50 percent loading factor to reflect additional expenses (administrative, marketing and claim assessment costs, and cost of capital), coastal communities that have the highest risk of wind damage from hurricanes in each of the four states we study will pay significantly more for insurance than would other regions in these states. This is particularly true in Texas, where Calhoun, Aransas, and Galveston counties would be charged over nine times the average for the entire state. The ratios for the most hazard-prone counties in the other three states are on the order of four to five times the average premium across the state.

13.1   Introduction

Who will pay for the losses from future catastrophes? This chapter provides a series of empirical analyses on how residential losses to homeowners due to hurricanes will be shared among the affected stakeholders under different market environments. The stakeholders we consider are uninsured homeowners, insured homeowners, all insurance policyholders, private insurers, private reinsurers, state insurers, and reinsurers, and general taxpayers.

We also examine the significant role that mitigation can play in reducing such losses. There are four principal objectives in undertaking these analyses:

• Determine the economic impact of a series of major hurricanes on the key stakeholders under the current disaster insurance programs in Florida, New York, South Carolina, and Texas. We denote this as the *status quo analysis*.

• Examine the ability of the insurance industry to provide coverage against hurricanes in each of these four states if they were able to charge risk-based premiums and adopt a maximum-exposure strategy. We denote this as the *competitive market analysis*.

• Analyze the impact of mitigation measures on the reduction of aggregate damage to homes and contents (ground-up losses) and insured losses from severe hurricanes in each of the four states.

• Characterize the relative magnitude of damage from hurricanes to the four metropolitan areas in relation to the state in which they are located: Miami, Florida, area (Miami-Dade County); New York City area (Bronx, New York, Queens, Kings, and Richmond counties); Charleston, South Carolina, area (Charleston, Berkeley, Colleton, and Dorchester counties); and Houston, Texas, area (Galveston, Harris, Fort Bend, Montgomery, Brazoria, Liberty, Waller, Chambers, Austin, and San Jacinto counties). The insured exposure at risk was provided by Risk Management Solutions (RMS) based on their latest research.

The maps in figures 13.1 depict the four states and the metropolitan areas (circled) on which these analyses are based.

13.2   Data Sources

In order to undertake these analyses, we obtained data from several complementary sources: the catastrophe modeling firm Risk Management Solutions (RMS), the rating agency A.M. Best, and the state insurance regulatory offices and state funds in Florida (Florida Hurricane Catastrophe Fund and Citizens Property Insurance Corporation) and Texas (Texas Windstorm Insurance Association).

State Exposure Data: Residential

Data on states' residential-only insured exposure to hurricane risk were provided by RMS. RMS used its proprietary U.S. Hurricane Industry Exposure Database, which contains residential exposures at the postal code level of resolution using a standard occupancy (e.g., single-family dwelling or multifamily dwelling) and construction (e.g., wood-frame or masonry) class for the standard coverages for building, contents, and time element costs (e.g., additional living expenses). These data provide information about the total insured values of residential structures in the four target states.

Figure 13.1
Counties and main cities in Florida, New York, South Carolina, and Texas. *Source:* Geology.com. *Note:* Metropolitan areas studied are circled.

South Carolina

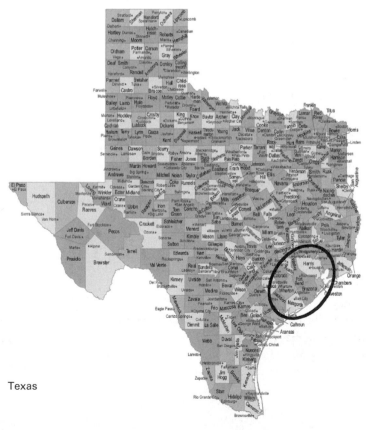

Texas

Figure 13.1
(continued)

Table 13.1
Total insured value of all dwelling types and residential/single-family homes and damage multipliers

State	TIV: All dwelling types (in $ billion)	TIV: Residential and single-family homes (in $ billion)	Damage multiplier
Florida	$1,769	$1,504	0.850
New York	$2,063	$1,749	0.847
South Carolina	$362	$321	0.888
Texas	$2,053	$1,857	0.904

Note: TIV = total insured value.

Our analyses in New York, South Carolina, and Texas were performed looking at both the wind and storm surge peril using the RMS U.S. Hurricane Model. While flooding losses are primarily covered by the National Flood Insurance Program (NFIP), it is assumed that a portion of the flooding from storm surge would be covered by private insurance (e.g., large commercial coverage). In Florida the residential exposure data came from the publicly available Florida Hurricane Catastrophe Fund (FHCF) through Paragon Strategic Solutions, the FHCF administrator. The RMS analyses in Florida did not include storm surge damage, because the FHCF insures only damage caused by the wind peril. The RMS model can analyze losses to multiple types of residential exposure, including, for example, single-family dwellings, mobile homes, condos, and rental properties. We used damage multipliers for each of the four states to isolate this single-family dwelling component of the total exposure at risk. Comparing the total insured value (TIV) of residential single-family homes to the TIV of all residential exposure yields the damage multiplier ($TIV_{Residential}/TIV_{Total}$).

Table 13.1 details the TIV for all residential structures and the TIV for residential single-family homes in each of the four states, along with the relevant damage multiplier.

The RMS U.S. Hurricane Model allows us to measure the following elements at a postal code level for each of the four states:

• Average annual loss (AAL) due to wind and storm surge peril, as applicable[1]

• Standard deviation of AAL

Data on Insurance Companies

The rating agency A.M. Best provided us with data on the 2006 statutory annual statements of individual insurance and reinsurance groups that included their total surplus and direct insurance premiums written, as well as the amount of homeowners' multiperil reinsurance coverage they assumed from both affiliates and nonaffiliates. A.M. Best also provided aggregate data on the gross and net probable maximum losses (PMLs) for hurricane events with a 100-, 250-, and 500-year return period for each of these groups. Probable maximum loss (PML) data came from the 2005 Supplemental Rating Questionnaires completed by all the insurers rated by A.M. Best. We used the PML data to estimate the amount of reinsurance and other risk transfer instruments available under the status quo program.

Note that A.M. Best provides group data and data from unaffiliated single companies. An unaffiliated single company is a stand-alone company that is not part of a group. A.M. Best provided us with the total surplus for each group of companies. This means that companies and their affiliates' surpluses were aggregated under one umbrella insurance group. One assumption inherent in this analysis is that the umbrella insurance group relies on its total surplus to determine how much insurance and reinsurance it will want to provide should it have the freedom to charge risk-based rates as assumed under the competitive market program.

Florida Office of Insurance Regulation Data

Insurers doing business in Florida are required by law to report statistical information to the Florida Office of Insurance Regulation (FLOIR). We used these data from its *Quarterly Supplement Report* (QUASR) to determine the insurer exposure in Florida. Because our analysis is undertaken using 2005 data from RMS, we also used the 2005 data from QUASR. Because we restricted our analysis of losses to single-family dwellings, we focused on the homeowners' exposure (including tenants and condo owners) from the QUASR data set. We used this exposure to develop individual insurer market shares to calculate the FHCF payouts on an individualized basis.

Data on State Funds

Given recent changes in the operation of state funds in Florida and Texas, we used the most recent information on their operation. The Florida Hurricane Catastrophe Fund (FHCF) provided us with 2007 information about its operations and surplus estimates. The data were compiled by Paragon, which also develops the reimbursement premium formula and the rates used in determining the FHCF's annual reimbursement premium. The FHCF annual reimbursement premiums are those paid by an insurer for its mandatory coverage. It does not include premiums of optional coverage above and below the standard coverage limit, Temporary Emergency Additional Coverage Options (TEACO) and Temporary Increase in Coverage Limit (TICL).

Data on Citizens Property Insurance Corporation, the state-run insurance company in Florida, were obtained from the same data sources used for other private insurers. We also obtained market share estimates for Citizens from news reports. A May 13, 2007, article in the *South Florida Sun-Sentinel* reported that Citizens' board chairman estimated its market share to be about 30 percent.[2] We recognize that this market share may increase substantially in the near future but use this figure for this analysis. Data on the Texas Windstorm Insurance Association (TWIA), the state-run insurance company in Texas, came from publicly available 2008 data, as well as the Insurance Information Institute.

American Housing Survey

Other housing statistical information came from the U.S. Census American Housing Survey (AHS), the largest, regular national housing sample survey in the United States. The U.S. Census Bureau conducts the AHS to obtain up-to-date housing statistics for HUD. The national sample covers an average 55,000 housing units. Each metropolitan area sample covers 4,100 or more housing units. National data are collected in odd-numbered years, and data for each of forty-seven selected metropolitan areas are collected every six years (not all metropolitan areas are collected at the same time). We used data from the following five metropolitan areas to project losses to uninsured homes: Tampa, Florida (1998); Miami/Fort Lauderdale, Florida (2002); Houston, Texas (1998); Dallas, Texas (2002); and Fort Worth/Arlington, Texas (2002).

13.3   Assumptions for the Status Quo Analysis

Our analysis of the status quo estimates how much insurance and reinsurance is provided by the public and private sectors in each of the four states we studied. We then examine the effects of hurricanes of different magnitudes and intensities in each of these states and four metropolitan areas based on the insurance programs currently in place. Should a hurricane occur tomorrow, and given the assumptions we have made, this analysis would specify who pays for the damage. We also discuss the nature and length of the ultimate loss sharing in Florida and Texas should their state-run funds have insufficient reserves to cover all homeowners' losses from the disaster.

Losses, Insurance Coverage, Take-Up Rate, Uninsured Projections, Reinsurance, and Mitigation Assumptions

To undertake a systematic analysis of insurance programs currently in place using data from the identified sources, we made a set of assumptions that we detail next.

Losses
Insurers' losses from hurricanes that occur in a particular state are determined by multiplying their market shares in that state by the total industry loss. This assumption implies that each insurer's portfolio of risks is distributed in the same manner across the entire state. While we recognize that this is a simplifying assumption, there is no systematic data collection publicly available on market share at a finer grain (e.g., postal code level).

Table 13.2
Take-up rates for selected American Housing Survey cities

City	Year	Take-up rate
Tampa, Florida	1998	93%
Miami/Fort Lauderdale, Florida	2002	87
Houston, Texas	1998	89
Dallas, Texas	2002	95
Fort Worth/Arlington, Texas	2002	92
Average		91

Take-Up Rate

Take-up rate (TUR), or market penetration, refers to the percentage of homeowners in a given state or metropolitan area who have purchased insurance against wind damage in Florida and wind and storm surge damage in the other states. The TUR enables one to derive the amount of losses to uninsured structures. We used AHS data to estimate the take-up rate for Tampa, Miami/Fort Lauderdale, Houston, Dallas, and Fort Worth/Arlington, as shown in table 13.2. Based on this analysis, we estimated the take-up rate for all four states to be 90 percent.

Mitigation

From the RMS U.S. Hurricane Model, losses were calculated on a ground up and gross basis, assuming an appropriate mitigation measure across the insured portfolio. The mitigation measures were based on various assumptions for the different regions. For example, in Florida, the requirements as defined by the Institute for Business and Home Safety's (IBHS) Fortified ... for Safer Living program were used to incorporate mitigation. Of course, this program is only for new construction. So, when we describe an analysis using these recommendations, it is the retrofit techniques that are aligned with the features of the Fortified program.[3] In New York, South Carolina, and Texas mitigation means the application of the latest building codes to the residential structures.

Uninsured Losses Projection

The TUR enables us to obtain an approximation of the residential uninsured losses. Loss calculations include the ground-up losses for insured structures only, as well as the gross losses, the portion of the ground-up losses covered by insurers. In order to determine the ground-up losses to uninsured structures, we had to extrapolate using the TUR.

We divided the ground-up losses by the TUR to determine the total ground-up losses assuming all structures were valued the same. Next, we subtracted the original value of ground-up losses to remove the insured structures from our new total figure. We used the ratio of the average uninsured home value (UHV) over the average insured home value (IHV) to estimate the value of the uninsured homes using the following formula:

Table 13.3
Ratio of insured to uninsured home values

Metropolitan area	Uninsured home value/ insured home value
Tampa, Florida	62%
Miami/Fort Lauderdale, Florida	73
Houston, Texas	53
Dallas, Texas	60
Fort Worth/Arlington, Texas	46
Average	59

Source: American Housing Survey

(Insured ground-up losses/take-up rate − Insured ground-up losses) · UHV/IHV.

We assumed that UHV/IHV = 60 percent based on the mean home values for insured and uninsured people from the AHS data on the five metropolitan areas in Florida and Texas, as shown in table 13.3.

The following example shows how we incorporate uninsured losses to obtain total losses from the wind peril. If the ground-up losses are $9 billion and the take-up rate is 90 percent, then we divide $9 billion by 90 percent to get total losses of $10 billion. But the additional $1 billion must be diminished because it represents uninsured structures, which are worth less than the insured structures we used to estimate the loss. We multiply this figure by 60 percent since we assume these homes are valued at 60 percent of the insured homes. This yields an uninsured value of $0.6 billion. This adjustment in value yields total losses of $9.6 billion. Nine billion dollars is the original value of ground-up loss, and $0.6 billion is our loss projection for the uninsured.

Reinsurance Assumptions and Calculations

Gross losses used in this analysis are calculated based on complete retention (i.e., there is no reinsurance and other risk transfer instruments in place). Note that hereafter when we refer to *reinsurance*, we mean all types of alternative risk transfer (ART) instruments such as industry loss warranties, catastrophe bonds, and sidecars.[4]

To estimate the aggregate amount of reinsurance, we rely on PML data from A.M. Best. We use the national pretax per-occurrence hurricane gross and net PMLs for the 100-, 250-, and 500-year return periods for ninety groups categorized within the personal lines and homeowners' segments using 2005 data. The ninety groups in the analysis represent companies that submitted a supplemental rating questionnaire to A.M. Best. Groups that provided the PML information verbally or in a group presentation are not included in the study.

Table 13.4
Estimating reinsurance percentages using PML data on homeowners' losses from hurricanes

Return period	Gross PML	Net PML	Net/ gross	Reinsurance (including alternative risk transfer)
100	21.3	8.5	39.7%	60.3%
250	33.3	16.1	48.3	51.7
500	44.7	25.4	56.9	43.1

Source: Data from A.M. Best; authors' calculations

Although some groups were omitted from the analysis, we believe this is an accurate portrayal of the industry. Furthermore, we used PML ratios, not the absolute value. These ratios from our sample should be generally applicable to the entire industry. The gross PML is the total projected loss from a catastrophic event for an insurer, while the net PML is the total projected loss from this event after subtracting reinsurance and other alternative risk transfer payments. The percentage of losses paid by reinsurance is derived using the following formula:

$$\% \text{ Reinsurance} = 1 - (\text{net PML}/\text{gross PML})$$

To illustrate, suppose that for a 100-year return period, an insurer had a gross PML from hurricanes in Florida of $500 million and a net PML of $300 million. Then equation 13.1 implies that the percentage Reinsurance = $1 - (\$300/\$500) = 40$ percent. A.M. Best estimated gross and net PMLs for the insurance industry from hurricanes using data at the group level for the 100-, 250-, and 500-year return periods. This enabled us to estimate the percentage of reinsurance that insurers had purchased for these catastrophic losses, as shown in table 13.4.

Because these reinsurance percentages are based on aggregate group PMLs, we feel they are accurate only for Florida hurricane coverage with no mitigation in place, since the losses comprise most of the nation's PML. Furthermore, reinsurance is linked to damage amounts instead of return periods. Considering the case of no mitigation in Florida, we find that gross (insured) losses are $76 billion at the 100-year return period level, $114 billion at the 250-year return period level, and $145 billion at the 500-year return period level. The gross losses for the other three states are somewhat lower. Based on PML analysis and discussions with several reinsurers, we developed the following assumptions for reinsurance percentages for the spectrum of gross loss amounts, as shown in table 13.5.

The private reinsurance in place to cover wind and storm surge losses in New York, South Carolina, and Texas is estimated by multiplying the gross losses by the relevant percentage in table 13.5. In Florida, the FHCF provides significant amounts of reinsurance to many insurers at rates more generous than those we assumed existed for private reinsurance in table 13.5. In the cases where reinsurance by the FHCF exceeds our estimates of

Table 13.5
Percentages of reinsurance as a function of catastrophic loss

Gross loss	Reinsurance
$0–10 billion	10%
$10–20 billion	20
$20–30 billion	30
$30–50 billion	40
$50–90 billion	60.3
$90–120 billion	51.7
$120–145 billion	43.1

the amount of private reinsurance in place, private reinsurance is assumed to be 0 and total reinsurance is equal to the reinsurance provided by the FHCF.

Private reinsurance = Max(0; Total reinsurance − reinsurance by FHCF).

Operation of Florida State Funds

Florida currently plays a significant role in providing insurance and reinsurance to home-owners through Citizens and the FHCF, respectively. We provided a detailed description of these two entities in chapter 2, so here we focus on key assumptions regarding the operation of these state funds.

Citizens

Citizens provides insurance to homeowners in high-risk areas and others who cannot obtain coverage in the open, private insurance market. For our analysis, we assumed Citizens had a market share of 30 percent for the base case scenario, a significant increase compared to its market share a few years ago. Citizens, which was designed to be the insurer of last resort, has recently become the largest provider of residential coverage against wind in Florida.

If Citizens does not have enough money to pay its claims, we assume that it will recoup its entire deficit over time against all policyholders in the state. Specifically, Citizens assesses insurers, who then collect a surcharge from all their policyholders that is remitted to Citizens. The assessment is an obligation of the policyholders, not the insurers. A policyholder who fails to pay the assessment loses coverage. The assessment base to pay for Citizens' deficits has been expanded from homeowners' coverage to include auto and other lines of insurance, with the exception of medical malpractice and workers' compensation. These policyholders are now required to help pay for Citizens' 2005 deficit through a surcharge averaging 2 percent of their annual premium. In 2006, the state legislature allocated $715 million to reduce the amount of assessments policyholders would be required to pay. The remainder of the deficit, about $887 million, will be collected over a ten-year period.[5]

Florida Hurricane Catastrophe Fund

The FHCF was established to supplement private reinsurance and reimburse all insurers in Florida for a portion of their losses from catastrophic hurricanes. During the January 2007 special Florida legislative session, the capacity of the FHCF was expanded to $27.8 billion in reinsurance.

Post-Disaster Assessment

Since the FHCF has far less reserves than potential liabilities, the additional capacity that might be needed to meet all its claims following a severe hurricane would be funded by bonds supported by the FHCF's emergency assessment authority, which will assess all property and casualty lines of business, including surplus lines but excluding workers' compensation, accident and health, medical malpractice, and federal flood. Here again, all Floridians who purchased these types of insurance coverage will have to pay over the years when the FHCF encounters a shortfall in resources provided from reimbursement premiums and investment earnings. The assessment is limited to 6 percent annually for losses realized in any one year and 10 percent annually in the aggregate for all assessments for losses in all years.

FHCF Payout Calculation

We obtained 2005 data on the exposure of different insurers at the county level from FLOIR. These data are reported by insurers to the FLOIR under the QUASR system. Of these companies, 138 had homeowners' exposure in Florida, and we estimated the market share of each insurer i to be

$$MarketShare_i = Exposure_i / TotalExposure.$$

We then use the gross losses to estimate the gross loss by insurer i as follows:

$$Loss_i = MarketShare_i \cdot TotalGrossLosses.$$

Under the current arrangement between the FHCF and insurers in Florida, the FHCF will reimburse a fixed percentage of a participating insurer's losses from each covered event in excess of a per event retention and subject to a maximum aggregate limit for all events. The percentage of proportional reinsurance covered by the FHCF can be 45 percent, 75 percent, or 90 percent at the option of the insurer. The event retentions and limits vary by insurer according to a formula based on FHCF premiums. In order to calculate the payout from the FHCF to each insurer, we accessed data on the FHCF. With knowledge of the retention cap, the choice of proportional reinsurance rate (45 percent, 75 percent, or 90 percent) and the FHCF's obligation to pay an additional 5 percent of the calculated reimbursement figure for loss adjustment expenses, the FHCF payout to insurer i is determined by the following formula:

$$FHCF\ payout_i = Max[0; (Loss_i - retention_i)] \cdot (ReinsuranceRate_i) \cdot (1.05)$$

To illustrate the FHCF payout, consider an insurer with a $50 million retention that selected the 90 percent proportional reinsurance rate. If that insurer suffers $500 million losses, the FHCF will be responsible for $425.25 million [$405 million (i.e., 90 percent above the $50 million retention) × 1.05].

We sum all the individual payouts to insurers to obtain the total FHCF payout:

$$\text{FHCF } payout = \sum_i \{\text{Max}[0; (Loss - Retention_i)] \cdot (ReinsuranceRate_i) \cdot (1.05)\}$$

If the total payout is greater than $27.8 billion, the FHCF payout is capped at $27.8 billion because that is its defined maximum coverage. Then the $27.8 billion is multiplied by the damage multiplier ($TIV_{Residential}/TIV_{Total}$) to determine the portion of the payout going toward residential structures.[6] Note that the $27.8 billion includes the 5 percent loss adjustment expenses. The total losses would be $26.5 billion ($27.8/1.05), and the loss adjustment expense would be $1.3 billion ($26.5 billion × 5 percent). Note that for any given event, individual insurers may be capped out due to exhausting their coverage limit or FHCF payout. For example; in 2004, there were fifty-nine insurers that had FHCF losses in excess of their coverage limits, and in 2005 there were twelve such insurers.

Funding Arrangements

The 2007–2008 FHCF funding structure is displayed in figure 13.2. The $6.1 billion industry retention is the sum of the retentions (deductibles) of the individual insurers covered by the FHCF. Each insurer's retention is a per occurrence retention that is applied to each hurricane event during the FHCF's contract year. Insurers are assumed to have a 90 percent proportional reinsurance rate so that they are responsible for only 10 percent of the insurance wind losses from a hurricane above their share of the overall $6.1 billion retention. The FHCF structure uses a buy-down option below the aggregate industry overall retention level, temporary emergency additional coverage options (TEACO), which lowers the retention (deductible) of an insurer.[7] The FHCF offers an additional buy-up option above the FHCF limit, temporary increase in coverage limit (TICL), which can be chosen by the insurer to increase its coverage against catastrophic wind losses from hurricanes. TICL coverage applies when hurricane losses exceed an insurer's mandatory FHCF coverage. It acts to expand an insurer's limit of FHCF coverage.

The FHCF claims-paying capacity is the fund's balance as of December 31 of a contract year plus any reinsurance purchased by the FHCF plus the amount that can be raised through the issuance of revenue bonds. The 2007–2008 FHCF funding structure is used to analyze the FHCF shortfall should a severe hurricane occur. Table 13.6 compares the potential coverage as stated in the legislation to the actual coverage based on availability and insurer selections. We have estimated actual coverage using 2006 premiums.

The State Board of Administration (SBA) may make available an additional $4 billion of capacity, but this optional coverage is not currently offered to insurers. Mandatory layer

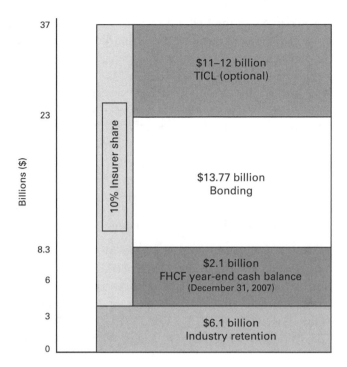

Figure 13.2
2007–2008 FHCF event funding structure

Table 13.6
FHCF funding structure for paying hurricane claims

	Potential coverage	Actual coverage based on selections
TICL layer	$12.000 billion	$11.428 billion
SBA optional limit	$4.000 billion	$0
Mandatory layer bonds	$13.767 billion	$13.767 billion
$10 million coverage option	$0.600 billion	$0.557 billion
TEACO	$6.000 billion	$0
Cash balance	$2.078 billion	$2.078 billion
Totals	$38.445 billion	$27.830 billion

bonds are the bonds taken out by the FHCF to pay for the regular (mandatory) coverage. The $10 million coverage option is available to certain limited apportionment companies and companies that participated in the Insurance Capital Build-Up Incentive Program. No insurer actually purchased TEACO since it is designed to be a last-resort coverage; private reinsurance was used as a substitute for TEACO. As a result, the total actual coverage of $27.8 billion is about $10.6 billion less than its potential coverage.[8] For our analyses of hurricane damage to homeowners, FHCF coverage is $23.6 billion the portion of the state fund that would be available for covering insurers' hurricane wind claims to residences. That represents the maximum level of claims the fund will be responsible for in our analysis. We discuss how the FHCF can finance such a level of claims (using future reinsurance premiums collected against insurers or ex post assessment against all policyholders in the state).

Operation of the Texas Windstorm Insurance Association

In 1970, Hurricane Celia caused an estimated $310 million in insured losses in Texas ($1.55 billion in 2005 dollars).[9] Many insurers sustained significant losses and discontinued coverage in the state's exposed coastal communities. As a result, in 1971, the state created the Texas Catastrophe Property Insurance Association, which later became the Texas Windstorm Insurance Association (TWIA). The TWIA provides wind and hail coverage for Texas Gulf Coast property owners as an insurer of last resort. As such, the TWIA writes higher-risk policies than other carriers.

The TWIA writes policies in only the following fifteen counties, all of which are on the coast, as shown in figure 13.3.

Aransas	Galveston	Matagorda
Brazoria	Harris County (partial)*	Nueces
Calhoun	Jefferson	Refugio
Cameron	Kenedy	San Patricio
Chambers	Kleberg	Willacy

Insured Property

The number of structures insured by TWIA has been growing dramatically. In 2001, it had 68,756 policyholders; as of August 31, 2008, 224,468 policies were in place. In 1992, TWIA had about $5 billion exposure in these counties. As of December 31, 2008, TWIA had approximately $58.5 billion in direct exposure (building and contents coverage) on issued policies, not including loss of business coverage and additional living expense coverage. Due to underwriting procedures implemented after Hurricane Ike, there are an unusually large number of policies that have been bound but not issued that are not reflected in this

*Although not on the map in figure 13.3, the following portions of Harris County, located inside the city limits and east of Highway 146 are also included: LaPort, Morgan's Point, Pasadena, Seabrook, and Sore Acres.

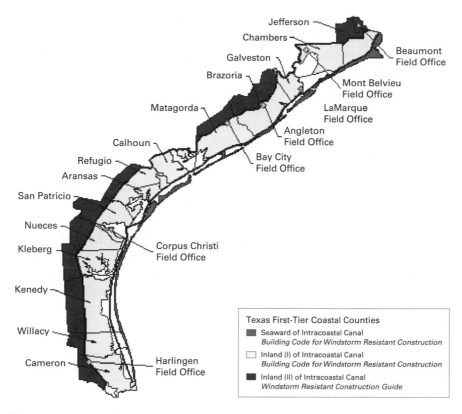

Figure 13.3
Coastal counties where coverage is provided by TWIA

total. When business interruption and additional living expense coverage are included, the total TWIA exposure rises to over $68.4 billion.

Residential and commercial policyholders can purchase TWIA coverage up to the following statutory limits:

- Residential: Dwelling building and contents: $1.7 million

- Apartment, condo, townhouse: Contents only: $350,000

- Mobile home: Building and contents: $84,000

- Commercial: Commercial building and contents: $4 million

How the TWIA Operates
All companies licensed to write property insurance in Texas are required to contribute to the TWIA as pool members. Any excess and surplus lines carriers that are affiliated with a member company are also included. TWIA is governed by a nine-member board of

directors, comprising five insurance company representatives, two agent representatives, and two consumer representatives. While our analysis focuses on residential property only, the TWIA covers residential and commercial structures as well as miscellaneous items such as signs, fences, flagpoles, and swimming pools.

The TWIA operates similarly to a standard insurance company. It issues policies, collects premiums, and pays claims. Any profits accrued are deposited annually into the Catastrophe Reserve Trust Fund, which provides one source of funding in the event of a catastrophic loss or series of losses, as detailed in the funding arrangement section below.

Market Share

The TWIA estimates that its 2008 share of the coastal residential market where it is authorized to do business is 55.3 percent. The average annual losses (AAL) of the coastal areas where TWIA does business relative to the total AAL in Texas was calculated. It ranges from 53.6 percent if there is no mitigation in place to 46.7 percent if there is mitigation in place. Given the 55.3 percent market share for TWIA in these coastal areas, this translates to a 26 to 30 percent overall market share (with mitigation and without mitigation, respectively) in Texas. As of December 31, 2008, TWIA had approximately $58.5 billion in direct exposure (building and contents coverage) on issued policies.

Funding Arrangements

The 2008–09 funding structure for TWIA is shown in figure 13.4. Texas statute requires that losses to the TWIA be paid from the following sources in this order:

1. $100 million assessed against members of TWIA

2. The current reserve in the Catastrophe Reserve Trust Fund, which acts as the TWIA surplus

3. Any reinsurance

4. $200 million assessed against members of the association, nonreimbursable

5. Unlimited additional assessments against members of the association, reimbursable through premium tax credits over five or more years

The amount of reinsurance recoverable by the TWIA is contractual. For the 2008 storm season, $1.5 billion in reinsurance coverage was purchased by the TWIA. The amount paid from the Catastrophe Reserve Trust Fund (CRTF) is based on the actual fund balance, which was approximately $500 million at the beginning of the 2008 storm season. Given current premiums and reinsurance expenses, average noncatastrophic losses, and no catastrophic losses, the TWIA expects to be able to contribute an average of $50 million annually to the CRTF. Unexpected growth, changes in reinsurance costs, noncatastrophic losses significantly above or below historic averages, or any catastrophes could materially affect the amount of any contribution to the CRTF.

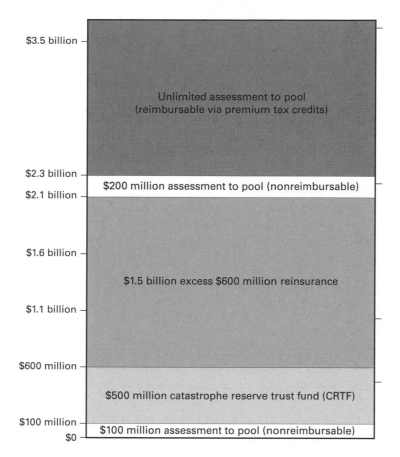

Figure 13.4
Funding structure of the TWIA (2008–09). *Source:* Texas Windstorm Insurance Association (TWIA)

The premium tax credit provision in the TWIA statute has never been executed because losses have never exceeded the relevant threshold. In the event of an assessment in this layer, TWIA member companies would claim up to 20 percent of their assessment annually as a credit against their Texas premium taxes for five or more years.[10] TWIA representatives indicated to us that the Texas Windstorm Insurance Association was seeking solutions to pay losses and avoid compromising the Texas General Revenue Fund should a major hurricane make landfall in a coastal area of the state.

As a result of the storms that hit Texas in 2008, the funding structure for TWIA has changed significantly. The CRTF was used in its entirety to pay claims from Hurricanes Dolly and Ike. As of December 31, 2008, $921.5 million had been paid by TWIA for Hurricanes Dolly and Ike. The TWIA assessed the entire $300 million nonreimbursable available to them from member companies and has had to use the unlimited, reimbursable layer. The Texas legislature will most likely address TWIA funding with potentially significant changes during 2009.

Mitigation

In undertaking our series of analyses, we assume two extreme cases regarding mitigation in place: no mitigation or full mitigation on all residential homes. As our analysis reveals, mitigation plays a critical role in reducing losses associated with the different major hurricanes we analyze.

13.4   Status Quo Analysis

Comparisons across the Four States

We use the following base case assumptions for our analyses of current insurance programs in place. Table 13.7 provides a dollar comparison of the impact of a 1-in-100-year return period loss event on the different stakeholders for each of the four states. An explanation of each column of this table is described below:

• *Losses to uninsured homes:* Losses to homeowners who do not have insurance.

• *Losses to insured homes:* Losses to homeowners who have insurance after claims reimbursements. These residual losses include deductibles and payments above the coverage limit.

• *State insurer:* Losses to Citizens in Florida (this amount is the level of claims that Citizens will be responsible for under different scenarios) and the TWIA in Texas after reinsurance reimbursements.

• *State assessment to insurers:* Losses paid by TWIA pool members (private insurers in Texas).

• *Private insurers:* Losses to private insurers after reinsurance reimbursement.

• *Private insurers reimbursable tax credits:* Losses paid by TWIA pool members (private insurers in Texas), that can be recouped through future tax credits.

• *State reinsurer:* Losses to the FHCF in Florida only (that amount is the level of claims the FHCF will be responsible for under different scenarios; later we discuss how the fund will meet its claims if they are higher than its current reserves).

• *Private reinsurance:* Losses to private reinsurers.

Table 13.8 provides a percentage comparison of the impact of a 1-in-100-year return period loss event on the different stakeholders for each of the four states. Several observations are relevant regarding the distribution of losses between the affected parties.

Table 13.7
State comparison $ losses: 100-year return period: Hurricane without mitigation ($ billion)

State	Details	Homeowner losses			Insurer losses				Reinsurer losses	
		Total loss	Losses to uninsured homes	Losses to insured homes (below deductible and above limit)	State insurer (FL = Citizens, TX = TWIA)	State assessment to insurers (TWIA only)	Private insurers	Private insurers' reimbursable tax credits portion (TWIA only)	State reinsurer (FHCF only)	Private reinsurance
Florida	Return period: 100 Take-up rate: 90% Mitigation: No Reinsurance: 60.3% Citizens market share: 30% Citizens reserve: $4.18B FHCF reserve: $2.78B	$75.73	$4.73	$6.18	$7.72	—	$18.01	—	$23.59	$15.49
Texas	Return period: 100 Take-up rate: 90% Mitigation: No Reinsurance: 20%	16.6	1.04	1.08	0.4	$0.3	8.59	$2.29	—	2.90
New York	Return period: 100 Take-up rate: 90% Mitigation: No Reinsurance: 10%	5.41	0.34	0.82	—	—	3.82	—	—	0.42
South Carolina	Return period: 100 Take-up rate: 90% Mitigation: No Reinsurance: 10%	4.13	0.26	0.21	—	—	3.29	—	—	0.37

Table 13.8
State comparison (percentage): 100-year return period: Hurricane without mitigation ($ billion)

State	Details	Total loss	Homeowner losses		Insurer losses				Reinsurer losses	
			Losses to uninsured homes	Losses to insured homes	State insurer (FL = Citizens, TX = TWIA)	State assessment to insurers (TWIA only)	Private insurers	Private insurers' reimbursable tax credits portion (TWIA only)	State reinsurer (FHCF only)	Private reinsurance
Florida	Return period: 100 Take-up rate: 90% Mitigation: No Reinsurance: 60.3% Citizens market share: 30% Citizens reserve: $4.18B FHCF reserve: $2.78B	$75.73	6%	8%	10%	—	24%	—	31%	20%
Texas	Return period: 100 Take-up rate: 90% Mitigation: No Reinsurance: 20%	16.6	6	7	2	2%	52	14%	—	17
New York	Return period: 100 Take-up rate: 90% Mitigation: No Reinsurance: 10%	5.41	6	15	—	—	71	—	—	8
South Carolina	Return period: 100 Take-up rate: 90% Mitigation: No Reinsurance: 10%	4.13	6	5	—	—	80	—	—	9

Differences in State Losses

Florida is by far the most exposed of the four states we studied. A 1-in-100-year return period loss event is estimated to produce total losses of $75.7 billion in Florida, $16.6 billion in Texas, $5.4 billion in New York, and $4.1 billion in South Carolina. As shown in appendix 13A, total losses at the 250-year return period level are $114.2 billion in Florida, $26.1 billion in Texas, $11.4 in New York, and $6.5 billion in South Carolina. Total losses at the 500-year level are $144.9 billion in Florida, $35.5 billion in Texas, $17.4 billion in New York, and $8.7 billion in South Carolina. (See appendix 13A.)

Homeowners' Losses after a 500-year Event

Due to the nature of our analysis, the losses to homeowners are derived from the take-up rate and estimates of ground-up loss, based on the assumption that uninsured home values are 60 percent of the insured homes in any given state. These assumptions result in uninsured homeowners in all states paying for 6 percent of the total 500-year return period loss. Insured homeowners are relatively well protected against large catastrophes, generally suffering less than 4 to 11 percent of the total losses.

State Fund Losses after a 500-year Event

In Florida, Citizens will incur only 14 percent of total losses even though it is assumed to have a market share of 30 percent. This is because Citizens is heavily reinsured by the FHCF for the 500-year return period loss ($9.45 billion in reinsurance coverage in 2009). TWIA would be responsible for only 1 percent of the losses in Texas, so that private insurers in that state would incur a higher percentage of the losses from the 500-year return period hurricane loss than those marketing policies in Florida.

Figure 13.5 details the losses sustained by homeowners, insurers, and reinsurers in each of the four states for events at the 50-, 100-, 250-, and 500-year return period levels when there are no mitigation measures in place. Private insurers in New York and South Carolina pay for a significant portion of the total losses, but the actual dollar amounts are much lower than in Florida and Texas.

We now analyze the residential losses that would be sustained by Citizens and the FHCF from the 500-year return period loss in 2009 and determine who ultimately will pay for these losses. Citizens will be responsible for $20.6 billion in claims from its policyholders, and the FHCF will be responsible for $23.6 billion in claims from the insurers it covers with respect to residential damage.[11] As of December 31, 2008, Citizens, which has become the largest provider of homeowners' insurance in the state, had $4.18 billion in reserves (claims available from surplus), another $4.17 billion of pre-event liquidity, and had purchased nearly $10 billion of reinsurance coverage ($9.45 billion from the FHCF and $.44 billion from private reinsurers). In other words, at the end of 2008, Citizens had $18.24 billion in claims-paying capacity to cover its losses from a future hurricane. Given that Citizens expects to collect about $2.8 billion in premiums during 2009, our analysis reveals that the state-run insurer would be able to handle its $20.6 billion insured losses

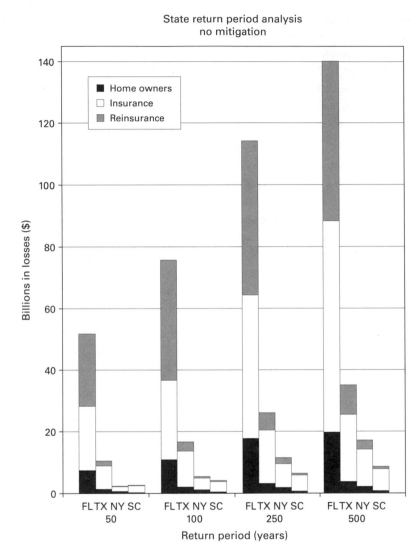

Figure 13.5
Homeowner, insurer, and reinsurer losses (initial claims) from hurricanes with 50- to 500-year return periods for
Florida, Texas, New York, and South Carolina

from a 500-year hurricane during the coming season. The major challenge is that as of 2009, the FHCF had reserves of $2.79 billion, and expected premiums for 2009 of $1.3 billion to cover reinsurance claims should a severe hurricane occur in the coming years. There are at least two possible ways the resulting deficit can be absorbed: ex post assessment (recoupment process) or use of future premiums.

Ex Post Assessment (Recoupment Process)

The first possibility is for the FHCF to assess the entire $19.51 (i.e., $23.6 − $2.79 − $1.3) deficit against all insurers, who in turn can assess it back to their policyholders.[12] Table 13.9 compares the original claims distribution to all stakeholders in Florida under a 1-in-500-year return period loss event (see table 13A.3 in the appendix) with the loss-sharing arrangements if the FHCF decides to finance 100 percent of the claims above $4.09 billion (reserves and premiums in 2009) through ex post assessments. We assume that the recoupment is assessed only to insured residential homeowners. In reality, the recoupment will be made against both residential and commercial policyholders in the state. Policyholders will now pay a total of $34.81 billion rather than the original $15.3 billion (table 13.9).

Use of Future Premiums

The second possibility is for the FHCF to issue some type of bond or access other types of debt so it can repay the debt over time using future premiums collected in the state. How long would it take the FHCF to repay claims above its current reserves if it followed this strategy?

To address this question, we assumed a growth in claims-paying capacity by the FHCF through premiums collected over time ($1.3 billion per year). Furthermore, we assumed no hurricane during the intervening years. Investment income on the premium or the balance carried forward is not included. Under these assumptions, it will take the FHCF until 2024 to repay its total losses from this 500-year hurricane (see figure 13.6), assuming there were no damaging hurricanes during this period.

Impact of Mitigation

The above analyses were undertaken with the assumption that no mitigation measures were in place to protect homes. Now we assume that all of the residential structures are fully mitigated.[13] Table 13.10 indicates the differences in losses for hurricanes with return periods of 100, 250, and 500 years for each of the four states we are studying when these loss-reduction measures are in place.

The analyses reveal that mitigation has the potential to significantly reduce losses from future hurricanes, ranging from 61 percent in Florida for a 100-year return period loss to 31 percent in New York for a 500-year return period loss. Appendix 13B depicts these differences graphically.

Table 13.9
Original claim distribution and ultimate loss sharing after 100% postdisaster assessment: 500-year return period without mitigation in Florida ($ billion)

Details	Total loss	Homeowner losses		Insurer losses		Reinsurer losses	
		Losses to uninsured homes	Losses to insured homes (below deductible and above limit)	Citizens	Private insurers	FHCF	Private reinsurance
Return period: 100	Original claims						
Take-up rate: 90%	$144.9	$9.1	$15.3	$20.6	$48.0	$23.6	$28.3
Mitigation: No	Ultimate loss distribution						
Reinsurance: 60.3%	$144.9	$9.1	$34.81	$20.6	$48.0	$4.08	$28.3
Citizens market share: 30%							
Citizens reserve: $4.18B							
FHCF reserve: $2.78B							

ªThe increase here assumes that the entire deficit of the FHCF is recouped only against homeowners who have wind coverage. In reality, the deficit would be recouped against all lines of insurance, with the exception of medical malpractice and workers' compensation.

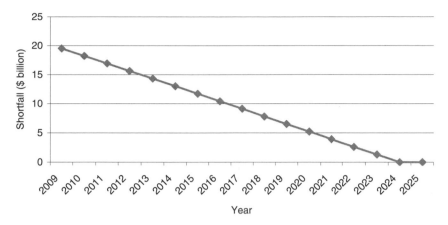

Figure 13.6
Number of years for the FHCF to recoup claims from a 500-year hurricane above its current reserve using future premiums. *Note:* The paying capacity assumes no event during the recoupment period.

Focus on Metropolitan Areas in the Four States

The total insured value (TIV) for each state is assumed to be equivalent to the total amount at risk in the state. Miami-Dade County represents 9 percent of Florida's $1.8 trillion TIV. The New York City area counties comprise 3 percent of New York's $2.1 trillion TIV. The Charleston area counties represent 15 percent of South Carolina's $0.36 trillion TIV, and the Houston area counties comprise 26 percent of Texas's $2.1 trillion TIV. Table 13.11 shows that the four metropolitan areas we selected comprise a much larger proportion of the ground-up losses than would be implied by looking at their percentage of the TIV in each of their respective states (without mitigation).

These regions are subject to a disproportionate hurricane risk than other parts of their states. This was not a surprise, as we intentionally chose the riskiest counties for this segment of our analysis.

13.5 Assumptions and Methodology for the Competitive Market Analysis

Databases

The competitive market analysis relied on two data sets. Projections of insurance industry losses (with and without mitigation) for different locations and return periods were used, as previously discussed for the status quo analysis.

A.M. Best provided us with publicly available data on 1,379 insurance and reinsurance groups. From this data set, we had the direct premiums written (DPW) for homeowners'

Table 13.10
Money saved (reduced losses) from full mitigation for different return periods

State	100-year event		250-year event		500-year event	
	Unmitigated losses	Savings (reduced losses) from mitigation	Unmitigated losses	Savings (reduced losses) from mitigation	Unmitigated losses	Savings (reduced losses) from mitigation
Florida	$84 billion	$51 billion 61%	$126 billion	$69 billion 55%	$160 billion	$83 billion 52%
New York	6 billion	2 billion 39	13 billion	5 billion 37	19 billion	7 billion 35
South Carolina	4 billion	2 billion 44	7 billion	3 billion 41	9 billion	4 billion 39
Texas	17 billion	6 billion 34	27 billion	9 billion 32	37 billion	12 billion 31

Table 13.11
Metropolitan area regions' share of state ground-up losses for different return periods without mitigation

Region	100-year event			250-year event			500-year event		
	State loss	Region loss	Percentage of state loss	State loss	Region loss	Percentage of state loss	State loss	Region loss	Percentage of state loss
Miami-Dade	$84 billion	$18 billion	21%	$126 billion	$37 billion	29%	$160 billion	$58 billion	36%
New York City area	6 billion	1.4 billion	24	13 billion	4 billion	28	19 billion	6 billion	30
Charleston area	4 billion	2.4 billion	56	7 billion	4 billion	60	9 billion	6 billion	60
Houston area	17 billion	15 billion	89	27 billion	25 billion	92	37 billion	34 billion	93

multiperil insurance in each of the four states. We were then able to derive a market share for each group i in each state using the following formula:

$$MarketShare_i = DPW_i/TotalDPW.$$

There are seventy-five groups with DPW in Florida, one hundred groups with DPW in New York, sixty-two groups with DPW in South Carolina, and sixty-eight groups with DPW in Texas. The A.M. Best data also included the total surpluses of each of the groups, which we used to determine the amount of coverage they would offer in the competitive market.

For Florida, we use the DPW to estimate market share in the competitive market analysis, and exposure to estimate market share in calculating the FHCF payout in the status quo analysis. This is because we had exact exposure data from the FLOIR, which allowed us to calculate a more precise estimate of the FHCF payout. These data did not extend to the other three states, and this information was not relevant to our competitive market analysis since it assumes there are no state funds in existence. Insurance is provided only by private insurers, and reinsurance is provided only by reinsurers or other alternative risk transfer instruments.

General Assumptions

In undertaking the analyses of a competitive insurance market, we made the following general assumptions:

• Total insurance is based on the amount of surplus each group is willing to put at risk in the particular state for the relevant hurricane return period.

• Insurers allocate their surplus to each state independently.

• Total surplus of insurance companies in a group is equal to total surplus for the entire group.[14]

• Reinsurance and other risk transfer amounts are identical to the status quo. This assumption can be justified given that reinsurers are not restricted by state regulators under the status quo.

Insurance Calculation

To determine the amount of insurance coverage offered in the competitive market, we focused on the surpluses of the top twenty-five insurers by market share in each state. The data for these twenty-five insurers in each of the four states are in appendix 13C. These companies typically represent more than 90 percent of the private market for homeowners' coverage. This surplus data came from A.M. Best for every company except for State Farm,[15] which is unique in that it has separate entities for different lines of insurance. We took the sum of the surpluses from its five property companies instead of using the A.M.

Best figure. To determine how much capacity insurers are willing to provide to cover hurricane risk under a competitive market, we assumed that each insurance group would risk 10 percent of its surplus to provide coverage for a 100-year, 250-year, or 500-year return period loss. This 10 percent figure was confirmed by the insurers and rating agencies with whom we spoke as a reasonable assumption for these analyses. In reality, of course, the determination by each insurer as to how much surplus it is willing to assign to a specific risk (e.g., wind damage) in a given state depends on its financial characteristics and the distribution of its portfolio in other states and countries. The capacity that insurers are willing to offer is also likely to vary with the return period of the catastrophic event under consideration and the price they can charge for providing coverage. More specifically, we have:

Insurance offered by insurer $i = 0.10 \cdot (Total\ surplus\ of\ insurer\ i)$

By aggregating the amount of coverage provided by each insurer in the state, we obtained the amount of coverage available to cover losses from hurricanes. For example, there was about $150 billion of surplus available amongst the top twenty-five private insurers operating in Florida. We thus assumed that $15 billion would be available for coverage against wind damage in the competitive market in Florida. We derived the percentage of the residential market covered in each of the states when no reinsurance was in place by using the following formula:

$$\text{Percentage of market covered in state Y} = \frac{\text{Insurance offered in state Y}}{\text{Gross loss in state Y}}$$

In a complementary series of analyses, we also calculated the percentage of total insurers' surplus that would have to be allocated against insured losses from hurricanes in each state so that all residential structures would be provided with full coverage. These figures were determined by the following formula:

$$\text{Necessary percentage of surplus for full coverage in state Y} = \frac{\text{Gross loss in state Y}}{\text{Total surplus}}$$

We conducted this analysis of competitive market insurance for the 100-year, 250-year, and 500-year return period losses both with and without mitigation in place. A separate analysis was undertaken to account for the impact of reinsurance and other risk transfer instruments on insurers' ability to provide coverage.

Insurer Surplus Assumption

We used the surplus from the top twenty-five insurers within each state for undertaking our base case analyses. We also examined other amounts of total surplus in 2006, including the total surplus of the top insurers writing coverage that comprise 95 percent of the market and the total surplus of all insurers writing coverage in the state (100 percent of the market). The increase in coverage as we expanded the pool of insurers is not large, as shown in table 13.12.

Note on Competitive Market Insurer Surpluses

The competitive market insurer surplus allocations may differ from how these companies actually allocate their surpluses. This is a theoretical analysis of what these companies are capable of doing based on their total conglomerate surplus reported in the A.M. Best data set. However, in practice they may make their capital allocation decisions differently.

13.6   Competitive Market Analysis

Our specific interest in undertaking this analysis is to determine how much coverage insurers could provide in each of the four states. We focus on losses at the 100-, 250-, and 500-year return periods and vary assumptions regarding mitigation in place and availability of reinsurance (whether it is provided by traditional reinsurance or alternative risk transfer instruments). We study two cases: first, insurers do not have any way to reinsure part of their exposure; second, we introduce additional capacity to insurers provided by reinsurance.

Case 1: No Reinsurance

We first examine the case where none of the homes had adopted mitigation measures and insurers could not rely on reinsurance to protect themselves against future damage. Even when insurers are entirely on their own, our analysis shows that using the strategy of allocating 10 percent of surplus, they will have enough capacity to be able to provide protection to all homeowners in New York and South Carolina for the 100-, 250-, and 500-year loss event, as shown in table 13.13. The hurricane damage even for a 500-year loss in New York and South Carolina will be sufficiently small that insurers would not have to commit a large percentage of their surplus to be able to provide full protection against all residential structures in the area. For example, insurers providing wind coverage in New York State would have to commit only 2.5 percent of their surplus to cover total losses to homes (except for the deductible portions of the policy) from a 100-year loss. This percentage would increase to 8.9 percent for a hurricane with a 500-year return period loss. The percentage of surplus required in South Carolina to cover hurricanes with these return periods would be even smaller than in New York.

Private insurers in Florida and Texas would need financial backup to cover all the wind losses from a severe hurricane if homeowners have not undertaken mitigation measures. Even for a 100-year return period loss in Florida, the total amount of insurance in place would cover only 23.8 percent of the loss. Insurers providing wind coverage in Florida would have to allocate 42 percent of their surplus to provide full coverage to homeowners

Table 13.12
Industry surplus analysis for top 25 insurers, and insurers comprising 95 to 100 percent of the market

	Top 25 companies			95% of the market			100% of the market		
State	Number of companies	Market share	Surplus ($ billions)	Number of companies	Market share	Surplus ($ billions)	Number of companies	Market share	Surplus ($ billions)
Florida	25	91.7%	$154.4	32	94.9%	$164.3	75	100.0%	$205.2
New York	25	93.2	167.8	29	95.0	168.7	100	100.0	225.6
South Carolina	25	95.2	175.0	25	95.2	175.0	62	100.0	203.7
Texas	25	95.3	139.2	25	95.3	139.2	68	100.0	195.7

Table 13.13
Percentage of loss covered and required surplus for full coverage by insurers with no reinsurance ($ billion)

State	Surplus	Return period (years)	Gross losses	Amount of coverage (10% of surplus)	Market covered	Surplus necessary for full coverage
No mitigation of current homes						
Florida	$154.4	100	$64.8	15.4	23.8%	42.0%
		250	96.4	15.4	16.0	62.5
		500	120.5	15.4	12.8	78.1
New York	167.8	100	4.2	16.8	100.0	2.5
		250	9.6	16.8	100.0	5.7
		500	14.9	16.8	100.0	8.9
South Carolina	175.0	100	3.7	17.5	100.0	2.1
		250	5.8	17.5	100.0	3.3
		500	7.7	17.5	100.0	4.4
Texas	139.2	100	14.5	13.9	96.2	10.4
		250	22.9	13.9	60.7	16.5
		500	31.4	13.9	44.4	22.5
Full mitigation of current homes						
Florida	154.4	100	23.7	15.4	65.1	15.4
		250	42.9	15.4	36.0	27.8
		500	58.9	15.4	26.2	38.2
New York	167.8	100	2.4	16.8	100.0	1.4
		250	5.8	16.8	100.0	3.5
		500	9.4	16.8	100.0	5.6
South Carolina	175.0	100	2.0	17.5	100.0	1.1
		250	3.3	17.5	100.0	1.9
		500	4.7	17.5	100.0	2.7
Texas	139.2	100	9.4	13.9	100.0	6.7
		250	15.2	13.9	91.4	10.9
		500	21.1	13.9	65.9	15.2

against this event. In Texas, the loss would be less severe than in Florida, so that insurers would be able to offer close to full protection (96.2 percent) against a 100-year loss but not against the 250- or 500-year return period loss (table 13.13).

The situation improves considerably in these two states if all homes are required to adopt cost-effective mitigation measures, as shown in the bottom portion of table 13.13. In Florida, insurers would now be able to cover 65.1 percent of the losses from a 1-in-100-year return period loss event when mitigation was in place, without having to rely on reinsurance (see chapter 7) or alternative risk transfer (ART) instruments (see chapter 8). A similar story emerges for homes in Texas, where full coverage will be provided for a 1-in-100-year return period loss event if all residential structures had adopted mitigation measures specified in current building codes.

Table 13.14
Percentage of losses covered and required surplus for full coverage by insurers with reinsurance in place ($ billion)

State	Surplus	Return period (years)	Gross losses	Rein-surance coverage	Unrein-sured losses	Amount of coverage (10% of surplus)	Market covered	Surplus necessary for full coverage
No mitigation of current homes								
Florida	$154.4	100	$64.8	39.1	$25.7	15.4	60.0%	16.7%
		250	96.4	49.8	46.6	15.4	33.1	30.2
		500	120.5	51.9	68.6	15.4	22.5	44.4
New York	167.8	100	4.2	0.4	3.8	16.8	100.0	2.3
		250	9.6	1.9	7.7	16.8	100.0	4.6
		500	14.9	3.0	11.9	16.8	100.0	7.1
South Carolina	175.0	100	3.7	0.4	3.3	17.5	100.0	1.9
		250	5.8	0.6	5.2	17.5	100.0	3.0
		500	7.7	0.8	7.0	17.5	100.0	4.0
Texas	139.2	100	14.5	2.9	11.6	13.9	100.0	8.3
		250	22.9	6.9	16.1	13.9	86.7	11.5
		500	31.4	12.5	18.8	13.9	74.0	13.5
Full mitigation of current homes								
Florida	154.4	100	23.7	20.8	2.9	15.4	100.0	1.9
		250	42.9	23.6	19.3	15.4	80.1	12.5
		500	58.9	35.5	23.4	15.4	66.0	15.1
New York	167.8	100	2.4	0.2	2.1	16.8	100.0	1.3
		250	5.8	0.6	5.2	16.8	100.0	3.1
		500	9.4	1.9	7.5	16.8	100.0	4.5
South Carolina	175.0	100	2.0	0.2	1.8	17.5	100.0	1.0
		250	3.3	0.3	3.0	17.5	100.0	1.7
		500	4.7	0.5	4.2	17.5	100.0	2.4
Texas	139.2	100	9.4	1.9	7.5	13.9	100.0	5.4
		250	15.2	3.0	12.2	13.9	100.0	8.8
		500	21.1	6.3	14.8	13.9	94.2	10.6

Case 2: Reinsurance in Place

With reinsurance in place, we made the same assumption as in case 1 regarding allocation of insurer surplus to homeowners' insurance, but used different estimates of insured losses. We subtracted the total reinsurance obtained from the status quo analysis so insurers had to cover only their unreinsured losses instead of their total gross losses.

As shown in table 13.14, when reinsurance is available, the private insurance market is able to cover all the losses in Texas from a 100-year return period loss, 86.7 percent of the 250-year losses, and 74 percent of the 500-year losses for a 1-in-500-year return period loss event even if homes had not undertaken mitigation measures. In Florida, 60 percent of the 100-year return period losses will be covered from a 1-in-100-year return period loss event, but the majority of the 250-year and 500-year losses will still be uninsured for 1-in-250-year and 1-in-500-year return period loss events if mitigation measures had not been adopted by homeowners. Should all homes be mitigated, there will be less than full coverage in Texas only for the 1-in 500-year loss event and in Florida for the 250-year and 500-year loss events.

13.7   Impact of Insurance Premiums Reflecting Risk

We conclude this series of analyses by determining the loss cost for Florida, New York, South Carolina, and Texas and counties in these states as a basis for determining premiums that reflect risk for covering wind damage. To determine these premiums one needs to augment the expected average annual loss by using a loading factor.

Assumptions for the Analysis

Loss Cost per $1,000
In order to do our analysis at the county level, we summed the average annual loss (AAL) and total insured value (TIV) from the relevant postal codes to obtain the appropriate figures for each county. The loss cost per $1,000 of coverage for each county i was determined by the following formula:

$$Loss\ cost_i = AAL_i/(TIV_i) \cdot \$1,000$$

To illustrate, suppose a particular county has an AAL = $1 million and TIV = $20 million. This implies that a loss cost for homes in this county would be $50 per $1,000 of coverage.

Loading Factor
In addition to the loss cost, we assume insurers incorporate a loading factor (λ) into their pricing to cover administrative, marketing and claims processing costs and the cost of capital. As discussed in chapter 6, each policy the insurer sells imposes its own capital burden. If an additional policy were sold without adding to the insurer's overall capital, there would normally be a small increase in the likelihood that the insurer could default. Just how much of an increase would depend on the riskiness of the policy and its covariance with other policies and assets held by the insurer. The appropriate allocation of capital to a policy would be that required to maintain the insurer's credit status; the addition of the policy and the accompanying capital would leave the insurer with the same credit status as before. We thus define a fair price for insurance as a premium that provides a fair rate of return on invested equity.

Let k be the ratio of capital to expected losses for the insurer to maintain its credit rating. Here we will use $k = 1$, a value that many property liability insurers use for their combined book of business.[16]

In addition to paying claims, the insurer is assumed to set aside capital for covering additional expenses (X) in the form of commissions to agents and brokers, and underwriting and claims assessment expenses. For this example suppose $k = 1$ and $X = \$200$. Given the risk characteristics of the portfolio, we assume that investors in insurance companies require a return on equity (ROE) of 15 percent to compensate for risk. The insurer invests its funds in lower-risk vehicles that yield an expected return r of 5 percent. What premium π would the insurer have to charge its policyholders to cover them against hurricanes and to secure a return of 15 percent for its investors? Using the hypothetical example in chapter 6 (section 6.4) the premium is: $\pi = \$1274$, so that the loading factor is $\lambda = .274$.

In the analysis that follows, we will use a value of $\lambda = .5$ (a 50 percent loading factor). This is still a conservative estimate, as it does not take into account reinsurance costs associated with catastrophic risks and other expenses that the insurer incurs in modeling catastrophic risk by either purchasing commercial models or using their own in-house modeling capability, nor does it include state and federal taxes which the insurer has to pay as any other business.[17]

Statewide Prices

Prices for the entire state were determined using the same procedure as for the individual counties, except the postal code data were aggregated for the entire state.

Determination of Loss Cost and Insurance Premiums

Table 13.15 specify the loss costs and premiums with a 50 percent loading factor for hurricane wind damage for the ten counties with the highest risk within each state, as well as any counties from the metropolitan areas we studied that were not among the top ten. The loss costs and premiums for the entire state are specified at the bottom of the table for each state. We also specify ratios of the county/state premium so one can appreciate how much more (or less) insurers would have to charge in areas that have a significant hurricane risk relative to other parts of the state in order to cover their expected claims payments. The counties from our designated metropolitan areas in each of the four states are in bold type in table 13.15. Appendix 13D presents tables that include all the counties in the four states that we studied.

The data reveal that coastal counties subject to hurricane risk will pay significantly higher premiums than other portions of the state. This is particularly true in Texas, where Calhoun, Aransas, and Galveston counties are charged over nine times the average for the entire state. For the other three states, the differences are less extreme. In the case of Florida, the risk-based premiums do not include any losses from storm surge, so they are likely to be somewhat higher when this cause of damage is incorporated. It is important to remember that premiums based on loss costs are likely to be somewhat lower than homeowners' insurance premiums, since a standard policy covers losses from other causes, such as fire and theft.

Table 13.15
Loss costs and insurance premiums for hurricane wind-insured damage in counties with highest risk

	Price rank	County	Loss cost per $1,000	Premium with 50% loading	County/state premium ratio
Florida	1	Monroe	$16.22	$24.32	4.62
	2	Franklin	6.84	10.26	1.95
	3	Martin	6.69	10.03	1.90
	4	**Miami-Dade**	**6.48**	**9.73**	**1.85**
	5	Palm Beach	6.47	9.71	1.84
	6	Indian River	5.67	8.51	1.62
	7	Broward	5.64	8.46	1.61
	8	Collier	5.04	7.56	1.44
	9	Saint Lucie	4.68	7.02	1.33
	10	Santa Rosa	4.46	6.69	1.27
		Entire state	**3.50**	**5.25**	
New York	1	Suffolk	0.38	0.56	4.10
	2	Nassau	0.17	0.25	1.85
	3	**Richmond**	**0.12**	**0.17**	**1.26**
	4	**Queens**	**0.10**	**0.15**	**1.10**
	5	**Kings**	**0.08**	**0.12**	**.89**
	6	Westchester	0.08	0.12	.88
	7	Rockland	0.07	0.11	.78
	8	**Bronx**	**0.07**	**0.10**	**.71**
	9	Putnam	0.06	0.09	.69
	10	Dutchess	0.04	0.06	.43
	14	**New York (Manhattan)**	**0.02**	**0.04**	**.27**
		Entire state	**0.09**	**0.14**	
South Carolina	1	Georgetown	2.69	4.04	4.74
	2	**Charleston**	**2.62**	**3.93**	**4.61**
	3	Horry	2.11	3.17	3.72
	4	Beaufort	2.10	3.15	3.70
	5	**Colleton**	**1.37**	**2.05**	**2.41**
	6	**Berkeley**	**1.20**	**1.80**	**2.12**
	7	Jasper	0.92	1.38	1.62
	8	**Dorchester**	**0.85**	**1.27**	**1.49**
	9	Williamsburg	0.81	1.21	1.42
	10	Marion	0.65	0.97	1.14
		Entire state	**0.57**	**0.85**	
Texas	1	Calhoun	4.60	6.89	10.53
	2	Aransas	4.56	6.84	10.45
	3	**Galveston**	**3.95**	**5.92**	**9.05**
	4	Matagorda	3.19	4.79	7.32

Table 13.15
(continued)

Price rank	County	Loss cost per $1,000	Premium with 50% loading	County/state premium ratio
5	**Chambers**	**2.59**	**3.88**	**5.93**
6	**Brazoria**	**2.44**	**3.65**	**5.59**
7	Nueces	2.32	3.48	5.32
8	San Patricio	2.27	3.40	5.19
9	Cameron	2.08	3.12	4.77
10	Jackson	2.04	3.07	4.69
17	**Fort Bend**	**1.07**	**1.61**	**2.46**
19	**Liberty**	**1.02**	**1.53**	**2.34**
22	**Harris**	**0.81**	**1.22**	**1.86**
28	**Waller**	**0.57**	**0.85**	**1.39**
29	**Austin**	**0.50**	**0.75**	**1.14**
34	**San Jacinto**	**0.38**	**0.56**	**.86**
36	**Montgomery**	**0.32**	**0.48**	**.74**
	Entire state	**0.44**	**0.65**	

Note: Counties in bold are in our designated metropolitan areas.

Summary

This chapter provides a series of analyses to evaluate how catastrophe losses would be shared among different stakeholders under the status quo using data provided by Risk Management Solutions on the exposure at risk and expected losses, A.M. Best data on insurance groups, and data from the state funds in Florida and Texas. We estimate the distribution of losses to homeowners, insurers, and reinsurers for return period loss events of 1-in-100 years, 1-in-250-years, and 1-in-500 years for Florida, New York, South Carolina, and Texas and metropolitan areas in each of these states with and without mitigation in place (status quo analysis).

We also determine the ability of the private market to offer insurance protection if companies are permitted to charge rates that reflect risk (competitive market analysis). The analysis reveals that insurers would not need reinsurance in order to be able to provide protection to most homeowners in New York, South Carolina, and Texas, but would have to rely on private reinsurance or other alternative risk transfer instruments to provide coverage to the majority of homes in Florida. If all single-family residences were required to adopt mitigation measures, the private sector should be able to provide full insurance protection in all four states without having to allocate a significant portion of its surplus to the hurricane risk. The chapter concludes with an analysis of loss costs and premiums reflecting risks and the cost of capital in the counties most subject to hurricane damage in each of the four states. These premiums are compared with the state average to show the degree of variation in the hurricane risk.

APPENDIX 13A: COMPARISON OF LOSSES AT THE 250- AND 500-YEAR RETURN PERIOD

Table 13A.1
250- and 500-year return state comparisons. Event: 250-year return period without mitigation ($ billion)

State	Details	Homeowner losses			Insurer losses				Reinsurer losses	
		Total loss	Losses to uninsured homes	Losses to insured homes	State insurer (FL = Citizens, TX = TWIA)	State assessment to insurers (TWIA only)	Private insurers	Private insurers' reimbursable tax credits portion (TWIA only)	State reinsurer (FHCF only)	Private reinsurance
Florida	Return period: 250 Take-up rate: 90% Mitigation: No Reinsurance: 60.3% Citizens market share: 30% Citizens reserve: $4.18B FHCF reserve: $2.78B	$114.2	$7.1	$10.6	$14.0	—	$32.6	—	$23.6	$26.2
Texas	Return period: 250 Take-up rate: 90% Mitigation: No Reinsurance: 20%	26.1	1.6	1.5	0.4	$0.3	11.9	$4.6	—	5.7
New York	Return period: 250 Take-up rate: 90% Mitigation: No Reinsurance: 10%	11.4	0.7	1.1	—	—	7.7	—	—	1.9
South Carolina	Return period: 250 Take-up rate: 90% Mitigation: No Reinsurance: 10%	6.5	0.4	0.3	—	—	5.2	—	—	0.6

Table 13A.2
State comparisons. Event: 250-year return period without mitigation ($ billion)

State	Details	Total loss	Homeowner losses		Insurer losses				Reinsurer losses	
			Losses to uninsured homes	Losses to insured homes	State insurer (FL = Citizens, TX = TWIA)	State assessment to insurers (TWIA only)	Private insurers	Private insurers' reimbursable tax credits portion (TWIA only)	State reinsurer (FHCF only)	Private reinsurance
Florida	Return period: 250 Take-up rate: 90% Mitigation: No Reinsurance: 60.3% Citizens market share: 30% Citizens reserve: $4.18B FHCF reserve: $2.78B	$114.2	6%	9%	12%	—	29%	—	21%	23%
Texas	Return period: 250 Take-up rate: 90% Mitigation: No Reinsurance: 20%	26.08	6	6	2	1%	46	18%	—	22
New York	Return period: 250 Take-up rate: 90% Mitigation: No Reinsurance: 10%	11.44	6	10	—	—	67	—	—	17
South Carolina	Return period: 250 Take-up rate: 90% Mitigation: No Reinsurance: 10%	6.46	6	4	—	—	80	—	—	9

Table 13A.3
State comparisons. Event: 500-year return period without mitigation ($ billion)

State	Details	Homeowner losses			Insurer losses				Reinsurer losses	
		Total loss	Losses to uninsured homes	Losses to insured homes	State insurer (FL = Citizens, TX = TWIA)	State assessment to insurers (TWIA only)	Private insurers	Private insurers' reimbursable tax credits portion (TWIA only)	State reinsurer (FHCF only)	Private reinsurance
Florida	Return period: 500 Take-up rate: 90% Mitigation: No Reinsurance: 60.3% Citizens market share: 30% Citizens reserve: $4.18B FHCF reserve: $2.78B	$144.9	$9.1	$15.3	$20.6	—	$48.0	—	$23.6	$28.3
Texas	Return period: 500 Take-up rate: 90% Mitigation: No Reinsurance: 20%	35.5	2.2	1.9	0.4	$0.3	14.0	$6.9	—	9.7
New York	Return period: 500 Take-up rate: 90% Mitigation: No Reinsurance: 10%	17.4	1.1	1.3	—	—	11.9	—	—	3.0
South Carolina	Return period: 500 Take-up rate: 90% Mitigation: No Reinsurance: 10%	8.7	0.5	0.4	—	—	7.0	—	—	0.8

Table 13A.4
State comparisons. Event: 500-year return period without mitigation ($ billion)

State	Details	Homeowner losses			Insurer losses				Reinsurer losses	
		Total loss	Losses to uninsured homes	Losses to insured homes	State insurer (FL = Citizens, TX = TWIA)	State assessment to insurers (TWIA only)	Private insurers	Private insurers' reimbursable tax credits portion (TWIA only)	State reinsurer (FHCF only)	Private reinsurance
Florida	Return period: 500 Take-up rate: 90% Mitigation: No Reinsurance: 60.3% Citizens market share: 30% Citizens reserve: $4.18B FHCF reserve: $2.78B	$144.9	6%	11%	14%	—	33%	—	16%	20%
Texas	Return period: 500 Take-up rate: 90% Mitigation: No Reinsurance: 20%	35.46	6	5	1	1%	40	20%	—	27
New York	Return period: 500 Take-up rate: 90% Mitigation: No Reinsurance: 10%	17.36	6	8	—	—	69	—	—	17
South Carolina	Return period: 500 Take-up rate: 90% Mitigation: No Reinsurance: 10%	8.66	6	4	—	—	81	—	—	9

APPENDIX 13B: EFFECTS OF MITIGATION ON HURRICANE RISK

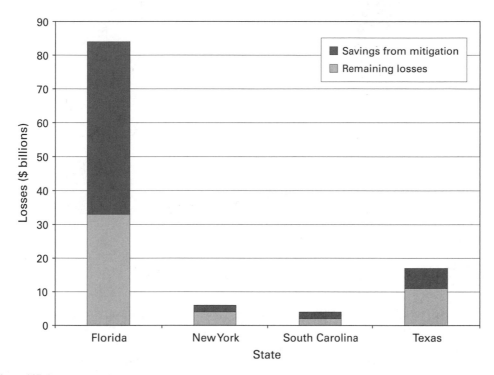

Figure 13B.1
Money saved (reduced losses) from full mitigation for a 100-year event

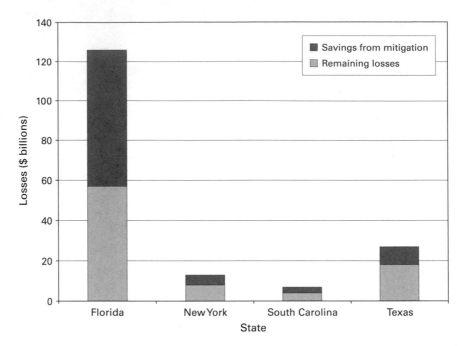

Figure 13B.2
Money saved (reduced losses) from full mitigation for a 250-year event

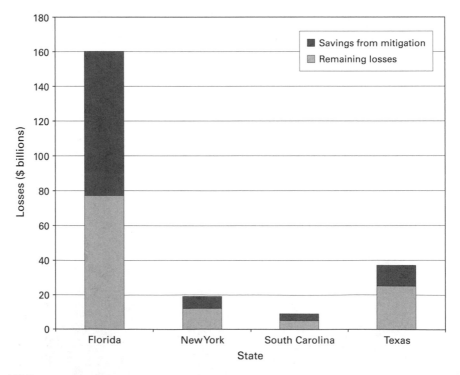

Figure 13B.3
Money saved (reduced losses) from full mitigation for a 500-year event

APPENDIX 13C: MARKET SHARE ANALYSIS FOR THE TOP TWENTY-FIVE INSURERS IN FLORIDA, NEW YORK, SOUTH CAROLINA, AND TEXAS

Table 13C.1
Market share analysis for the top twenty-five insurers in Florida

Rank	Company name	Company surplus (billions)	DPW market share	Surplus market share	DPW market share (excluding Citizens)
1	State Farm Group	$12.8	19.7%	8.3%	23.9%
2	Citizens Property Insurance Corporation	0.0	17.7	0.0	0.0
3	Allstate Insurance Group	19.2	7.2	12.5	8.7
4	Tower Hill Group	0.1	4.7	0.0	5.7
5	Universal P&C Insurance Co.	0.1	4.6	0.0	5.6
6	USAA Group	11.7	4.3	7.6	5.2
7	Nationwide Group	12.8	4.1	8.3	4.9
8	Liberty Mutual Insurance Companies	12.1	3.0	7.9	3.7
9	American Strategic Insurance Companies	0.2	3.0	0.1	3.6
10	Universal Insurance Group of Puerto Rico	0.2	2.5	0.1	3.1
11	American International Group	27.0	2.2	17.5	2.7
12	Chubb Group of Insurance Companies	11.3	2.1	7.3	2.6
13	United Property and Casualty Insurance Co.	0.1	1.9	0.0	2.3
14	Hartford Insurance Group	14.5	1.9	9.4	2.3
15	Travelers Insurance Companies	20.2	1.8	13.1	2.2
16	Gulfstream Property and Casualty Insurance Co.	0.0	1.6	0.0	2.0
17	GeoVera Insurance Group	0.1	1.5	0.1	1.8
18	Southern Farm Bureau Group	1.8	1.2	1.2	1.5
19	Sunshine State Insurance Company	0.0	1.2	0.0	1.5
20	Cypress Holdings Group	0.0	1.2	0.0	1.5
21	Farmers Insurance Group	5.3	1.1	3.4	1.3
22	Florida Family Insurance Company	0.0	1.0	0.0	1.2
23	Allianz of America	3.8	0.9	2.5	1.1
24	Philadelphia Insurance Group	1.0	0.8	0.7	1.0
25	Coral Insurance Company	0.0	0.7	0.0	0.8

Table 13C.2
Market share analysis for the top twenty-five insurers in New York

Rank	Company name	Company surplus (billions)	DPW market share	Surplus market share
1	Allstate Insurance Group	$19.2	19.1%	11.5%
2	State Farm Group	12.8	14.6	7.6
3	Travelers Insurance Companies	20.2	11.3	12.0
4	Chubb Group of Insurance Companies	11.3	10.0	6.7
5	Liberty Mutual Insurance Companies	12.1	6.3	7.2
6	Central Services Group	0.3	4.1	0.2
7	Nationwide Group	12.8	4.0	7.7
8	MetLife Auto and Home Group	1.9	3.4	1.1
9	Tower Group Companies	0.2	2.2	0.1
10	USAA Group	11.7	2.0	7.0
11	Hartford Insurance Group	14.5	2.0	8.7
12	Allianz of America	3.8	1.9	2.3
13	American International Group	27.0	1.5	16.1
14	White Mountains Insurance Group	3.3	1.4	2.0
15	Unitrin	1.2	1.2	0.7
16	Hanover Insurance Group Property and Casualty Co.	1.5	1.1	0.9
17	Preferred Mutual Insurance Company	0.1	1.1	0.1
18	Amica Mutual Group	2.1	1.0	1.2
19	Farmers Insurance Group	5.3	0.9	3.1
20	Andover Companies	0.7	0.8	0.4
21	Sterling Insurance Company	0.0	0.8	0.0
22	Utica National Insurance Group	0.7	0.7	0.4
23	Security Mutual Insurance Company	0.0	0.7	0.0
24	Main Street America Group	0.6	0.6	0.3
25	Erie Insurance Group	4.3	0.6	2.6

Table 13C.3
Market share analysis for the top twenty-five insurers in South Carolina

Rank	Company name	Company surplus (billions)	DPW market share	Surplus market share
1	State Farm Group	$12.8	26.0%	7.3%
2	Allstate Insurance Group	19.2	14.9	11.0
3	Nationwide Group	12.8	8.9	7.3
4	Southern Farm Bureau Group	1.8	6.8	1.1
5	USAA Group	11.7	6.8	6.7
6	Travelers Insurance Companies	20.2	6.6	11.5
7	American International Group	27.0	3.9	15.4
8	Farmers Insurance Group	5.3	3.9	3.0
9	Auto-Owners Insurance Group	4.8	2.9	2.8
10	Assurant Solutions	0.9	2.1	0.5
11	GeoVera Insurance Group	0.1	1.7	0.1
12	Liberty Mutual Insurance Companies	12.1	1.7	6.9
13	Safeco Insurance Companies	3.8	1.0	2.2
14	Chubb Group of Insurance Companies	11.3	1.0	6.4
15	Hartford Insurance Group	14.5	0.9	8.3
16	State Auto Insurance Companies	1.6	0.9	0.9
17	Companion Property and Casualty Group	0.1	0.7	0.1
18	Allianz of America	3.8	0.7	2.2
19	American National P&C Group	0.7	0.7	0.4
20	Horace Mann Insurance Group	0.3	0.7	0.2
21	MetLife Auto and Home Group	1.9	0.6	1.1
22	Balboa Insurance Group	0.7	0.6	0.4
23	Selective Insurance Group	1.0	0.5	0.6
24	Zurich Financial Services NA Group	6.2	0.5	3.6
25	Homesite Group	0.2	0.4	0.1

Table 13C.4
Market share analysis for the top twenty-five insurers in Texas

Rank	Company name	Company surplus (billions)	DPW market share	Surplus market share
1	State Farm Group	$12.8	29.3%	9.2%
2	Allstate Insurance Group	19.2	15.7	13.8
3	Farmers Insurance Group	5.3	12.6	3.8
4	USAA Group	11.7	7.4	8.4
5	Travelers Insurance Companies	20.2	5.7	14.5
6	Nationwide Group	12.8	4.0	9.2
7	Southern Farm Bureau Group	1.8	2.6	1.3
8	Chubb Group of Insurance Companies	11.3	2.4	8.1
9	Liberty Mutual Insurance Companies	12.1	1.9	8.7
10	Hartford Insurance Group	14.5	1.6	10.4
11	Republic Companies Group	0.2	1.5	0.1
12	Safeco Insurance Companies	3.8	1.3	2.7
13	NLASCO Group	0.1	1.0	0.1
14	Texas FAIR Plan Association	0.0	1.0	0.0
15	American Strategic Insurance Companies	0.2	1.0	0.1
16	Amica Mutual Group	2.1	0.9	1.5
17	Auto Club Enterprises Insurance Group	3.2	0.7	2.3
18	Cypress Holdings Group	0.0	0.7	0.0
19	Unitrin, Inc.	1.2	0.7	0.9
20	State National Companies	0.1	0.6	0.1
21	American National P&C Group	0.7	0.6	0.5
22	GeoVera Insurance Group	0.1	0.5	0.1
23	Allianz of America	3.8	0.5	2.7
24	MetLife Auto & Home Group	1.9	0.5	1.3
25	Colonial Insurance Group	0.0	0.4	0.0

APPENDIX 13D: LOSS COSTS AND INSURANCE PREMIUMS FOR WIND COVERAGE IN ALL COUNTIES IN FLORIDA, NEW YORK, SOUTH CAROLINA, AND TEXAS

Table 13D.1
Loss costs and insurance premiums for hurricane wind insured damage in all counties in Florida

Rank	County	Loss costs per $1,000	50% loading	Ratio to state
1	Monroe	$16.22	$24.32	4.62
2	Franklin	6.84	10.26	1.95
3	Martin	6.69	10.03	1.90
4	Miami-Dade	6.48	9.73	1.85
5	Palm Beach	6.47	9.71	1.84
6	Indian River	5.67	8.51	1.62
7	Broward	5.64	8.46	1.61
8	Collier	5.04	7.56	1.44
9	Saint Lucie	4.68	7.02	1.33
10	Santa Rosa	4.46	6.69	1.27
11	Manatee	4.20	6.30	1.20
12	Lee	4.19	6.28	1.19
13	Walton	4.15	6.22	1.18
14	Sarasota	4.14	6.21	1.18
15	Escambia	4.04	6.06	1.15
16	Okaloosa	4.00	6.00	1.14
17	Gulf	3.98	5.96	1.13
18	Pinellas	3.87	5.81	1.10
19	Charlotte	3.29	4.94	0.94
20	Brevard	3.09	4.63	0.88
21	Okeechobee	3.07	4.61	0.87
22	Glades	2.91	4.37	0.83
23	Hendry	2.88	4.32	0.82
24	Bay	2.80	4.20	0.80
25	De Soto	2.23	3.34	0.64
26	Wakulla	1.89	2.83	0.54
27	Pasco	1.84	2.76	0.52
28	Hillsborough	1.70	2.55	0.48
29	Dixie	1.54	2.30	0.44
30	Levy	1.47	2.20	0.42
31	Hardee	1.45	2.18	0.41
32	Volusia	1.44	2.15	0.41
33	Hernando	1.41	2.12	0.40

Table 13D.1
(continued)

Rank	County	Loss costs per $1,000	50% loading	Ratio to state
34	Washington	1.40	2.09	0.40
35	Flagler	1.32	1.99	0.38
36	Saint Johns	1.28	1.92	0.36
37	Taylor	1.26	1.89	0.36
38	Highlands	1.23	1.84	0.35
39	Liberty	1.09	1.63	0.31
40	Citrus	1.07	1.61	0.31
41	Gilchrist	1.05	1.58	0.30
42	Nassau	1.04	1.55	0.30
43	Calhoun	1.02	1.52	0.29
44	Polk	0.97	1.45	0.28
45	Holmes	0.85	1.27	0.24
46	Osceola	0.82	1.23	0.23
47	Lake	0.78	1.17	0.22
48	Sumter	0.75	1.12	0.21
49	Duval	0.74	1.11	0.21
50	Lafayette	0.70	1.05	0.20
51	Marion	0.65	0.98	0.19
52	Putnam	0.64	0.97	0.18
53	Jackson	0.64	0.95	0.18
54	Seminole	0.62	0.93	0.18
55	Jefferson	0.60	0.90	0.17
56	Orange	0.60	0.90	0.17
57	Gadsden	0.60	0.90	0.17
58	Leon	0.59	0.89	0.17
59	Suwannee	0.54	0.82	0.16
60	Madison	0.52	0.78	0.15
61	Clay	0.48	0.72	0.14
62	Alachua	0.46	0.69	0.13
63	Columbia	0.39	0.58	0.11
64	Union	0.37	0.55	0.10
65	Bradford	0.32	0.48	0.09
66	Hamilton	0.31	0.46	0.09
67	Baker	0.23	0.34	0.07
Total	All counties	3.51	5.27	1.00

Table 13D.2
Loss costs and insurance premiums for hurricane wind insured damage in all counties in New York

Rank	County	Loss cost per $1,000	50% loading	Ratio to state
1	Suffolk	$0.38	$0.56	4.10
2	Nassau	0.17	0.25	1.85
3	Richmond	0.12	0.17	1.26
4	Queens	0.10	0.15	1.11
5	Kings	0.08	0.12	0.89
6	Westchester	0.08	0.12	0.88
7	Rockland	0.07	0.11	0.78
8	Bronx	0.07	0.10	0.71
9	Putnam	0.06	0.09	0.69
10	Dutchess	0.04	0.06	0.43
11	Columbia	0.04	0.05	0.40
12	Ulster	0.03	0.05	0.35
13	Orange	0.03	0.05	0.35
14	New York	0.02	0.04	0.27
15	Rensselaer	0.02	0.03	0.22
16	Greene	0.02	0.03	0.21
17	Washington	0.02	0.03	0.19
18	Albany	0.01	0.02	0.15
19	Saratoga	0.01	0.02	0.15
20	Sullivan	0.01	0.02	0.14
21	Warren	0.01	0.02	0.11
22	Schenectady	0.01	0.01	0.10
23	Montgomery	0.01	0.01	0.09
24	Clinton	0.01	0.01	0.08
25	Schoharie	0.01	0.01	0.08
26	Essex	0.01	0.01	0.07
27	Fulton	0.01	0.01	0.06
28	Delaware	0.01	0.01	0.06
29	Herkimer	0.00	0.01	0.04
30	Otsego	0.00	0.01	0.04
31	Hamilton	0.00	0.00	0.03
32	Chenango	0.00	0.00	0.03
33	Oneida	0.00	0.00	0.03
34	Broome	0.00	0.00	0.02
35	Madison	0.00	0.00	0.02
36	Cortland	0.00	0.00	0.02
37	Tioga	0.00	0.00	0.02
38	Lewis	0.00	0.00	0.02

Table 13D.2
(continued)

Rank	County	Loss cost per $1,000	50% loading	Ratio to state
39	Seneca	0.00	0.00	0.01
40	Cayuga	0.00	0.00	0.01
41	Tompkins	0.00	0.00	0.01
42	Franklin	0.00	0.00	0.01
43	Saint Lawrence	0.00	0.00	0.01
44	Jefferson	0.00	0.00	0.01
45	Oswego	0.00	0.00	0.01
46	Yates	0.00	0.00	0.01
47	Onondaga	0.00	0.00	0.01
48	Wayne	0.00	0.00	0.01
49	Ontario	0.00	0.00	0.01
50	Schuyler	0.00	0.00	0.01
51	Chemung	0.00	0.00	0.00
52	Steuben	0.00	0.00	0.00
53	Monroe	0.00	0.00	0.00
54	Livingston	0.00	0.00	0.00
55	Genesee	0.00	0.00	0.00
56	Orleans	0.00	0.00	0.00
57	Wyoming	0.00	0.00	0.00
58	Chautauqua	0.00	0.00	0.00
59	Cattaraugus	0.00	0.00	0.00
60	Niagara	0.00	0.00	0.00
61	Allegany	0.00	0.00	0.00
62	Erie	0.00	0.00	0.00
Total	All counties	0.09	0.14	1.00

Table 13D.3
Loss costs and insurance premiums for hurricane wind insured damage in all counties in South Carolina

Rank	County	Loss costs per $1,000	50% loading	Ratio to state
1	Georgetown	$2.69	$4.04	4.74
2	Charleston	2.62	3.93	4.61
3	Horry	2.11	3.17	3.72
4	Beaufort	2.10	3.15	3.70
5	Colleton	1.37	2.05	2.41
6	Berkeley	1.20	1.80	2.12
7	Jasper	0.92	1.38	1.62
8	Dorchester	0.85	1.27	1.49
9	Williamsburg	0.81	1.21	1.42
10	Marion	0.65	0.97	1.14
11	Hampton	0.55	0.83	0.97
12	Clarendon	0.50	0.75	0.88
13	Dillon	0.38	0.57	0.67
14	Florence	0.36	0.54	0.63
15	Orangeburg	0.36	0.53	0.63
16	Allendale	0.31	0.46	0.54
17	Bamberg	0.27	0.40	0.47
18	Calhoun	0.25	0.37	0.43
19	Darlington	0.20	0.30	0.35
20	Lee	0.20	0.30	0.35
21	Sumter	0.19	0.28	0.33
22	Marlboro	0.18	0.28	0.32
23	Barnwell	0.15	0.23	0.27
24	Chesterfield	0.06	0.09	0.11
25	Kershaw	0.06	0.09	0.10
26	Aiken	0.04	0.06	0.07
27	Lexington	0.04	0.06	0.07
28	Richland	0.04	0.06	0.07
29	Fairfield	0.02	0.02	0.03
30	Lancaster	0.02	0.02	0.03
31	Edgefield	0.02	0.02	0.03
32	Saluda	0.01	0.02	0.02
33	Newberry	0.01	0.01	0.01
34	Mccormick	0.01	0.01	0.01
35	Chester	0.01	0.01	0.01
36	Greenwood	0.00	0.00	0.00
37	Abbeville	0.00	0.00	0.00
38	Laurens	0.00	0.00	0.00

Table 13D.3
(continued)

Rank	County	Loss costs per $1,000	50% loading	Ratio to state
39	York	0.00	0.00	0.00
40	Union	0.00	0.00	0.00
41	Cherokee	0.00	0.00	0.00
42	Anderson	0.00	0.00	0.00
43	Spartanburg	0.00	0.00	0.00
44	Greenville	0.00	0.00	0.00
45	Pickens	0.00	0.00	0.00
46	Oconee	0.00	0.00	0.00
Total	All counties	0.57	0.85	1.00

Table 13D.4
Loss costs and insurance premiums for hurricane wind insured damage in all counties in Texas

Rank	County	Price	50% loading	Ratio to state
1	Calhoun	$4.60	$6.89	10.53
2	Aransas	4.56	6.84	10.44
3	Galveston	3.95	5.92	9.05
4	Matagorda	3.19	4.79	7.32
5	Chambers	2.59	3.88	5.93
6	Brazoria	2.44	3.65	5.58
7	Nueces	2.32	3.48	5.32
8	San Patricio	2.27	3.40	5.19
9	Cameron	2.08	3.12	4.77
10	Jackson	2.04	3.07	4.69
11	Refugio	2.01	3.01	4.60
12	Jefferson	1.72	2.58	3.95
13	Kenedy	1.54	2.30	3.52
14	Willacy	1.53	2.30	3.52
15	Orange	1.41	2.12	3.24
16	Wharton	1.39	2.08	3.18
17	Fort Bend	1.07	1.61	2.46
18	Victoria	1.06	1.58	2.42
19	Liberty	1.02	1.53	2.34
20	Goliad	0.91	1.37	2.09
21	Kleberg	0.90	1.34	2.05
22	Harris	0.81	1.22	1.86
23	Brooks	0.80	1.20	1.83
24	Hardin	0.76	1.14	1.74
25	Jim Wells	0.75	1.12	1.71
26	Hidalgo	0.72	1.09	1.66
27	Bee	0.65	0.98	1.50
28	Waller	0.57	0.85	1.30
29	Austin	0.50	0.75	1.14
30	Colorado	0.48	0.72	1.11
31	De Witt	0.47	0.70	1.08
32	Newton	0.46	0.69	1.05
33	Lavaca	0.38	0.57	0.87
34	San Jacinto	0.38	0.56	0.86
35	Jasper	0.35	0.52	0.80
36	Montgomery	0.32	0.48	0.74
37	Duval	0.29	0.44	0.67
38	Live Oak	0.29	0.44	0.67
39	Karnes	0.29	0.43	0.66

Table 13D.4
(continued)

Rank	County	Price	50% loading	Ratio to state
40	Washington	0.24	0.35	0.54
41	Tyler	0.22	0.34	0.51
42	Jim Hogg	0.20	0.30	0.45
43	Fayette	0.19	0.29	0.44
44	Starr	0.19	0.29	0.44
45	Grimes	0.19	0.28	0.43
46	Mcmullen	0.18	0.27	0.41
47	Gonzales	0.18	0.26	0.40
48	Polk	0.16	0.25	0.38
49	Walker	0.13	0.20	0.31
50	Wilson	0.12	0.18	0.28
51	Sabine	0.10	0.16	0.24
52	Burleson	0.10	0.16	0.24
53	Trinity	0.10	0.16	0.24
54	Lee	0.08	0.13	0.19
55	Atascosa	0.07	0.11	0.17
56	Madison	0.07	0.11	0.16
57	Caldwell	0.06	0.09	0.14
58	San Augustine	0.06	0.09	0.13
59	Guadalupe	0.06	0.09	0.13
60	Zapata	0.05	0.08	0.13
61	Bastrop	0.05	0.07	0.11
62	Brazos	0.04	0.06	0.09
63	Angelina	0.04	0.06	0.09
64	La Salle	0.04	0.06	0.09
65	Webb	0.03	0.05	0.08
66	Houston	0.03	0.05	0.08
67	Frio	0.03	0.04	0.07
68	Comal	0.02	0.03	0.05
69	Robertson	0.02	0.03	0.05
70	Milam	0.02	0.03	0.05
71	Hays	0.02	0.03	0.05
72	Nacogdoches	0.02	0.03	0.04
73	Leon	0.02	0.03	0.04
74	Bexar	0.02	0.02	0.04
75	Medina	0.01	0.02	0.03
76	Shelby	0.01	0.02	0.03
77	Dimmit	0.01	0.01	0.02
78	Williamson	0.01	0.01	0.02

Table 13D.4
(continued)

Rank	County	Price	50% loading	Ratio to state
79	Cherokee	0.01	0.01	0.02
80	Falls	0.01	0.01	0.01
81	Bell	0.01	0.01	0.01
82	Travis	0.01	0.01	0.01
83	Freestone	0.01	0.01	0.01
84	Kendall	0.01	0.01	0.01
85	Anderson	0.00	0.01	0.01
86	Blanco	0.00	0.01	0.01
87	Limestone	0.00	0.01	0.01
88	Zavala	0.00	0.01	0.01
89	Panola	0.00	0.01	0.01
90	Rusk	0.00	0.00	0.01
91	Coryell	0.00	0.00	0.01
92	Navarro	0.00	0.00	0.01
93	Uvalde	0.00	0.00	0.00
94	Mclennan	0.00	0.00	0.00
95	Bandera	0.00	0.00	0.00
96	Burnet	0.00	0.00	0.00
97	Henderson	0.00	0.00	0.00
98	Gregg	0.00	0.00	0.00
99	Lampasas	0.00	0.00	0.00
100	Harrison	0.00	0.00	0.00
101	Bosque	0.00	0.00	0.00
102	Gillespie	0.00	0.00	0.00
103	Llano	0.00	0.00	0.00
104	Smith	0.00	0.00	0.00
105	Hill	0.00	0.00	0.00
106	Upshur	0.00	0.00	0.00
107	Hamilton	0.00	0.00	0.00
108	Maverick	0.00	0.00	0.00
109	Marion	0.00	0.00	0.00
110	Kerr	0.00	0.00	0.00
111	Van Zandt	0.00	0.00	0.00
112	Rains	0.00	0.00	0.00
113	Kaufman	0.00	0.00	0.00
114	Ellis	0.00	0.00	0.00
115	Johnson	0.00	0.00	0.00
116	Wood	0.00	0.00	0.00
117	Camp	0.00	0.00	0.00

Table 13D.4
(continued)

Rank	County	Price	50% loading	Ratio to state
118	Franklin	0.00	0.00	0.00
119	Mills	0.00	0.00	0.00
120	Morris	0.00	0.00	0.00
121	Cass	0.00	0.00	0.00
122	Hunt	0.00	0.00	0.00
123	Titus	0.00	0.00	0.00
124	Somervell	0.00	0.00	0.00
125	Mason	0.00	0.00	0.00
126	Hood	0.00	0.00	0.00
127	San Saba	0.00	0.00	0.00
128	Hopkins	0.00	0.00	0.00
129	Rockwall	0.00	0.00	0.00
130	Bowie	0.00	0.00	0.00
131	Real	0.00	0.00	0.00
132	Erath	0.00	0.00	0.00
133	Red River	0.00	0.00	0.00
134	Delta	0.00	0.00	0.00
135	Brown	0.00	0.00	0.00
136	Comanche	0.00	0.00	0.00
137	Parker	0.00	0.00	0.00
138	Tarrant	0.00	0.00	0.00
139	Dallas	0.00	0.00	0.00
140	Collin	0.00	0.00	0.00
141	Lamar	0.00	0.00	0.00
142	Palo Pinto	0.00	0.00	0.00
143	Eastland	0.00	0.00	0.00
144	Edwards	0.00	0.00	0.00
145	Fannin	0.00	0.00	0.00
146	Mcculloch	0.00	0.00	0.00
147	Denton	0.00	0.00	0.00
148	Val Verde	0.00	0.00	0.00
149	Kinney	0.00	0.00	0.00
150	Jack	0.00	0.00	0.00
151	Wise	0.00	0.00	0.00
152	King	0.00	0.00	0.00
153	Andrews	0.00	0.00	0.00
154	Archer	0.00	0.00	0.00
155	Armstrong	0.00	0.00	0.00
156	Bailey	0.00	0.00	0.00

Table 13D.4
(continued)

Rank	County	Price	50% loading	Ratio to state
157	Baylor	0.00	0.00	0.00
158	Borden	0.00	0.00	0.00
159	Brewster	0.00	0.00	0.00
160	Briscoe	0.00	0.00	0.00
161	Callahan	0.00	0.00	0.00
162	Carson	0.00	0.00	0.00
163	Castro	0.00	0.00	0.00
164	Childress	0.00	0.00	0.00
165	Clay	0.00	0.00	0.00
166	Cochran	0.00	0.00	0.00
167	Coke	0.00	0.00	0.00
168	Coleman	0.00	0.00	0.00
169	Collingsworth	0.00	0.00	0.00
170	Concho	0.00	0.00	0.00
171	Cooke	0.00	0.00	0.00
172	Cottle	0.00	0.00	0.00
173	Crane	0.00	0.00	0.00
174	Crockett	0.00	0.00	0.00
175	Crosby	0.00	0.00	0.00
176	Culberson	0.00	0.00	0.00
177	Dallam	0.00	0.00	0.00
178	Dawson	0.00	0.00	0.00
179	Deaf Smith	0.00	0.00	0.00
180	Dickens	0.00	0.00	0.00
181	Donley	0.00	0.00	0.00
182	Ector	0.00	0.00	0.00
183	El Paso	0.00	0.00	0.00
184	Fisher	0.00	0.00	0.00
185	Floyd	0.00	0.00	0.00
186	Foard	0.00	0.00	0.00
187	Gaines	0.00	0.00	0.00
188	Garza	0.00	0.00	0.00
189	Glasscock	0.00	0.00	0.00
190	Gray	0.00	0.00	0.00
191	Grayson	0.00	0.00	0.00
192	Hale	0.00	0.00	0.00
193	Hall	0.00	0.00	0.00
194	Hansford	0.00	0.00	0.00
195	Hardeman	0.00	0.00	0.00

Table 13D.4
(continued)

Rank	County	Price	50% loading	Ratio to state
196	Hartley	0.00	0.00	0.00
197	Haskell	0.00	0.00	0.00
198	Hemphill	0.00	0.00	0.00
199	Hockley	0.00	0.00	0.00
200	Howard	0.00	0.00	0.00
201	Hudspeth	0.00	0.00	0.00
202	Hutchinson	0.00	0.00	0.00
203	Irion	0.00	0.00	0.00
204	Jeff Davis	0.00	0.00	0.00
205	Jones	0.00	0.00	0.00
206	Kent	0.00	0.00	0.00
207	Kimble	0.00	0.00	0.00
208	Knox	0.00	0.00	0.00
209	Lamb	0.00	0.00	0.00
210	Lipscomb	0.00	0.00	0.00
211	Loving	0.00	0.00	0.00
212	Lubbock	0.00	0.00	0.00
213	Lynn	0.00	0.00	0.00
214	Martin	0.00	0.00	0.00
215	Menard	0.00	0.00	0.00
216	Midland	0.00	0.00	0.00
217	Mitchell	0.00	0.00	0.00
218	Montague	0.00	0.00	0.00
219	Moore	0.00	0.00	0.00
220	Motley	0.00	0.00	0.00
221	Nolan	0.00	0.00	0.00
222	Ochiltree	0.00	0.00	0.00
223	Oldham	0.00	0.00	0.00
224	Parmer	0.00	0.00	0.00
225	Pecos	0.00	0.00	0.00
226	Potter	0.00	0.00	0.00
227	Presidio	0.00	0.00	0.00
228	Randall	0.00	0.00	0.00
229	Reagan	0.00	0.00	0.00
230	Reeves	0.00	0.00	0.00
231	Roberts	0.00	0.00	0.00
232	Runnels	0.00	0.00	0.00
233	Schleicher	0.00	0.00	0.00
234	Scurry	0.00	0.00	0.00

Table 13D.4
(continued)

Rank	County	Price	50% loading	Ratio to state
235	Shackelford	0.00	0.00	0.00
236	Sherman	0.00	0.00	0.00
237	Stephens	0.00	0.00	0.00
238	Sterling	0.00	0.00	0.00
239	Stonewall	0.00	0.00	0.00
240	Sutton	0.00	0.00	0.00
241	Swisher	0.00	0.00	0.00
242	Taylor	0.00	0.00	0.00
243	Terrell	0.00	0.00	0.00
244	Terry	0.00	0.00	0.00
245	Throckmorton	0.00	0.00	0.00
246	Tom Green	0.00	0.00	0.00
247	Upton	0.00	0.00	0.00
248	Ward	0.00	0.00	0.00
249	Wheeler	0.00	0.00	0.00
250	Wichita	0.00	0.00	0.00
251	Wilbarger	0.00	0.00	0.00
252	Winkler	0.00	0.00	0.00
253	Yoakum	0.00	0.00	0.00
254	Young	0.00	0.00	0.00

IV CREATING INNOVATIVE SOLUTIONS

14 Proposed Innovations for Dealing with Catastrophic Risks

Key Findings

Two principles provide guidelines for the development of new catastrophe insurance programs. *Principle 1: Premiums reflecting risk* are designed to provide signals to individuals regarding the hazards they face and encourage the adoption of cost-effective mitigation measures. *Principle 2: Dealing with equity and affordability issues* addresses ways to provide special treatment to homeowners currently residing in hazard-prone areas (e.g., low-income uninsured or inadequately insured homeowners).

To provide protection to homeowners in hazard-prone areas, two innovations are proposed based on the above principles. *Innovation 1:* Long-term homeowners' insurance could be tied to a mortgage, thus stabilizing a homeowner's premiums over time. Home improvement loans can encourage the adoption of cost-effective loss-reduction measures. *Innovation 2:* A program of insurance vouchers, similar in concept to food stamps, could assist low-income residents in disaster-prone areas so they can purchase adequate insurance coverage.

Several specific insurance-related proposals have been initiated that involve the private and public sectors. *A coastal hurricane zone* has been proposed with regulations established by the federal government and consistent across states within the zone. After several years of operation, any surplus of underwriting operation would be redistributed to homeowners or deficits met through surcharges. Such a system would allow insurers to make long-term commitments of capital to provide coverage against wind damage from hurricanes in high-risk zones. *A national catastrophe fund* has been proposed as a financial backstop for state catastrophe funds and to augment private reinsurance. *Auctioned reinsurance contracts* could be developed by the federal government to cover truly cataclysmic events. *Alternative risk transfer instruments* offered by the financial market to cover catastrophic losses could be expanded through innovative products, making this market much more liquid than it is today and thus providing additional capacity.

A data collection and information-sharing platform could be created to inform the private sector and policymakers on the extent of insurance penetration. Despite the series of recent catastrophes, the United States does not have any system in place to ascertain on a national scale who has purchased insurance coverage and how much, and who is uninsured. We propose the creation of a national insurance data collection system to better understand the level of coverage of homeowners against future disasters. The implementation of this concept could be achieved at a very small cost through the Internal Revenue Service, with homeowners answering a few questions about their property insurance coverage on their federal IRS tax returns.

In-depth analyses are needed to evaluate these proposed innovations and concepts. All raise important questions regarding the economic effectiveness, equitability, and feasibility of current disaster management programs. Addressing these issues to ensure well-reasoned public policy requires a series of in-depth analyses that go beyond the scope of the present book.

There are risks and costs to a program of action. But they are far less than the long-range risks and costs of comfortable inaction.
—John F. Kennedy (1917–1963)

14.1 Two Guiding Principles

Given the significant increase in damage from hurricanes and other natural disasters and the growing population and assets in high-risk areas, we need a new approach for insuring these risks and encouraging individuals who reside in hazard-prone areas to undertake effective mitigation measures. Two principles should guide the development of new programs for reducing future losses and allocating the costs of disasters in an efficient and equitable manner:

Principle 1: Premiums reflecting risk. Insurance premiums should be based on risk to provide signals to individuals as to the hazards they face and encourage them to engage in cost-effective mitigation measures to reduce their vulnerability to catastrophes.

Principle 2: Dealing with equity and affordability issues. Any special treatment given to homeowners currently residing in hazard-prone areas (e.g., low-income uninsured or inadequately insured homeowners) should come from general public funding, not through insurance premium subsidies.

The application of principle 1 would provide a clear signal of likely damage to those currently residing in areas subject to natural disasters and those who are considering moving into these regions. Risk-based premiums would also enable insurers to provide discounts to homeowners and businesses that invest in cost-effective loss-reduction mitigation measures. If insurance premiums are not risk based, insurers have no economic incentive to offer these discounts. In fact, they prefer not to offer coverage to these property owners because it is a losing proposition in the long run if they are forced to charge artificially low premiums.

Principle 2 reflects a concern for some residents in high-hazard areas who will be faced with large premium increases if insurers are permitted to adhere to principle 1. As noted throughout this book, regulations imposed by state insurance commissioners keep premiums in many regions subject to hurricane damage artificially lower than the risk-based level. If insurers are permitted to charge premiums that reflect risk, homeowners residing in hurricane-prone areas would pay considerably more for coverage than they do today. Therefore, there might be a need for a transition period, so that over time (e.g., three to five years), premiums would increase to the risk-based level. Doing so might actually also reduce the premiums paid by other policyholders, who are currently paying more than their risk-based exposure in order to subsidize those in highly exposed areas.[1]

Note that principle 2 applies only to individuals who currently reside in a hazard-prone area. Those who decide to move to the area in the future should be charged premiums that reflect the risk. If they were provided with financial assistance from public sources to purchase insurance, the resulting public policy would directly encourage development in hazard-prone areas and exacerbate the potential for catastrophic losses from future disasters.

14.2 Developing Different Insurance Programs Using the Two Guiding Principles

The two principles can be used to design any insurance program where there are data available for developing premiums reflecting risk. As discussed in chapter 6, catastrophe models have been developed to estimate the likelihood and damages resulting from future disasters of different magnitudes and intensities. Although there is uncertainty surrounding the estimates from these catastrophe models, they have been widely used by insurers and reinsurers to better determine their exposure and price the risk.

Premiums Reflecting Risk

The first step in developing an insurance program that would adhere to principle 1 is to estimate the risk-based rates that would apply to different regions of the country. In chapter 13 we presented rates that reflect the risk for hurricane wind-related damage for counties in Florida, New York, South Carolina, and Texas. We also specified how this translates into premiums when insurers used a loading factor to cover the costs of marketing policies, assessing and paying claims after a loss. The appropriate loading factor also integrates the cost of capital that private insurers need to access to cover catastrophic events and maintain their ratings while earning a high enough return for investors to want to allocate funds to the insurance company.

A major issue that needs to be addressed is how to reach agreement on a given risk assessment and the role that state regulators will play in the process. We believe that to enable insurers to charge premiums that reflect risk, regulators should not be involved in matters pertaining to rate setting. If a truly competitive market were allowed to operate, insurers would not engage in price gouging since they would be undercut by another competing company that could profitably market policies at a lower price. Regulators would still have an important role to play in other aspects of the insurance operation, such as making certain that insurers have sufficient surplus to protect unsuspecting consumers against the possibility of their becoming insolvent following the next severe disaster.

Affordability of Coverage

The second step in the process relates to the affordability and equity issues indicated in principle 2. The analyses in chapter 11 reveal that many homeowners who supposedly cannot afford insurance (because their income is below a predefined threshold, say, 125 or 200 percent of poverty level), actually do purchase coverage, and some people who can afford it are not buying it. In chapter 11 we also addressed the question of equity. If changes in premiums are distributed unevenly across households, one might take the view that those subject to very large increases are not being treated fairly and justly. More specifically, if premiums are raised in high-hazard areas so as to reflect risk, those residents may feel they are treated unjustly relative to others with similar homes whose premiums remain unchanged.

To deal with these issues of equity and affordability, we recommend that some type of insurance voucher be provided by the state or federal government. This type of in-kind assistance, rather than an unrestricted grant, ensures that the recipients will use the funds for obtaining insurance rather than having the freedom to spend the money on other goods and services. The goal would be to alleviate displacement and homelessness after a major disaster. It would also assure fast economic recovery of the affected area by making sure people receive adequate insurance payments to rebuild their houses and make it possible to continue to remain in the area. If this system were applied to a low-income family in a hazard-prone area, this family would pay an insurance premium that reflects its risk, and then be reimbursed by the state in which they reside for a portion of the increased cost of insurance over the prior year's policy. The amount of reimbursement would be determined by their income and the insurance premium they are charged.

Several existing programs could serve as models for developing such a voucher system in the United States.

Food Stamp Program

Under the U.S. food stamp program, a family is given vouchers to purchase food based on their annual income and family size. The idea for the program was born in the late 1930s, revived as a pilot program in 1961, and extended nationwide in 1974. The current program structure was implemented in 1977 with a goal of alleviating hunger and malnutrition by permitting low-income households to obtain a more nutritious diet through normal purchasing of food from grocery stores. Food stamps are available to most low-income households with limited resources regardless of age, disability status, or family structure. Households, except those with elderly or disabled members, must have gross incomes below 130 percent of the poverty line. All households must have net incomes below 100 percent of the poverty line to be eligible.[2] The program is funded entirely by the federal government. Federal and state governments share administrative costs, with the federal government contributing nearly 50 percent. In 2007, the budget for the federal food stamp program was $35 billion,[3] distributed to over 26 million food stamp participants, including 1.2 million in Florida, 1.8 million in New York, and 2.4 million in Texas.[4] It would be of value to determine whether these same people also lack proper insurance against natural disasters. If so, these homeowners could comprise a test group for an insurance voucher program.

Low-Income Home Energy Assistance Program
The mission of this program is to assist low-income households that pay a high proportion of their income for home energy in meeting their immediate energy needs. Eligibility is based on criteria similar to the food stamp program. The funding is provided by the federal government but is administered by the states and federally recognized tribes or insular areas (e.g., Guam, Puerto Rico, Virgin Islands) to help eligible low-income homeowners and renters meet their heating or cooling needs.[5] The federal government became involved in awarding energy assistance funds to low-income households as a result of the increase in oil prices resulting from the Organization of Petroleum Exporting Countries oil embargo in 1973. Between 2000 and 2007, the annual appropriation of this program has averaged $2 billion.[6]

Universal Service Fund
The Universal Service Fund (USF) was created by the Federal Communications Commission in 1997 to ensure that consumers in all regions of the nation have access to and pay rates for telecommunications services that are reasonably comparable to those in urban areas.[7] To achieve this goal, the program provides discounts to all households in particular high-cost areas (e.g., rural areas) so they all pay the same subsidized rate regardless of income. Then there are universal service programs that are strictly aimed at low-income households, regardless of whether they live in high-cost or low-cost areas.[8] Under the Telecommunications Act of 1996, all telecommunication carriers that provide service internationally and between states pay contributions into the USF. The carriers may build this factor into their billing systems if they choose to recoup this amount from their customers. Between 1998 and 2006, more than $50 billion has been disbursed by this fund.

Who Should Fund Insurance Vouchers?

These programs have different methods to subsidize low-income families for specific goods and services. With respect to homeowners' insurance, funding for vouchers could be provided in several ways that mirror these programs.

General Taxpayer

If one takes the position that everyone in society is responsible for assisting those who reside in hazard-prone areas and cannot afford insurance coverage, then one could use general taxpayer revenue from the federal government to cover the costs of insurance vouchers. This is similar to the food stamp program and the Low Income Home Energy Assistance Program.

State Government

An alternative (or complementary) source of funding would come from taxes paid by residents or commercial enterprises, or both, in states exposed to natural disasters. One argument for this type of funding arrangement is that states obtain significant financial benefits from economic development in their jurisdictions through the collection of property taxes or other state revenue such as gasoline taxes, state income taxes, or sales taxes. If residents in coastal areas derive greater benefits from the economic development in these regions than others in the state, they should be taxed proportionately more than those residing inland.

Insurance Policyholders

A special tax could be levied on insurance policyholders to provide vouchers to those currently residing in hazard-prone areas who require special treatment. The rationale for this type of tax would be that all homeowners (as opposed to all taxpayers) should be responsible for helping to protect those who cannot afford protection. The justification for such a program would be similar to the rationale for establishing the USF for telecommunication service: providing affordable telephone service to all residents in the country.

14.3   Long-Term Homeowners' Insurance

Nature of the Program

This volatility in catastrophe losses and the market and regulatory reactions after the 2004 and 2005 hurricane seasons in the United States raises the following question for insuring catastrophe risks in the future: How can one smooth the cost of coverage over time to avoid the radical changes in the market environment from year to year that have recently occurred? To address the problem of volatility of insurance premiums and homeowners' failure to protect their property against disaster, we propose a new approach to providing homeowners' coverage: long-term insurance contracts (LTI) rather than the usual annual policies on residential property.[9] The precedent for LTI contracts in the United States goes back to Benjamin Franklin, who started the Philadelphia Contributionship for the Insuring of Houses from Fire in 1752. It eventually became the Green Tree Mutual Assurance Company, which closed its doors in 2004.[10] There is an interesting benchmark from the mortgage market as well. Jaffee, Kunreuther, and Michel-Kerjan (2008) show that while home loans today are typically long-term (20- or 30-year maturity), until the Great Depression, such long-term mortgages were rare. Prior to the Depression, U.S. bank mortgages were commonly short-term (maturities of 1 to 4 years), with the full principal due at maturity.

One consideration is whether long-term homeowners' insurance should be required on all residential property. This would not be a radical change from the current situation: homeowners who have a mortgage are normally required by the bank that finances the loan to purchase coverage against wind damage for the length of the mortgage. Similarly, those in flood-prone areas are required to purchase flood insurance under the National Flood Insurance Program if they have a federally insured mortgage. Insurance coverage is required today for other consumer purchases. Today in all states, motorists must show proof of financial responsibility on their automobile insurance policy or bodily injury and property damage liability in order to register their car.

For a long-term insurance policy to be feasible, insurers would have to be able to charge a premium that reflects their best estimate of the risk over that time period (say, ten or twenty-five years) (principle 1). The uncertainty surrounding these estimates could be reflected in the premium as a function of the length of the insurance contract (see section 6.3) in much the same way that the interest rate on fixed-rate mortgages varies between fifteen-, twenty-five-, and thirty-year loans. Insurance vouchers could be provided to homeowners who cannot afford coverage if premiums reflect risk (principle 2).

The obvious advantage of a long-term insurance contract from the point of view of policyholders is that it provides them with stability and an assurance that their property is protected for as long as they own it. This has been a major concern in hazard-prone areas where insurers have cancelled policies following severe disasters such as those that occurred during the 2005 hurricane season. With a long-term insurance policy in place, homeowners in hazard-prone areas would be protected following the next disaster, providing them with financial resources for recovery and reducing the need for liberal disaster assistance.

Encouraging Adoption of Mitigation Measures

Long-term insurance provides economic incentives for homeowners to invest in mitigation, whereas current annual insurance policies (even if they are risk based) are unlikely to do so. To highlight this point, consider the following simple example in which we do not impose a loading factor when pricing insurance. Suppose a family could invest $1,500 to strengthen the roof of its house so as to reduce the damage by $30,000 from a future hurricane with an annual probability of 1 in 100. An insurer charging a risk-based premium would be willing to reduce the annual charge by $300 (1/100 × $30,000) to reflect the lower expected losses that would occur if a hurricane hit the area in which the policyholder was residing. If the house was expected to last for ten or more years, the net present value of the expected benefit of investing in this measure would exceed the up-front cost at an annual discount rate as high as 15 percent.

Under current annual insurance contracts, many property owners would be reluctant to incur the $1,500 expenditure, because they would get only $300 back each year and are likely to consider only the benefits over the next few years when making their decisions. If they underweight the future, the expected discounted benefits would likely be less than the $1,500 up-front costs. In addition, budget constraints could discourage them from investing in the mitigation measure. Other considerations would also play a role in a family's decision not to invest in these measures. The family may not be clear how long they will reside in the house or whether their insurer would reward them again when their policy is renewed.

A twenty-year required insurance policy ties the contract to the property rather than to the individual. In fact, the homeowner could take out a $1,500 home improvement loan tied to the mortgage at an annual interest rate of 10 percent, resulting in payments of $145 per year. If the insurance premium was reduced by $300, the savings to the homeowner each year would be $155. Alternatively, this loan could be incorporated as part of the mortgage at even a lower interest rate than 10 percent.

These mitigation loans would constitute a new financial product. A bank would have a financial incentive to provide this type of loan, since it is now better protected against a catastrophic loss to the property, and the insurer knows that its potential loss from a major disaster is reduced. Moreover, the general public will now be less likely to have large amounts of their tax dollars going for disaster relief—a win-win-win-win situation for all![11]

There is an additional benefit to insurers in having banks encourage individuals to invest in cost-effective mitigation measures. The cost of reinsurance, which protects insurers against catastrophic losses, should now decrease. If reinsurers know that they are less likely to make large payments to insurers because each piece of property in a region now has a lower chance of experiencing a large loss, then they will reduce their premiums to the insurer for the same reason that the insurer is reducing its premium to the property owner.

Suppose that an insurer had 1,000 identical insurance policies in a particular area and that each would expect to make claims payments of $40,000 following a hurricane if homeowners had not strengthened their roofs. The insurer's loss from such a disaster would be $40 million. Suppose also that the insurer would want to have $25 million in coverage from a reinsurer to protect its surplus. If the hypothetical hurricane has a 1 in 100 chance of hitting the region where these families reside, the expected loss to a reinsurer would be $250,000 and the premium charged to the insurer would reflect this. If the bank required that all 1,000 homes had their roofs mitigated to meet the local building code and each homeowner's loss were reduced to $10,000, then the insurer's total loss would be $10 million should all 1,000 homes be affected, and it would not require reinsurance. This savings would be passed on by the insurer to the homeowner in the form of a lower premium.

In addition to all these benefits, LTI would also reduce transaction costs from the consumer's and insurer's point of view. More specifically, an insurer who offers an LTI policy has reduced marketing costs since this is only incurred at the time the contract is offered instead of every year. Similarly, consumers with one-year policies whose contracts are canceled at the end of the year are able to avoid the search costs of looking for another policy by buying an LTI policy. The expected social welfare benefits to the consumer based on a long-term policy can be quite substantial.

Open Issues and Questions

A number of issues and questions associated with the development of a long-term insurance policy that have a direct impact on insurers and homeowners, and indirect effects on other stakeholders, require further research and analysis.

Nature of the Contract

Long-term insurance could be offered by insurers in the form of a fixed-price contract (FPC) for the full term of the policy (e.g., twenty years) or an adjustable premium contract (APC) at a variable premium with guaranteed renewal for the term of the policy. The annual premium would be reset based on an index that would have to be simple and transparent. Policyholders will want the option to terminate the contract; mortgage markets provide examples of both good and bad practices. On FPCs, formal arrangements to make the insurer whole through provisions such as yield maintenance and defeasance (the two most common methods for dealing with prepayment costs on commercial mortgages) may be necessary.[12] On APCs, the borrower would want the right to terminate the contract without cost within a certain time period of a premium increase notification (e.g., three months).[13]

Protection against Catastrophic Losses

One would also need to know how the rating agencies will view long-term FPC commitments since the insurer is now locked into the premium even if the expected losses rise. To protect itself against possible increases in the probability of catastrophic losses over time, insurers marketing FPCs would have to be able to invest in catastrophe bonds or other forms of securitized risks. Some type of government guarantee might be necessary to deal with both insurers' and policyholders' concerns with respect to the ability to pay claims in the future following a catastrophic loss. As for the pricing of the product, FPC premiums would likely be somewhat higher than APC premiums to protect insurers against an increase in the risk during the contract period. This behavior would be similar to the pricing of fixed-rate mortgages relative to adjustable-rate mortgages.

One of the central issues will be how high the price of a long-term contract will be, given the ambiguities associated with the risk and the capital costs for covering catastrophic losses. Without some type of protection against large losses through long-term risk transfer instruments (which currently do not exist) or a government reinsurance program at the state or federal level, the premiums for FPCs are likely to be extremely high, so that there would be little demand for this type of coverage.[14]

Understanding the Contract

Those who purchase insurance policies often have a difficult time understanding the terms of the contract: what risks are covered, what risks are not, and the basis for being charged a specific rate. The problem is likely to be compounded for a long-term insurance contract. There is an opportunity for insurers to educate consumers as to the basis for the premiums they charge by providing more detail on the types of risks covered and the amounts charged for different levels of protection. More specifically, insurers could break down the premium into coverage against fire, theft, wind damage, and other losses included in a homeowners' policy and explain how and why the premium varies with the length of the long-term contract. It would be beneficial for insurers to reveal this information so that homeowners are able to make better decisions by understanding the nature of the contract and what alternative options cost them. They will then be able to make trade-offs between costs and expected benefits—something that is impossible for them to do today. Thaler and Sunstein (2008) argue for this type of information disclosure by proposing a form of government regulation termed RECAP: record, evaluate and compare alternative prices. They recommend that the government not regulate prices but require disclosure practices —not in a long, unintelligible document but in a spreadsheet-like format that includes all relevant formulas.

Institutional Details

Some questions regarding institutional details require further analysis and discussion with key stakeholders:

• Under what circumstances could property owners change their insurance policy over time?

• What role would the modeling companies and the scientific community studying climate play in providing estimates for developing risk-based premiums and suggesting a rationale for changes over time as new risk models become available?

• How would insurers deal with significant changes in risk estimates over time?

• What types of risk transfer instruments would have to emerge from the reinsurance market as well as from the capital markets to protect insurers against catastrophic losses and changes in risk estimates over time?

• What role would the public sector play in providing protection against catastrophic losses?

• How concerned will consumers be at possible insolvencies of insurers providing long-term contracts, and what steps should be taken to protect homeowners should this occur?

Whether long-term insurance will be attractive to insurers, homeowners, regulators, and other relevant stakeholders is uncertain. What is clear is that we need innovative programs for reducing future losses from disasters that involve the public and private sectors. For insurance to play an important role in this regard, one needs to understand what a policy can and cannot do as a function of the nature of the risk, the type of coverage provided by the insurer, and the premium structure.

14.4   All-Hazards Insurance

The long-term contract addresses the issue of time diversification.[15] Another proposed program to consider is all-hazards insurance. Current insurance programs for residents in hazard-prone areas are segmented across perils. Standard homeowners' and commercial insurance policies, normally required as a condition for a mortgage, cover damage from fire, wind, hail, lightning, winter storms, and volcanic eruption. Earthquake insurance can be purchased for an additional premium. Flood insurance is offered through the National Flood Insurance Program (NFIP).

Features of the Program

An all-hazards insurance policy, if developed, should adhere to the two principles of premiums reflecting risk, equity, and affordability. The idea of an insurance program where all natural disasters are covered by a single policy has been adopted in other countries. In 1954, Spain formed a public corporation, the Consorcio de Compensacion de Seguros, that today provides mandatory insurance for so-called extraordinary risks, including natural disasters and political and social events such as terrorism, riots, and civil commotion. Such coverage is an add-on to property insurance policies that are marketed by the private sector. The Consorcio pays claims only if the loss is not covered by private insurance, if low-income families did not buy insurance, or the insurance company fails to pay because it becomes insolvent. The government collects the premiums, and private insurers market the policies and handle claims settlements.[16]

In France, a mandatory homeowners' policy covers a number of natural disasters, along with terrorism risk. The main difference comes at the reinsurance level, which is partially provided by a publicly owned reinsurer, the Caisse Centrale de Reassurance, for flood, earthquakes, and droughts with an unlimited government guarantee.[17]

Advantages of All-Hazards Insurance

Consider an insurer who wishes to market homeowners' coverage in different parts of the United States. With risk-based rates, it would collect premiums that reflect the earthquake risk in California, hurricane risk on the Gulf Coast, tornado damage in the Great Plains states, and flood risk in the Mississippi Valley. Each of these risks is independent of the others. This higher premium base and the diversification of risk across many hazards reduce the likelihood that the insurer would suffer a loss that exceeds its surplus in any given year for a given book of business.

An all-hazards homeowners' policy should also be attractive to both insurers and policyholders in hurricane-prone areas because it avoids the costly process of having an adjuster determine whether the damage was caused by wind (today covered by private insurers and state-run companies in certain states) or water (today covered by the National Flood Insurance Program). As noted in chapter 2, this problem of differentiating wind damage from water damage was particularly challenging following Hurricane Katrina. Across large portions of the coast, all that remained of demolished buildings were foundations and stairs, making it difficult to determine the cause of damage. In these cases, insurers may decide to pay the coverage limits rather than incur litigation costs to determine whether the damage came from water or wind. For a house still standing, this process is somewhat easier since one knows, for example, that roof destruction is likely to be caused by the wind and water marks in the living room are signs of flooding.[18]

An all-hazards policy would also deal with the problem that insurers currently face with respect to fire damage caused by earthquakes. Even if a homeowner has not purchased an earthquake insurance policy, it will be able to collect for damages from a fire caused by an earthquake. In the case of the 1906 San Francisco earthquake, most of the damage was caused by fire, and insurers were obligated to cover these losses. In this sense, homeowners' insurance actually covers a portion of earthquake losses even though this coverage is excluded from the policy.

Another reason for having an insurance policy that covers all hazards is that there will be no ambiguity by the homeowner as to whether she has coverage. Many residing in the Gulf Coast believed they were covered for water damage from hurricanes by their homeowners' policies. The attractiveness of insurance that guarantees that the policyholder will have coverage against all losses from disasters independent of cause has been demonstrated experimentally by Kahneman and Tversky (1979). They showed that 80 percent of their responders preferred such coverage to what they termed "probabilistic insurance," where there was some chance that a loss was not covered. What matters to an individual is the knowledge that she will be covered if her property is damaged or destroyed, not the cause of the loss.

Another advantage of all-hazards homeowners' insurance is that it may address some of the issues that currently plague the NFIP. As noted recently by the U.S. Government Accountability Office, only half of the properties eligible for flood insurance are covered by it. Furthermore, a number of properties that suffered water damage from Hurricane Katrina were not eligible to purchase flood insurance under the NFIP. Moreover, some of those who did have flood insurance and suffered large losses from the rising waters were able to cover only a portion of their losses, because the maximum coverage limit for flood insurance under the NFIP is $250,000 on building property and $100,000 on contents.

Naturally, an all-hazards insurance policy will be more expensive than the standard homeowners' policy because it is more comprehensive. If premiums are based on risk, however, then policyholders would be charged only for hazards that they face. Thus, a homeowner in the Gulf Coast would theoretically be covered for earthquake damage but would not be charged anything for this additional protection if the area in which she resides is not seismically active. In promoting this all-hazard coverage, one needs to highlight this point to the general public, who may otherwise feel that they are paying for risks that they do not face.

Disadvantages of All-Hazards Insurance

The major disadvantage of an all-hazards insurance program with premiums reflecting risk (principle 1) is that it will force insurers to raise their prices considerably to cover the potential damage in hazard-prone areas. A large increase in premium could be viewed by homeowners as unjustified, and there would be significant resistance to paying for this coverage. For high-income residents who have second homes on the coast, there is an economic rationale for them to pay the cost of their insurance. For lower-income residents, some type of insurance voucher may have to be provided so that these homeowners can afford coverage (principle 2).

Many insurers are likely to resist all-hazards insurance because they may fear the possibility of even larger losses than they have suffered to date owing to the increase of their exposure. Some rightly note that if both wind and water damage were to be included in homeowners' policies, the losses from future Hurricane Katrinas to private insurers would be considerably higher. Others might argue that insurers would have also collected more premiums over the years. To assume the additional risk, there would be a need for a substantial increase in insurers' surplus or increased capacity through reinsurance, insurance-linked securities, state funds, or federal reinsurance.

There will also be special needs facing small insurers operating in a single state that have smaller surplus than larger firms and are limited in their ability to diversify their risk. These insurers may find that the variance in their losses increases by incorporating the flood and earthquake risks as part of a homeowners' policy. For example, a Louisiana insurance company providing protection against hurricane damage might find the variance in losses to be higher than it is today if both wind and water damage were covered under a homeowners' policy. For these companies to compete with larger firms, they would have to be able to protect themselves against catastrophic losses through either private- or public-based risk transfer instruments that would not price them out of the market.

Insurers that market an all-hazards insurance policy face an additional challenge in trying to convince homeowners that they will pay only for risks that they actually face. One way for insurance companies to do this is to itemize the cost of different types of coverage on the policy itself in much the way current homeowners or automobile insurance breaks up the cost for different types of protection. If a family living on the Gulf Coast knew that it would be paying $3,000 for wind coverage, $1,500 for water coverage, $500 for fire coverage, and nothing for earthquake coverage, it would not complain about covering damage from seismic risk facing California homeowners. Such an itemized list of coverage would also highlight the magnitude of risks of living in that particular area, another role that insurance can play—a signal as to how hazardous a particular place is likely to be.

14.5   Making Insurance-Linked Securities a More Liquid Market

Since finding a way to cover losses from truly cataclysmic events is of major concern, the development of new types of insurance-linked securities is worth pursuing. Chapter 8 discusses current instruments and proposes innovations to transfer additional exposure to financial markets so that a more liquid market for providing protection against catastrophic losses can develop.

14.6   Creation of a Data Collection and Information-Sharing Entity

Another innovation to consider is that one develops more granular data collection on insurance coverage and claims payment over time: the evolution of different lines of coverage in specific locations. With the increased population in coastal regions, we need to better understand and quantify who has insurance coverage and the amount of protection they have. We propose the creation of a data collection entity to determine the degree of insurance penetration in different parts of the country. The implementation of this concept could be achieved at a very small cost through the Internal Revenue Service (IRS), with homeowners answering a few questions about their property insurance coverage for flood, earthquake, and wind on their annual tax returns. The IRS could collect this information and make it available on an aggregate level (e.g., postal zone) so that individuals cannot be identified. By providing more detailed data on the degree of insurance protection of homeowners, it should be possible to develop much more effective strategies for reducing losses and aiding recovery from future natural disasters.

14.7   Other Proposals for Financing Catastrophic Losses

We now turn to three other proposals advocated recently to address the issue of financing catastrophic losses from natural disasters: auctions for federal reinsurance contracts, a federally regulated coastal hurricane zone, and a national catastrophe fund. We describe these proposals without making any judgment as to their economic effectiveness, equitability, and feasibility, since this would require a series of in-depth analyses that go beyond the scope of this book.

Auctions for Federal Reinsurance Contracts

In the aftermath of Hurricane Andrew in 1992 and the Northridge earthquake in 1994, Lewis and Murdock (1996) developed a proposal that the federal government offer catastrophe reinsurance contracts that would be auctioned annually in order to provide the private sector with more capacity to handle truly extreme events. The U.S. Treasury Department would auction a limited number of contracts indexed on the aggregate direct insured losses occurring as a result of a catastrophic natural disaster. Originally Lewis and Murdock proposed contracts covering losses between $25 billion and $50 billion but then modified this so that private insurers, reinsurers, or state pools could select any trigger level that did not crowd out coverage available in the private market.[21] The design of such contracts would have to be specified, and a more detailed analysis would have to be undertaken to determine the potential impact of such an auction mechanism on the relevant stakeholders.

Creation of a Coastal Hurricane Zone

One way to address the challenge of lack of liquidity to cover catastrophic losses from hurricanes is to establish a multistate zone in which risks are diversified and the market regulated at a federal level.[19]

In 2008, The Travelers Companies proposed the creation of federally regulated coastal hurricane wind zones from Texas to Maine. Private insurers would still market residential homeowners policies covering wind damage from named storms, but an independent board created by the federal government would regulate and oversee all aspects of wind underwriting by private insurers including pricing.

The rationale for this proposal is that the current system, wherein each state regulates and oversees its own insurance market, has led to regulatory inconsistency and unpredictability with respect to rates, coverages, and underwriting rules for insurers and customers alike following major hurricanes. Properly designed and executed, coastal hurricane wind zones would provide a more stable set of rules that would allow insurers to make long-term commitments of capital to those areas for wind risks, thus increasing the availability of insurance. Federal oversight would also ensure that rates are actuarially sound, so that premiums reflect the risks being taken (principle 1). This would be achieved through the certification of wind-risk models by the federal oversight board. Rate competition would still exist through independent company rating plans filed with the independent board. States would continue their regulatory oversight of all other perils.

Beyond this federal oversight, the proposed coastal hurricane wind zones would also include a mechanism to equitably adjust premiums after periods during which wind-risk models become misaligned with actual loss results. If actual wind-related losses over a multiyear period were less than anticipated, an insurer would be required to provide a prospective premium credit to policyholders. This would eliminate the perception that insurers are "winning" and customers are "losing" if the wind does not blow.

A cost-based federal reinsurance mechanism for extreme events would be funded by actuarially sound rates paid by insurers, with the savings passed on to the consumers. A federal reinsurance mechanism would also address the issue of availability since insurers with stable reinsurance coverage for extreme events should be willing to write more coverage for homes in coastal areas.

To reduce losses from inevitable hurricanes, federal, state, and local governments have another critical role to play in promoting risk-mitigation programs. Foremost in this regard is the adoption and enforcement of federal guidelines for enhanced building codes for both new construction and renovations. The use of storm shutters and impact-resistant windows should be encouraged through economic incentives. Coastal states would be entitled to federal grants if they adopt a proposed federal building code and related mitigation measures. In addition, insurers would be required to provide meaningful premium credits to those insureds who took the steps necessary to strengthen their homes and make them less susceptible to loss. Other loss-mitigation plans include prudent land use management, such as acknowledging the importance of coastal wetlands in minimizing a hurricane's impact upon landfall.

National Catastrophe Fund

ProtectingAmerica.org, a national coalition of emergency management officials, first responders, disaster relief agencies, nonprofits, businesses, and insurers created in 2005, has proposed comprehensive, integrated approach to increase preparedness, reduce losses, and improve protection from natural catastrophes. Included in the recommended approach would be a privately funded, actuarially sound national catastrophe fund to serve as a financial backstop for state catastrophe funds to provide more protection at lower cost for consumers.[20] The backstop is designed to strengthen the United States' financial infrastructure to deal more effectively and efficiently with major catastrophes by augmenting capacity provided by private reinsurance.

A portion of private insurance company revenues would be deposited into the national catastrophe fund, which would provide reinsurance to state catastrophe funds for losses above a specified amount. The fund, which would be self-supporting except for $10 million in start-up costs, would be operated on a tax-exempt, not-for-profit basis and administered by the U.S. Treasury Department. Premiums would be set on an actuarially sound basis to ensure that rates reflect the risk that consumers face and to avoid subsidization of consumers in high-risk areas by consumers in lower-risk areas (principle 1). State catastrophe funds that purchase reinsurance from the national fund would be required to set aside up to 35 percent of investment income from the state fund for prevention, mitigation, and public education programs.

Private insurance companies would be required to meet all their obligations before using the state catastrophe fund to pay claims. The state catastrophe fund would discharge its financial obligations before the national fund is accessed. This would mean that the national fund would cover only losses from mega-catastrophes that cause damage of such magnitude that private insurers and state catastrophe plans are at significant risk of financial collapse or consumers would be exposed to serious availability or affordability challenges. Since the national catastrophe fund would be exempt from taxation and have no profit load, it could charge lower rates than the private market and pass those savings on to consumers.

This proposal also raises the following questions that need to be considered:

· How much private reinsurance and insurance-linked securities capacity will be available to deal with mega-catastrophic losses today?

· Would a backstop mechanism help guard against insolvency risk of insurers and/or reinsurers?

· What should be the threshold at which such a national fund is triggered (e.g., $50 billion, $100 billion, or $200 billion), and what is the basis for this level?

· The proposed solution would be privately funded, but what would happen if truly extreme events occurred in the first few years of operation of the fund?

· Would the creation of such a national fund crowd out innovative private sector solutions?

Summary

This chapter examines strategies for satisfying two complementary objectives: providing financial protection to homeowners in hurricane-prone areas through insurance and reducing losses through cost-effective mitigation measures. Two principles should guide the policy debate as to what should constitute a sustainable efficient and equitable solution for managing and financing large-scale natural disasters in the United States: *Principle 1:* premiums reflecting risk, and *Principle 2:* dealing with equity and affordability issues.

To enable insurers to charge premiums reflecting risk, regulators should not be involved in matters pertaining to rate setting. To deal with issues of equity and affordability, we recommend that the state or federal government provide an insurance voucher. Funding for these vouchers could come from the general taxpayer, taxes paid by residents or commercial enterprises, or both, in states exposed to natural disasters, or insurance policyholders.

Based on these two principles, we have highlighted several insurance programs and proposed some innovations for both the private and public sectors: long-term insurance; all-hazards insurance, making insurance-linked securities a more liquid market; the creation of a data collection and information-sharing entity; auctions for federal reinsurance contracts; creation of a coastal hurricane zone; and creation of a national catastrophe fund.

15 Winning the War against the Weather and Other Extreme Events

Human beings have always been infatuated with gambling because it puts us head-to-head against the fates, with no holds barred. We enter this daunting battle because we are convinced we have a powerful ally: Lady Luck will interpose herself between us and the fates (or the odds) to bring victory to our side.
—Peter L. Bernstein, *Against the Gods: The Remarkable Story of Risk*, 1996.

Fortune cannot aid those who do nothing.
—Sophocles (496–405/6 B.C.)

15.1 The Myth of Low-Probability/High-Consequence Events

While the analysis in this book has dealt with one type of catastrophe (weather-related hazards) and one country (the United States), we believe that the framework and analysis in this book applies to a much broader set of extreme events than natural disasters and can also be extended to other countries.

In the first few years of the twenty-first century, the world has experienced a spate of unprecedented catastrophes that require us to rethink our approach to reduce future losses and deal with these events in a more proactive way. In the United States on September 11, 2001, a superpower was challenged on its own soil by terrorists, making national security the top priority on the U.S. agenda. The event has had an enduring impact on the rest of the world. In August 2003, a massive failure of the electric power distribution system in the United States and Canada demonstrated how short-term competitive pressure can jeopardize our critical infrastructure. The resulting blackout deprived over 50 million North Americans of electricity, some for several days. More broadly, the protection of our critical but aging infrastructure is not yet viewed as a national priority. Within a fifteen-month period in 2004 and 2005, seven major hurricanes made landfall in the United States. Hurricane Katrina, a violent but long-anticipated hurricane, overwhelmed a vulnerable coastline in August 2005, met an unprepared government, inflicted lasting damage on a population and destroyed a major portion of New Orleans, a historic landmark. And in 2008, a financial crisis occurred with severe global impacts that are still unfolding as this book goes to press.

Catastrophes in developing countries are often even more destructive with respect to the toll they take on human lives when they occur. The December 2004 tsunami in Thailand, Indonesia, and other Asian countries was responsible for the deaths of over 280,000 people in just a few hours owing to lack of an alert system. A few weeks after a major cyclone killed over 140,000 in Myanmar in April 2008, an intense earthquake in the Sichuan province in China caused nearly 50,000 deaths and forced China to rethink its national strategy for dealing with major natural disasters.

Conventional wisdom holds that major accidents and disasters are low-probability events. From the viewpoint of any individual or community these events may indeed have a small chance of occurring. However, when one expands the lens to include a state or country or the global community, catastrophic risks have a much higher likelihood of occurring. It is somewhat sobering to learn from an analysis by Risk Management Solutions that there is a 1-in-6 probability that at least $10 billion dollars of insured properties will be destroyed by hurricanes in Florida next year. This is equivalent to the chance of getting the number 3 when one tosses a die—hardly a low probability. If we extended the time horizon from one year to ten years while keeping the population of Florida constant, the likelihood of damage exceeding this amount would be greater than 5 in 6. With economic development in coastal areas of this state and increased intensity of hurricanes as a result of global warming, we are almost certain to experience a disaster of $10 billion or greater in Florida in the next decade. In fact, if one extends the event space to include all natural disasters and the sample space to encompass the globe, then it should be clear that we have to modify our definition of a low-probability event. In other words, we expect large-scale catastrophes to unfold at an accelerating rhythm in the coming years. What can and should be done to meet this new challenge?

15.2   A Five-Pillar Strategy

A more coherent strategy is needed to link risk assessment, risk perception, and risk management for dealing with extreme events here and abroad. To highlight the importance of these three elements, we propose a five-pillar strategy that implicitly guided our analysis of natural disasters in this book. We illustrate each of these pillars by showing how they apply to the natural hazard problem as well as to other extreme events. Concrete solutions to deal with these issues are suggested when we introduce the fifth pillar.

Pillar 1: Problem Characterization   *One needs to highlight the nature of the problem, the affected stakeholders, and their objectives.*

With respect to the natural hazard problem, the focus of our analysis in this book is on homeowners in regions affected by hurricanes and floods. Some other key stakeholders are the insurance/reinsurance industry, state insurance commissioners, financial institutions, capital markets, rating agencies, as well as the real estate industry and local governments. Homeowners value living in a safe home that meets their basic needs. The insurers' objectives are to provide coverage against natural disasters at prices that enable them to make a profit. The state insurance commissioners are concerned with having insurers offer coverage to homeowners at prices that are affordable but do not lead to insolvencies of insurers following the next hurricane.

For extreme events such as terrorism, pandemics, power failures, and financial crises, it will be important to single out the different stakeholders and their objectives relative to the problem of concern. It is very likely that one will discover conflicting objectives among the relevant interested parties. For example, the managers of divisions within an organization may be reluctant to invest in cost-effective risk-reducing measures because the required upfront expenditures have a negative impact on the profitability of their operations and hence may reduce their bonuses at the end of the year. The Chief Executive Officer (CEO) and Chief Financial Officer (CFO) may value these investments but be unaware that their division heads have not undertaken these measures. It is important for those in charge to understand the stakeholder map and their associated agendas, values and objectives.

Pillar 2: Risk Assessment *One needs to characterize the likelihood and consequences of the extreme events being studied and the uncertainties surrounding these estimates.*

A useful tool for conveying this information is an exceedance probability (EP) curve, which specifies the likelihood that the dimension of interest (e.g., dollar losses, number of fatalities) will exceed different magnitudes. For the natural disaster problem, our principal focus was on the likelihood that hurricanes of different magnitudes and intensities would cause dollar losses (L) to homeowners' property in a given region that exceeded a given level L^*. We were also interested in how certain the catastrophe modeling community was with respect to these point estimates so that one gained insight into the confidence intervals surrounding the EP curve.

We have developed EP curves for losses from natural hazards, and a similar analysis could be undertaken for variables of interest with respect to other extreme events. For example, if one were studying pandemics then one would want to know the likelihood that the population contracting a particular disease during a given period in a given geographic area would exceed prespecified values and the uncertainty surrounding these estimates.

One should recognize though that it is not always possible to construct such EP curves without having very wide confidence bands surrounding them. Today it is challenging to estimate the likely damage and fatalities from a future terrorist attack in any part of the world or the consequences of a cyber-attack on business interruption losses. Yet even for such circumstances experts should be able to compare the *relative* likelihood of different events by constructing specific scenarios (e.g., a terrorist attack in a large urban area compared to a similar mode of attack in a less populated region). These types of assessments are particularly useful in determining how to allocate limited resources for reducing future losses from specific events or across different risks.

Pillar 3: Interdependencies *One should recognize the interdependencies associated with specific extreme events and their impacts on other stakeholders.*

These interdependencies have both *spatial* and *time* dimensions associated with them. At the spatial level, a poorly designed house that is hit by a hurricane can cause damage to other structures nearby if, for example, the roof blows off and flies into a neighbor's well-designed home, which would otherwise have suffered minimal damage. With respect to time, if there is disruption in services provided by utilities (e.g., electricity, water) from a hurricane, then homeowners may be forced to leave their homes until the infrastructure is repaired even though these residents had invested in risk reduction measures that effectively protected their property. A specific example is the major storm surge from Hurricane Katrina in 2005, which was partially caused by wetland losses that occurred slowly over decades. The rate of wetland loss is about 24 square miles per year today, or about one football field of wetlands lost off the Louisiana coast every 38 minutes (Kousky and Zeckhauser 2006). This creates the conditions for even more devastating storm surge in the future.

It is highly likely that any extreme event will cause a set of non-trivial interdependencies that need to be examined in more detail. For example, the August 2003 power failures in the northeastern United States and Canada were caused by a Ohio utility, a weak link in a highly interconnected system. With respect to the 2008 financial crisis, the potential collapse of the American International Group (A.I.G.), the world's largest insurer, was the result of a 377-person London unit known as A.I.G. Financial Products that was run with almost complete autonomy from the parent company (Morgenson 2008). These interdependencies are often the consequence of globalization. The 2008 food crisis is another example. Faced with the need for short-term positive return during a global financial turmoil, speculators on financial markets invested heavily in products that they fully understood. And what could be more basic than food: rice, wheat, corn, and so forth in a market-based economy—prices of those commodities started reflecting this growing demand and food prices increased. As they increased, food became even more attractive as an investment, fueling the demand, and prices rose even more. From January 2007 to April 2008, the price of rice on the Chicago Board of Trade increased by over 100 percent. (Data available at www.cbot.com). From a simple financial perspective, this strategy made sense. But these actions would soon have impacts thousands of miles away. With about 1 billion people living on $1 per day—the official threshold of absolute poverty—soaring prices increased hunger around the world. We are not saying that traders were directly responsible for the deaths of hundreds of people in Africa and Asia, but we foresee such interdependent risks to be even more salient in the coming years.

Pillar 4: Behavioral Biases and Choice Heuristics   *Expert risk assessments and laypersons' risk perceptions often differ significantly. One needs to understand the nature of the behavioral biases and heuristics utilized by individuals and organizations in making decisions.*

One of the most important biases humankind suffers from is myopia, or a focus on short-time horizons. A related heuristic is the failure to take into account the consequences of a future large-scale disaster by assuming *it will not happen*. These two behavioral characteristics account for many homeowners' failure to invest in cost-effective loss reduction measures in hurricane- or flood-prone areas. By focusing only on the potential benefits from making their homes safer over the next two or three years, it is hard for them to justify incurring the high upfront cost of the investment even though the risk reduction measures will in fact be effective for twenty or thirty years. If a homeowner perceived that a hurricane damaging his property would not occur in his lifetime, then he would not even consider investing in any loss reduction measure.

Similar behavior can be observed with respect to most extreme events until after they happen. Even after the first terrorist attack in the garage of the World Trade Center in 1993, which cost insurers over $750 million, they continued to include terrorism as an unnamed peril in their policies. The decision to ignore this threat and not to charge a penny for terrorism the following years made insurers and their reinsurers fully liable for the $35 billion of insured losses resulting from the September 11, 2001, attacks. Following 9/11, most insurers in the United States and Europe began to exclude terrorism from most of their commercial policies. Those who provided this coverage charged extremely high premiums to their clients (Kunreuther and Pauly 2005). In the same spirit, only after the Bhopal chemical accident in 1984 were regulations passed requiring firms to develop risk management plans for reducing the likelihood of future disasters occurring. It appears as if we are often battling a war that has already wreaked havoc on individuals and their possessions.

Pillar 5: Catastrophe Risk Management   *Catastrophe risk management strategies should address the problem under study, be based on experts' assessments of the risk, recognize interdependencies, and address behavioral biases and heuristics used by decision makers.*

The capabilities of the private sector should be used to develop catastrophe risk management strategies in combination with public sector initiatives. In the context of natural disasters, we have proposed the development of long-term contracts such as multiyear insurance policies with premiums reflecting risk and multiyear financial loans to encourage homeowners to invest in cost-effective loss reduction measures. Given the vulnerability associated with poorly designed structures, there is a need for well-enforced building codes when building new structures in hazard-prone areas (Jaffee, Kunreuther, and Michel-Kerjan 2008).

Turning to other extreme events, we believe that similar risk management strategies may be appropriate for reducing future losses. Rather than assuming that an event will not happen, one should develop worst-case scenarios to determine whether there are steps that can be taken to reduce their impacts. For example, with respect to the recent financial crisis, there has been extensive documentation about how the subprime mortgage crisis could have easily been predicted if one had developed scenarios where housing prices fell nationally by a large amount. In the context of natural hazards, the *New Orleans Times Picayune* had a series of articles in 2002 predicting Hurricane Katrina, and *National Geographic* had an article in October 2004 characterizing the devastation that a disaster such as Katrina could deliver to the city. The disaster occurred ten months later. The challenge is to develop economic incentives for rewarding individuals and organizations for taking these scenarios seriously before a disaster occurs, as there are often competing interests that demand immediate attention after a catastrophe.

There are also opportunities for developing long-term contracts that take the behavioral biases and heuristics utilized by decision makers into account. For example, the standard *annual* bonus system practiced by many organizations could be modified so that bonuses are contingent on multiyear performance. This might induce managers to more systematically consider the potential consequences of their immediate actions in the long-run and to pay more attention to worst-case scenarios rather than hoping that they will not occur in their terms of office. In the same vein, presenting probabilities of extreme events in the context of a multiyear horizon may also lead individuals to pay attention to the resulting outcomes. For example, rather than providing information in terms of a 1-in-100 chance of an event occurring next year, one could indicate that the chance of at least one of these events occurring in the next twenty-five years is greater than 1 in 5. This is one way to make probabilities more salient.

We also need well-designed regulations to cope with the growing interdependencies that are likely to exist with respect to many of these risks. It was only after 9/11 that strict baggage-transfer security regulations were imposed in airports around the country, mandated by the federal government and financed by a security tax charged against all passengers. Before the terrorist attacks, each airline was expected to institute its own system and pay for these measures. Yet all airlines were vulnerable to poor screening by other connecting airlines. This was the case with the Pan Am 103 crash in 1988 when an uninspected bag was placed on a Malta Airlines flight at a small unsecured airport in Malta, transferred in Frankfurt to a Pan Am feeder line, and then loaded onto Pan Am 103 in London's Heathrow Airport. The bomb was designed to explode above 28,000 feet, a height normally first attained on this route over the Atlantic Ocean. The plane exploded over Lockerbie, Scotland, killing all 243 passengers and 16 crew members and 11 people on the ground. There was nothing Pan Am could have done to prevent the crash unless it inspected all transferred bags, a costly practice only followed by El Al airlines at that time (Lockerbie Verdict, 2001).

15.3   The Need for Bold Initiatives to Deal with Interdependent Risks

The increasing globalization of economic and social activities worldwide is also reshaping the risk landscape from the more traditional local and relatively well-defined risks to global and often highly uncertain situations where the impacts can be devastating. The leitmotiv becomes *interdependency* on a large scale and requires a paradigm shift from traditional risk management strategies. We believe the research community, working in collaboration with leaders from the private and public sectors, can provide insights into how to deal with this new and more complex environment. In this spirit, we present below two new initiatives that deal with these issues.

World Economic Forum's Global Risk Network

This network was established by the World Economic Forum (WEF) in 2006 in response to a concern that the international community and global businesses did not respond adequately to a changing global risk landscape. The Global Risk Network involves a partnership between the WEF and Citigroup, Marsh & McLennan, Swiss Re, Zurich, and the Wharton Risk Management and Decision Processes Center at the University of Pennsylvania. One of its main goals is to aggregate information about global risks from many private sector organizations and to act as a clearinghouse for future risk-reduction and risk-financing proposals. In this sense, the initiative is a work in progress.

The Global Risk Network methodology involved selecting twenty-three risks, ranging from international terrorism, climate change, natural disasters, and pandemics to asset price collapse, liability regimes, and critical infrastructure disruption. A survey of experts estimated a range of likelihoods and potential losses associated with these risks on a five-to-ten-year horizon. The Global Risk Network expanded the standard (probability, severity) framework for assessing individual risks by analyzing the correlations between each of these risks and the other twenty-two risks using data provided by a number of risk experts. An example of this correlation matrix, which reflects how one risk can affect another risk, which in turn affects another, is displayed in figure 15.1.

Figure 15.1 provides decision makers with some perspective on other issues that could affect their core businesses, which they may otherwise not have considered in their strategic planning process. The large-scale destabilization from events such as the anthrax scare and the SARS epidemic came as a surprise to many managers, signaling that the interdependencies associated with global risks need to be more fully understood and internalized in risk management strategies by firms and governmental organizations. Likewise, it should not come as a surprise that a change in climate in some parts of the world could lead to aggravated living conditions (e.g., impact of severe repetitive droughts or floods on access to drinkable water and food), which in turn could exacerbate local conflicts and destabilize the geopolitical balance in that region, with ripple effects on other parts of the world. This

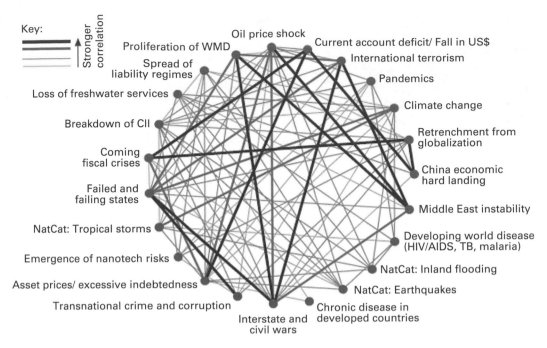

Figure 15.1
New approach to deal with global risks: correlation matrix. *Source:* World Economic Forum (2007).

initiative results in the *Global Risks Report* that is released at the annual meeting in Davos. (More details can be found at www.weforum.org/en/initiatives/globalrisk.)

In 2008, recognizing that new international responses were needed and that some international organizations created sixty years ago might not be ideally structured to respond quickly to new challenges of the twenty-first century, the World Economic Forum formed Global Agenda Councils (GACs) on the foremost topics in the global arena. For each of these areas, a dedicated WEF GAC convenes experts and leaders to capture state-of-the-art knowledge with the purpose of integrating their ideas on innovative strategies with those of other GACs as part of a global collaboration effort. GACs represent a transformational innovation in global governance, creating multistakeholder groups for the purpose of advancing knowledge as well as collaboratively developing solutions for the most crucial issues on the global agenda. The GACs are expected to challenge prevailing assumptions, monitor trends, map interrelationships, and address knowledge gaps. Equally important, GACs will also propose solutions, devise strategies and evaluate the effectiveness of actions using measurable benchmarks. In an environment marked by short-term orientation and silo-thinking, where companies and industries focus on their own activities without necessarily considering their global impacts, this bold initiative is designed to foster interdisciplinary and long-range thinking in addressing the prevailing challenges on the global agenda. (For more details on the Global Agenda Councils see www.weforum.org/en/about/GlobalAgendaCouncils/index.)

OECD Network on Financial Management of Large-Scale Catastrophes

The Organization for Economic Cooperation and Development (OECD) and its thirty member countries offer a setting in which governments can compare their experiences using different risk management strategies, seek answers to common problems, identify good practices, and coordinate domestic and international policies. It is a forum where peer pressure can act as a powerful incentive to improve policy. In an increasingly globalized economy, the OECD recently recognized that the interdependencies associated with disasters have global implications, and therefore governments need to be proactive prior to the occurrence of catastrophic events rather than hope they will not occur on their watch.

To address these issues and develop sound policies in a timely fashion, the OECD has established an International Network on the Financial Management of Large-Scale Catastrophes in 2006. Under the guidance of a high-level advisory board, whose members are not employed by the OECD, the network promotes the exchange of information and experiences among policymakers, industry, and academia. The board plays a leading role in identifying and discussing the major policy issues related to the financial management of large-scale catastrophes. It also performs advisory functions to the OECD Secretary-General and to the Insurance and Private Pensions Committee and the Committee on Financial Markets in the drafting of guidelines, good practices, recommendations, and principles. (More details on the board's activities can be found at www.oecd.org/daf/fin/catrisks.)

Both these initiatives recognize that firms, governments, nongovernmental organizations, and international organizations need to take into account interactions at an international level when developing their strategic plans as national boundaries assume less importance. They also illustrate how these issues are now on the agenda of decision makers at the highest level of their organizations. More companies now realize that a single event can seriously jeopardize their activities, if not their own existence. As a result, a growing number of boards of directors and government cabinets are incorporating the importance of management of extreme events into their strategic planning process.

It is often the case that events destabilizing one's organization are those that occur outside of normal routines. Training top decision makers to deal with these "it cannot happen" scenarios has become a critical element of success in managing large-scale risks in a new era of catastrophes. But one thing is clear: proactive leaders will be the ones to glean the benefits from initiatives that reduce the potential impacts of future catastrophic events on their own activities and those of other stakeholders.

15.4   At War with Ourselves

We typically think of a war as combat against a particular enemy. However, for most global risks, the battlefield and the warriors are not clearly defined. Natural hazards have always been part of our environment. But we often choose to ignore these hazards, or believe we are immune from them. In fact, one of the main reasons why the war against the weather has escalated is the desire of many people to reside in high-risk areas. The economic development of Florida highlights this point: the population of the state by 2010 will have grown by 600 percent since 1950. Most of this development has taken place in coastal areas subject to hurricane risk because property owners enjoy the sun and shore and disregard the dangers they face from an extreme event. As Peter Bernstein wrote in his seminal book *Against the Gods*, we believe that "Lady Luck will interpose herself between us and the fates (or the odds) to bring victory to our side" (pp. 11–12).

The paradox in waging a war against the weather and other extreme events is that we might very well be our own worst enemy. As individuals, we may decide to build in risky areas. As entrepreneurs in the private sector, we may decide to locate our businesses in these hazard-prone regions. As decision makers in the public sector, we may permit millions of people to reside and businesses to operate in these areas without requiring them to adopt appropriate risk reduction measures. In refusing to take steps in a proactive manner to reduce our vulnerabilities, the seeds for future disasters are created that will affect our future well-being and social welfare. The same can certainly be said of the many extreme events that have unfolded in the past few years. Fortune cannot aid those who do nothing.

Abbreviations

AAAS	American Association for the Advancement of Science
ABI	Association of British Insurers
AHS	American Housing Survey
CBO	Congressional Budget Office
CEA	California Earthquake Authority
CEIOPS	Committee of European Insurance and Occupational Pensions Supervisors
CME	Chicago Mercantile Exchange
CPIC	Citizens Property Insurance Corporation
CRS	Community Rating System
CRTF	Catastrophe Reserve Trust Fund
DBPM	Dade, Broward, Palm Beach and Monroe counties
FEMA	Federal Emergency Management Agency
FHCF	Florida Hurricane Catastrophe Fund
FIA	Federal Insurance Administration
FIFA	Federation Internationale de Football Association
FIGA	Florida Insurance Guaranty Association
FLOIR	Florida Office of Insurance Regulation
FRPCJUA	Florida Residential Property and Casualty Joint Underwriting Association
FWUA	Florida Windstorm Underwriting Association
GAO	Government Accountability Office
GIS	Geographic information systems
HUD	U.S. Department of Housing and Urban Development
IBHS	Institute for Business and Home Safety

ICC	International Code Council
ISO	Insurance Services Office
JUA	Florida Residential Property and Casualty Joint Underwriting Association
LCPIC	Louisiana Citizens Property Insurance Corporation
LIHEAP	Low Income Home Energy Assistance Program
MCH	Miami Children's Hospital
MMC	U.S. National Institute of Building Science's Multihazard Mitigation Council
NAIC	National Association of Insurance Commissioners
NCCI	National Council on Compensation Insurance
NFIP	National Flood Insurance Program
NOAA	National Oceanic and Atmospheric Administration
NYMEX	New York Mercantile Exchange
OECD	Organization for Economic Cooperation and Development
PCIAA	Property Casualty Insurers Association of America
PIPSO	Property Insurance Plans Service Office
RMS	Risk Management Solutions
SBA	State Board of Administration (of Florida)
SBA	Small Business Administration
SCDOI	South Carolina Department of Insurance
TWIA	Texas Windstorm Insurance Association
USF	Universal Service Fund
WRMA	Weather Risk Management Association

Glossary

actuarially fair rates   rates that reflect the expected loss.

additional living expenses (ALE)   extra charges covered by homeowners' policies over and above the policyholder's customary living expenses, such as when the insured requires temporary shelter due to damage by a covered peril that makes the home temporarily uninhabitable.

adjustable premium contract (APC)   a variable premium with guaranteed renewal for the term of the policy.

adverse selection   a situation where sellers have information that buyers do not (or vice versa) about some aspect of product quality; in insurance, a situation where the people who have insurance are more likely to make a claim than the average population used by the insurers to set their rates.

affordability   a household's having enough income to buy the quantity of the good that meets well established (social sector) norms of adequacy at a total cost that leaves them with enough income to live on without falling below some poverty standard.

alternative risk transfer (ART)   the use of financial techniques other than traditional insurance and reinsurance to provide risk-bearing entities with coverage or protection. Alternative risk transfer instruments grew out of a series of insurance capacity crises in the 1970s through 2000s that drove purchasers of traditional coverage to seek more robust ways to protect themselves against catastrophic losses.

attachment point   the point at which excess insurance or reinsurance limits apply. For example, an insurer's retention on a given reinsurance contract can be $100 million; $100 million is the "attachment point" above which the reinsurer will start covering the insurer (see also exhaustion point).

average annual loss (AAL)   the average or expected loss for an insurance exposure unit or a set of exposures per year.

base flood elevation (BFE)   the elevation shown on flood insurance rate maps (FIRMs) for indicating the water-surface elevation resulting from a flood that has a 1 percent chance of equaling or exceeding that level in any given year.

basis risk   the imperfect correlation between the actual losses suffered by a company or individual and the payments received from a risk transfer instrument designed to cover these losses.

Best's Capital Adequacy Ratio (BCAR)   an integrated review of an insurer's underwriting, financial and asset leverage used by A.M. Best to test the impact of scenarios that affect an insurer's financial outcomes.

Building Code Effectiveness Grading Schedule (BCEGS)   assesses the building codes in effect in a particular community and how the community enforces its building codes, with special emphasis on mitigation of losses from natural hazards.

capacity   total limit of liability that a company or the insurance industry can assume, according to generally accepted criteria for solvency.

capital markets   markets in which corporate equity and longer-term debt securities are issued and traded.

catastrophe bond (cat bond)   a corporate bond that requires the purchasers to forgive or defer some or all payments of interest or principal if the catastrophe loss surpasses a specified amount or trigger.

catastrophe loss   economic loss resulting from a large-scale disaster.

catastrophe model   computer-based model that estimates losses from natural or man-made hazards, such as earthquakes, floods, hurricanes, and acts of terrorism.

catastrophe risk   potential economic loss or other negative impact associated with large-scale disasters.

cedant   an insurer transferring all or part of a risk to another party, such as a reinsurer.

coinsurance   the sharing of the insured losses incurred by a policyholder with her insurer.

collateralized debt obligation (CDO)   a type of asset-backed security and structured credit product. CDOs are constructed from a portfolio of fixed-income assets that are divided into tranches and serve as an important funding vehicle for fixed-income assets.

community rating system (CRS)   a system by which communities are rated for their mitigation efforts beyond those required by the National Flood Insurance Program (NFIP) for its policyholders.

competitive rating (CR) systems   a system in which, in theory, regulators essentially rely on the private market to set premiums and do not attempt to constrain them.

correlated losses   the simultaneous occurrence of many losses from a single catastrophe or disaster.

cost-benefit analysis (CBA)   a type of economic evaluation for ranking alternative projects in which both the costs and consequences of different interventions are expressed in monetary units.

credit default swap (CDS)   a credit derivative between two counterparties, whereby one makes periodic payments to the other and receives the promise of a payoff if a third party defaults.

credit derivatives   a contract that enables a user, such as a bank, to better manage its credit risk; a way of transferring credit risk to another party.

credit risk   the possibility that a party will default on payments (recoverables) it owes to another party.

cross-subsidies   when insurance is priced below cost for particular geographic areas or groups of policyholders, a portion of their losses over time is covered by premiums collected in other areas or from other groups of policyholders.

deductible   the dollar amount or percentage of an insured loss that the policyholder must cover before any claims are paid by the insurer.

demand surge   the sudden increase in construction costs following a catastrophe.

direct premiums written (DPW)   property and casualty premiums collected by a primary insurer from its policyholders that are not adjusted for reinsurance costs.

exceedance probability (EP) curve   a graphical representation of the probability that a certain level of risk will be surpassed during a future time period. The most common form of an EP curve is the probability that an economic loss will be exceeded on an annual basis.

excess of loss reinsurance   a type of reinsurance contract in which a premium is paid by an insurer to a reinsurer covering losses above a certain threshold or retention level.

exhaustion point   the limit of the payout on an insurance or reinsurance contract.

expected loss   the sum of the probabilities of each insured event multiplied by the estimated dollar amount of the loss from each of these events.

exposure   in a catastrophe model, the properties at risk from a natural or man-made hazard.

FAIR Plans (Fair Access to Insurance Requirements)   a pooling arrangement to insure risks that cannot obtain coverage in the private market because of high risk over which insurers may have no control.

federal poverty line (FPL)   the level set by the federal government that states how much money, an individual or families of varying sizes need to live a basic existence.

file and use   a system in which insurers may implement rates it is required to file without prior regulatory approval; in practice, regulators may disapprove such rates before they are implemented.

fixed-price contract (FPC)   a contract where the annual premium is constant for the full term of the policy.

Flood Insurance Rate Maps (FIRM)   official map of a community that has delineated both the special hazard areas and the risk premium zones applicable to the community.

geographic information systems (GIS)   an organized collection of computer hardware, software, and geographic data designed to efficiently capture, store, update, manipulate, analyze, and display all forms of geographically referenced information.

gross loss   the portion of the ground-up losses covered by an insurer after subtracting deductibles and reinsurance.

ground-up loss   total amount of loss sustained by an insurer before any policy deductibles or reinsurance are applied.

Herfindahl-Hirschman Index (HHI)   a measure of the concentration of an industry.

homeowners' insurance   a comprehensive insurance package policy covering an owner-occupied residence for losses due to fire, theft, and certain other perils including hurricane winds; policies exclude damage from surface water (e.g., floods, storm surges.) and earth movement.

indemnity contract   a contract in which one insurance company charges a premium to provide funds to another insurance company to cover a stated portion of the loss it may sustain under its insurance policies. See *reinsurance*.

indicated loss cost (ILC)   the expected loss (including loss adjustment expense) per exposure unit for a defined rating classification based on actuarial analysis.

industry loss warranties (ILWs)   type of reinsurance or derivative contract through which one party purchases protection based on the total loss to the entire insurance industry arising from an event rather than his or her own losses.

insolvency risk   possibility that an insurer or reinsurer will become bankrupt and be unable to pay all or a portions of its claims obligations.

insurable risk   an event that meets a set of criteria so that an insurer is willing to provide coverage against it.

insurance rate   the cost per unit of insurance purchased; usually reflects expected losses from a series of events combined with loss adjustment expense, overhead, and profit.

insurance-linked securities (ILS)   instruments by which insurance risk is transferred in capital markets contracts; these include catastrophe bonds, industry loss warrantees, sidecars, and catastrophe futures contracts.

Joint Underwriting Association (JUA)   a pooling arrangement among companies that share risks that cannot be accommodated by a sole insurer in the private market.

layer   a prespecified range of potential claims (e.g., $200–$500 million) to be covered by an insurer or reinsurer if the insured loss exceeds the lower limit (I.E. $200 million).

loss on line (LOL)   amount of expected loss from a predefined layer of coverage of reinsurance.

mitigation   measures taken to reduce or eliminate damage or loss from natural or man-made hazards.

moral hazard   careless behavior caused by the presence of insurance that increases the expected claims filed by policyholders.

noncompetitive rating (NCR) systems   a system in which regulators may approve the rates that insurers file rather than relying on market competition.

ordinary least squares regression   a statistical technique used in econometrics to find the best linear fit from given data.

portfolio   the full set of policies covered by an insurance company.

power dissipation index (PDI)   the sum of the maximum one-minute sustained wind speed cubed, at six-hourly intervals, for all periods when the cyclone is at least tropical storm strength.

pre-FIRM   in the National Flood Insurance Program, refers to structures constructed prior to the development of a flood insurance rate map (FIRM) for a community, and for which rates are subsidized.

premium   the price of insurance protection for a specified period of time defined in the insurance contract (normally, one year).

probable maximum loss (PML)   representing the largest economic loss likely to occur for a given policy or a set of policies when a catastrophic event occurs.

pro rata reinsurance   type of reinsurance in which premiums and losses are shared by the cedant and insurer on a proportional basis.

probability   likelihood of an event occurring during a specified period of time.

rate making   the process by which insurance rates, or the cost per unit of insurance purchased, is established.

rate on line (ROL)   a percentage derived by dividing the (re)insurance premium by the (re)insurance limit; the inverse is known as the payback or amortization period. For example, a $10 million catastrophe cover with a premium of $2 million would have a rate on line of 20 percent and a payback period of 5 years.

reinsurance   purchase of insurance by an insurer from another insurance company (the reinsurer) for the purpose of spreading risk and reducing the insurer's losses from catastrophic events.

return on equity (ROE)   rate of return per dollar of stockholders' equity; measures a firm's efficiency at generating profits from every dollar of net assets (assets minus liabilities) and shows how well a company uses investment dollars to generate earnings growth.

return period   expected time between a certain magnitude of loss event; defined as the inverse of the annual exceedance probability. For example, a return period of 100 years corresponds to an annual exceedance probability of 1 percent.

risk transfer   method by which an individual or company reduces its risk from a natural or man-made hazard by reassigning the risk to another entity.

securitization   process of taking an illiquid asset or group of assets and, through financial engineering, transforming them into securities that are then sold to investors (e.g., the issuance of a catastrophe bond).

Sharpe ratio   A relative measure of a portfolio's return-to-risk ratio; calculated as the return above the risk-free rate divided by its standard deviation; often used to determine the amount of excess return required by investors for an additional unit of risk.

sidecar   special-purpose company that provides reinsurance coverage exclusively to its sponsor (a reinsurer or a large insurer) by issuing securities to investors.

Solvency II   the updated set of regulatory requirements for insurance firms operating in the European Union.

special flood hazard areas (SFHA)   FEMA-identified high-risk flood area where flood insurance is mandatory for properties.

take-up rate (TUR)   percentage of homeowners in a given state or metropolitan area who have purchased insurance against a particular risk.

total insured value (TIV)   value of all the assets covered by an insurance contract.

tsunamis   tidal waves usually resulting from Pacific Ocean hurricanes, earthquakes, and volcanic eruptions.

underwriting   process of selecting risks to insure and determining in what amounts and on what terms the company will accept the risk.

use and file   practice in some states of permitting insurers to implement new rates for a brief period (usually thirty days) before filing them with the insurance commissioner, who may then disapprove the rates if not in compliance with legal requirements.

weather derivative   insurance or securities product used as a hedge by energy-related businesses and others whose sales tend to fluctuate depending on the weather.

Write-Your-Own (WYO)   program under which private insurance companies sell and service flood insurance for the National Flood Insurance Program; they assume no risk but are reimbursed for their expenses.

Notes

Chapter 1

1. This figure excludes payment by the U.S. National Flood Insurance Program for damage due to 2005 flooding (over $20 billion in claims).

2. Munich Re and Swiss Re, the two leading reinsurers in the world, do not use the same definition of catastrophic losses. Natural disasters inflicting insured losses above $38.7 million or total losses above $77.5 million are considered a major catastrophe by Swiss Re (we use this threshold in figure 1.2); Munich Re considers a higher threshold, which explains the difference between figures 1.1 and 1.2. For example, when Munich Re estimated insured loss from natural disasters at about $42 billion in 2004, Swiss Re's estimate was over $52 billion. As a result, most figures used in the literature regarding the evolution of catastrophe loss actually underestimate the real effect on insurers.

3. Grossi and Kunreuther (2005).

4. Swiss Re (2007a).

5. This section is based on Kunreuther and Michel-Kerjan (2007).

6. Association of British Insurers (2005).

7. Mills and Lecomte (2006).

8. This proportion varies depending on the definition of "coastal counties" one considers; for instance, taking a more restrictive definition (i.e., any county that has a coastline bordering the open ocean or associated sheltered water bodies, or a county that contains V zones (as defined by the U.S. National Flood Insurance Program), one finds that the proportion of the population living in such counties is 30 percent). In any event, this proportion is significant and growing (Crowell et al., 2007).

9. Crossett, Culliton, Wiley, and Goodspeed (2004).

10. The NFIP is a public insurance program created in 1968. Insurers play the role of intermediaries between the policyholders and the federal government. Following Hurricane Katrina, the program had to borrow $20 billion from the federal government in 2006 to meet its claims. Congress is considering modifying the program substantially. For a more detailed discussion of the NFIP, see chapter 4.

11. Munich Re (2000).

12. For additional data on the economic impact of future catastrophic hurricanes, see Financial Services Roundtable (2007, chap. 2).

13. These estimates might vary, depending on underlying assumptions over such a long period of time, such as inflation, population growth, and wealth normalization in the studied area; moreover, mitigation and building codes will have an important impact on total losses.

14. This section is based on Kunreuther and Michel-Kerjan (2007).

15. For more details on the scientific evidence regarding climate change and its impact, see Stern Review (2006) and Intergovernmental Panel on Climate Change (2007).

16. Category 4 hurricanes have sustained winds from 131 to 155 miles per hour; Category 5 systems, such as Hurricane Katrina at its peak over the Gulf of Mexico, have sustained winds of 156 miles per hour or more.

17. Hoyos, Agudelo, Webster, and Curry (2006).

18. See, for instance, the exchange between Pielke, Landsea, and Emanuel (2005), Chan (2006), and Webster et al. (2006).

19. Landsea, Harper, Hoarau, and Knaff (2006).

20. Michaels (2006).

21. Kossin, Knapp, Vimont, Murnane, and Harper (2007).

22. Kossin et al. (2007).

23. World Meteorological Organization (2006); Goldenberg, Landsea, Mestas-Nunez, and Gray (2001).

24. For more discussion on this issue, see Mills (2005) and Höppe and Pielke (2006).

25. We were not able to access similar data for Texas, so the Texas map (figure 1.7) shows only counties and major cities for this state.

26. Meaner (2006).

27. U.S. Government Accountability Office (2002).

28. Kunreuther (2006).

29. U.S. Government Accountability Office (2007a, p. 25).

30. Insurance Research Council and Insurance Institute of Property Loss Reduction (1995).

31. Wharton Risk Center (2005).

32. See Klein (1995, 2007) and Grace et al. (2005); see Klein (2007) for a more detailed discussion of insurance regulatory policies in general and specific to natural disaster risk.

33. Roth (1998).

34. Lecomte and Gahagan (1998).

35. U.S. Government Accountability Office (2007a, p. 16).

36. See Grace et al. (2006) and Grace and Klein (2006) for a more detailed discussion of insurers' considerations and actions in dealing with correlated loss exposures and catastrophic risk.

37. See chapter 8 for more details.

38. Risk Management Solutions (2007).

Chapter 2

1. This chapter is based on Klein (2007).

2. The McCarran-Ferguson Act (enacted in 1945) still serves as the principal federal statute that establishes the framework for state and federal roles in regulating insurance. The act delegates most of the regulatory authority to the states but also retains the authority of the federal government to supersede state regulation where it specifically chooses to do so. Over the years, the federal government has imposed laws and policies in certain areas and could do so in the future. Legislation to create an optional federal regulatory charter for insurers has been introduced but not enacted. Other legislation has been introduced to establish a federal reinsurance program for natural catastrophes, and related bills and proposals have been introduced or discussed.

3. Grace and Klein (2007) documents insurer withdrawals from Florida.

4. One example is the Florida legislature's enactment of a moratorium on policy terminations following Hurricane Andrew.

5. Klein (1995).

6. Surplus lines or nonadmitted insurers typically are not licensed in the states in which they write business and are subject to less regulation than licensed insurers. Regulators permit surplus lines insurers to underwrite certain insurance coverages or risks for which the supply of coverage from licensed insurers is deemed to be inadequate.

7. U.S. regulators are considering changes to this policy that would reduce collateral requirements for foreign reinsurers based on some system of grading the financial condition of the foreign reinsurer or the quality of its regulation. See Klein and Wang (2007). Recently New York and Florida proposed to revise the collateral requirements they impose on non-U.S. reinsurers.

8. Researchers have sought to measure regulatory stringency and its effects in different ways. This research suggests that greater stringency may have some effect on the net price of insurance, at least in the short term, or other effects that tend to have negative impacts on consumers.

9. In theory, insurers might seek to charge higher rates to low-risk insureds to partially or completely offset the effect of constraints on rates for high-risk insureds.

10. Technically the change in an insurer's overall rate level is calculated as the exposure-weighted average of the changes in the rates for each rate classification.

11. For example, one proxy used is the difference between the rate levels that insurers have filed versus the rate levels that regulators have approved. Another proxy has been survey-based insurer ratings of the regulatory environment in various states. Both measures are imperfect, but some studies have revealed fairly robust results when different stringency measures are tested. See Klein, Phillips, and Shiu (2002).

12. This might be labeled as the sticker-shock effect. In normal markets, rate increases less than 10 percent tend not to encounter significant resistance. In markets hit by a major hurricane, consumer and regulatory tolerance may even be somewhat greater. However, there is a limit to this tolerance even in markets that are subject to high hurricane risk.

13. Grace, Klein, and Kleindorfer (2004).

14. Earlier in 2006, Allstate Floridian received a rate increase of 16.3 percent, and Allstate Floridian Indemnity received a rate increase of 24.4 percent.

15. In August 2008, Allstate reached a settlement with the FLOIR on disputes regarding its pricing and underwriting. Under the terms of the settlement, Allstate agreed to lower its rates 5.6 percent, write 100,000 additional policies over the next three years, and pay a $5 million fine.

16. South Carolina Department of Insurance (2007).

17. Proponents of government catastrophe reinsurance might contend that such programs would help to lower and stabilize rates, but insurers' views on the need for such programs differ, and this book does not attempt to resolve this debate.

18. "Fla. Subpoenas State Farm over Nonrenewal Plans" (2007).

19. "N.Y. Stops Insurers from Tie-Ins for Coastal Customers" (2007).

20. As an element of comparison, the federal National Flood Insurance Program, which covers homeowners against flood, has a maximum $5,000 deductible, independent of the level of coverage (see our analysis of homeowners' choice of flood deductible in chapter 4).

21. There is an understanding between private insurers and the federal government that the NFIP should be the source of flood coverage up to the limits provided by the program. Private insurers then may sell excess flood coverage over the NFIP limits.

22. There has been some criticism of the adequacy of federal flood mapping.

23. *Buente* v. *Allstate*. Civil Action No. 1:05CV712 LTS-JMR L.T. Senter, Jr., Senior Judge, April 11, (2006).

24. Treaster (2007).

25. In Re Katrina Canal Breaches Consolidated Litigation, No. 05-4182 (E.D. La. Nov. 27, 2006).

26. Property Casualty Insurers Association of America (PCIAA); Lehman Brothers Equity Research; Insurance Information Institute.

27. Some established insurers may still find this preferable if insolvency costs are spread broadly across all insurers and other lines. Also, state and federal laws allow insurers to recover at least some of their guaranty association assessments through rate surcharges or tax credits or deductions.

28. FAIR is the acronym for Fair Access to Insurance Requirements.

29. Louisiana established a similar mechanism in 2004.

30. Milliman (2007).

31. Information obtained from CPIC's Web site at http://www.citizensfla.com.

32. These data are somewhat imprecise in that they reflect Citizens' percentage of all property insurance premiums in the state. Also, the Florida data reflect only the residential property JUA in 2001 and Citizens' market share, 2002–2005, based on all of its premiums, including those for high-risk policies previously insured by the Florida wind pool.

33. Information on FLOIR's takeout plan can be accessed at http://www.floir.com/TakeoutCompanies.aspx.

34. In the matter of Citizens Property Insurance Corporation, Case No. 94539-08, Order Approving CPIC's Personal Residential and Commercial Residential Non-bonus Takeout Plans, http://www.floir.com/pdf/Executed _Order.pdf (July 24, 2008).

35. South Carolina Department of Insurance (2007).

36. Florida Hurricane Catastrophe Fund (2007).

Chapter 3

1. This chapter is drawn from a more detailed analysis of market conditions in coastal states by Grace and Klein (2007).

2. For example, when production is pushed beyond some point, communication and coordination among workers and units within a firm can suffer, leading to diminishing productivity. See Varian (1992) for an explanation of firm cost functions.

3. See Klein and Kleindorfer (2003).

4. See, for example, "Allstate Considers More Cancellations," *Tampa Tribune*, May 19, 2006.

5. Market concentration is measured by the HHI where a higher value implies greater market concentration.

6. Grace and Klein (2007).

7. In figure 3.2 we also include data for the state of Louisiana as an element of comparison.

8. The average premium will reflect coverage adjustments as it is based on the premiums that insureds actually pay.

9. Grace and Klein (2007).

10. In chapter 4 we discuss the premium change in these counties for public flood insurance, which has been less significant in the past few years.

11. See Grace, Klein, and Kleindorfer (2004).

12. The term *long run* can be ambiguous in the context of catastrophe risk. In homeowners' insurance markets not subject to catastrophic risk, five to ten years might be sufficient for insurers to balance out their profits and losses. However, in homeowners' insurance markets subject to catastrophic risk, it may take much longer for profits and losses to balance out (presuming that rates were set at adequate levels). This makes it difficult to assess whether profits approximate a fair rate of return over the long run.

13. All of the data used in these profit calculations are based on statutory financial statements filed by insurers. These profit measures are developed and calculated expressly by the National Association of Insurance Commissioners for regulators and others to use to determine the profits and losses of insurers by line and by state. They include allocations of all costs and all income (including investment income attributable to reserves for unearned premiums and unpaid losses) for a specific line of business in and specific state. The formulas used by the NAIC are complex and are documented in NAIC (2007). Insurers' dismal assessment of their financial performance in homeowners' insurers is reflected by the fact that a number of insurers have exited Florida and other coastal states, and others have substantially reduced their coastal exposures.

Chapter 4

1. This chapter is drawn from Michel-Kerjan and Kousky (2008).

2. Overman (1957), Gerdes (1963), and Anderson (1974). Recently this assessment has been changing. Swiss Re, for example, has argued that floods are insurable by private companies, given an appropriate partnership with

government. (See Menzinger and Brauner 2002.) It is interesting to see how different countries have handled the flood hazard differently. For example, private insurers provide flood coverage in the United Kingdom.

3. This bill superseded the Federal Flood Insurance Act of 1956 by implementing a federally run national flood program (the 1956 act was limited in scope, requiring, for example, that where "reasonably priced" private coverage was available, the federal insurance would not be).

4. Grossman (1958).

5. Pasterick (1998).

6. Congressional Budget Office (2007). The subsidy applies only to the first $35,000 of coverage on the building and $10,000 on contents, although the mean and median claims in 2004 were below these limits.

7. Pasterick (1998); Wetmore et al. (2006). Subsidized properties become required to pay actuarial rates only when they are damaged at half the property value or are improved creating in increase in value of 50 percent (Congressional Budget Office, 2007).

8. PricewaterhouseCoopers (1999).

9. Hayes, Spafford, and Boone (2006).

10. Congressional Budget Office (2007). (For more on the effects of eliminating NFIP subsidies, see PricewaterhouseCoopers 1999.)

11. See, for example, Criss and Shock (2001).

12. Center for Sustainable Communities (2006).

13. Anderson (1974).

14. Anderson (1974), Kunreuther (1979), Power and Shows (1979). For more detail on this point, see chapter 5.

15. Anderson (1974); Federal Emergency Management Agency (2002b).

16. Kriesel and Landry (2004).

17. Dixon, Clancy, Seabury, and Overton (2006).

18. Three significant flood events in 1992 (Texas flood, Hurricane Andrew, and a nor'easter) generated over $500 million in insured losses; a March storm and the floods in the Midwest in 1993 also generated $500 million of payments by the NFIP. The Texas floods in October 1994, the Louisiana floods in May 1995, and Hurricane Opal cost the NFIP over $1.2 billion.

19. The price does, of course, vary by flood zone, but averaging across all policies at the national level is also telling.

20. Given that the premiums also included fees paid for administrative expenses to insurers participating in the WYO program, the implicit probability of flooding is actually even lower than that.

21. Prices for NFIP insurance are set nationally and vary by flood zone (see appendix 4A) and characteristics of the house. They do not vary by state or locality, so the numbers reported here reflect the variety in flood risk by state, variation in the composition of who buys insurance, and how much coverage is bought per policy—a function of the value of homes.

22. We thank Tim Scoville and Ed Pasterick for sharing this data set and the claims data set for our research project and for helpful discussions on the practical operation of the program.

23. As discussed earlier, there has been an important controversy on the quality of these maps, especially in the aftermath of Hurricane Katrina and the breach of the levees in New Orleans.

24. We provide the full definition of each zone in appendix 4A.

25. Commercial (nonresidential) buildings are eligible for up to $500,000 in building coverage and up to $500,000 on personal property. According to FEMA, as of June 2007, nearly 2 million of the 5.4 million policies in force had building coverage only, 3.4 million had both building and contents coverage, and 100,000 had contents coverage only.

26. Not surprisingly, several private insurers, including AIG and Chubb, offer private insurance in excess of the NFIP policy limits. However, the same problems of insurability that the NFIP was established to address affect private programs. To our knowledge, AIG offers its coverage in only a handful of states, including California, Colorado, Connecticut, Illinois, and Massachusetts (Silverman 2005). The Chubb Group is offering its policies

only in Arizona, Colorado, Illinois, Idaho, Indiana, Michigan, and Utah (Best's Review 2006). Therefore, private flood insurance is not available in the areas where homeowners need it the most. We are not aware, however, of any exhaustive data set that contains this information for the state of Florida that we could access.

27. The findings are more consistent with the goal-based model of insurance decision making discussed in chapter 5.

28. Kunreuther et al. (1978).

29. Results previously published show that policyholders would choose a lower deductible but also a lower limit on the policy, focusing mainly on noncatastrophic loss. For instance, in his survey of insurance buyers, Eldred (1980) found that 68 percent of the automobile policies and 69 percent of the homeowners' policies that had the lowest deductible also had liability limits of $25,000 or less, even though insurance professionals and consumer publications agreed that a $100,000 personal liability limit is necessary to afford reasonable protection.

30. Hurricane Katrina made its first landfall in Florida as a Category 1 hurricane on August 25, before moving to the Gulf of Mexico and becoming a Category 3 hurricane when it hit landfall again three days later in Louisiana.

31. Hurricane Dennis made landfall in Florida on July 11, 2005, as a Category 3 hurricane.

32. In 2005, the average premium in Santa Rosa County was $411; in Escambia, it was $423. These floods then correspond more or less to a fifteen- to twenty-year event if NFIP rate are actuarially based (this is a conservative assumption since rates are also supposed to cover management costs).

33. Miami was ranked twenty-third with an average $929 in claims per policy over this period of time; Palm Beach was fifty-ninth with $148.

34. Ordinary least-squares linear regression technique minimizes the sum of the squared differences between the predicted and observed values.

35. See appendix 4B for the percentage of properties located in an SFHA for each county in Florida.

36. Having a basement also slightly reduces the claims; the coefficient is -0.08490.

37. Looking at changes in average premium per policy, we see from table 4.8 that the policy premiums have not seen the same decrease between 2000 and 2005. This is the case because over time, more people have selected a lower deductible and increased the maximum limit on their policy (as we discussed earlier). In other words, the average premiums per policy remained about the same, but the quantity of insurance purchased increased significantly, which diminished the cost, measured as premium per thousand dollars of coverage.

38. Council of Economic Advisors (2007).

39. Indeed, the NFIP borrowed from the Treasury only three times prior to 2005 and repaid all three loans with interest (Jenkins 2005). (Under current law, FEMA is required to repay all funds for the NFIP borrowed from the Treasury). The 2005 hurricanes, however, have taxed the NFIP's financial soundness, as shown in figure 4.8. FEMA had about $23 billion in claims from Hurricanes Katrina, Rita, and Wilma, close to double the amount paid over the program's lifetime (King 2006).

40. We are grateful to Ed Pasterick from the NFIP for providing us with these data.

41. Pasterick (1998).

42. See U.S. Government Accountability Office (2007b) for a detailed description of FEMA's payments to participating insurers.

43. This estimation is in the range of loading factors insurers use when selling their own policy to reflect administrative costs beyond their estimates of actuarial cost of the coverage. In fiscal years 2005 and 2006, payments to WYO insurers were even larger because the WYO insurance companies received payments in these years for settling an unprecedented number and dollar amount of claims for the major 2004 and 2005 hurricanes.

44. Until 1986, the salaries, program expenses, and mapping costs were paid by an annual appropriation from Congress. From 1987 to 1990, these costs were paid out of premiums collected. Starting in 1991, a federal policy fee of $25 was added to every policy (increased to $30 in 1995) to cover salaries and administrative costs.

45. We have not included in that description the $400 million spent for interest expenses by the program over this 1968–2005 period.

46. U.S. Government Accountability Office (2007b).

47. U.S. Government Accountability Office (2006).
48. U.S. Government Accountability Office (2006).
49. Overman (1957).
50. Wetmore et al. (2006).
51. On the property value aspect, see Kunreuther (1968).
52. Wetmore et al. (2006).
53. Appendix 4A is from FEMA, U.S. Department of Homeland Security.

Chapter 5

1. The first two sections of this chapter are based on Kunreuther and Pauly (2006b).
2. The amount of disaster assistance is assumed to have no impact on the uninsured losses that a person can write off for tax purposes.
3. Kunreuther, Novemsky, and Kahneman (2001).
4. Kunreuther and Pauly (2004).
5. For empirical evidence on the use of threshold models of choice in protective decisions, see Camerer and Kunreuther (1989).
6. McClelland, Schulze, and Coursey (1993).
7. Kunreuther et al. (1978).
8. Buchanan (1975), Coate (1995).
9. Moss (2002).
10. Dacy and Kunreuther (1968).
11. Reeves (2004, 2005).
12. Michel-Kerjan (2008). After a major disaster, a governor may determine that the recovery appears to be beyond the combined resources of both the state and local governments and that federal assistance may be needed. In requesting supplemental federal assistance through a presidential declaration under the Robert T. Stafford Disaster Relief and Emergency Assistance Act, 42 U.S.C. secs. 5121–5206 (Stafford Act), the governor must certify that the severity and magnitude of the disaster exceed state and local capabilities. Following a FEMA regional and national office review of the request and the findings of the preliminary damage assessment, FEMA provides the president an analysis of the situation and a recommended course of action. See http://www.fema.gov/media/fact_sheets/declaration_process.shtm for a complete description of the process and criteria. Neither federal law nor FEMA regulations provide a precise definition of what is and what is not a disaster.
13. Congressional Research Service (2005).
14. This section is based on Krantz and Kunreuther (2007).
15. Kunreuther, Sanderson, and Vetschera (1985).
16. Tobin and Calfee (2005).
17. Lowenstein, Weber, Hsee, and Welch (2001); Finucane, Alhakami, Slovic, and Johnson (2001).
18. Bell (1982), Loomes and Sugden (1982), Braun and Muermann (2004).
19. Bell (1985).
20. Rottenstreich and Hsee (2001), Sunstein (2003).
21. Kunreuther et al. (1978).
22. Shafir, Simonson, and Tversky (1993).
23. Hogarth and Kunreuther (1995).

Chapter 6

1. Stone also introduces a constraint regarding the stability of the insurer's operation. Insurers have traditionally not focused on this constraint in dealing with catastrophic risks but reinsurers have, as discussed in the next chapter.

2. Kunreuther, Meszaros, Hogarth, and Spranca (1995).

3. See chapter 14 for a detailed discussion of this concept.

4. For a survey of adverse selection issues, see Dionne, Doherty, and Fombaron (2000).

5. Henriet and Michel-Kerjan (2008).

6. Lecomte and Gahagan (1998).

7. Francis (2005).

8. See Doherty (2000) for more details.

9. Doherty (2000).

10. A.M. Best (2006).

11. Insurance Journal (2006).

12. Fleckenstein (2006).

13. The material in the first three parts of this section is based on Grossi and Kunreuther (2005, chap. 2).

14. Kozlowski and Mathewson (1995).

15. The EP curve is equivalent to the standard cumulative distribution function.

16. We thank Jack Nicholson of the Florida Hurricane Catastrophe Fund (FHCF) for providing us with the FHCF database and Patricia Grossi and Robert Muir-Wood of Risk Management Solutions for their analyses of the FHCF data. They provided us with the relevant EP curves and tables presented in this section.

17. We use here the new generation of models developed by RMS in 2006.

18. The coefficient of variation is the ratio of the standard deviation of a given variable to its mean.

Chapter 7

1. See Kreps (1990) for a mathematical treatment as to how this constraint affects reinsurers' decisions on whether to offer coverage.

2. Reinsurers are not regulated by states as to what premiums they can charge.

3. We thank Sean Mooney of Guy Carpenter who provided us with relevant material, including an unpublished draft of his paper "Pricing" (1999), which helped us to better determine how reinsurers price different layers of coverage.

4. Kreps (1990).

5. For more details on this model, see Kreps (1990) and Feldblum (1990).

6. We thank Patricia Grossi and Robert Muir-Wood from Risk Management Solutions for undertaking these analyses, which are based on the RMS 2006 models. See chapter 2 (section 2.5) for a discussion of the Florida Hurricane Catastrophe Fund (FHCF).

7. Grossi and Muir-Wood (2008).

8. State Board of Administration of Florida (2006).

9. State Board of Administration of Florida (2006).

10. We do not have price information for Citizens' reinsurance program in subsequent years.

11. Guy Carpenter (2007a).

12. Guy Carpenter (2008).

13. Guy Carpenter (2007b) and personal communication with Sean Mooney, January 20, 2009.

Chapter 8

1. This chapter is based on Michel-Kerjan and Morlaye (2008).

2. Lewis (2007).

3. For a comprehensive discussion of alternative risk transfers markets at the beginning of the 2000s, see Lane (2002), Dischel (2002), and Hartwig and Wilkinson (2007).

4. We give the example of a derivative swap, which is the most commonly used ILW contract. But it does not have to be. There could be a first indemnity-trigger (loss encounter by the buyers), then a second trigger based on industry loss. There could also be several thresholds with which are associated different payments.

5. Zeng (2000).

6. Lane (2006).

7. State Board of Administration of Florida (2006). Data for 2008 were provided by Justin Maletsky at Goldman Sachs and Enda McDonnell at Access Reinsurance, personal communication January 20, 2009.

8. For a theoretical treatment of optimal risk hedging through a bond, see Barrieu and El Karoui (2002).

9. Note that before the 2004 and 2005 hurricane seasons, the largest bond issued ever was the $470 million Zen-kyoren's Phoenix in 2003 to cover earthquakes in Japan. Since then, we have witnessed the issuance of much larger cat bonds, such as the $1.2 billion bond issued by State Farm in 2007 (Merna Re). The bond provides a three-year cumulative aggregate excess-of-loss catastrophe reinsurance to State Farm for multiple perils in the United States and some other countries, including hurricane, earthquake and fire following, tornado, hailstorm, winter storm, and brush fire.

10. Kunreuther and Michel-Kerjan (2004).

11. The cat bonds were part of a $450 million reinsurance transaction with European Finance Reinsurance, a wholly owned subsidiary of the reinsurance company Swiss Re. Swiss Re retained $290 million of the contract exposure and issued $160 million in cat bonds with a three-year maturity through a special-purpose vehicle, CAT-Mex.

12. The figure combines bonds for natural disasters in the United States and abroad, as well as the first liability cat bond (Avalon Re), issued by Oil Casualty Company in 2005 for $405 million.

13. Personal correspondence of Erwann Michel-Kerjan with Michael Millette, Goldman Sachs, December 20, 2007.

14. Although not all the relevant insurance claims affecting this issue have been processed, the bonds are trading as though a complete loss is expected.

15. Moyer (2006).

16. British Bankers Association (2006).

17. The first deal was made in July 1996, when Aquila Energy structured a dual-commodity hedge for Consolidated Edison Co. The transaction involved ConEd's purchase of electric power from Aquila for August. The price of the power was agreed to, but a weather clause was embedded into the contract. This clause stipulated that Aquila would pay ConEd a rebate if August turned out to be cooler than expected. The measurement of this was referenced to cooling degree days (CDDs) measured at New York City's Central Park weather station. If total CDDs were from 0 to 10 percent below the predefined expected level, the company received no discount to the power price, but if total CDDs were 11 to 20 percent below normal, ConEd would receive a $16,000 discount.

18. Weather Risk Management Association (2007).

19. For a discussion of the developments in ILS markets, see Butt (2007), De Mey (2007), Wu and Soanes (2007), Ramella and Madeiros (2007), and Csiszar (2007).

20. The European directive for reinsurance will make securitization of risks easier for the insurance market with the recognition of the special purpose reinsurance vehicle. The directive is due to be translated into national law by 2008 in the European Union.

21. In both cases, limits in available capacity were also a strong force driving the issue of ILS.

22. Swiss Re (2007b).

23. The Sharpe ratio is a measure of the excess return on a risk-adjusted target of return, divided by volatility of the product. It is a key indicator for investors as it helps discriminate between investments with the same level of risks measured by volatility of expected return.

24. See "Catastrophe bonds. Ports and storms," *The Economist*, 2007.

25. This new initiative is very encouraging almost ten years after the CBOT stopped trading such options. The NYMEX product is based on the final aggregate annual ISO's PCS loss estimate for the contract year (three years available to trade). The CME product is settled on a parametric index for individual hurricanes making landfall in the United States (there are contracts for three subsequent hurricane landfalls in five U.S. regions available to trade).

26. For instance, what is the probability of a dirty bomb exploding in Europe this year? What would be the direct and indirect impacts of such an attack? Michel-Kerjan and Pedell (2006).

27. For a discussion on other similar multifunction instruments, see Barrieu and Loubergé (forthcoming).

Chapter 9

1. Gron (1994), Winter (1988).

2. The so-called pecking order theory explains the preference for internal capital. In addition to the direct transaction costs of external capital, there are also agency costs, which take the form of controls to prevent insiders from diverting wealth to themselves. For details, see Myers and Majluf (1984).

3. State Board of Administration of Florida (2006).

4. Doherty and Posey (1997).

5. Strictly, the average risk per policy converges to zero as the number of policies in the pool gets very large. Thus, the average burden of risk in a large pool is close to zero.

6. Borch (1962).

Chapter 10

1. Portions of this section came from Grace, Klein, Kleindorfer, and Murray (2004).

2. Gal-or (1983).

3. Kunreuther (1998).

4. Klein (1998, 2007).

5. See Bartlett, Klein, and Russell (1999) for a discussion of how regulation-imposed insurance price subsidies may be sustained for a period of time.

6. For a further discussion of this point, see Grace, Klein, and Kleindorfer (GKK) (2004).

7. In our first-stage regression which we use for both the supply and demand equations, we include the following additional instrumental variables: log of capital and surplus, indicator for coastal county, change in population, and percentage area of the county covered by water.

8. Group operations would not be expected to subsidize business in a specific state, but group capital and diversification could help insurers deal with the random element of the risks they underwrite.

9. The elasticity is a result of the fact that we employ a logarithmic transformation to variables on both sides of the regression estimation equation.

10. Grace et al. (2004) used the price markup as a measure of price rather than average premiums.

11. Only owner-occupied single- or multiunit residential structures are eligible for homeowners' insurance, with the limit on multiunit structures usually set at four or five units. Dwellings that are not owner-occupied or structures that have more than four or five units typically would be covered under a commercial property insurance policy.

12. Some qualification of this statement is warranted. Many personal lines insurers offer both home and auto insurance and offer a discount if a consumer buys both products from them. This suggests that there are at least

economies of scope for insurers, if not for consumers. However, economies of scope or consumer benefits may not exist for the cross-selling of insurance products other than auto and home insurance.

13. It is ironic that the regulators view this as a way of undercapitalizing their Florida subsidiaries, and the state has prohibited new formation of these state-specific companies. This is likely because the state regulators desire to use the surplus of the entire company (rather than just the subsidiary) in pricing homeowners' insurance in Florida.

14. Owners of a failed insurer lose the value of their equity holdings in the company. However, their personal assets are not at risk to cover any deficits (negative surplus) of the failed company. Hence, owners of incorporated or limited liability insurers can gain the upside of any bets on the market, but they do not pay the full cost of the downsides of such bets. Also, owners can extract value from insurers they own through dividends or other means, which reduces the amount of equity bound in the company should it fail. This strategy can be particularly attractive in underwriting property insurance in catastrophe-prone areas because profits can be relatively high in storm-free years, which have tended to be more frequent than years in which hurricanes have caused heavy losses.

15. In 2006, companies rated in the B range represented 49 percent of the policies written, while companies with any type of A rating had approximately 26 percent of the market. This leaves the C and unrated companies with approximately 25 percent of the market. Also see chapter 2 and Klein (2007) for a more detailed discussion of regulatory conflicts of interest in adequately overseeing the financial condition and risk of insurance companies writing home insurance in hurricane prone states.

16. See, for example, Cummins and Weiss (2000).

17. As Willig (1976) has shown, this form, with constant marginal utility of income, is appropriate for demand modeling when the good in question does not absorb a significant fraction of the homeowner's budget, a reasonable assumption in the case of insurance (the typical homeowners' insurance premium is around $300 to $500 and somewhat higher in catastrophe-prone areas). This is not to say, of course, that there are no income effects to consumers, only that the marginal utility of income for each consumer is assumed constant over the range of policy options offered.

18. Note that we do not consider the effects of taxes in this model. See Myers and Cohn (1987) and Cummins (1990). For a more detailed discussion of price in the insurance context, see also Cummins, Weiss, and Zi (1998) for a related empirical study of price and profitability using frontier efficiency methods.

19. Grace et al. (2004).

20. The R^2 represents the degree to which the model explains the data; an R^2 close to zero implies no explanatory power. If R^2 is 1, the model fits the data perfectly.

21. Currently, we do not have a method of determining indicated loss costs for Texas. ISO, until quite recently, did not provide indicated loss costs for Texas. Thus, we have no base loss costs or a methodology to calculate the estimated loss costs. The difference in contracts employed in the analysis is due to the fact that we could not initially estimate indicated loss costs for all contracts. For example, ISO relativities are specific to a given deductible of, say, $500 or $1,000. If the deductible is $750, there may not be relativity for a $750 deductible in the manual. We would then interpolate the result in order to obtain a "cost relativity" for the contract. We interpolated missing information and estimated the indicated loss costs (ILCs) for all contracts except for Texas, for which we had no information regarding ILCs. We have undertaken some simple tests to determine if there is any systematic bias in the set of contracts we employ in this analysis and did not discern appreciable differences. Also, the ILC contains both catastrophic- and noncatastrophic-indicated loss costs in a total indicated loss cost calculation.

22. It is our impression, based on anecdotal information (see chapter 2), that rates in South Carolina and New York have been closer to "adequate" levels than in Florida. This is partly due to the lower level of risk in these other states as well as indicated by fewer and smaller disputes between insurers and regulators over the rates that insurers are allowed to charge.

23. See chapter 4 for a discussion of deductibles on flood insurance policies in Florida.

24. Kunreuther and Pauly (2006a).

Chapter 11

1. The federal poverty line within the forty-eight contiguous states is $9,800 per year for a single person and increases by $3,400 for each additional person in the household.

2. Perhaps the few homes with mortgages but without insurance are ones in which the principal of the mortgage has fallen so low that the lender's interest is less than the salvage value of the property, and so the lender is less strict in requiring insurance.

3. Bundorf and Pauly (2006).

4. U.S. Department of Housing and Urban Development, "Affordable Housing," http://www.hud.gov/offices/cpd/affordablehousing/index.cfm as of December 7, 2007.

5. For more details on this concept of affordability see Congressional Budget Office, Future Investment in Drinking Water and Wastewater Infrastructure, November 2002, Appendix C.

Chapter 12

1. For further discussion and recommendations as to ways to reduce future disaster losses through mitigation, see Financial Services Roundtable (2007).

2. For more details on these and other measures, see Laska (1991).

3. U.S. National Institute of Building Science (2005).

4. U.S. National Institute of Building Science (2005, vol. 1, p. 7).

5. International Code Council (2006). http://www.iccsafe.org/government/adoption.html, as of December 2008.

6. U.S. Government Accountability Office (2007c).

7. Insurance Services Office, Inc. Building Code Effectiveness Classifications http://www.iso.com/products/2400/prod2409.html as of September 2007.

8. Insurance Services Office (2006). ISO's Building Code Effectiveness Grading Schedule http://www.isomitigation.com/bcegs/0000/bcegs0001.html.

9. U.S. Government Accountability Office (2007c, pp. 39–40).

10. U.S. Government Accountability Office (2007c, p. 38).

11. More recent building codes were established in 2004 and again in 2007. See www.FloridaBuilding.org.

12. Institute for Business and Home Safety (2007).

13. Citizens Property Insurance Corporation (2006); State Farm Florida Insurance Company, Homeowners: FPL-10.509, 8/15/2006; First Floridian Auto and Home Insurance Company (Travelers of Florida), Filing 06-05323: Homeowners Premium Section, Rev 4/23/2006; Allstate Floridian Insurance Company, Homeowners Manual, 4/22/2002.

14. This section is based on Kunreuther (2006). Portions of this chapter are reprinted from Kunreuther, Meyer, and Michel-Kerjan (2007).

15. A discussion of alternative flood reduction measures can be found in Laska (1991) and Federal Emergency Management Agency (1998).

16. Kunreuther et al. (1978).

17. Thaler (1999).

18. Kunreuther, Onculer, and Slovic (1998).

19. Lowenstein and Prelec (1991).

20. Tversky and Shafir (1992).

21. Magat, Viscusi, and Huber (1987), Camerer and Kunreuther (1989).

22. Hogarth and Kunreuther (1995).

23. Oberholzer-Gee (1998).

24. Kunreuther and Pauly (2005).

25. Brinkley (2006).

26. Meyer (2006).

27. Meyer (2006).

28. Kunreuther (1996).

29. Kunreuther et al. (1978).

30. Palm, Hodgson, Blanchard, and Lyons (1990); Burby, Bollens, Kaiser, Mullan, and Sheaffer (1988); Laska (1991).

31. Goodnough (2006).

32. Michel-Kerjan (2008).

33. Personal communication.

34. U.S. Government Accountability Office (2007c).

35. In Auerswald et al. (2006), we analyze in great detail this same mitigation challenge but in the case of protection of critical infrastructure services (electricity, transportation, telecommunications, defense, health systems, banking and finance, etc).

36. A more detailed description of the two examples in this appendix can be found on FEMA's Web site, http://www.fema.gov/plan/prevent/bestpractices/kat_fl.shtm.

Chapter 13

1. By definition, the average annual loss (AAL) is the sum over all possible events of the expected losses associated with each of these individual events in a given state or postal zone and for a given year.

2. Bushouse (2007). This figure is consistent with other estimates; see, for instance, Holborn (2007).

3. For the features of the "Fortified..." program, see http://www.ibhs.org/publications/downloads/20071106 _084937_30401.pdf.

4. See chapter 8 for a more detailed discussion of these insurance-linked securities.

5. Insurance Information Institute (2007).

6. We thank Jack Nicholson, the Chief Operating Officer of the Florida Hurricane Catastrophe Fund, for many insightful discussions on the operation of the fund.

7. In 2007, no insurers selected this coverage.

8. More details can be found at http://www.sbafla.com/fhcf/ as of December 2007.

9. We thank Jim Oliver and Jim Murphy of the Texas Windstorm Insurance Association for discussions we had on the nature of the association's operations.

10. If a company's potential tax credit were greater than its tax liability, it could carry over the additional credit to future years. In this case, a company with a small tax liability or a large assessment (or both) might require significantly more than five years to fully recoup its assessment. Under no circumstance would a company be able to recoup its assessment in less than five years, as the maximum annual credit is 20 percent of the assessment.

11. The actual figure, including commercial coverage, would be higher.

12. Personal correspondence with Jack Nicholson, January 12, 2009.

13. We are assuming that because these measures are incorporated in building codes they are cost-effective. In other words, the discounted long-term expected benefits from the mitigation measure over the projected life of the house is greater than its upfront costs. By obtaining detailed cost estimates for specific mitigation measures incorporated in building codes or Florida's *Fortified...for Safer Living* program, one could rank their relative cost-effectiveness.

14. State Farm, which groups its companies differently, is the exception. See note 15 for a full explanation of how we handled this special case.

15. State Farm is a parent company that has an atypical structure in that it divides its subunits by line of business. Other companies do not separate their surpluses at all or they do it based on state-level companies, which still handle all of the different types of insurance. The A.M. Best data gave the total surpluses for entire conglomerate companies. Typically this entire surplus is available for property insurance since the companies are not separate entities. However, State Farm separates property insurance so its A.M. Best figure is too high. In order to rectify

this, we used the sum of the surpluses for State Farm's property insurance subsidiaries: State Farm Fire and Casualty: $8.95 billion; State Farm General (California): $1.85 billion; State Farm Florida: $0.72 billion; Texas Lloyds: $1.29 billion; Total: $12.81 billion.

16. Doherty (2000).

17. For more details on this point, see chapter 6 (section 6.4).

Chapter 14

1. See Kunreuther (2007c) for more details as to why we need these principles for developing new approaches for dealing with disasters. http://opim.wharton.upenn.edu/risk/library/oped_NYT2007%2708%2725.pdf.

2. More details can be found at http://www.frac.org/html/federal_food_programs/programs/fsp.html.

3. See U.S. Department of Agriculture FY 2006 Budget Summary and Annual Performance Plan. http://www.usda.gov/documents/FY07budsum.pdf.

4. Food Research and Action Center, http://www.frac.org/data/FSPparticipation/2007_06.pdf.

5. For instance, at the end of August 2007, Secretary of Health and Human Services Mike Leavitt announced that $50 million in emergency energy assistance would be given to twelve states that experienced much hotter temperatures than normal during the summer.

6. See U.S. Department of Health and Human Services at http://www.acf.hhs.gov/programs/liheap.

7. For more details on this program, see http://www.usac.org/about/universal-service as of September 2007.

8. We thank Genio Staranczak for insightful comments on the operation of the fund.

9. This section is based on Kunreuther (2007a, 2008) and Jaffee, Kunreuther, and Michel-Kerjan (2008).

10. The Philadelphia Contributionship and other insurance companies selling perpetual policies require a large fixed payment at the time of insurance purchase. The interest earned on this "insurance investment" covers the annual premiums on the property. We thank Felix Kloman for calling attention to this type of long-term insurance relationship. Kloman has favored long-term commitments and partnerships between the insurer and insured for many years, having written columns on the topic in his publication, *Risk Management Reports*, in September 1994 and October 1995.

11. Kunreuther (2006).

12. See http://www.rivkinradler.com/rivkinradler/Publications/newformat/200302weissman.shtml for additional details on these two contractual arrangements. For a fuller discussion of the defeasance option, see Dierker, Quan, and Torous (2005).

13. Failure to require this condition has created major problems for subprime mortgages.

14. A related question is whether long-term contracts are immune to renegotiation when there are changes in the level of the perceived risks. What protection does the insurance and reinsurance industry have if one discovers that the dikes in New Orleans are not built to specification and companies have a large book of business in the area with rates fixed for the next ten years? We appreciate Paul Kleindorfer raising this point (personal communication, November 21, 2007).

15. This section draws on Kunreuther (2007b).

16. Freeman and Scott (2005).

17. Michel-Kerjan and de Marcellis-Warin (2006).

18. Towers Perrin (2005).

19. This section is based on Fishman (2007a). The basic concepts also appeared in Fishman (2007b). Jay Fishman is CEO of Travelers Companies. For further details on this proposal, see www.coastalplan.com.

20. More details on the National Catastrophe Fund can be found at http://www.protectingamerica.org/pdf/WhitePaper_US.pdf, as of September 2007.

21. Cummins, Lewis, and Phillips (1999).

References

"Allstate Considers More Cancellations." (2006). *Tampa Tribune*, May 19.

Allstate Floridian Insurance Company. (2002). *Homeowners Manual*, 4/22/2002.

A.M. Best. (2006). *Methodology: Catastrophe Analysis in A.M. Best Rating*. A.M. Best, April. Oldwick, NJ.

American Re. (2002). *Topics: Annual Review of North American Natural Catastrophes 2001*. American Re. Princeton, NJ.

Anderson, D. R. (1974). "The National Flood Insurance Program: Problems and Potential." *Journal of Risk and Insurance* 41: 579–599.

Association of British Insurers. (2005). "Financial Risks of Climate Change." Association of British Insurers. London.

Auerswald, P., L. Branscomb, T. LaPorte, and E. Michel-Kerjan. (2006). *Seeds of Disaster, Roots of Response. How Private Action Can Reduce Public Vulnerability*. New York: Cambridge University Press.

Barrieu, P., and N. El Karoui. (2002). "Reinsuring Climatic Risk Using Optimally Designed Weather Bonds." *Geneva Papers Risk and Insurance Theory* 27: 87–113.

Barrieu, P., and H. Loubergé. (forthcoming). "Hybrid Cat-Bonds." *Journal of Risk and Insurance*.

Bartlett, D., R. W. Klein, and D. Russell. (1999). "Attempts to Socialize Costs in Voluntary Insurance Markets: The Historical Record." *Journal of Insurance Regulation* 17: 478–511.

Bell, D. (1982). "Regret in Decision Making Under Uncertainty." *Operations Research* 30: 961–981.

Bell, D. (1985). "Disappointment in Decision Making Under Uncertainty." *Operations Research* 33: 1–27.

Benfield Group. (2007). "Global Reinsurance Market Review." Benfield Group, January. London.

Bernstein, P. (1996). *Against the Gods: The Remarkable Story of Risk*. New York: John Wiley and Sons.

Best's Review. (2006) "High Water Mark: Privatizing Flood." July 1.

BestWire. (2009). "Florida Panel Suggests Rate Increase for State-Run Homeowners Insurer." January 7.

Borch, K. (1962). "Equilibrium in a Reinsurance Market." *Econometrica* 30: 424–444.

Bramley, G. (1991). *Bridging the Affordability Gap in 1990*. Birmingham, England: BEC Publications.

Braun, M., and A. Muermann. (2004). "The Impact of Regret on the Demand for Insurance." *Journal of Risk and Insurance* 71: 737–767.

Brinkley, D. (2006). *The Great Deluge: Hurricane Katrina, New Orleans, and the Mississippi Gulf Coast*. New York: HarperCollins.

British Bankers Association. (2006). *BBA Credit Derivatives Report 2006*. London: BBA Enterprises.

Buchanan, J. (1975). "The Samaritan's Dilemma." In *Altruism, Morality and Economic Theory*, edited by E. Phelps. New York: Russell Sage Foundation, 71–85.

Buente versus Allstate. (2006). U.S. District Court, Southern District of Mississippi. Civil action No. 1:05CV712 LTS-JMR L.T. April 11.

Bundorf, M. K., and M. V. Pauly. (2006). "Is Health Insurance Affordable for the Uninsured?" *Journal of Health Economics* 25: 650–673.

Burby, R. (2006). "Hurricane Katrina and the Paradoxes of Government Disaster Policy: Bringing About Wise Governmental Decisions for Hazardous Areas." *Annals of the American Academy of Political and Social Science* 604: 171–191.

Burby, R. J., S. Bollens, E. J. Kaiser, D. Mullan, and J. R. Sheaffer. (1988). *Cities under Water: A Comparative Evaluation of Ten Cities' Efforts to Manage Floodplain Land Use.* Boulder, CO.: Institute of Behavioral Science, University of Colorado.

Burby, R. J., B. A. Cigler, S. P. French, E. J. Kaiser, J. Kartez, D. Roenigk, D. Weist, and D. Whittington. (1991). *Sharing Environmental Risks: How to Control Governments' Losses in Natural Disasters.* Boulder, Colo.: Westview.

Bushouse, K. (2007). "Citizens' Growth Called Risky: All Floridians Could Pay If Major Storm Hits." *Fort Lauderdale Sun-Sentinel*, May 13.

Butt, M. (2007). "Insurance, Finance, Solvency II and Financial Market Interaction." *Geneva Papers on Risk and Insurance* 32: 42–45.

Cabantous, L. (2007). "Ambiguity Aversion in the Field of Insurance: Insurers' Attitude to Imprecise and Conflicting Probability Estimates." *Theory and Decision* 62: 219–235.

Camerer, C., and H. Kunreuther. (1989). "Decision Processes for Low Probability Events: Policy Implications." *Journal of Policy Analysis and Management* 8: 565–592.

"Catastrophe Bonds: Ports and Storms." (2007). *Economist*, August 4–10, 64.

Center for Sustainable Communities. (2006). *Pennypack Creek Watershed Study.* Center for Sustainable Communities, Temple University. Philadelphia, PA.

Chan, J. (2006). "Comment on 'Changes in Tropical Cyclone Number, Duration, and Intensity in a Warming Environment.'" *Science* March 24, 1713.

Citizens Property Insurance Corporation. (2006). *Homeowners Policy Program Manual General Rules*, Ed. 4/01/2006.

Coate, S. (1995). "Altruism, the Samaritan's Dilemma, and Government Transfer Policy." *American Economic Review* 85: 46–57.

Cohen, L., and R. Noll. (1981). "The Economics of Building Codes to Resist Seismic Shocks." *Public Policy* (Winter): 1–29.

Congressional Budget Office. (2002). Future Investment in Drinking Water and Wastewater Infrastructure, November 2002, Appendix C. http://www.cbo.gov/ftpdocs/39xx/doc3983/11-18-watersystems.pdf.

Congressional Budget Office. (2007). *Value of Properties in the National Flood Insurance Program.* Washington, D.C.: CBO.

Congressional Research Service. (2005). "Federal Stafford Act Disaster Assistance: Presidential Declarations, Eligible Activities, and Funding." Washington, D.C.: Congressional Research Service, Library of Congress.

Council of Economic Advisors. (2007). *The Economic Report of the President.* Washington, D.C.: Council of Economic Advisors.

Criss, R. E., and E. L. Shock. (2001). "Flood Enhancement Through Flood Control." *Geology* 29: 875–878.

Crossett, K. M., T. J. Culliton, P. C. Wiley, and T. R. Goodspeed. (2004). *Population Trends Along the Coastal United States: 1980–2008.* Silver Spring, Md.: National Oceanic and Atmospheric Administration.

Crowell, M., S. Edelman, K. Coulton, and S. McAfee. (2007). "How Many People Live in Coastal Areas?" *Journal of Coastal Research* 23 (5): iii–vi.

Csiszar, E. (2007). "An Update on the Use of Modern Financial Instruments in the Insurance Sector." *Geneva Papers on Risk and Insurance* 32: 319–331.

Cummins, J. D. (1990). "Multi-Period Discounted Cash Flow Rate-Making Models in Property-Liability Insurance." *Journal of Risk and Insurance* 57: 79–109.

Cummins, J. D., C. Lewis, and R. Phillip. (1999). "Pricing Excess-of-Loss Reinsurance Contracts against Catastrophe Loss." In *The Financing of Catastrophe Risk*, edited by K. Froot. Chicago: University of Chicago Press.

Cummins, J. D., and M. A. Weiss. (2000). "Analyzing Firm Performance in the Insurance Industry Using Frontier Efficiency and Productivity Methods." In *Insurance Handbook*, edited by G. Dionne. Boston: Kluwer.

Cummins, J. D., M. A. Weiss, and H. Zi. (1998). "Organizational Form and Efficiency: An Analysis of Stock and Mutual Property-Liability Insurers." Working papers 98–19, Federal Reserve Bank of Philadelphia.

Cutler, D. M., and R. J. Zeckhauser. (2004). *Extending the Theory to Meet the Practice of Insurance.* Washington, D.C.: Brookings Institute.

Dacy, D., and H. Kunreuther. (1968). *The Economics of Natural Disasters.* New York: Free Press.

De Mey, J. (2007). "Insurance and the Capital Markets." *Geneva Papers on Risk and Insurance* 32: 35–41.

Dierker, M., D. Quan, and W. Torous. (2005). "Pricing the Defeasance Option in Securitized Commercial Mortgages." *Real Estate Economics* 33: 663–680.

Dionne, G., N. Doherty, and N. Fombaron. (2000). "Adverse Selection in Insurance Markets." In *Handbook of Insurance*, edited by G. Dionne. Boston: Kluwer.

Dischel, R. (2002). *Climate Risk and the Weather Market: Financial Risk Management with Weather Hedges.* London: Risk Books.

Dixon, L., N. Clancy, S. A. Seabury, and A. Overton. (2006). *The National Flood Insurance Program's Market Penetration Rate: Estimates and Policy Implications.* Santa Monica, CA: RAND.

Doherty, N. (2000). *Integrated Risk Management.* New York: McGraw-Hill.

Doherty, N., and L. L. Posey. (1997). "Availability Crises in Insurance Markets: Optimal Contracts with Asymmetric Information and Capacity Constraints." *Journal of Risk and Uncertainty* 15: 55–80.

Dowling, V. J. (2006a). *IBRN Weekly*, August 28.

Dowling, V. J. (2006b). *IBRN Weekly*, October 2.

Eldred, G. W. (1980). "How Wisely Do Consumers Select Their Property and Liability Insurance Coverages?" *Journal of Consumer Affairs* 14: 288–306.

Ellsberg, D. (1961) "Risk, Ambiguity, and the Savage Axioms." *Quarterly Journal of Economics* 75: 643–669.

Emanuel, K. (2005). Increasing destructiveness of tropical cyclones over the past 30 years. *Nature* 436: 686–688.

Federal Emergency Management Agency. (1998). "Retrofitting: Six Ways to Prevent Your Home from Flooding." Washington, D.C.: Federal Emergency Management Agency, June.

Federal Emergency Management Agency. (2002a). "Community Wind Shelters, Background and Research." Washington, D.C.: Federal Emergency Management Agency, August.

Federal Emergency Management Agency. (2002b). "National Flood Insurance Program: Program Description." Washington, D.C.: Federal Emergency Management Agency.

Feldblum, S. (1990). "Risk Loads for Insurers." *Proceedings of the Casualty Actuarial Society* 77: 160–195.

Financial Services Roundtable. (2007). *Blue Ribbon Commission on Mega-Catastrophes Comprehensive Report.* Financial Services Roundtable. Washington, D.C.

Finucane, M. L., A. Alhakami, P. Slovic, and S. M. Johnson. (2001). "The Affect Heuristic in Judgments of Risks and Benefits." *Journal of Behavioral Decision Making* 13 (1): 1–17.

First Floridian Auto and Home Insurance Company (Travelers of Florida). *Filing 06-05323: Homeowners Premium Section*, Rev 4/23/2006.

Fishman, J. (2007a). "'Something's Gotta Give': A Private Market-Based Hurricane Wind Concept." Paper presented at the American Risk and Insurance Association Annual Meeting, Quebec City, Canada, August 6.

Fishman, J. (2007b). "Before the Next 'Big One' Hits." *Wall Street Journal*, August 27.

"Fla. Subpoenas State Farm over Nonrenewal Plans." *National Underwriter*, August 7, 2007.

Fleckenstein, M. (2006). "Rating Agency Recalibrations." In *The Review Cedant's Guide to Renewals 2006*, edited by G. Dobie. Informa UK Limited.

Florida Hurricane Catastrophe Fund. (2007). *Fiscal Year 2005–2006 Annual Report.* Tallahassee, Fla.: Florida Hurricane Catastrophe Fund.

Francis, T. (2005). "CEO Says Allstate Adjusts Storm Plan: Interview of Edward Liddy." *Wall Street Journal*, September 5, C1–C3.

Freeman, P., and K. Scott. (2005). "Comparative Analysis of Large Scale Catastrophe Compensation Schemes." In *Catastrophic Risks and Insurance*. Paris: Organization for Economic Cooperation and Development. July. OECD Publishing.

Froot, K. (1999). *The Financing of Catastrophe Risk*. Chicago: University of Chicago Press.

Froot, K., and P. O'Connell. (1999). "The Pricing of U.S. Catastrophe Reinsurance." In *The Financing of Catastrophe Risk*, edited by K. Froot. Chicago: University of Chicago Press, 195–232.

Gal-or, E. (1983). "Quality and Quantity Competition." *Bell Journal of Economics* 14: 590–600.

Gerdes, V. (1963). "Insuring against Flood Peril." *Journal of Insurance* 30: 547–553.

Gladwell, M. (2000). *The Tipping Point*. New York: Little, Brown.

Godard, O., C. Henry, P. Lagadec, and E. Michel-Kerjan. (2002). *Traité des nouveaux risques* (Treatise on New Risks), Folio Inédit 100. Paris: Gallimard.

Goldenberg, S. B., C. W. Landsea, A. M. Mestas-Nunez, and W. M. Gray. (2001). "The Recent Increase in Atlantic Hurricane Activity: Causes and Implications." *Science* 293: 474.

Goodnough, A. (2006). "As Hurricane Season Looms, State Aim to Scare." *New York Times*, May 31.

Grace, M. F., and R. W. Klein. (2006). "After the Storms: Property Insurance Markets in Florida, Center for Risk Management and Insurance." Working paper, Georgia State University.

Grace, M. F., and R. W. Klein. (2007). "Hurricane Risk and Property Insurance Markets." Working paper, Georgia State University, December.

Grace, M. F., R. W. Klein, and P. R. Kleindorfer. (2004). "Homeowners Insurance with Bundled Catastrophe Coverage." *Journal of Risk and Insurance* 71: 351–379.

Grace, M. F., R. W. Klein, P. R. Kleindorfer, and M. Murray. (2004). *Catastrophe Insurance: Supply, Demand and Regulation*. Boston: Kluwer.

Grace, M. F., R. W. Klein, and Z. Liu. (2005). "Increased Hurricane Risk and Insurance Market Responses." *Journal of Insurance Regulation* 24: 2–32.

Grace, M. F., R. W. Klein, and Z. Liu. (2006). "Mother Nature on the Rampage: Implications for Insurance Markets." Paper presented at the National Bureau of Economic Research, February 20.

Gron, A. (1994). "Capacity Constraints and Cycles in Property-Casualty Insurance Markets." *Rand Journal of Economics* 25: 110–127.

Grossi, P., and H. Kunreuther, eds. (2005). *Catastrophe Modeling: A New Approach to Managing Risk*. New York: Springer.

Grossi, P., and R. Muir-Wood. (2008). "The Allocation of Reinsurance Costs for U.S. Catastrophe Insurance Rating." Risk Management Solutions.

Grossman, D. A. (1958). "Flood Insurance: Can a Feasible Program Be Created?" *Land Economics* 34: 352–357.

Guy Carpenter. (2006). *The World Catastrophe Reinsurance Market*. New York: Guy Carpenter and Company, LLC.

Guy Carpenter. (2007a). "U.S. Reinsurance Renewals at January 1, 2007." New York: Guy Carpenter and Company, LLC.

Guy Carpenter. (2007b). "The World Catastrophe Reinsurance Market: New Capital Stabilizes Market." New York: Guy Carpenter and Company, LLC., September. New York.

Guy Carpenter. (2008). "2008 Reinsurance Market Review: Near Misses Call for Caution." Guy Carpenter and Company, LLC.

Guy Carpenter. (2009). "Catastrophe Losses, Credit Crisis Push Reinsurance Pricing Upwards, According to Guy Carpenter Review." New York: Guy Carpenter and Company, LLC, January 5.

Harrington, S. E., and G. Niehaus. (2001). "Government Insurance, Tax Policy, and the Affordability and Availability of Catastrophe Insurance." *Journal of Insurance Regulation* 19: 591–612.

Hartwig, R., and C. Wilkinson. (2007). "An Overview of the Alternative Risk Transfer Market." In *Handbook of International Insurance: Between Global Dynamics and Local Contingencies*, edited by D. Cummins and B. Venard. New York: Springer.

Hayes, T. L., D. R. Spafford, and J. P. Boone. (2006). *Actuarial Rate Review.* Washington, D.C.: Federal Emergency Management Agency.

Heal, G., and H. Kunreuther. (2005). "You Can Only Die Once: Interdependent Security in an Uncertain World." In *The Economic Impacts of Terrorist Attacks,* edited by H. W. Richardson, P. Gordon, and J. E. Moore II. Cheltenham, U.K.: Edward Elgar.

Henriet, D., and E. Michel-Kerjan. (2008). "Looking at Optimal Risk-Sharing in a Kaleidoscope: The (Market Power, Information) Rotational Symmetry." Working paper, Wharton Risk Management and Decision Processes Center, The Wharton School, University of Pennsylvania, Philadelphia.

Hogarth, R., and H. Kunreuther. (1995). "Decision Making under Ignorance: Arguing with Yourself." *Journal of Risk and Uncertainty* 10: 15–36.

Holborn. (2007). "Florida 2007 Update: Law Changes and Market Responses." Holborn Corporation, June 1. New York.

Höppe, P., and R. Pielke, eds. (2006). *Report of the Workshop on Climate Change and Disaster Losses,* May 25–26, Hohenkammer, Germany. October.

Hoyos, C., P. A. Agudelo, P. J. Webster, and J. A. Curry. (2006). "Deconvolution of the Factors Contributing to the Increase in Global Hurricane Intensity." *Science* 312: 94–97, April 7.

Hsee, C. K., and H. Kunreuther. (2000). "The Affection Effect in Insurance Decisions." *Journal of Risk and Uncertainty* 20: 149–59.

Huber, O., R. Wider, and O. Huber. (1997). "Active Information Search and Complete Information Presentation in Naturalistic Risky Decision Tasks." *Acta Psychologica* 95: 5–29.

In re Katrina Canal Breaches Consolidated Litigation. (2006). No. 05-182 (E.D. La.).

Institute for Business and Home Safety. (2007). "The Benefits of Modern Wind Resistant Building Codes on Hurricane Claim Frequency and Severity—A Summary Report." Institute for Business and Home Safety. Tampa, FL.

Insurance Information Institute. (2007). "Issues Update: Residual Markets." Insurance Information Institute, August. New York, NY.

Insurance Journal. (2006). "S&P to Implement New Way to Assess Insurer Cat Risk." March 31.

Insurance Research Council and Insurance Institute of Property Loss Reduction. (1995). *Coastal Exposure and Community Protection: Hurricane Andrew's Legacy.* Wheaton, Ill.: IRC, and Boston: IIPLR.

Insurance Services Office. (2006). ISO's Building Code Effectiveness Grading Schedule http://www.isomitigation .com/bcegs/0000/bcegs0001.html.

Intergovernmental Panel on Climate Change. (2007). *Climate Change 2007,* Intergovernmental Panel on Climate Change, January. Geneva, Switzerland.

International Code Council. (2006). http://www.iccsafe.org/government/adoption.html, as of September 2007.

Jaffee, D., H. Kunreuther, and E. Michel-Kerjan. (2008). "Long Term Insurance (LTI) for Addressing Catastrophe Risk." Working paper #14210, U.S. National Bureau of Economic Research, Cambridge, MA.

Jenkins, W. O. (2005). "Federal Emergency Management Agency: Challenges Facing the National Flood Insurance Program," GAO-06-174T. U.S. Government Accountability Office, Washington, DC.

Kahneman, D., and A. Tversky. (1979). "Prospect Theory: An Analysis of Decision under Risk." *Econometrica* 47: 263–291.

King, R. O. (2006). "National Flood Insurance Program: Treasury Borrowing in the Aftermath of Hurricane Katrina (Order Code RS22394)." Washington, D.C.: Congressional Research Service.

Klein, R. W. (1995). "Insurance Regulation in Transition." *Journal of Risk and Insurance* 62: 363–404.

Klein, R. W. (1998). "Regulating Catastrophe Insurance: Issues and Options." In *Earthquake Insurance: Public Policy Perspectives from the Western United States Earthquake Insurance Summit,* Western States Seismic Policy Council, pp. 105–124.

Klein, R. W. (2007). "Catastrophe Risk and the Regulation of Property Insurance: A Comparative Analysis of Five States." Working paper, Georgia State University, December.

Klein, R. W., and P. R. Kleindorfer. (2003). "Regulation and Markets for Catastrophe Insurance." In *Advances in Economic Design,* edited by Murat R. Sertel and Semih Koray. Berlin: Springer-Verlag.

Klein, R. W., R. D. Phillips, and W. Shiu. (2002). "The Capital Structure of Firms Subject to Price Regulation: Evidence from the Insurance Industry." *Journal of Financial Services Research* 21: 79–100.

Klein, R. W., and S. Wang. (2007) "Catastrophe Risk Financing in the United States and the European Union: A Comparison of Alternative Regulatory Approaches." Paper presented at the New Forms of Risk Sharing and Risk Engineering: A SCOR-JRI Conference on Insurance, Reinsurance, and Capital Market Transformations, Paris, September 20–21.

Kossin, J. P., J. R. Knapp, D. L. Vimont, R. J. Murnane, and B. A. Harper. (2007). "A Globally Consistent Reanalysis of Hurricane Variability and Trends." *Geophysical Research Letters*, Vol. 34. L04815.

Kousky, C., and R. Zeckhauser. (2006). "JARring Actions that Fuel the Floods." In *On Risk and Disaster: Lessons from Hurricane Katrina*, edited by R. J. Daniels, D. F. Kettl, and H. Kunreuther. Philadelphia: University of Pennsylvania Press.

Kozlowski, R. T., and S. B. Mathewson. (1995). "Measuring and Managing Catastrophe Risk." 1995 discussion papers on Dynamic Financial Analysis, Casualty Actuarial Society, Arlington, Virginia.

Krantz, D. H., and H. Kunreuther. (2007). "Goals and Plans in Decision Making." *Judgment and Decision Making* 2: 137–168.

Kreps, R. (1990). "Reinsurer Risk Loads from Marginal Surplus Requirements." *Proceedings of the Casualty Actuarial Society* 77: 196–203.

Kriesel, W., and C. Landry. (2004). "Participation in the NFIP: An Empirical Analysis for Coastal Properties." *Journal of Risk and Insurance* 71: 405–420.

Kunreuther, H. (1968). "The Case for Comprehensive Disaster Insurance." *Journal of Law and Economics* 11: 133–163.

Kunreuther, H. (1979). "The Changing Societal Consequences of Risks from Natural Hazards." *Annals of the American Academy of Political and Social Science* 443: 104–116.

Kunreuther, H. (1996). "Mitigating Disaster Losses through Insurance." *Journal of Risk and Uncertainty* 12: 71–187.

Kunreuther, H. (1998). "The Role of Insurance in Dealing with Catastrophe Risks from Natural Disasters." In *Alternative Approaches to Insurance Regulation*, edited by R. W. Klein. Kansas City: National Association of Insurance Commissioners.

Kunreuther, H. (2006). "Disaster Mitigation and Insurance: Learning from Katrina." *Annals of the American Academy of Political and Social Science* 604: 208–227.

Kunreuther, H. (2007a). "Challenges for the U.S. and Asia." In *Asian Catastrophe Insurance*, edited by C. Scawthorn and K. Kobayashi. London: Incisive Media, Ltd.

Kunreuther, H. (2007b). "Reflections on U.S. Disaster Insurance Policy for the 21st Century." In *Risking House and Home: Disasters, Cities, Public Policy*, edited by J. Quigley and L. Rosenthal. Berkeley, CA.: Berkeley Public Policy Press.

Kunreuther, H. (2007c). "Who Will Pay for the Next Hurricane?" *New York Times*, August 25.

Kunreuther, H. (2008). "Reducing Losses From Catastrophic Risks Through Long-Term Insurance and Mitigation." *Social Research*, "Disasters: Recipes and Remedies." 75:3.

Kunreuther, H., R. Ginsberg, L. Miller, P. Sagi, P. Slovic, B. Borkan, and N. Katz. (1978). *Disaster Insurance Protection: Public Policy Lessons.* New York: Wiley.

Kunreuther, H., J. Meszaros, R. Hogarth, and M. Spranca. (1995). "Ambiguity and Underwriter Decision Processes." *Journal of Economic Behaviour and Organization* 26: 337–352.

Kunreuther, H., R. J. Meyer, and E. Michel-Kerjan. (2007). "Strategies for Better Protection against Catastrophic Risks." Invited paper for the Conference on the Behavioral Foundations of Policy, Princeton University, October.

Kunreuther, H., and E. Michel-Kerjan. (2004). "Challenges for Terrorism Insurance in the United States." *Journal of Economic Perspectives* 18: 201–214.

Kunreuther, H., and E. Michel-Kerjan. (2007). "Climate Change, Insurability of Large-Scale Disasters and the Emerging Liability Challenge." *Penn Law Review* 155(6): 1795–1842.

Kunreuther, H., N. Novemsky, and D. Kahneman. (2001). "Making Low Probabilities Useful." *Journal of Risk and Uncertainty* 23: 103–120.

Kunreuther, H., A. Onculer, and P. Slovic. (1998). "Time Insensitivity for Protective Measures." *Journal of Risk and Uncertainty* 16: 279–299.

Kunreuther, H., and M. Pauly. (2004). "Neglecting Disaster: Why Don't People Insure against Large Losses?" *Journal of Risk and Uncertainty* 28: 5–21.

Kunreuther, H., and M. Pauly. (2005). "Terrorism Losses and All-Perils Insurance." *Journal of Insurance Regulation* 23: 3.

Kunreuther, H., and M. Pauly. (2006a). *Insurance Decision-Making and Market Behavior.* Boston: Now Publishers.

Kunreuther, H., and M. Pauly. (2006b). "Rules Rather Than Discretion: Lessons from Hurricane Katrina." *Journal of Risk and Uncertainty* 33: 101–116.

Kunreuther, H., and R. Roth, Sr. (1998). *Paying the Price: The Status and Role of Insurance against Natural Disasters in the United States.* Washington, D.C.: Joseph Henry Press.

Kunreuther, H., W. Sanderson, and R. Vetschera. (1985). "A Behavioral Model of the Adoption of Protective Activities." *Journal of Economic Behavior and Organization* 6: 1–15.

Kydland, F., and E. Prescott. (1977). "Rules Rather Than Discretion: The Inconsistency of Optimal Plans." *Journal of Political Economy* 85: 473–491.

Lalonde, D. (2005). "Risk Financing." In *Catastrophe Modeling: A New Approach to Managing Risk*, edited by P. Grossi and H. Kunreuther. New York: Springer.

Landsea, C. W., B. A. Harper, K. Hoarau, and J. A. Knaff. (2006). "Can We Detect Trends in Extreme Tropical Cyclones?" *Science* 313: 452–454.

Lane, M., ed. (2002). *Alternative Risk Strategies.* London: Risk Waters Group.

Lane, M. (2006). "How High Is Up? The 2006 Review of the Insurance Securitization Market." *Lane Financial*, April.

Laska, S. B. (1991). *Floodproof Retrofitting: Homeowner Self-Protective Behavior.* Boulder: Institute of Behavioral Science, University of Colorado.

Lecomte, E., and K. Gahagan. (1998). "Hurricane Insurance Protection in Florida." In *Paying the Price: The Status and Role of Insurance against Natural Disasters in the United States*, edited by H. Kunreuther and R. Roth, Sr. Washington, D.C.: Joseph Henry Press, 97–124.

Lerner, J., R. Gonzalez, D. Small, and B. Fischhoff. (2003). "Effects of Fear and Anger on Perceived Risks of Terrorism: A National Field Experiment." *Psychological Science* 14: 144–150.

Lewis, C., and L. Murdock. (1996). "The Role of Government Contracts in Discretionary Reinsurance Markets for Natural Disasters." *Journal of Risk and Insurance* 63: 567–597.

Lewis, M. (2007). "In Nature's Casino." *New York Times Magazine*, August 26.

Lockerbie Verdict. (2001). *Her Majesty's Advocate, v. Abdelbaset Ali Mohmed Al Megrahi and Al Amin Khalifa Fhimah*, Case No.: 1475/99. High Court of Justiciary at Camp Zeist—January 31.

Loomes, G., and R. Sugden. (1982). "Regret Theory: An Alternative Theory of Rational Choice under Uncertainty." *Economic Journal* 92 (368): 805–824.

Lowenstein, G., and D. Prelec. (1991). "Negative Time Preference." *American Economic Review* 81: 347–352.

Lowenstein, G. F., E. U. Weber, C. K. Hsee, and N. Welch. (2001). "Risk as Feelings." *Psychological Bulletin* 127: 267–286.

Magat, W., K. W. Viscusi, and J. Huber. (1987). "Risk-Dollar Tradeoffs, Risk Perceptions, and Consumer Behavior." In *Learning About Risk*, edited by W. Viscusi and W. Magat. Cambridge, Mass.: Harvard University Press, 83–97.

McClelland, G., W. Schulze, and D. Coursey. (1993). "Insurance for Low-Probability Hazards: A Bimodal Response to Unlikely Events." *Journal of Risk and Uncertainty* 7: 95–116.

Meaner, M., ed. (2006). *Pennypack Watershed Study.* Ambler, Pa.: Temple University, Center for Sustainable Communities, August.

Menzinger, I., and C. Brauner. (2002). "Floods Are Insurable!" Zurich: Swiss Reinsurance Company.

Meyer, R. J. (2006). "Why We Under-Prepare for Hazards." In *On Risk and Disaster: Lessons from Hurricane Katrina*, edited by R. J. Daniels, D. F. Kettl, and H. Kunreuther. Philadelphia: University of Pennsylvania Press, 153–174.

Michaels, P. (2006). "Is the Sky Really Falling? A Review of Recent Global Warming Scare Stories." Washington, D.C.: Cato Institute.

Michel-Kerjan, E. (2008). "Disasters and Public Policy: Can Market Lessons Help Address Government Failures." In *Proceedings of the 99th National Tax Association Conference*, Boston, MA.

Michel-Kerjan, E., and N. de Marcellis-Warin. (2006). "Public-Private Programs for Covering Extreme Events: The Impact of Information Distribution on Risk-Sharing." *Asia-Pacific Journal of Risk and Insurance* 1(2): 21–49.

Michel-Kerjan, E., and C. Kousky. (2008). "Come Rain or Shine: Evidence on Flood Insurance Purchases in Florida." Joint working paper, Wharton School of the University of Pennsylvania and Kennedy School of Government, Harvard University, March.

Michel-Kerjan, E., and F. Morlaye. (2008). "Extreme Events, Global Warming, and Insurance-Linked Securities: How to Trigger the 'Tipping Point.'" *Geneva Papers on Risk and Insurance* 33: 153–176.

Michel-Kerjan, E., and B. Pedell. (2006). "How Does the Corporate World Cope With Mega-Terrorism? Puzzling Evidence from Terrorism Insurance Markets." *Journal of Applied Corporate Finance* 18(4): 61–75.

Milliman. (2007). *Analysis of Florida Legislative Reform: Special Session, January 2007.* San Francisco, Calif.: Milliman, April 30.

Mills, E. (2005). "Insurance in a Climate of Change." *Science* 308: 1040–1044.

Mills, E., and E. Lecomte. (2006). "From Risk to Opportunity: How Insurers Can Proactively and Profitably Manage Climate Change." *Ceres*, August.

Morgenson, G. (2008). "Behind Insurer's Crisis, Blind Eye to a Web of Risk." *New York Times*, September 28, p. 1.

Moss, D. (2002). *When All Else Fails: Government as the Ultimate Risk Manager*, Cambridge, Mass.: Harvard University Press.

Moyer, L. (2006). "Hedge Funds' Sidecars." *Fortune*, July 27.

Munich Re. (2000). "Topics 2000: Natural Catastrophes—The Current Position." Special issue.

Munich Re. (2008). "Catastrophe Figures for 2008 Confirm That Climate Agreement Is Urgently Needed." December 29.

Myers, S., and R. Cohn. (1987). "A Discounted Cash Flow Approach to Property-Liability Insurance Rate Regulation." In *Fair Rate of Return in Property-Liability Insurance*, edited by D. Cummins and S. E. Harrington. Norwell, Mass.: Kluwer.

Myers, S., and N. Majluf. (1984). "Corporate Investment and Financing Decisions When Firms Have Information That Investors Do Not Have." *Journal of Financial Economics* 13: 187–222.

National Association of Insurance Commissioners (NAIC). (2007). *Profitability By Line By State in 2006.* Kansas City, MO: National Association of Insurance Commissioners.

"N.Y. Stops Insurers from Tie-Ins for Coastal Customers." (2007). *National Underwriter*, August 27.

Oberholzer-Gee, F. (1998). "Learning to Bear the Unbearable: Towards an Explanation of Risk Ignorance." Mimeo., Wharton School, University of Pennsylvania.

Overman, E. S. (1957). "The Flood Peril and the Federal Flood Insurance Act of 1956." *Annals of the American Academy of Political and Social Science* 309: 98–106.

Palm, R. (1981). *Real Estate Agents and Special Studies Zones Disclosure.* Boulder: Institute of Behavioral Science, University of Colorado.

Palm, R., M. Hodgson, R. D. Blanchard, and D. Lyons. (1990). *Earthquake Insurance in California: Environmental Policy and Individual Decision Making.* Boulder, CO.: Westview Press.

Pasterick, E. T. (1998). "The National Flood Insurance Program." In *Paying the Price: The Status and Role of Insurance Against Natural Disasters in the United States*, edited by H. Kunreuther and R. J. Roth, Sr. Washington, D.C.: Joseph Henry Press.

Pielke, R., Jr., C. W. Landsea, and K. Emanuel. (2005). *Nature* 438, 22–29.

Power, F. B., and E. W. Shows. (1979). "A Status Report on the National Flood Insurance Program, Mid 1978." *Journal of Risk and Insurance* 46: 61–76.

PricewaterhouseCoopers. (1999). *Study of the Economic Effects of Charging Actuarially Based Premium Rates for Pre-FIRM Structures.* PricewaterhouseCoopers, LLP.

Ramella, M., and L. Madeiros. (2007). "Bermuda Sidecars: Supervising Reinsurance Companies in Innovative Global Markets." *Geneva Papers on Risk and Insurance* 32: 345–363.

Reeves, A. (2004). "Plucking Votes from Disasters." *Los Angeles Times*, May 12.

Reeves, A. (2005). "Political Disaster? Electoral Politics and Presidential Disaster Declarations." Cambridge, MA: Kennedy School of Government, Harvard University.

Risk Management Solutions. (2007). "Hurricane Model Re-Certified by Florida Commission." Press release, June 25.

Roth, R. J. Jr. (1998). "Earthquake Insurance Protection in California." In *Paying the Price: The Status and Role of Insurance Against Natural Disasters in the United States*, edited by H. Kunreuther and R. Roth, Sr. Washington, D.C.: Joseph Henry Press, 67–95.

Rottenstreich, Y., and C. K. Hsee. (2001). "Money, Kisses, and Electric Shocks: On the Affective Psychology of Risk." *Psychological Science* 12: 185–190.

Schelling, T. (1978). *Micromotives and Macrobehavior.* New York: Norton.

Schoemaker, P., and H. Kunreuther. (1979). "An Experimental Study of Insurance Decisions." *Journal of Risk and Insurance* 46: 603–618.

Shafir, E., I. Simonson, and A. Tversky. (1993). "Reason-Based Choice." *Cognition* 49 (1–2): 11–36.

Silverman, R. (2005). "Insurers Introduce Flood Coverage Aimed at Costly Homes." *Wall Street Journal*, September 1.

Smith, A. (1966). *The Theory of Moral Sentiments* (1759). New York: Kelley.

South Carolina Department of Insurance. (2007). *Coastal Property Insurance Issues in South Carolina.* Columbia, SC: South Carolina Department of Insurance, January.

State Board of Administration of Florida. (2006). *A Study of Private Capital Investment Options and Capital Formation Impacting Florida's Residential Insurance Market.* State Board of Administration of Florida, September 19. Tallahassee, FL.

State Farm Florida Insurance Company. (2006). Homeowners: FPL-10.509, 8/15/2006.

Stern Review. (2006). *The Economics of Climate Change.* London: H. M. Treasury, December.

Stone, J. (1973). "A Theory of Capacity and the Insurance of Catastrophic Risks: Part I and Part II." *Journal of Risk and Insurance* 40: 231–243, 339–355.

Sunstein, C. (2003). "Terrorism and Probability Neglect." *Journal of Risk and Uncertainty* 26: 121–136.

Swiss Re. (2007a). "Natural Catastrophes and Man-Made Disasters in 2006." *Sigma*, no. 2.

Swiss Re. (2007b). "Insurance Linked Securities Market Update." August.

Swiss Re. (2008a). "Natural Catastrophes and Man-Made Disasters in 2007: High Losses in Europe." *Sigma*, no. 1.

Swiss Re. (2008b). Media release. December 18.

Sydnor, J. (2006). "Abundant Aversion to Moderate Risk: Evidence from Homeowners Insurance." Berkeley: University of California, Berkeley.

Thaler, R. (1999). "Mental Accounting Matters." *Journal of Behavioral Decision Making* 12: 183–206.

Thaler, R., and C. Sunstein. (2008). *Nudge: The Gentle Power of Choice Architecture.* New Haven, Conn.: Yale University Press.

Tobin, R., and C. Calfee. (2005). *The National Flood Insurance Program's Mandatory Purchase Requirement: Policies, Processes, and Stakeholders.* Washington, D.C.: American Institute for Research.

Towers Perrin. (2005). "Hurricane Katrina: Analysis of the Impact on the Insurance Industry." http://www.towersperrin.com/tillinghast/publications/reports/Hurricane_Katrina/katrina.pdf.

Treaster, J. (2007). "State Farm Ends New Property Coverage in Mississippi." *New York Times*, February 15.

Tversky, A., and E. Shafir. (1992). "Choice under Conflict: The Dynamics of Deferred Decision." *Psychological Science* 3: 358–361.

U.S. Department of Agriculture FY 2006 Budget Summary and Annual Performance Plan. http://www.usda.gov/documents/FY06budsum.pdf as of August 2008.

U.S. Department of Housing and Urban Development, "Affordable Housing," http://www.hud.gov/offices/cpd/affordablehousing/index.cfm as of December 7, 2007.

U.S. Government Accountability Office. (2002). *Flood Insurance: Extent of Noncompliance with Purchase Requirements is Unknown.* Washington, D.C.: Government Accountability Office, June 21.

U.S. Government Accountability Office. (2006). *National Flood Insurance Program: New Processes Aided Hurricane Katrina Claims Handling, But FEMA's Oversight Should Be Improved.* Washington, D.C.: Government Accountability Office, December.

U.S. Government Accountability Office. (2007a). *Natural Disasters: Public Policy Options for Changing the Federal Role in Natural Catastrophe Insurance,* Washington, D.C.: Government Accountability Office, November.

U.S. Government Accountability Office. (2007b). *National Flood Insurance Program: FEMA's Management and Oversight of Payments for Insurance Company Services Should Be Improved.* Washington, D.C.: Government Accountability Office September.

U.S. Government Accountability Office. (2007c). *Natural Hazard Mitigation: Various Mitigation Efforts Exist But Federal Efforts Do Not Provide a Comprehensive Strategic Framework.* Washington, D.C.: Government Accountability Office, August.

U.S. House of Representatives. (2007). "A Bill: Homeowner's Insurance Protection Act." H.R. 91, 110th Congress, 1st session, Washington, D.C.: January 4.

U.S. National Institute of Building Science. (2005). "Natural Hazard Mitigation Saves: An Independent Study to Assess the Future Savings from Mitigation Activities." Washington, D.C.: Multihazard Mitigation Council.

Varian, H. R. (1992). *Microeconomic Analysis*, 3rd ed. New York: Norton.

Weather Risk Management Association. (2007). "Strong Demand Seen for Weather Risk Management Contracts: Annual WRMA Survey Shows Industries Regard Weather Risk Tools as Essential." Miami, Fla.: Weather Risk Management Association, May 11.

Webster, P. J., J. A. Curry, J. Liu, and G. J. Holland. (2006, March 24). "Response to Comment on 'Changes in Tropical Cyclone Number, Duration, and Intensity in a Warming Environment.'" *Science* 311, 1713c.

Webster, P., G. J. Holland, J. Curry, and H. R. Chang. (2005). "Changes in Tropical Cyclone Number, Duration, and Intensity in a Warming Environment." *Science* 309: 1844–18465.

Wetmore, F., G. Bernstein, D. Conrad, L. Larson, D. Plasencia, R. Riggs, J. Monday, M. F. Robinson, and M. Shapiro. (2006). *An Evaluation of the National Flood Insurance Program: Final Report.* Washington, D.C.: American Institutes for Research.

Wharton Risk Center. (2005). "Lessons from Katrina: Déjà vu All Over Again." *Risk Management Review*, Fall.

Willig, R. D. (1976). "Consumer's Surplus without Apology." *American Economic Review* 66: 589–597.

Winter, R. (1988). "The Liability Insurance Crisis and the Dynamics of Competitive Insurance Markets." *Yale Journal of Regulation* 5: 455–499.

World Economic Forum. (2007). "Global Risks 2007, A Global Risk Network Report." Geneva, Switzerland.

World Meteorological Organization. (2006). "Statement on Tropical Cyclones and Climate Change." WMO Sixth International Workshop on Tropical Cyclones, San Jose, November.

Wu, Y. C., and D. Soanes. (2007). "Insurance and the Fixed Income Capital Markets." *Geneva Papers on Risk and Insurance* 32: 46–57.

Zeng, L. (2000). "On the Basis Risk of Industry Loss Warranties." *Journal of Risk Finance* 1(4): 27–32.

Study Directors and Other Lead Authors

Direction of the Study

Howard C. Kunreuther is the Cecilia Yen Koo Professor of Decision Sciences and Public Policy at the Wharton School and codirector of the Risk Management and Decision Processes Center. He has a long-standing interest in ways that society can better manage low-probability, high-consequence events related to technological and natural hazards and has published extensively on the topic, including *On Risk and Disaster: Lessons from Hurricane Katrina* (with Ronald J. Daniels and Donald F. Kettl, 2006); *Catastrophe Modeling: A New Approach to Managing Risks* (with Patricia Grossi, 2005); and *Paying the Price: The State of Natural Disaster Insurance in the United States* (with John Roth, Sr., 1998). He is the recipient of the Elizur Wright Award for the publication that makes the most significant contribution to the literature of insurance.

Kunreuther is cochair of the World Economic Forum's Global Agenda Council on "Leadership and Innovation for Reducing Risks from Natural Disasters." He is a founding member of the High Level Advisory Board on Financial Management of Large-Scale Catastrophes of the Organization for Economic Cooperation and Development (OECD); a Fellow of the American Association for the Advancement of Science; a member of the National Earthquake Hazards Reduction Program's Advisory Committee on Earthquake Hazards Reduction; and a Distinguished Fellow of the Society for Risk Analysis, receiving the Society's Distinguished Achievement Award in 2001. He received his Ph.D. in economics from the Massachusetts Institute of Technology.

Erwann O. Michel-Kerjan is managing director of the Wharton Risk Management and Decision Processes Center at the Wharton School, where he also teaches Value Creation in the Wharton M.B.A. program. His work focuses on developing strategies and policies for managing and financing extreme events, primarily natural disasters and megaterrorism, optimal catastrophe risk sharing in public-private partnerships, climate change, the economics of national security, energy interdependence, and nonproliferation. His work also includes projects on critical services protection in collaboration with the defense industry and federal agencies.

Michel-Kerjan is a founding member and elected chairman of the OECD High Level Advisory Board on Financial Management of Large-Scale Catastrophes established by the Secretary General of the OECD in 2006. He also serves on the World Economic Forum's Global Agenda Council on Natural Disasters.

He has studied at McGill and Harvard and joined Wharton in 2002 after he completed his doctoral studies in economics and mathematics at the Ecole Polytechnique in Paris, where he is currently a Faculty Research Associate.

Michel-Kerjan has authored or coauthored more than forty publications at the crux of financial management and global risk governance, and his views regularly appear in the leading media. His first book was *Treatise on New Risks* (with O. Godard, C. Henry, and P. Lagadec, 2002). From 2003 to 2005 he served on the OECD Task Force on Terrorism Insurance, which published *Terrorism Insurance in OECD Countries* in July 2005, and in 2005 he co-led, with Howard Kunreuther, the Wharton initiative *TRIA and Beyond* on the future of terrorism risk financing in the United States. His most recent book, *Seeds of Disaster, Roots of Response: How Private Action Can Reduce Public Vulnerability* (with P. Auerswald, L. Branscomb, and T. LaPorte, 2006), is the first to analyze the private efficiency–public vulnerability trade-off in the context of extreme event management.

In 2007, Michel-Kerjan was named a Young Global Leader by the World Economic Forum (Davos), a five-year nomination bestowed to recognize and acknowledge the most extraordinary leaders of the world under the age of forty.

Other Lead Authors

Neil A. Doherty is the Frederick H. Ecker Professor of Insurance and Risk Management and chair of the Department of Insurance and Risk Management at the Wharton School. One of his principal areas of interest is corporate risk management focusing on the financial strategies for managing risks that traditionally have been insurable. Such strategies include the use of existing derivatives, the design of new financial products, and the use of capital structure. He has written several books in this area, including *Corporate Risk Management: A Financial Exposition* (1985); *The Financial Theory of Insurance Pricing* (with S. D'Arcy, 1987); and *Integrated Risk Management* (2000). Doherty is also interested in the economics of risk and information. His papers on adverse selection, the value of information, and the design of insurance contracts with imperfect information and related issues have appeared in the *Journal of Risk and Insurance*, *Journal of Political Economy*, *Quarterly Journal of Economics*, *Journal of Public Economics*, *Journal of Finance*, and *Journal of Risk and Uncertainty*, among others. He is a coauthor of *Managerial Economics* (with B. Allen and K. Weigelt, 2003).

Martin F. Grace is the James S. Kemper Professor of Risk Management and associate director and research associate of the Center for Risk Management and Insurance Research at Georgia State University in Atlanta, Georgia. His research has been published in various journals in economics and insurance concerning the economics and public policy aspects of insurance regulation and taxation, with a focus on industrial organization and econometrics. In particular, he has undertaken various studies of the efficiency of insurance firms, insurance taxation, optimal regulation of insurance in a federal system, and solvency regulation. His latest book is *Regulation, Pricing and Demand in Catastrophe Insurance Markets* (with Robert Klein, Paul Kleindorfer, and Michael R. Murray, 2003).

Grace is a former president of the Risk Theory Society and is an associate editor of the *Journal of Risk and Insurance*. He earned both a Ph.D. in economics and J.D. from the University of Florida.

Robert W. Klein is director of the Center for Risk Management and Insurance Research and an associate professor of risk management and insurance at Georgia State University in Atlanta. He is a leading expert on insurance regulation and markets, with twenty-five years of experience as a regulator and an academic researcher.

He has written numerous articles, books, and monographs on various topics in insurance and its regulation, including the structure and performance of insurance markets, insurance regulation and public policy, and the political economy of risk and insurance. His research has encompassed many areas of insurance and its regulation, including catastrophe risk and associated issues for insurance markets and public policy. He has testified frequently at legislative and regulatory hearings on significant issues affecting insurance consumers and the industry.

Prior to joining Georgia State University in September 1996, Klein was the director of research and chief economist for the National Association of Insurance Commissioners. He also has served as staff economist for the insurance department and state legislature in Michigan. He has a B.A., M.A., and Ph.D. in economics from Michigan State University. He is a Sloan Fellow at the Financial Institutions Center at the Wharton School of Business. He has served on the board of directors for the American Risk and Insurance Association and currently serves on the editorial boards for the *Journal of Insurance Regulation and Risk Management* and *Insurance Review*.

Mark V. Pauly is Bendheim Professor in the Department of Health Care Management at the Wharton School of the University of Pennsylvania. He is professor of health care management, insurance and risk management, and business and public policy at the Wharton School and professor of economics in the School of Arts and Sciences at the University of Pennsylvania. He received a Ph.D. in economics from the University of Virginia.

Pauly is a former commissioner on the Physician Payment Review Commission and an active member of the Institute of Medicine. One of the nation's leading health economists, he has made significant contributions to the fields of medical economics and health insurance. His classic study on the economics of moral hazard was the first to point out how health insurance coverage may affect patients' use of medical services. Subsequent work, both theoretical and empirical, has explored the impact of conventional insurance coverage on preventive care, on outpatient care, and on prescription drug use in managed care.

Pauly is a coeditor-in-chief of the *International Journal of Health Care Finance and Economics* and an associate editor of the *Journal of Risk and Uncertainty*. He has served on Institute of Medicine panels on public accountability for health insurers under Medicare and on improving the financing of vaccines. He is a former member of the advisory committee to the Agency for Health Care Research and Quality and, most recently, a member of the Medicare Technical Advisory Panel.

Index